CIRCULAR KNITTING WORKSHOP

Essential Techniques to Master Knitting in the Round

Margaret Radcliffe

photography by
JOHN POLAK

Storey Publishing

*The mission of Storey Publishing is to serve our customers by
publishing practical information that encourages
personal independence in harmony with the environment.*

Edited by Gwen Steege
Art direction and book design by Mary Winkelman Velgos

Cover and interior photography by © John Polak Photography, except for paper textures pages
21, 46, 50, 70, 74, 114, 121, 126, 131, 140, 152, 209, 214, 246, 262 and 286 by © Nicholas Belton/
iStockphoto.com, and pages 3, 19, 25, 30, 42, 69, 112, 118, 135, 137, 157, 165, 170, 175, 176, 198, 234,
and 238 by © Marek Ludzen/iStockphoto.com
Pattern diagrams and how-to illustrations by Leslie Anne Charles
Knitting technique illustrations by Alison Kolesar

Indexed by Nancy D. Wood
Technical editing by Charlotte Quiggle

Storey Publishing
210 MASS MoCA Way
North Adams, MA 01247
www.storey.com

Printed in the China by R. R. Donnelley
10 9 8 7 6 5 4 3 2

LIBRARY OF CONGRESS CATALOGING-IN-PUBLICATION DATA

Radcliffe, Margaret (Margaret K. K.)
  Circular knitting workshop / by Margaret Radcliffe.
    p. cm.
  Includes index.
  ISBN 978-1-60342-999-3 (pbk.)
  1. Knitting. 2. Knitting—Patterns. I. Radcliffe, Margaret. II. Title.
TT825.R25 2012
746.43'2—dc23
     2011025033

CONTENTS

To David,
who makes it all
possible

WHY KNIT CIRCULARLY?

If you already knit in the round, you probably already know the answer to this question. Circular knitting lets you work on the right side of the fabric all the time. It's especially suited to some knitting techniques, like stranded color work. There are few or no seams to be joined. It's convenient to carry around — circular needles don't poke the passenger next to you in the plane or on the bus and you don't need to worry about dropping one of a set of needles or a needle poking through your bag and taking off on an unsupervised excursion of its own. Many knitters find that circular knitting is easier on their hands or arms, because they hold the needles and support the work-in-progress differently than when knitting flat. Some knitters love the meditative flow of knitting in the round — it goes on and on without any interruptions for turning or switching hands.

I myself am a firm believer in what I call "knitterly solutions." A knitterly solution is an approach to a project that makes it easier to knit, while producing better results than working it conventionally or as the instructions dictate. Knitterly solutions are straight-forward and uncomplicated, making work on a project more comfortable, leaving the knitter more relaxed, and resulting in a more enjoyable experience and better results all around. In other words, knitterly solutions are based on what knitting naturally does well.

Once you're familiar with the staggering range of circular knitting's possibilities, you'll see that some projects just beg to be made in the round because it's so much more efficient and effective than flat knitting. To take just one example, sewing together a garment made entirely of lace so that all the seams look flawless can be an incredibly frustrating and time-consuming process and is likely to end in failure because it's nearly impossible to sew seams neatly in a lacey knitted fabric. But work the same project circularly, eliminating the seams, and not only do you end up with a garment that looks better, you don't have to spend the additional time sewing up.

Why This Book?

Sometimes it's easiest to define a thing by what it is *not*. This is *not* a book of patterns for circular projects. So what *is* in this book? First of all, there's a wide-ranging discussion of circular knitting techniques, with enough detail so that those unfamiliar with circular knitting will be able to get started just using this book and so that those already enamored of knitting in the round will discover new approaches and applications of techniques. Second, this book is packed with work-shop projects — the kinds of projects I find most useful to teach circular garment and accessory construction in my knitting classes. The projects are small, with instructions for just one size, and designed to teach as much as possible with a minimum expenditure of knitting effort. You'll find the technical discussions, including a chapter on converting flat patterns to circular, in chapters 1–4 and workshop projects in chapters 5–10.

This is a book to learn from and to refer back to. In writing it, I have tried to introduce you to the broadest possible range of uses for circular knitting, from the obvious (hats) to the obscure (sideways cuff-to-cuff sweaters) so that you thoroughly understand how to construct any shape circularly and can apply your knowledge to all your future knitting. When you knit from pattern instructions, it will be easier to stay oriented as you work the project, and you'll better understand the designer's choices, be able to question them, and know how to make adaptations. If you design for yourself, you'll have an arsenal of techniques at your disposal, offering multiple approaches to every project.

Before You Start

Each of the workshop projects includes:
• **An introductory section.** This highlights the specific techniques you will learn, lists the required needles, yarn and other supplies, and notes the gauge and finished measurements of the project pictured.
• **Instructions for making the project.** These are for just one small size. You'll find cross references to techniques and details discussed elsewhere in the book. If I don't specifically tell you where to find additional information and explanations, check the appendix for details.

• **Variations on the project.** A discussion in each project tells you how to make it any size you like and suggests possible variations, such as how to make a sock from the toe up rather than from the top down.

In the introduction to each project you will find the following note: *Match the project's gauge if you want finished measurements to match pattern instructions.* This is because, for purposes of learning the techniques, it doesn't matter if you use the same thickness of yarn, use the suggested needle size, or work at the suggested gauge; however (and this is a big *however*), you need to understand that if you work with a different yarn weight or at a different gauge, your project will not be the same finished size or the fabric will not behave like the original. This is fine if you just want to learn the techniques. On the other hand, if you want to have a nice-looking, well-proportioned, satisfying finished product to be displayed proudly to your admiring public, you will need either to use the yarn weight specified and match the suggested gauge, or to exercise your own good judgment. When you substitute a different weight of yarn keep the following in mind:

• **You'll need to use a different size needle.** For thicker yarn, use larger-sized needles. For thinner yarn, use smaller-sized needles. Substitute a needle size appropriate for the yarn you're using so that the resulting fabric is neither too thick and stiff nor too loose and floppy, because either extreme will make the project more difficult to work and produce poor results.

• **The yarn amount specified will not be correct.** If you substitute a thicker yarn you'll need more yards. With a thinner yarn you'll need fewer yards.

• **You will get a different gauge.** The number of stitches and rounds per inch or centimeter will not match the instructions for the project shown. If there are any measurements given within the instructions (for example, "Knit for 3"/7.6 cm from cast on"), they will not result in the same proportions in your project as they do in the original. You can accept that the project may end up short and fat or tall and skinny, or you can adjust the measurement given and work until the length looks right to you.

Where to Begin?

If you've never worked circularly before, start with casting on, joining, and working on a single circular needle in chapters 1 and 2. This will introduce you to the basics of circular knitting. Then pick a simple project at the beginning of chapter 5 and try it out. You'll want to refer to chapter 3 for any finishing techniques where you may need a little help. Next, try working on double-pointed needles, two circular needles, or Magic Loop (page 46). Again, you'll want to refer to chapters 1 and 2 to cast on and work circularly, then find a project in chapter 5 where you can test out your new skills.

Once you have some experience working in the round, or if you are already familiar with it, you can explore circular knitting any way you like. You could read through all of the technical information in part 1 and then look for projects that use the techniques that interest you, or you can find projects that look interesting and then refer back to the techniques chapters for explanations.

The workshop projects are organized with the easiest types of projects in the early chapters, followed by progressively more complex constructions in later chapters. Within each chapter, the projects are arranged so that the most basic are at the beginning and the most demanding are at the end. Each project is designed to introduce something not used anywhere else, and most provide experience in several new techniques. So, if you want to learn basic construction techniques for many kinds of projects, you can start by working all the most basic projects (a bag, a hat, a shawl, a sock, a mitten, and a vest) from the beginning of each chapter. Or, if you want to explore a particular type of garment, like socks, you could start with the basic sock and then work all the way through the chapter trying out more and more challenging socks and different types of needles.

Whatever approach you take, be prepared to challenge yourself. Learning something new is almost always uncomfortable and can sometimes even be frightening. That's one of the reasons why it's best to begin with a small project as a learning exercise. Once you've completed the workshop project, you'll approach your full-sized creation with the confidence to put your newly learned skills to good use.

Margaret Radcliffe

GETTING STARTED

If you have always knit flat and never circularly, you probably have a lot of questions about what kind of needles to use for which projects and how to get started. This chapter includes a discussion of how to cast on, how to choose the perfect cast on, how to join the knitting into a circle, and how to solve some of the most frequent problems that new circular knitters encounter.

Most of the time getting started on circular knitting is really not very different from getting started in flat knitting. Choose needles based on what will fit the project most comfortably, and choose a cast on based on how you want it to behave. There will almost always be several types of needles and different cast ons to choose from. Make your final selection the one you personally are most comfortable with.

Because circular knitting offers a huge amount of flexibility in constructing seamless projects, there will be special cases, such as the Closed Cast Ons described on pages 22–30, where you want your cast on to do more than just put stitches on the needle. Once again, pick whichever one suits you and your project best, and don't be afraid to try something new. After all, what's the worst that can happen? If the results are not what you expect, you might need to unravel and try it again. No big deal, right?

NEEDLES FOR CIRCULAR KNITTING

There are two types of needles used for knitting in the round: circular needles and double-pointed needles.

Circular needles have a flexible cable connecting two needle points. They are designed to be used singly to knit a tube that fits comfortably around them, but they can also be used in other ways, either singly or employing multiple needles. We'll investigate these possibilities in chapter 2.

Double-pointed needles are straight and inflexible, with points at both ends, and are traditionally used in sets of four or five, but there are also ways to knit circularly on just two or three of them.

Both types of needles come in a wide variety of lengths. Double-pointed needles are most frequently found in lengths from 5" (13 cm) to 8" (20 cm), but a few manufacturers make them 4" (10 cm), 10" (25 cm) and even 16" (40 cm) long. Circular needles are usually sold in lengths from 16" (40 cm) to 40" (100 cm), but needles as short as 9" (23 cm) and as long as 60" (150 cm) are also available. Circular needles are also available in sets, with cables of various lengths and interchangeable points in a range of sizes.

When using these needles in the traditional way, the shortest circular needles (less than 16"/40 cm) are used to knit narrow tubes such as socks, mittens, gloves, or the sleeves of small children's garments. The 16" (40 cm) size is used for sweater sleeves and hats. The medium lengths (24"/60 cm to 40"/100 cm) are used for the bodies of sweaters. And the longest needles (47"/120 cm and over) are used for large projects such as blankets or shawls, or for the Magic Loop method of knitting smaller items

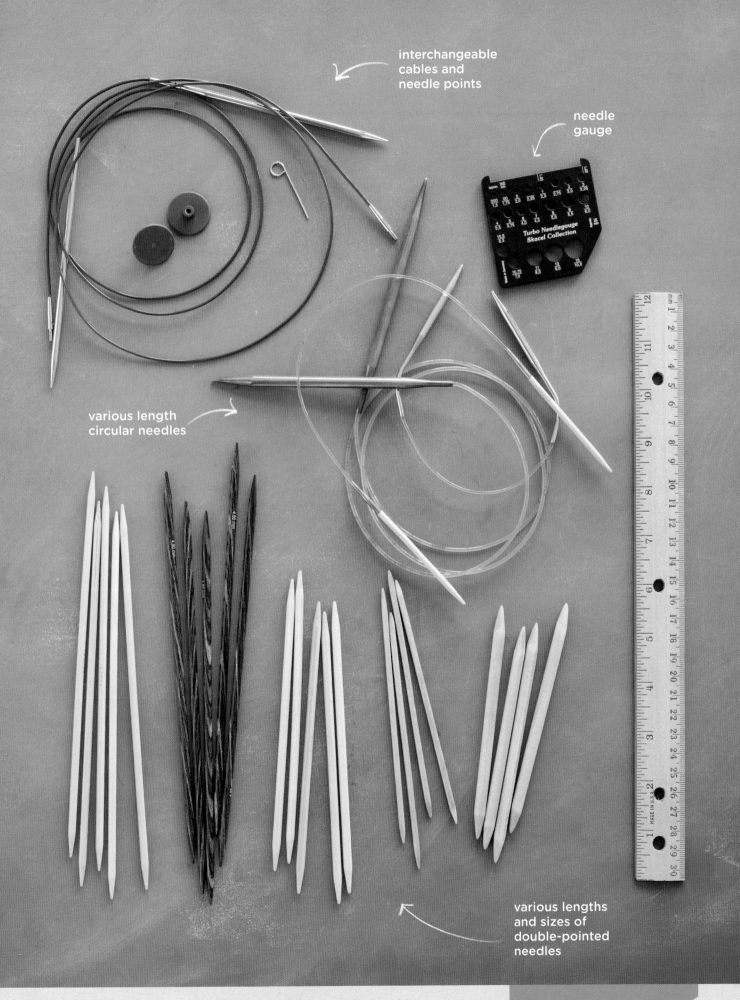

interchangeable
cables and
needle points

needle
gauge

various length
circular needles

various lengths
and sizes of
double-pointed
needles

(for a discussion of the Magic Loop, see Knitting with One Long Circular: The Magic Loop, page 46).

Double-pointed needles can be used for any sized tube, as long as it's not so large the stitches slip off the ends of the needles. Short double points (4"/10 cm and 5"/13 cm) are particularly suited for socks, gloves, and mittens, because the very small fingers and thumbs are comfortably worked on these short needles. Longer double points (7"/18 cm to 8"/20 cm) are perfect for hats and sleeves, but the versatility of these needles means that they, too, can be used for much smaller projects. The longest of the double-pointed needles, at 16" (40 cm), are now rarely used, having been replaced by the more convenient (and less lethal) circular needles. They were traditionally used to knit Shetland lace and larger tubes such as sweater bodies.

Knitters are blessed these days with the wide availability of needles made from a variety of materials. Double-pointed needles, while no longer made out of ivory, can be found in everything from coated steel to bamboo, ebony, and casein. Circular needles' points are made from all the same materials as double-pointed needles. The critical details to note when choosing needles are listed below. The first two apply to all needles, the remainder only to circular needles.

Material and finish. The choice of material varies from knitter to knitter. Tight knitters frequently prefer slippery coated metal needles, while loose knitters lean toward bamboo or wooden needles, because additional friction helps prevent the stitches from slipping off.

Points. The shape of the needle tips produced by different manufacturers varies significantly. Those that are more blunt or rounded work well for plain knitting.

Those with longer, pointier tips are better if you are working stitch manipulations like cables, increases, or decreases. Some are so sharp they can poke holes in your fingers! You may find that you prefer different shapes for different types of yarn and different types of knitting. This is an excellent rationale for building a large and varied collection of needles.

Join between cable and rigid needle. The smoother the join is, the easier it is to feed stitches from the cable up onto the needle.

Cable. These are generally made of some kind of plastic or nylon, and are either monofilament (like fishing line) or hollow tubes. They vary in flexibility, and most knitters prefer the thinner, more flexible cables. Some knitters detest the hollow cables, finding that their stitches don't slide easily along them. As with everything in knitting, each individual has his or her own taste. When needles with stiff cables are stored coiled up, they tend to stay coiled, which can be very annoying when you try to knit with them. To relax the coil, hold the points and dip the cable momentarily into a pot of boiling water, then stretch the needle out so the cable is straight as it cools. To prevent this problem, store the needles suspended by the cable with the points hanging down.

Point length. Some circular needles have much longer rigid points than others. Some knitters prefer longer points, because they find the needle ends more comfortable to hold. Others prefer shorter points because they are easier to move to form the stitches.

OFF TO A GOOD START: CASTING ON AND JOINING

Let's start at the very beginning with the cast on. You may practice using any cast on you like.

For circular needles, cast on enough stitches to fit comfortably from one tip to the other **A**.

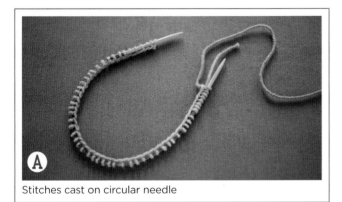

Stitches cast on circular needle

For double-pointed needles, cast the stitches you need onto one needle, then slip some of the stitches to two **B** or three **C** more needles so that they are divided more or less evenly among the needles. It's usually best to begin by slipping the first stitch you cast on (assuming you used the Long-Tail Cast On or began with a slip-knot), because that stitch won't pull loose. The working yarn should be on the right needle point (unless you are a mirror-image knitter and work from left to right across your needle instead of in the standard direction). Before you join the beginning and end of the round, check to be sure the cast on isn't twisted around the needle(s) at any point **D**. The best way to do this is to lay

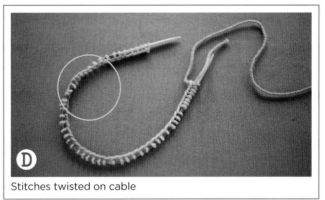

Stitches twisted on cable

the needle(s) down on a clear, flat surface and take a good look. Straighten out the cast on so it runs around the inside of the needle(s). If it passes over or under a needle at any point, straighten it out. When you begin knitting stitches from the left needle point, the knitting will be joined into a round. If you are using a circular needle, knit from one point onto the other **E**. If you are using double-pointed needles, pick up an empty needle and begin knitting onto it from the next needle to the left **F**.

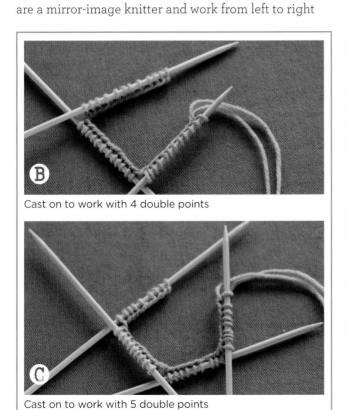

Cast on to work with 4 double points

Cast on to work with 5 double points

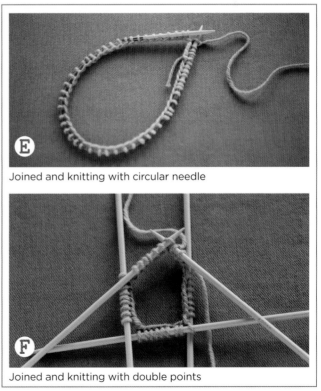

Joined and knitting with circular needle

Joined and knitting with double points

SOLVING CAST-ON PROBLEMS

Some cast-on problems are unique to circular knitting. You may end up with the wrong side of the cast on facing out. A too-tight cast on may make it impossible to work around on a circular needle. A too-loose cast on will let double-pointed needles fall right out. Certain cast ons, especially the Half-Hitch and Cable Cast Ons, spiral around the needle naturally, which can make them nearly impossible to untwist before joining the beginning and end of round, and some are difficult to slide from the cable onto the points of circular needles.

Choosing Right vs. Wrong Sides

Depending on what cast on you use and which side of that cast on you like best, you may end up with the wrong side facing out. When you work the Long-Tail Cast On, the stitches are placed on the right-hand needle, with what's normally considered the "right" side facing you. In flat knitting, you'd turn and work the first row across the back of the cast on, but in circular knitting, you'll just join the beginning and end of round and continue with the front of the cast on facing out.

On the other hand, the Knitted and Cable Cast Ons place all the stitches on the left-hand needle. When you've completed the cast on, the working yarn is at the right end of the needle, the tail from the cast on is at the other end of the needle and what is usually considered the "right" side is facing you. In flat knitting you'd work back across the cast on on the right side from this point. In circular knitting you'd turn it around so that the working yarn is attached to the right needle point and this makes the back of the cast on face out. To deal with this situation, there are two things you can do.

• Keep the right side facing you and knit one row flat, then join into a round and continue circularly. When you weave in the ends later, use the cast-on tail to close the small gap at the edge.

• Keep the right side facing you and join by holding the cast on tail together with the working yarn and work the first one or two stitches, then drop the tail of yarn and continue with just the working yarn. The tail serves to join the beginning and end of round. When you come to the double-stranded stitches at the beginning of the next round, be sure to knit the double strands as a single stitch.

There's really no need to worry ahead of time about which side will be facing out. When you finish casting on and are ready to join the beginning and end of round, take a good look at the bottom edge and decide which side you want to show, then adapt your joining technique accordingly.

Avoiding Tight Cast Ons

You cast on the required number of stitches on the correct length circular needle, but they won't stretch around the needle. What went wrong? Your cast on is too tight. Here are several things you can do to loosen up.

• **Use a different cast on.** Choose a cast on that stretches more. For example, the Cable Cast On (page 302) tends to be less stretchy than the Long-Tail Cast On (pages 302–303) and could be causing your problem.

• **Spread out the stitches.** Place the stitches slightly farther apart on the needle as you cast on. If you tend to scrunch them tightly together while casting on, then this is probably a good solution for you.

• **Use a larger needle.** Cast on using a larger needle, then switch to the correct size for the first round. This changeover can be fiddly to execute when joining the beginning and end of round. If you have a set of interchangeable circular needles (see page 11), cast on with points one size larger, then change the points to the correct size just before joining and working the first round. If you don't have interchangeable needles, slip or knit all the stitches onto the correct-size needle before joining. If this puts you on the wrong side to begin working circularly, see Choosing Right vs. Wrong Sides (at left).

Avoiding Loose Cast Ons

You were planning to use a set of double-pointed needles, but after you cast on they keep falling out of the stitches, making it impossible to start the knitting.

• **Use a different cast on.** Choose a cast on that's tighter. For example, the Half-Hitch Cast On (page 302) hugs the needle very tightly until it's worked on the first round.

• **Spread out the stitches.** After you've cast on and distributed them among the set of double points, spread the stitches out as far as possible along each needle and they'll grip it more firmly.

• **Work one row before joining.** Firmly work one row across the cast on, then distribute the stitches among the needles and join the beginning and end of round.

AVOIDING THE JOG

Unless you take measures to prevent it, most ways of joining the cast on to knit circularly tend to leave a noticeable stair step or jog and a long, stringy gap at the join. Here are three methods for creating a smoother join.

#1: Use the tail

Knit the first stitch or two using the tail from the cast on held together with the working yarn. This also has the advantage of preventing a long gap where the beginning and end of the cast on meet.

Knit first stitch with both tail and working yarn.

#2: Swap the first and last stitch

Swap first and last stitches.

Before you begin knitting, slip one stitch purlwise from the left needle to the right needle, then insert the left needle into the second stitch on the right needle and lift it over the slipped stitch. Leave this stitch on the left needle and the first and last stitch of the cast on will have traded places. Begin knitting as usual, or use the cast-on tail held together with the working yarn for the first few stitches to prevent a gap from forming.

#3: Add an extra stitch

Cast on one extra stitch. To join, slip one stitch purlwise from the right needle to the left needle. Holding the cast-on tail together with the working yarn, knit 2 together which will join the first and last stitches of the cast on. When you come to the first stitch at the beginning of the next round, be sure to knit the two strands together, treating them as one stitch.

Slip the extra stitch to the left needle.

Knit extra stitch together with first stitch.

Avoiding a Twisted Cast On

Spread the stitches out around your needle(s). Lay the knitting down flat and look for the cast-on edge going all the way around the inside of the needle(s). If that edge doesn't cross over or under the needle at any point, then it's not twisted. If your needle(s) are too short, however, the cast-on stitches will be compacted together and ruffle, making it very difficult to tell whether the cast on is twisted. Here are some solutions that may help:

• **Use extra needles.** Move the stitches to a longer needle or divide them among more needles (either an additional circular needle or double-pointed needles).

• **Work a few rows flat before joining.** Use the tail to seam the small opening at the cast on.

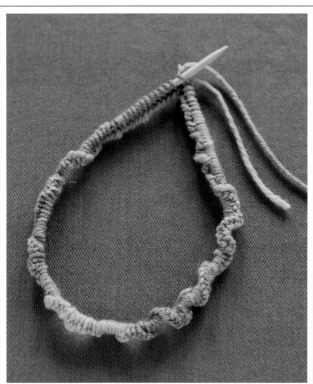

Twisted Cast On. Too many stitches squeezed on the needle make it difficult to avoid a twist when joining.

Preventing Cable Hang Ups

When you use the Half-Hitch Cast On, the cast-on stitches stretch around the cable of the needle and are pulled tight, then refuse to loosen up enough to slide onto the rigid needle at the end of the cable. Try one of these:

• **Use a different cast on.** The Long-Tail, Knitted, or Cable Cast Ons will all be easier to work with.

• **Work one row flat before joining.** The knitted stitches one row above the cast on will be much easier to work with. Use the tail to seam the small opening at the cast on.

Preventing Loose First Stitches

Loose first stitches are only a problem when you use a cast on that doesn't start with a slipknot, like the Half-Hitch Cast On.

• **Start with a slipknot.** When you begin casting on, place a slipknot on the needle, then begin placing half hitches on the needle. The slipknot counts as the first cast-on stitch.

FIVE BASIC CAST ONS

As I said earlier, you can choose any cast on you like for circular knitting, but you may find that there are circumstances where the cast on needs specific properties. For example, the top of a sock needs to be very stretchy to fit comfortably over the calf, and starting a hat from the center or a sock from the toe up is very different from starting the open bottom of a sweater.

Stretchy cast ons are best for the edges of many circular projects, including the tops of socks, the cuffs of mittens, the necks of sweaters, and the edges of shawls and scarves knit from the perimeter to the center. Unfortunately, some of the most stretchy cast ons do not wear well, so they aren't a good choice for areas that need to withstand a lot of abuse, like the cuffs of sweaters.

Let's start with the most common cast ons: Half-Hitch, Knitted, Cable, Ribbed Cable, and Long-Tail. Most knitters use at least one of these on a regular basis, and they are all appropriate for circular knitting. For any you are not familiar with, see specific instructions in the appendix (pages 302–303).

#1: Half-Hitch Cast On.

This cast on is also called the Backward-Loop or E-Wrap Cast On. It's formed by placing half hitches repeatedly on the needle. It can be difficult to knit into on the first row, difficult

to tension consistently, and difficult to slide from the cable onto the points of circular needles. It also tends to spiral around the needle and frequently looks loose. On the other hand, it's perfect for short cast ons where you want the least bulk possible, like the beginning of an I-cord or the center of a hat.

#2: Knitted Cast On.

This cast on is easiest for new knitters to learn, because each stitch is knitted out of the last and then slipped onto the left needle. Those

who hold the yarn in their left hand may find it more difficult to work than those who hold the yarn in their right hand. The Knitted Cast On is easier to work into on the first row or round than the Half-Hitch Cast On. While it's nice and stretchy, it frequently appears loose.

#3. Cable Cast On.

This variation on the Knitted Cast On involves knitting up each new stitch between the previous two. It makes a neat, firm, ropelike edge. It can sometimes be too firm, so it's best not

used along an edge that needs to stretch a great deal. Like the Half-Hitch Cast On, the Cable Cast On spirals around the needle, which can make it difficult to join the beginning and end of the round without twisting.

#4. Ribbed Cable Cast On.

In a further variation, the Cable Cast On is worked by alternately knitting and purling new stitches between the last two on the needle. This is a perfect foundation for K1, P1 ribbing and stretches very nicely.

#5. Long-Tail Cast On.

Also called the Continental Cast On, this is the best all-around cast on. Once learned, it is extremely fast to work, has medium stretch, and produces a nice neat edge.

PROVISIONAL CAST ONS

Also sometimes called open cast ons, Provisional Cast Ons are worked with waste yarn and are designed to be easy to remove, leaving live stitches that can be placed on a needle. You can then knit another section onto these stitches, add an edging, or join the cast-on edge to another piece of knitting using Three-Needle Bind Off or Kitchener stitch. A Provisional Cast On is especially useful when beginning a garment with a hem. Two Provisional Cast Ons are explained in the Appendix (pages 303–304). The Tubular Cast On (at right) is easier if you use a Provisional Cast On.

STRETCHY CAST ON: TUBULAR

The advantages of a Tubular Cast On are that it has lots of stretch, there is no noticeable ridge along the edge, and it integrates especially well with K1, P1 ribbing. On the down side, it can appear bulky when worked in thick yarn and may look loose when relaxed. You will need contrasting waste yarn and a single strand of the working yarn.

❶ **With waste yarn,** using a Provisional Cast On (such as shown in photos 1–4) or the Half-Hitch Cast On (such as shown in photos 5 and 6) cast on half the stitches you need. This will usually be an even number, assuming you will be working K1, P1 ribbing after casting on. If you need an odd number of stitches, add an extra stitch now and adjust to the correct number by decreasing one stitch after the cast on is completed. Cut the waste yarn leaving a tail about 6" (15 cm) long.

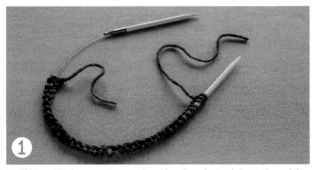

Half the stitches cast on using the Crocheted Cast On with waste yarn

❷ **Tie the working yarn** to the end of the waste yarn, leaving a tail about 6" (15 cm) long. Working flat, *yarn over, K1; repeat from * to end of row. You have doubled the number of stitches. To work a yarn over at the beginning of a row, just put the yarn in front of the right needle and knit the first stitch. Be sure to work

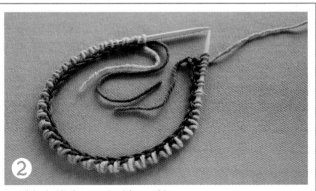

Doubled stitch count with working yarn

loosely or the yarn over will be difficult to work on the following round. Don't do anything special to join the beginning and end of round; just make sure it isn't twisted before beginning to work circularly in step 3.

❸ Working circularly, *K1, bring yarn to front, slip 1 purlwise, bring yarn to back; repeat from * to end of round. Note that you will slip the last stitch.

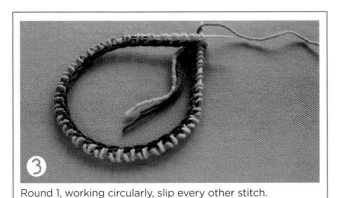
Round 1, working circularly, slip every other stitch.

❹ On the next round, *bring yarn to back, slip 1 purlwise, bring yarn to front, P1; repeat from * to end of round.

Round 2, completed

Repeat steps 3 and 4 at least once more.
❺ Work in K1, P1 ribbing or continue in whatever pattern you like.

Work pattern rounds (Half Hitch Cast On shown).

❻ After you've worked a couple of rounds, remove the waste yarn. If you used the Half-Hitch Cast On, cut the waste yarn every few stitches and pick out the pieces. If you used a Provisional Cast On, you can pull the waste yarn out in one piece or can cut it once or twice to make removal easier.

Remove waste yarn.

Finished edge

FIXING THE TENSION

Too loose. If the edge of your Tubular Cast On is loose, work the first row with the working yarn using a needle one or two sizes smaller. Note, however, that this will make it less stretchy. After it's completed, you can adjust the tension by teasing a little bit of yarn from each stitch with the tip of a knitting needle, working the slack over to the edge of the knitting.

Too tight. If you are a tight slipper, loosen up on the working yarn and spread out the stitches on the right needle point as you slip, or your edge will be too tight.

STRETCHY, DECORATIVE, AND DURABLE CAST ON: CHANNEL ISLANDS

The small picots of this cast on make a very nice edge for K1, P1 ribbing, garter stitch, or stockinette, and the additional strand of yarn used to cast on creates a more substantial, durable edge. You will need two balls of yarn.

❶ **Holding both strands together,** pull out lengths of yarn measuring about 1" (2.5 cm) for each stitch you are casting on (for example, you need about 10"/25 cm to cast on 10 stitches). The length of the tails recommended is for worsted weight yarn. If you are using thinner yarn you'll need less; with bulkier yarn, you'll need more. Make a single slipknot with both yarns at this point and place it on the needle. You now have four strands hanging from your needle. Cut off one of the strands that is attached to a ball.

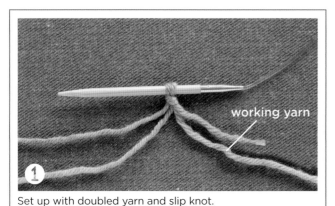
working yarn
Set up with doubled yarn and slip knot.

❷ **Hold the needle in your right hand** with your index finger on the slipknot. Wrap the double strand counterclockwise twice around your left thumb and hold the single strand over your left forefinger. Maintain tension on the strands in your left hand by holding them against your palm with the rest of your fingers.

Position the yarn.

❸ **Put one wrap of the single strand** around the needle by taking the needle point over the strand and behind it (making a yarn over). Insert the needle up through all the wraps on your thumb and over the strand on the index finger once again.

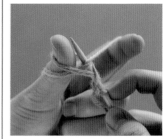
Make a yarn over.

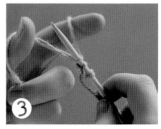
Insert the needle through the wraps and over the single strand.

❹ **Pull a new stitch out** through the thumb loops using the tip of the knitting needle and let the wraps slip off your thumb. Tighten the thumb strand.

❺ **Replace both the double and single strands** on your left hand, wrapping the double strand twice counterclockwise around your left thumb as in step 2.

Repeat steps 3–5. Each repeat will cast on two stitches. If you need an even number of stitches, adjust for this on the first row by knitting the two strands of the slipknot individually. If you need an odd number of stitches, knit the doubled strand of the slipknot as if it were one stitch.

Completed cast on

Finished edge

Two Hems for a Finished Edge

Hems provide an extra layer of thickness at the edge of a garment, so they can make sweater sleeves, sock tops, mitten cuffs, and hat bands extra warm. On the other hand, their bulk can cause unsightly bulges. To make a hem, begin with waste yarn and a Provisional Cast On (see page 18), then work in stockinette until the hem is as deep as you like. Decide what kind of edge you want.

Option 1: Folded Edge

Work one or two rounds in reverse stockinette (two rounds will make a squarer edge). To disguise the jog where the ends of the purl round are discontinuous, see Disguising the "Jog" in single pattern rounds (page 95).

Folded edge, right side

Folded edge, wrong side

Option 2: Picot Edge

Work *yo, K2tog; repeat from * around. To disguise the jog where the end of the picot round is discontinuous, see Disguising the "Jog," page 95.

Finished picot edge

Completing the Hem

Work in stockinette again until the length above the fold equals the length below the fold.

To join the two layers, remove the Provisional Cast On and place those stitches on extra double points or a spare circular needle Ⓐ. The lower edge will frequently have one stitch less than your working needle. Fold the hem to the inside and knit the stitches on the two layers together to join them Ⓑ. If there's an extra stitch on the outer layer, just knit it separately. Now continue with the body of your garment as usual.

Ⓐ Place the bottom stitches on needle(s).

Ⓑ Join the two layers.

TIP

Hems often bulge because the inner layer adds bulk. To prevent this, work the inner layer using thinner yarn, fewer stitches, or smaller needles.

WHY USE A CLOSED CAST ON?

Normally we work an open cast on: that is, we cast on all of our stitches, then join the beginning and end of round and begin working circularly. This leaves the bottom of the knitted tube open, which is why it's called an *open* cast on. But sometimes you'll need a *closed* cast on. For example, when starting at the toe of a sock or the bottom of a bag you'll need a closed cast on that forms a straight line. Or, if you're making a hat from the top down, you need to begin at the center point and work out in a circle. There are numerous excellent closed cast ons. Choose among them depending on the shape you are making, on whether you need firm, seamlike support or seamless stretch, and on which method you feel most comfortable working.

If you aren't already comfortable working circularly from an open cast on and can't work a tube using double-pointed needles, two circular needles, or the Magic Loop, skip to chapter 2 and get some practice before you attempt these cast-on methods.

To begin with a closed cast on, use double-pointed needles, two circular needles, or Magic Loop. Closed cast ons do not work with a single circular needle used the traditional way, because the knitting is too compressed, but you can shift to knitting around conventionally on a circular needle once the fabric has grown enough to make this comfortable.

Closed Center Cast On #1: Starting on Double Points

When you begin a top-down hat, a tip-down mitten, the center of a circular shawl, or the bottom of a bag, you'll need to start with a very few stitches and work out from there. This can be a very fiddly process until you are well underway. The needles flop, the tiny piece of fabric gets twisted, and double-pointed needles sometimes slip right out of their stitches. The method described here is designed so that you never need to set the needles down or separate them until the fabric is larger and more stable, making it less likely that the needles will twist or fall out. This approach can also be helpful when starting socks from the toe up if you're making a round toe rather than the traditional flat toe.

When beginning from the center, avoid a bulky cast on because it will leave a noticeable lump. The best cast on is the Half-Hitch Cast On (page 302). It has almost no bulk and can easily be tightened up later to get rid of the hole that always forms at the center point.

Starting on Double Points

Using double-pointed needles and the Half-Hitch method, cast on a total of 8 stitches this way: cast 4 stitches onto one needle, turn the needle over, slide the stitches to the other end **A**.

Hold a second needle together with the first needle in your left hand. Make sure the new needle is below the other needle. Cast 4 stitches onto this needle (*8 stitches total*) **B**.

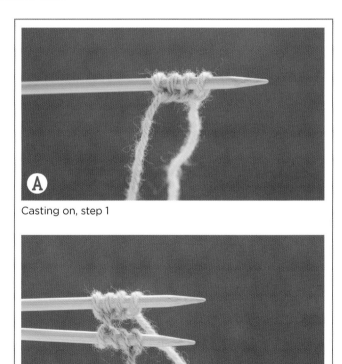

A Casting on, step 1

B Casting on, step 2

Round 1. Without turning, use a third needle to knit the first stitch on the upper needle. Pull the working yarn tight after this stitch to prevent a gap, and then knit across the rest of the needle **C**. Holding both needles

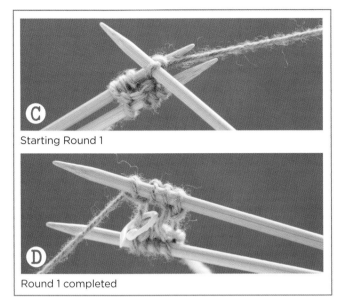

Starting Round 1

Round 1 completed

together, turn so the other needle is on top and the working yarn hangs from the right end of the needle. Knit across the upper needle. Put a split marker in your knitting at this point to mark the beginning of round **D**.

Round 2 (increase). Keeping the knit side facing you, rotate the needles so that the first needle is on top again. *K1, M1* across the first needle **E**. Rotate so the other needle is on top **F**, *K1, M1* across this needle to the end of the round **G**. (*16 stitches total*)

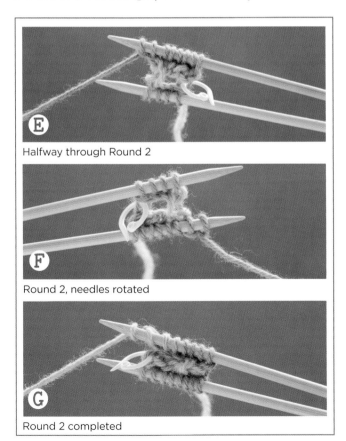

Halfway through Round 2

Round 2, needles rotated

Round 2 completed

Round 3. Rotate the needles again so that the first needle is on top. K4, then begin another empty needle and K4 to the end of the top needle **H**. Your knitting is now on three needles, and you can work around in the traditional manner. Using the needle you just emptied, K8 across the next needle to the end of the round **I**.

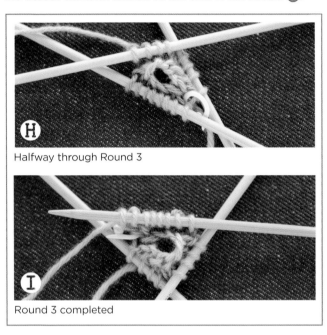

Halfway through Round 3

Round 3 completed

Round 4. Increase 8 stitches evenly spaced around; that is, work 2 stitches between each increase (*24 stitches total*) **J**.

Round 5. Knit across the first two needles. On the third needle, K6, begin using a fifth needle and K6 to the end of the round (*24 stitches remain, evenly divided with 6 stitches on each of four needles*) **K**.

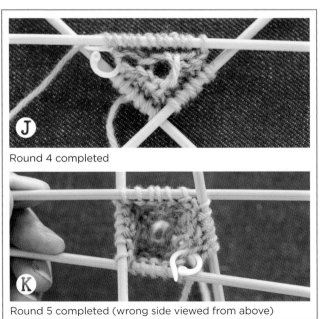

Round 4 completed

Round 5 completed (wrong side viewed from above)

MANAGING THE CENTER HOLE

Decorative approach. There will always be a small hole at the center of this cast on. If you're working a piece that's lacy, you may want to increase using yarn overs and leave the hole open as a decorative element **Ⓐ**.

Closing the hole. Use a yarn needle to neatly sew around all the cast-on stitches and then pull them up tight before weaving in the end on the wrong side **Ⓑ**.

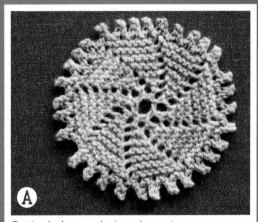

Ⓐ

Center hole as a design element

Ⓑ

Center hole closed

Using a Different Stitch Count

While the number of stitches you cast on and your rate of increase may vary depending on the shape you want to make (the example on the previous page has you casting on 8 stitches and increasing 8 stitches every other round), the basic approach is the same regardless of how many stitches you begin with and how often you increase. Begin by casting half of the stitches onto one needle, rotate and hold the second needle behind it, then cast on the other half of the stitches. Work around with a third needle until you have added more stitches, then divide the stitches on one needle between two needles on a plain knit round. You can arrange the stitches as I did, with half on one needle and a quarter on each of two other needles, or you can divide evenly among your needles. Adding a fourth needle is optional once you have enough stitches so that the knitting remains stable.

Starting on Two Circulars or Magic Loop

It's significantly easier to get started using two circulars or the Magic Loop than on a set of double-pointed needles. Circular needles don't fall out of the knitting, no matter how few stitches there are. When your stitches are cast on, just begin working circularly as usual on your needle(s) and increasing as described above. (See Working with Two Circulars, pages 44–45, or Knitting with One Long Circular: The Magic Loop, page 46.)

CLOSED CENTER CAST ON #2: STARTING WITH I-CORD

A variation on the cast on above is to begin with a short length of I-cord, which makes a nice start to a top-down hat.

❶ **Cast on** a convenient number of stitches for your I-cord. If you need to work with a multiple of 6, begin with 3 stitches; for a multiple of 8, start with 4; for a multiple of 10, begin with a 5-stitch I-cord. Work the I-cord for as long as you like (see Basic I-Cord, page 50). One inch or less will make a little stem. Longer cords can be knotted, sewn down to the top of the hat to form a loop, or left long for decorative effect (especially effective with a pom-pom or tassel attached to the end).

Cast on and work I-cord.

❷ **When your I-cord is complete,** knit across half the stitches, working a Make 1 (M1) with the working yarn after each stitch. Using a third needle, work across the second half of the stitches, still making an M1 after each stitch. You've doubled your stitches and the knitting is divided between two needles, exactly as it was when starting at the center without I-cord (page 22).

Double stitch count and divide between two needles.

❸ **Work as in Closed Center Cast On #1,** beginning with Round 1. You'll alternate plain knit rounds with increase rounds, and you'll introduce new needles as the work grows.

Continue to increase, introducing new needles as it grows.

❹ **To finish the I-cord,** tighten up the cast on and use a yarn needle to pull the tail of yarn through to the inside of the cord. You can either hide the tail inside the I-cord or, if you've made a short cord, weave it in on the wrong side near the base of the cord.

Finish the I-cord.

OTHER CENTER CAST ONS

- **Emily Ocker.** This center cast on can be easily closed up just by pulling on the yarn's tail. It begins by wrapping the yarn around your finger to form the center loop, then a crochet hook or knitting needle is used to make stitches around the hook in the same structure as an invisible cast on. (For illustrations of both methods see www.spellingtuesday.com/circular_co.html and techknitting.blogspot.com/2007/02/casting-on-from-middle-disappearing.html.)

- **Sandy Terp** (Moontide Lace Knitting Retreat, www.moonriselaceknitting.com). Use waste yarn to make a short I-cord, then change to the working yarn and begin increasing for the center of your project. When you're done, remove the waste yarn, leaving the open loops of working yarn to be closed up with the tail. It's a good idea to use smaller needles for the waste-yarn I-cord and the first round or two worked with the project yarn so that the center stitches aren't loose.

- **Marianne Kinzel.** In her *First Book of Modern Lace Knitting,* a center cast on for lace is made by working a chain of stitches with a crochet hook, forming it into a circle, and then picking up and knitting one stitch in each chain stitch.

STRAIGHT-LINE CAST ONS

When you begin knitting from the center of a rectangle or oval, from the bottom of a flat bag, or from the flat toe of a sock, you'll need to begin with a closed cast on that forms a line. It will probably fall at the point where, if working the project from the opposite direction, you would need to sew a closing seam. Make your choice among the cast ons on pages 26–30 based on whether you need a supported seam (for the bottom of a bag, for example) or whether you want the center of the knitting to be stretchy and the cast on seamless. Of course, you'll also decide based on which you find most comfortable to work.

Use a supported straight-line closed cast on such as #1 (at right) and #2 (page 28), when you want to control the stretch of your knitting or when you want it to wear better. The bottom of a flat bag will hold its shape better if begun with a supported cast on, for example, and the toe of a sock will stretch a bit less, holding its shape better and resisting wear. Supported cast ons have as much (or as little) stretch as the basic cast on you employ to begin them. You can expect the Long-Tail Cast On to have medium stretch, the Cable Cast On to be firm, and the Knitted and Half-Hitch Cast Ons to be the most stretchy.

All three of the methods described at right can be worked on double-pointed needles, two circular needles, or the Magic Loop (see Using Double-Pointed Needles, page 39, Working with Two Circulars, page 44, or Knitting with One Long Circular: The Magic Loop, page 46).

CLOSED STRAIGHT CAST ON #1: DOUBLE YOUR STITCHES

This is a less stretchy cast on.

❶ **Loosely cast on half** of the stitches you need, using any method you like, your working yarn, and your choice of needles. Work across, knitting into the front and back of every stitch, thus doubling the number of stitches.

Cast on and double stitch count

❷ **Gently slide the needle out** of the stitches, pinching the base of the cast on and being careful not to stretch it widthwise. The stitches will naturally spring to the front and to the back, alternating across the cast on. If any stitch clings to its neighbors, use the tip of a needle to gently encourage it into line.

Remove needle from stitches, allowing stitches to pop forward and back.

❸ **Carefully slip the needle** back into half of the stitches, either the front row or the back row. It doesn't matter which you do first.

Re-position half the stitches on one needle.

❹ Slip a second needle into the other row. (See box below for various needle styles.)

❹ Re-position remaining stitches on another needle.

Obviously, this method is best used for a small number of stitches — you wouldn't want to pull the needle out of 200 stitches and then try to pick them all back up! It's most appropriate for toe-up socks and tip-down mittens. An alternative to taking all the stitches off the needle, especially if it's a long cast on, is to slip them off in sections, placing them on two other needles as you work. The weight of the needles dangling in the air may make this difficult or cause unraveling, so work with a pillow on your lap and let the needles rest gently against it.

A Treasure Pouch started with this cast on

STITCHES ARRANGED ON VARIOUS NEEDLE STYLES

On double-pointed needles. Slip half of the stitches from one needle onto a third needle.

On two circular needles. You're all ready to start working in the round.

On a Magic Loop. Slip one end of your circular needle into the front row of stitches and the other into the back row of stitches. The needle tips should both point toward the working yarn.

On double points

On two circulars

With Magic Loop

CLOSED STRAIGHT CAST ON #2: CAST ON AND PICK UP

This cast on is worked as easily on many stitches as on just a few. If you are careful, it can look perfectly seamless on the right side, even though there's a slight ridge on the wrong side. This is another less stretchy cast on. **Cast on** half the number of stitches you need. Knit one row. Turn your knitting upside down so the bottom edge of the cast on is above the needle. With the knit side still facing you, neatly pick up and knit the second half of your stitches across the bottom of the cast on as shown in the box below. To make this appear seamless, carefully knit up your stitches *between* the cast-on stitches.

Fixing twisted stitches. If the cast on stitches appear twisted, insert the needle so they appear untwisted when picking up.

Too few stitches. You may come up one stitch short. If this happens, work an M1 increase with the working yarn at the end of the needle.

Using M1 to add an extra stitch

Completed almost-seamless cast on

STITCHES ARRANGED ON VARIOUS NEEDLE STYLES

Here's how to arrange your stitches on different needle styles:

On double-pointed needles. Use a second needle to pick up across the bottom edge.

On two circular needles. Push the live stitches to the center of the cable and use the second needle to pick up across the bottom edge.

On a Magic Loop. Push the live stitches onto the cable and then pick up stitches using the same needle.

On double points

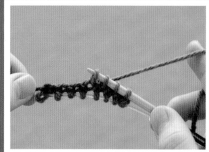
On two circulars

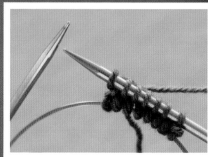
With Magic Loop

CLOSED STRAIGHT CAST ON #3: TURKISH

If you want a stretchy, seamless, closed straight-line cast on, there are several approaches you can take. My favorite method is the Turkish Cast On. Advantages of this method are that you don't need to worry about wrapping the yarn in the correct direction on each needle or about the length of the tail, which makes it good for longer cast ons.

The Turkish Cast On is most easily worked using two circular needles or the Magic Loop; the inflexibility of double-pointed needles makes it difficult to work the first round unless the tension is kept very loose. Sliding one half the stitches onto the cable of a circular needle allows some of the slack to be pulled into the facing stitches, making them easier to work. In spite of the difficulty inherent in working with double-pointed needles, I include instructions for using them because there will almost certainly be times when you don't have circular needles handy. If you are using double points, just ignore any of the instructions below that specifically refer to circular needles.

❶ **Hold two needle points** together in your left hand (both points of the same needle for Magic Loop, points of two separate circular needles, or two double-pointed needles). Begin with the tail of yarn hanging down *behind* the needles.

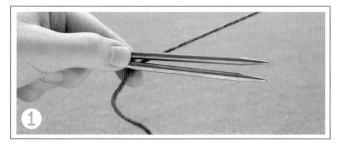

❷ **Wrap the yarn around both points,** making half as many wraps as the total stitches to be cast on. For example, if you need a total of 20 stitches (10 on one side of the cast on and 10 on the other), make 10 wraps. End with the working yarn hanging down in front of the points.

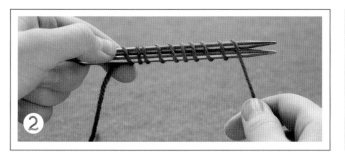

❸ **If you are working on one** or two circular needles, pull the needle through the lower half of the stitches so that they are on a cable.

❹ **Bring the working yarn up** *behind* the lower needle or cable.

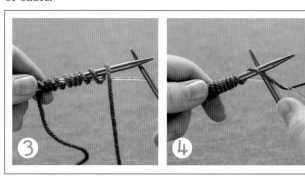

❺ **Knit across the upper needle.** The stitches will seem loose, but persevere to the end.

❻ **As you approach the end** of this needle, hold onto the tail to keep it from unwrapping. If it gets away from you, just rewrap the yarn.

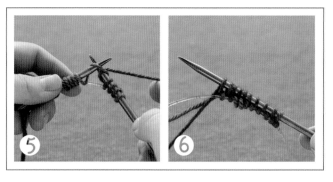

❼ **If you are working on one** or two circular needles, push the lower stitches up onto their needle point and pull the upper needle through so that the stitches you just knitted are on the cable. Regardless of needle type, rotate the knitting, and knit across the other half of the stitches.

❽ **After working across the top** of the cast on and the bottom of the cast on, you've completed one round, with the single cast-on row in the center of the round.

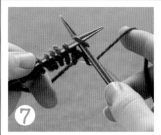
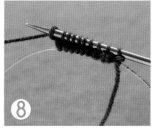

Anchoring the Tail

If you find it extremely annoying that the end comes unwrapped, there are two ways to deal with it.

• **Use a weight.** Steal a technique from machine knitters and place a clothespin or binder clip on that loose end to serve as a weight. This can be removed once the knitting is under way.

• **Use a slipknot.** Attach the end of the yarn to the lower needle using a slipknot to anchor it ❶. Wrap as usual (the slipknot doesn't count as a stitch) ❷. When you come to the slipknot for the first time at the beginning of the second row, slip it rather than knitting it ❸. When you come to the slipknot on the next round, drop it off the needle and unravel it.

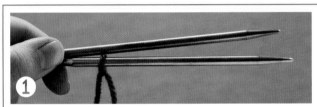
❶ Slipknot is used as anchor

❷ Wrap as usual.

❸ Round 2, slip the slipknot.

Adjusting the Number of Stitches

When casting on a lot of stitches, it may be difficult to keep track of how many wraps you've made, and if you try to count them, they may come undone. To be sure that you have enough stitches, leave a longish tail when you begin wrapping and add a few extra wraps at the end. As you knit across for the first time, count the stitches, or go back and count them after you've knit across. Unwind any excess wraps or, if you discover you're a few stitches short, just wrap the tail of yarn around the needle a few more times to create the necessary stitches.

OTHER STRAIGHT CAST ONS

• **Cat Bordhi.** To make a Moebius circularly, you have to cast on at the center and work out. Cat's Moebius cast on is by far the easiest and quickest and gives the best results. It's really just an invisible cast on, where the cable of the circular needle takes the place of waste yarn.

• **Judy Becker's Magic Cast-On.** This is an excellent cast on for toe-up socks, where you alternately cast on stitches onto the top and bottom needle.

• **Figure-8 Cast On.** Formed by holding two needle points together, then wrapping the yarn in the path of a figure 8, first on one needle, then on the other. The results are similar to the Turkish Cast On, but because half of the loops are wrapped in the opposite direction, you must take care to knit into the back of them on one needle on the first round so that they're not twisted.

DISCOVERING THE DIFFERENCE

From the outside, the Turkish Cast On can look very much like the "cast on and pick up" technique described on page 28. When you look at the inside, however, the difference is apparent. Casting on and picking up creates a noticeable seam on the inside of the toe, while the Turkish Cast On is truly seamless.

Turkish Cast On, outside

Turkish Cast On, inside

CASTING ON TO WORK IN PROGRESS

You'll sometimes need to add stitches in the middle of a round, for example to make a buttonhole or start a steek. The Long-Tail Cast On is difficult to use in most of these situations because you have only one strand of working yarn available, and it requires two strands. Your best bet is to choose one of the other basic cast ons for use at times like these.

• **Half-Hitch.** This is an excellent choice if you want no bulk and need to add only a few stitches.

• **Knitted.** Choose this if you want a very stretchy edge. Turn so the working yarn is attached to the needle in your left hand (even if the wrong side faces you) in order to work the Knitted Cast On.

• **Cable.** Use the Cable Cast On when you need a firm, neat edge or one that will stand up to abrasion. Like the Knitted Cast On, turn so the working yarn is attached to the needle in your left hand to execute this **A**.

Cable cast on

• **Ribbed Cable.** This cast on provides a neat edge with reduced curl. Just like the Knitted and Cable Cast Ons, turn so the working yarn is attached to the needle in your left hand to execute this.

• **Closing the Hole.** There will be a hole at the point where the cast on begins. There are two ways to deal with this problem:

• *Decrease.* To close this hole, when you come to it on the next round, pick up the long, loose strand between stitches **B**. Twist it and put it on the left needle **C**. Knit this twisted stitch together with the next stitch.

Knitted cable: Knit twisted and next stitch together.

Knitted cable: Twist loose strand.

• *Plan ahead.* Cast on one fewer stitch than specified. When you come to the beginning of the cast on in the next round, pick up the long strand between the stitches, twist it and put it on the left needle. This provides the additional stitch needed and there's no need to decrease.

A small hole may still remain: close it up using a nearby tail of yarn when you weave in the ends, or use a separate piece of yarn if there's none in the neighborhood.

WORKING CIRCULARLY

Working on a single circular needle the correct size for your project is by far the easiest way to work in the round. The circumference of the knitting should be the same as or larger than the length of your needle. If the needle is too long for the knitting, it won't stretch comfortably around and you'll have to fight to form each stitch. If you don't have a circular needle short enough, then the traditional solution is to use a set of double-pointed needles. Another solution is to use two circular needles or just one long circular needle with a very flexible cable.

Pitfalls of too many stitches. At the other end of the spectrum, it's amazing how many stitches you can squeeze onto a circular needle — easily three or four times the length of the needle — but there are situations when this is not a good idea:

• It's difficult to tell whether the cast on is twisted when joining the beginning and end of round.

• It's difficult to work if the knitting is too tightly crammed onto the needle.

• It's difficult to spread the work out to check for and correct mistakes.

• It's difficult to measure both length and width accurately.

• In some types of knitting, such as stranded colorwork or slipped-stitch patterns, it's difficult to maintain the correct tension, so the fabric becomes puckered.

If you find yourself in this position, but don't have a needle long enough, you can divide your knitting between two or more circular needles (see Working with Two Circulars, pages 44–45).

There are so many different ways to work circularly it can sometimes be difficult to decide which one to use. If you're a circular knitting neophyte, start with the easiest — a single circular needle with an open cast on. For a smaller tube, try working it on two circular needles, Magic Loop, or a set of double-points to see which you like best. With a little experience, you'll know exactly what needle configuration suits you best. To gain that experience, try out the basic projects in chapter 5, Starting with a Tube.

Using One Circular Needle . . .
The Traditional Way

If you aren't sure which needle(s) to use, the choice may be dictated by the needles you own or can easily purchase. If you have a choice of needles, then it's a matter of personal preference, familiarity, or what's most comfortable for the current project. Let's begin with the most traditional way: one circular needle.

❶ Find a needle that is slightly shorter than the circumference of your project. (See guidelines under the photos at right.)

❷ Cast on and join the beginning and end of round as described in Off to a Good Start: Casting On and Joining (page 13).

❸ Knit. Unlike flat knitting, you will never turn your knitting. Just continue in the same direction, with the knit side facing you. When you come to the point where the tail from the cast on is dangling, you've completed one round. You can place a marker on your needle at this point to keep track of the end of the round as the piece grows in length. To begin the next round, just keep on knitting. You're actually working in a long, smooth spiral. To make stockinette stitch, all you have to do is knit. Neat trick, eh?

Child's or adult's hat. A 16″ (40 cm) long needle should work.

Sweater body. A needle 24″ (60 cm) or longer is appropriate.

Socks or mittens. A very short 9″–11″ (23–28 cm) needle would be required. Needles this short can be hard to find and difficult to use because the rigid points are quite long in proportion to the cables, so I don't recommend them if you've never worked with circular needles before.

SOLVING CIRCULAR KNITTING PROBLEMS

Your stitches and the position of your knitting may look strange at first. Here's how to tell whether you've got a problem and how to fix it if you do.

Stitches Twisted?

Flat knitting, stitches not twisted

Circular knitting, stitches twisted

If your knitting is perfect when you work flat, but every stitch is twisted when you work circularly, it's because you are a special knitter! You use one of the alternative methods of knitting. You probably hold your yarn in the left hand, but some knitters who hold the yarn in the right hand encounter the same problem.

The "standard" method is to knit into the front of the stitch (**A** and **B**). When you purl, you wrap or pick the yarn in the opposite direction from the "standard" method, so these stitches are on the needle in the oppo-

A Standard position for stitch

B Standard method for knitting stitch

C Left leg forward (reversed from standard)

D Knit into back of reversed stitch to avoid twisting.

site direction from the knit stitches **C**. Knitting into the back of them on the following row prevents them from ending up twisted **D**.

Unfortunately, the method just described only works when you are alternating knit and purl rows. When you're knitting round and round, you never make any purl stitches, so you don't need to untwist them. When you knit or purl into the backs of them, as you normally do, they become twisted (**E** and **F**). Chances are, when you work garter stitch flat, all your stitches are twisted, too. To fix the problem, just work into the front of any

E Knitting into back of a standard stitch makes it twist.

F Purling into back of a standard stitch makes it twist.

G Purl into front of a standard stitch so it doesn't twist.

H Purl into back of a reversed stitch to untwist it.

stitch that's on the needle in the "standard" position (**B**, **C**) and into the back of any stitch that is on the needle in "reversed" position (**D**, **H**). There's no need for you to change your normal method of flat knitting, and there's no need to spend a lot of time deciding whether you originally knitted or purled a stitch. You just have to recognize how each stitch is positioned on the needle and correct for it as you go.

GETTING LOST?

If you put your knitting down and can't figure out which direction to go, check to see where the working yarn connects to the knitting. The stitch it's attached to is the last stitch you worked. You don't want to work it again! Put that end in your right hand, check to make sure the right side is facing you, and knit the first stitch from the left point to get started again.

Identifying right direction to proceed

INSIDE OUT?

You may find that the purl side of your tube is on the outside. Don't worry. Because of the way you position your hands while you work, the knitting just flipped to the inside of the needle. It's perfectly all right to continue with it inside out, but if it bothers you, poke it back through the center of the needle and it will be fixed. If you're still close to the cast on, it may flip back on you. Once it's a little longer it will stay put. Knitting with the tube inside out is not really a problem at all, just a matter of personal preference. In fact, it's very useful to feel comfortable working with it inside out, because you'll sometimes be in a situation where you can't just poke it back through the needle or where it improves your knitting. For example, when working stranded knitting, working inside out can prevent puckering.

Working with purl side facing out

PROBLEM SOLVING TWISTED KNITTING

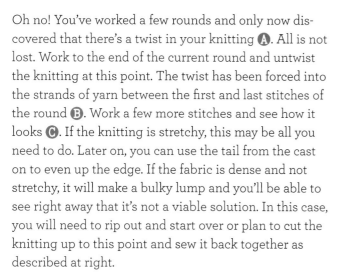

A

Twisted Knitting

B

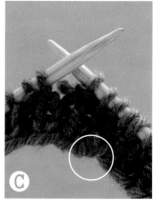

C

Untwist knitting at beginning of round.

Check to see how it looks.

Oh no! You've worked a few rounds and only now discovered that there's a twist in your knitting **A**. All is not lost. Work to the end of the current round and untwist the knitting at this point. The twist has been forced into the strands of yarn between the first and last stitches of the round **B**. Work a few more stitches and see how it looks **C**. If the knitting is stretchy, this may be all you need to do. Later on, you can use the tail from the cast on to even up the edge. If the fabric is dense and not stretchy, it will make a bulky lump and you'll be able to see right away that it's not a viable solution. In this case, you will need to rip out and start over or plan to cut the knitting up to this point and sew it back together as described at right.

Twists discovered more than a few rounds into the knitting are more of a challenge. You've invested significant time in the knitting at this point and don't want to waste all that effort. If you are an intrepid knitter, you can cut the knitting at the beginning/end of round, from the cast-on edge up to the needle, untwist it, and continue working. You should secure your stitches before cutting and seam the cut edges later — see the Steeked V-Neck Vest (pages 264–272) and the Side-to-Side Sweater (pages 287–301) for more information on preparing and cutting your knitting. If the cut will be unobtrusive, say at the bottom band of a vest or sweater, this may be a workable solution. If the cut will be very visible, or you just don't have the courage to cut, then you've no alternative but to rip out.

HOW MANY NEEDLES?

Some knitters prefer to place the stitches on three needles, while others use four. It's worth trying it both ways to see which you like better.

• **If the knitting seems uncomfortably stretched** at the corners of three needles, using four needles will enlarge the angle at each corner, easing the stretch.

• **If the knitting is too big to fit comfortably on three needles**, divide it among four so there will be fewer stitches on each needle. On the other hand, if the knitting is very floppy on four needles, it will usually be more stable on just three.

• **Match the number of needles to the repeat** of your shaping or your pattern stitch. If there's a multiple of three or six pattern repeats, then it may make more sense to divide among three needles. If you're working with multiples of four or eight, then four needles might make the work more coherent.

Using Double-Pointed Needles

The second basic method of working circularly is on sets of four or five double-pointed needles. You can use this method for tubes up to about 24" (61 cm) around. The advantage of double-pointed needles is that you can start from a very tiny tube and enlarge it (or start with a large tube and make it very narrow) without having to change to different needles. You can also fashion a tube smaller than would be possible or comfortable on any of the circular needles. Here's how it's done:

❶ **Cast on,** divide your stitches among three or four needles, pick up an empty needle, and join the beginning and end of round as described in Off to a Good Start: Casting On and Joining (page 13).

Cast on, divide among double points, and join to begin.

❷ **Use an empty needle** to knit across the needle to the left of the beginning/end of round. Insert it from the front to knit the first stitch.

Insert empty needle from front to begin knitting.

❸ **Work across as usual.** Remember that you are working with only the two needles that are actually knitting — the others are just holding the stitches until you get to them.

Work across, holding just the two working double points.

❹ **Continue knitting** until you come to the end of the first needle. It will now be empty. Slide the stitches you just worked to the center of the needle they are now on and spread them out. This will balance the needle to keep it from flopping to one side, and the stretched-out stitches will hug it more tightly, preventing the needle from falling out of the knitting.

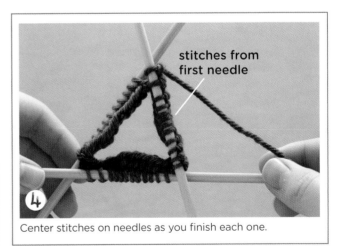

stitches from first needle

Center stitches on needles as you finish each one.

❺ **Rotate the knitting** slightly clockwise and knit across the next needle with the empty one.

Each time you empty a needle, use it to knit across the next needle. When you get back to where the tail of yarn from the cast on is hanging, you've completed one round.

SOLVING PROBLEMS WITH DOUBLE POINTS

Working on a set of double-pointed needles can be uncomfortable and unnerving at first because there are all those extra needles. In reality, you are still just knitting from one needle onto a second needle. The other needles are serving as stitch holders. Don't try to hold all of the needles — just hold onto the two working needles  Ⓐ. Don't try to push the others out of the way, however, as this will stretch the knitting and cause loose stitches where the needles meet. Instead, let the non-working needles just hang there with their upper points poking loosely through the circles of your fingers and thumbs. If the next needle points up outside your hand, let it stay there until it bumps up against your hand, then gather it in.

Let the needles not in use dangle.

Pieces worked on double-pointed needles can be very floppy and disorganized until they grow large enough so that the fabric supports the needles. If the dangling needles are too mobile and distracting, place a pillow on your lap and let the lower ends of the needles not in use rest gently on the pillow. This also helps to prevent slippery metal needles from sliding right out in the early stages of the knitting. Wooden or bamboo needles are not so slippery and may be easier to work with for those first few rounds.

Here are a few hints on dealing with the most common difficulties and frustrations when you're new to double points.

Loose Stitches

To prevent loose stitches where two needles meet, it's especially important to hold the needle points close together when starting a new needle. Follow these guidelines.

When you're knitting:

• Insert the new needle under the point of the needle you just finished and gather the tips of the three needles (the one you just finished, the one you're just starting, and the empty one you're knitting with) close together Ⓑ.

Insert new needle in front of the one you just finished, and keep all three needle tips close together.

• Knit the first stitch firmly, make sure things are still nice and cozy, with minimal space between the needles, and continue knitting Ⓒ.

Knit first stitch firmly.

When you're purling:

• Insert the new needle from the back, behind the needle that was just completed and make sure the three needle tips are all close together **D**. Purl the first stitch firmly and make sure the needles are still close together before continuing across.

D

To purl, insert new needle behind the one you just finished; keep the working needle tips close.

Working the first and last stitch of each needle on the tapered tip of the needle makes a smaller stitch and can help prevent looseness. You can also knit a few stitches from the next needle onto the current needle, but this just shifts the loose stitches in a spiral around the knitting; it may also make it more difficult to keep track of the beginning and end of round, pattern stitches, and shaping.

Sometimes the stitches aren't really any looser than the ones on either side, they're just distorted from being under tension between the needles. When the knitting is complete, take the tip of a needle and tease these stitches into a better shape so they look more like their neighbors. Stretch the knitting lengthwise, diagonally, and from side to side to help even out the stitches. Blocking under a little tension after the knitting is completed will also make the fabric look more consistent.

NEEDLE-YANKING DESPAIR

There is nothing more annoying than mistaking a working needle for the empty needle and accidentally pulling it out of the stitches, but this happens to every knitter. If it happens to you, stay calm. You can take emergency action. First, gather the knitting up in your hand so the loose stitches don't stretch. It's stretching the row horizontally that makes them unravel. Take the now-empty needle and slide it back into the stitches, from either right to left or left to right — it makes no difference with double-pointed needles **E**. Be careful not to pull on the stitches as you do this, because it will cause the following stitch to unravel. To prevent unraveling, pinch the base of each stitch and hold onto it while you slip in the needle.

If you have a thinner needle handy, you'll find it easier to slide into the dropped stitches. Some of your stitches will probably be on the needle the wrong way, and a few may have unraveled in spite of the care you took. Next time you work across that needle, make corrections as you go. If a stitch is on the needle backward, take it off and untwist it before working it, or work into the back to straighten it out. If a stitch has unraveled, fix the problem and put it back on the left needle before working the stitch on the current round **F**.

E

Prevent stitches from unraveling by pinching the base of the stitch as you slip the needle in.

F

Knit unraveled stitches back up, row by row, with a crochet hook.

USING MARKERS IN CIRCULAR KNITTING

You've probably already realized that you can't put ring markers on the ends of double-pointed needles because they fall right off again. The same thing happens at the ends when working with two or more circular needles. What are the alternatives?

Use the needles as markers. If you're not shifting stitches from needle to needle, you can keep track of sections of your knitting just by how you divide them between the needles. For example, put all of the front stitches of a sock on one needle, and divide the back stitches evenly between two more needles, with the beginning of round at the point between the two needles. You'll always know when you're working the front, because there are more stitches on that needle and you'll always know where the end of round is: between the two short needles.

Use the tail from the cast on. Leave a relatively long tail when you cast on. As you knit, keep track of the beginning/end of round by flipping the tail to the inside at the end of one round and back to the outside at the end of the next round. This weaves the tail through the knitting as you go and is very easy to remove later. It's particularly useful when you are increasing or decreasing in a swirl, because the farther you work, the harder it can be to see where the end of round falls. For better visibility, you can use a contrasting piece of yarn or crochet cotton instead. If you're worried about it slipping out, tie the end of it to the cast-on tail.

Using needles as markers for the front and back of a sock

Weaving up a contrasting-color yarn as a marker

MAKING SHIFT

You'll sometimes encounter situations where you need to work a stitch manipulation that requires stitches on two different needles. For example, a decrease where the first stitch is at the end of the current needle and the second is at the beginning of the next needle. For double decreases, where three stitches are worked together to become one, or for cables, which may be worked across even more stitches, the best thing to do is to slip the stitches so that they are all on one needle before attempting to work them. This may even occur across the beginning and end of round. If it does, just forge ahead, and replace any marker in the correct position on the needle when you're done. Shifting stitches between needles may make the knitting difficult to work because there are too many stitches on one needle and too few on another; rearrange them so it's comfortable to continue.

Split markers. Under the general heading "split markers" I include any markers that open so that you can stick them in a specific stitch, between two stitches in the fabric, or you can put them on or take them off the middle of a needle any time you want to. When they are attached to the knitting, they can't fall off the needles by accident. You can use the plastic markers shaped like short fat safety pins, actual safety pins (with or without the coil that catches in your knitting), or split-ring markers (rings with an opening; sometimes they overlap like tiny keyrings). Another fun option is to use earrings with a lever-back French clip, so they can be opened and closed; because they have something beautiful dangling from them, they're easy to spot in your knitting.

Split markers are especially useful placed in a stitch to indicate the center of a double increase or double decrease. A marker placed before or after a stitch gets in the way when working a double decrease (you have to remove it, work the decrease, and then replace it on the needle). When working double increases, a marker placed before or after the center stitch shifts one stitch over every time you increase, so it too must be removed from the needle and replaced every time you work the shaping. When increases are made using yarn overs, it's also easy for the marker to accidentally shift to the wrong side of the yarn over, causing future increases to be out of line. If you place the marker in the center stitch, however, it can remain there while you work the increase or decrease.

As the knitting grows, the marker will move further away from the needle. Once the decrease or increase pattern has been established, you may no longer need a marker to keep your place. If you find that you do need to rely on a marker, just move it up closer to the needle every so often — it's not necessary to do this on every round.

Using "safety pins" (orange) or split-ring markers (white)

BENEFITS OF WORKING WITH TWO CIRCULAR NEEDLES AT ONCE

Knowing how to knit on two circular needles can be a lifesaver in certain situations, and many knitters find they prefer two circulars to sets of double-points. The circulars allow you to knit pieces that are very large, very small, or constrained by their shape so that they don't fit comfortably on a single circular needle.

It can also be very convenient to knit the body of a sweater on two circular needles even if it would fit comfortably onto a single needle. Two needles allow it to lie flat for measurement or even to be tried on, without having to transfer it to a piece of yarn or to a longer needle .

You can avoid accidentally knitting onto the other needle if you use two needles whose cables or points are different colors or materials, but be aware that your gauge may vary slightly if you use different types of needles. They can also be different lengths — in fact some knitters prefer this — but they need to be the same size in diameter.

A Separate the front and back of a sweater so it's easy to try on and measure.

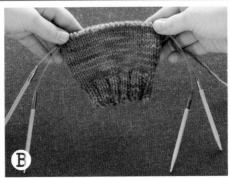
B Use two circular needles for projects too small to fit on one circular needle.

WORKING WITH TWO CIRCULARS

❶ Cast all the stitches onto one circular needle, then slip half of them to a second needle and fold the knitting in half with the right side (if one is identifiable) facing out. Make sure the cast on doesn't twist around the needles at any point.

You may join the beginning and end of round for stability, but it's certainly not required. I have found that the easiest, least fiddly method of joining in this situation is to knit the first stitch using the cast-on tail and the working yarn held together (see page 15).

❷ Slide the back half of the stitches to the center of their needle's cable with the working yarn hanging from the right-hand side of the knitting; leave the ends dangling. Slide the front half of the stitches onto the needle point closest to where the working yarn is attached. Knit across the stitches on this needle using the other end of the same needle.

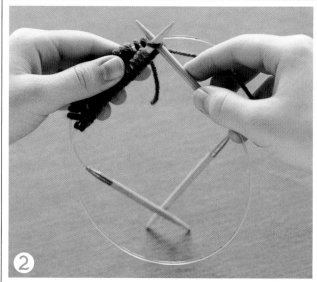

Slide back half of stitches onto cable, and front half onto front needle point.

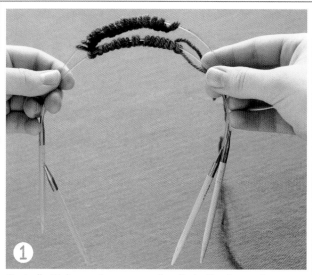

Cast all stitches onto one needle, slip half onto another needle, then fold in half.

WORKING WITH MORE THAN TWO

When you have a very large project, you may want to divide the knitting onto several circular needles. This will let you work more easily, because the stitches aren't squashed together, and you can lay it out flat to get accurate measurements. Just as when working with two circulars, knit the stitches from each needle onto that same needle as you work around.

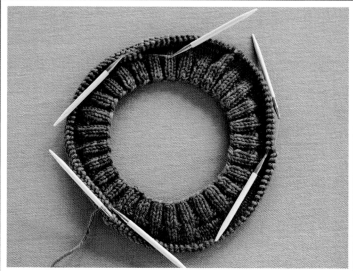

Use additional circulars for very large items or to lay flat to measure accurately.

❸ Slide the stitches you just knitted to the center of their needle's cable, turn the knitting so the other half is facing you, and slide the stitches now in front to the right point of their needle, closest to the working yarn. Knit these stitches with the other end of their own needle.

❹ The working yarn and the cast-on tail are now attached at the same side of the knitting, which means you've completed a full round.

Repeat steps 2 through 4 to continue knitting in the round. Remember that you never knit any stitches from one needle to the other. Don't worry about loose stitches as you begin each needle. Because the last stitch worked is hanging from the thinner cable of its needle, it will tighten up, preventing any looseness where the two needles meet. If you are a firm knitter, be careful not to pull too tightly when beginning a new needle — a "seam" of tight stitches would be very noticeable in your finished project.

The tail from the cast on marks the beginning and end of round. The halfway point is where the knitting divides between the two needles on the opposite side. You don't need any markers for these points. If you need to mark any other locations in between, just place a marker on one of the needles.

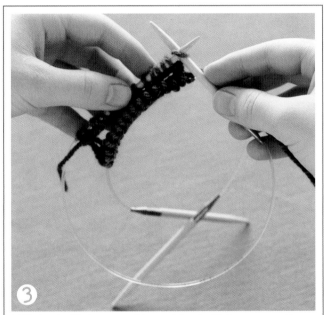

With back stitches on cable, and front stitches on needle point, use other end of front needle to knit.

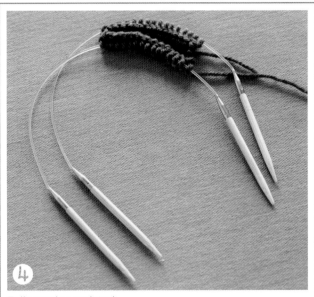

Full round completed.

KNITTING WITH ONE LONG CIRCULAR: THE MAGIC LOOP

For many years, knitters have been managing to knit smaller tubes on longer needles by pulling out a loop of the cable every so often. More recently, Sarah Hauschka perfected an even better method, which she and Bev Galeskas documented in the booklet from Fiber Trends called "The Magic Loop." The Magic Loop method allows knitters to use one very long circular needle to knit small items or to more easily work shapes where conventional approaches are impossible. The needle should be about 40"–47" (100–120 cm) long and must have a very flexible cable, or you'll fight with it the whole time. It's possible to work the Magic Loop using a shorter needle, but it's not always comfortable.

Sock knitted on Magic Loop

Bottom of bag knitted on Magic Loop

"HALF" A MAGIC LOOP

Throughout the book, when describing how to work a project on the Magic Loop, I'll refer to "half of the loop." This means one-half of the knitting on the loop, which is divided between the "front half" and the "back half." The front half is the half of the stitches on the side of the needle closest to you. The back half is the half of the stitches farthest away from you. In some cases, there may not be the same number of stitches on each needle, but they are still called "halves." I also refer to the "first half" of the loop and the "second half." Starting from the beginning of round, the stitches you knit first are the first half. The stitches between the first half and the end of the round are the second half. When instructions are given for working on two circular needles and on the Magic Loop, there may be references to the "first needle," "second needle," "front needle," or "back needle." On the Magic Loop, these are the same as the "first half," "second half," and so on.

Working with the Magic Loop

❶ Cast on. Find the center of the cast on, where half of the stitches are to the right and half are to the left, and pull a loop of the cable through at this spot.

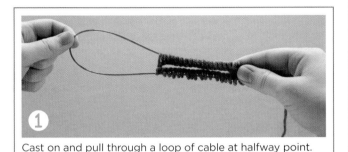
Cast on and pull through a loop of cable at halfway point.

❷ Slide the stitches up onto the points of the needles, keeping the knitting folded in half. Before you start knitting, make sure the cast on isn't twisted around the needle at any point and the working yarn is hanging at the right end of the back needle. If this would place the wrong side of your cast on facing out, then work one row flat before beginning to work circularly.

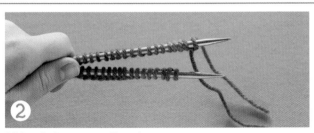
Slide stitches to needle points.

❸ The working yarn should be hanging from the right end of the back needle. Pull the back needle point through to the right so that there is enough slack to knit easily across the front, but there is still a loop of cable at the left, between the two halves of the knitting.

Slide back stitches to cable, leaving a loop at the halfway point, ready to knit the first half.

❹ Knit across the front half of the Magic Loop. The working yarn will now be attached at the left side of the knitting.

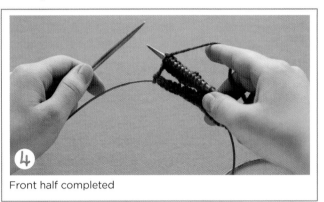
Front half completed

❺ Push the stitches on the back half of the Magic Loop up onto the point of the back needle and turn in preparation for knitting across.

Ready to knit the second half

Repeat steps 3–5. Each time you knit across half of the Magic Loop, you've completed half a round. When you reach the place where the cast-on tail is hanging, you've reached the end of the round and are ready to begin a new round. Notice that you always leave a loop of cable at the other side of the knitting when you complete one half of the knitting and that there are always two loops of the cable (one at each side) when you are knitting across. If you find that you accidentally pull out the cable loop at the far end, place markers at the beginning of round and the halfway point to make it easy to reestablish the loop.

The instructions above make an open cast on; that is, the bottom of the tube is open. For a closed cast on, which you'll use to begin at the toe of sock, the tip of a mitten, the top of a hat, or the bottom of a bag, see Closed Straight Cast Ons on pages 26–30.

KNITTING TWO TUBES AT A TIME

Using either two circular needles or the Magic Loop, you can also knit two tubes at a time. Those who suffer from so-called Second-Sock or Second-Sleeve Syndrome (the inability to complete, or sometimes even to begin, the second of a knitted pair) find knitting two at a time to be a remedy for this chronic condition. Interestingly, I've never known a knitter to complain of Second-Mitten Syndrome, although perhaps those afflicted with it prefer to stay in the closet.

Working two at a time requires two separate balls of yarn, one for each tube. If your project requires more than one color of yarn, then you'll need two balls of each color so that you can use a separate ball for each tube. These basic instructions refer to anything knit circularly that you need to make two of: socks, mittens, sleeves, and so on. You'll notice that I refer to the things being knitted generically as "tubes."

❶ **Cast on half** of the stitches of the *first tube* (shown in gold), then use a second ball of yarn to cast on half of the stitches for the *second tube* (shown in olive) on the same needle.

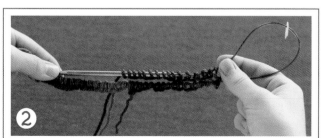

Cast on first half stitches for each tube, using separate balls of yarn for each.

❷ **If you are using two circular needles,** begin using the second needle now. For Magic Loop, just continue with the same long needle. Using the same ball of yarn, cast on the other half of the stitches for the *second tube.* For Magic Loop, pull a loop of the cable out at the halfway point of the *second tube* (which you just finished casting on). You may want to place a marker at this point before you cast on the second half of the stitches, to make it easier to find the center point of the tube.

Cast on second half of stitches for second tube, on either a second circular needle or the second half of a Magic Loop.

❸ **Using the same needle,** but the other ball of yarn, snug the needle up close to the first half of the *first tube* and cast on the second half of its stitches.

Cast on second half of stitches for first tube.

Regardless of whether you're using one needle or two needles, proceed this way:

❹ **Work across the first half** of the first tube.

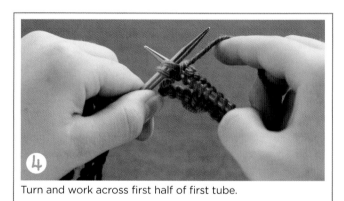

Turn and work across first half of first tube.

❺ **Change to the other ball of yarn** and work across the first half of the second tube.

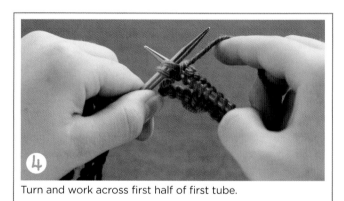

Using other ball of yarn, work across first half of second tube.

6 **Turn and work across** the second half of the second tube. Change to the other ball of yarn and work across the second half of the first tube.

Repeat steps 4 through 6.

Turn and work second half of second tube, and then second half of first tube.

First round completed on both tubes.

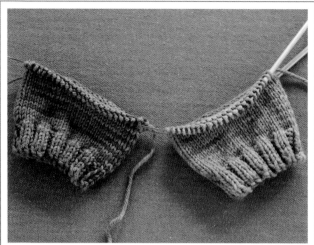

Progress! As pieces lengthen, you'll find it's easier to stay oriented.

TIPS FOR WORKING TWO AT A TIME

Socks. If you are working a heel with a heel flap, you work back and forth just on half of the stitches to make the flat sections of the knitting. The other halves of the socks hang from the other section of cable, waiting for circular knitting to begin again at the gussets. To work both heel flaps at the same time, work across the right sides of both sock heels, then turn and work across the wrong sides. Repeat until the heel flaps are complete.

Mittens. It's best to work the thumbs separately. They are just too fiddly to work two at a time.

Gloves. It would be possible, but not very practical, to work the fingers and the thumb for one glove at

the same time, with a separate ball of yarn for each digit. Yes, that means five balls of yarn! The stitches for each half of a digit would be divided between the two sections of cables. Theoretically, it would also be possible to do this for both gloves at the same time, but that would require 10 balls of yarn!

Sleeves. Sleeves can be worked circularly up to the underarm. If there is any underarm or sleeve cap shaping, this must be worked flat after binding off for the underarm. The flat sections, of course, can be worked for both sleeves at the same time, just as described for heel flaps above.

Three Ways to Make I-Cord

In her book *Knitting Without Tears* (1971), Elizabeth Zimmermann refers to this knitted cord as "Idiot's Delight." By the time *Knitter's Almanac* was published in 1974, she was calling it "idiot-cord." I haven't been able to discover who shortened it to "I-cord," or exactly when, but by the mid-1990s the term was in wide popular use. This narrow knitted cord can be made using a child's Knitting Nancy or knitting spool, or a hand-cranked I-cord maker, but it's also quick and easy to make using two double-pointed needles.

Basic I-Cord

Cast on 3 or 4 stitches. The best cast on to use is the Half-Hitch (see page 302) because it's not bulky. Hold the needle so that the working yarn hangs from the left end of the needle.

❶ **Without turning,** slide the stitches to the right end of the needle and put it in your left hand.

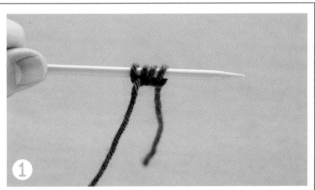

Slide stitches to right without turning, and hold needle in your left hand.

❷ **Pull the working yarn across** the back, knit across. The first stitch tends to be loose, so pull firmly on the yarn after you complete that stitch.

Pull working yarn across back, and knit first stitch.

Repeat steps 1 and 2 until I-cord is the desired length. The back of the cord tends to be a bit loose. Pull the cord and stretch it to even up the stitches.

To finish off the cord, cut the yarn and pull the end through all the stitches. Use a yarn needle to hide the cut ends inside the tube.

Finish. Thread tail through a yarn needle and draw it up through tube.

TIP

If you prefer, instead of sliding the stitches to the other end of the needle and moving the needle to your left hand in step 1, you may just slip the stitches from the right needle back to the left needle. This also allows you to make I-cord on any type of needle, not just double-points.

Purled I-Cord

Work purled I-cord exactly the same as regular knitted I-cord, but pull the yarn across the front, rather than across the back.

To make purled I-cord, pull yarn across front, then knit across.

Wider I-Cord

Wider I-cord can be worked over more stitches, but there will be a gap at the back that you'll need to close up.

❶ **Cast on one fewer stitch** than you really want. Work your I-cord to the desired length, pulling the yarn across the back, but don't worry about closing the gap completely.

❶ For wide I-cord, cast on one fewer stitch than you need; there will be a gap in the back.

❷ **Before finishing off the end of the cord,** use a crochet hook to make one more column of stitches from the loose strands at the back. Insert the crochet hook into the lowest strand from above and rotate it to make a twisted loop on the hook. This "casts on" one additional stitch at the beginning of the cord.

❷ Use a crochet hook to "cast on" one stitch using lowest strand in gap.

❸ **Hook the loose strands up,** row by row, just as you would to fix a dropped stitch.

❸ Hook up loose strands row by row.

When you have hooked the top strand through to form a stitch, place it on the needle, at the end away from the working yarn. Then cut the yarn and pull it through all of the stitches. It's a good idea to work a short length at first to test out your tension: it may take a little experimentation to make the strands across the gap just the right length so that the added column matches the rest of the stitches.

Making Circular Swatches

Gauge swatches for circular knitting should be made circularly. This is because your knit stitches and your purl stitches may differ slightly in size, so that fabric knit flat may be looser or tighter than the same fabric knit circularly. You can deal with the circular swatch issue several different ways. If a project will require both flat knitting and circular knitting, then it's important to make both circular and flat swatches to insure that the gauge is identical using both techniques. Assuming that you are familiar with how to make small flat swatches, I have only provided some hints for circular swatching here.

Make a small tube. Using double-pointed needles, two circular needles, or the Magic Loop, make a tube at least 9" (23 cm) in circumference and at least 5" (25 cm) long. This gives you enough width so that you can flatten it and measure at least 4" (10 cm) of stitches and rows.

Make an even smaller tube. You can also make a smaller tube, which you cut open to measure. While you don't have to knit as much, your gauge on a very small tube may be different from what you get on a larger piece of knitting. Also, if you cut the swatch, you can't unravel the yarn and re-use it.

Make a small tube.

Cut it at the beginning of round, and flatten it to measure.

Work an open-backed swatch. Work a narrow piece of knitting on a double-pointed needle or a circular needle, while carrying the yarn very loosely across the back so that you can work across again on the right side. The loose yarn allows you to lay the swatch flat to measure; carrying it across the back lets you work every row on the right side.

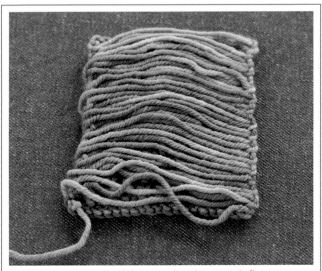
Loose yarn across back lets you lay the swatch flat to measure.

Start a hat. This is particularly nice if you plan to make a sweater — you'll end up with a matching hat. Cast on enough stitches for about 18"–20" (46–51 cm) and get to work. When the hat is 3"–4" (7.5–10 cm) tall, measure to see if the gauge is correct.

Start a sleeve. If you're making a sweater from the bottom up, start one of the sleeves first, work for a few inches and see if the gauge is correct. If it is, keep going and finish the sleeve. If not, unravel and adjust your needle size. The beauty of this method is that you don't end up with a useless gauge swatch, and you get the immediate gratification of starting your sweater without any preparation.

MEASURING GAUGE

No matter how you make your swatch, the technique for measuring gauge is the same: Lay your swatch on a smooth surface and place a ruler on top of it to hold it flat, if necessary. Count the number of stitches across 4" (10 cm) or more. A longer length is better because it gives you a bigger, more representative sample. Avoid measuring at the edge of a swatch, where the stitches may not be consistent. On a circular swatch, this is usually not a problem, but on one where loose strands are carried across the back, the edge stitches are usually very loose. Divide the total number of stitches by the number of inches (or centimeters) to get stitches per inch (or centimeter). This may not be an even number of stitches. For example, 18 stitches across 4" (10 cm) is 4½ stitches per inch and 1.8 stitches per centimeter.

Make note of the stitch and row gauge and of the dimensions of your swatch, then wash and dry it as you would the finished project. There may be some shrinkage or the yarn may expand when washed, changing the stitch or row gauge. If the overall dimensions of the swatch have not changed after washing, then the original gauge should still be correct. If the dimensions have altered, measure the stitch and row gauges again for accuracy. Remember to allow for shrinkage or expansion as you knit so that the project will come out the correct size after washing.

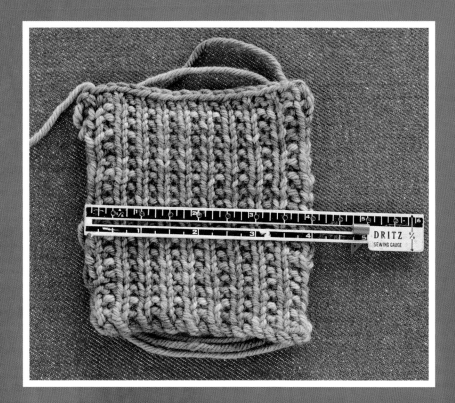

chapter 3

FINISHING
TECHNIQUES

Most circular garments are seamless. In fact, you will find no instructions for sewing seams anywhere in this chapter on finishing. If you love to knit and hate to sew (like so many other knitters), you'll agree that this is a tremendous benefit of circular knitting. Aside from seaming, however, finishing circular garments well involves exactly the same techniques as finishing flat garments: binding off, picking up stitches, and weaving in ends. Pay attention to these details, and your finishing can be as perfect as your knitting. When you need to bind off, choose your bind off based on its function. Should it be stretchy or firm? Open or closed? Decorative or unnoticeable? If you hate to weave in ends, work them in as you go or hide them inside a hem or binding. Plan any shaping along the edges to make it easy to pick up neatly for borders or sleeves.

Binding off in circular knitting is much the same as binding off in flat knitting, but there are a few special circumstances where a particular bind off might be a better choice, as well as situations where the basic bind off could be either too tight or too loose. Luckily, there are techniques that let you fine tune your bind off to your project. Instructions for bind offs mentioned in this book that are not covered in chapter 3 can be found in the Appendix.

MAKING THE BIND OFF LOOK CONTINUOUS

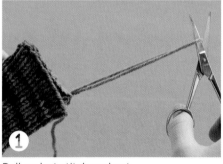

① Pull up last stitch and cut.

② Sew under both legs of first bound-off stitch.

③ Go back down through last stitch.

④ Adjust tension and weave in end.

OPEN BIND OFFS FOR CIRCULAR KNITTING

Open bind offs are just normal bind offs around an opening, like the top of a bag or the cuff of a sleeve, but, in fact, these two situations call for bind offs with different qualities. Because the top of a bag needs to hold its shape or the bag will stretch, it requires a supportive bind off. The cuff of a sleeve, on the other hand, needs to stretch quite a bit to pass comfortably over the hand and to allow the wearer to push or roll up the sleeve.

Supportive Open Bind Offs

The supportive bind off that you almost certainly already know is the basic bind off: knit two stitches, pass the first one over, knit another stitch, pass the second stitch over this third stitch, and so on across the row. This bind off has a tendency to be tighter than the knitting it finishes, but that's just perfect for a supportive bind off. You'll want to use this firm bind off around necks, armhole edges, the tops of bags, and anywhere else that's under tension and might stretch out of shape.

One-Over-Two Bind Off

If you need even more support, for example to create a gathered edge, try the One-Over-Two Bind Off.

❶ **K3, *pass the first** of these stitches over the other two, K1; repeat from * until only 2 stitches remain. Pass the right stitch off over the left stitch.

K3, pass the first stitch over the other 2.

❷ **To join the beginning and end of round,** refer to Making the Bind Off Look Continuous at left. The edge will look perfect, but the first stitch of the round below it will be a little loose, and there will be a small hole. Cleverly use the tail to close up this hole when you weave it in.

Use the tail to make the bind off continuous and close the hole.

If you end your bind off the usual way, by pulling the cut end of the yarn through the last stitch, there will be a noticeable gap in the bind off between the beginning and end of round. Here's a way to fix that:

❶ When you have just one stitch left on your needle at the end of the bind off, pull the last stitch loose so it's about 6" (15 cm) tall. Cut the yarn at the top of the loop, leaving a 4"–6" (10–15 cm) end.

❷ Use a yarn needle to sew with this tail under the two legs of the first stitch you bound off.

❸ Go back down through the last stitch. This re-forms the final stitch of the bind off, around the first stitch, making a continuous chain.

❹ Adjust the tension so that the joined stitch is the same size as its neighbors, and weave all the ends in on the wrong side.

Stretchy Open Bind Offs

In some circumstances you'll want a very stretchy open bind off: the tops of socks (so that they don't dig into the wearer's calves), the bottom of hats (so they don't leave a crease across the forehead), and the bottom of sweaters (because there's nothing so unflattering around your hips as a tight edge that makes the sweater bulge out!). Another place that's not quite so obvious is the outer edge of a circular piece of knitting, like a shawl, coaster, or doily. A normal bind off will make the edge cup up, and it will be impossible to flatten it; a longer or stretchier bind off will let the outer edge lie flat.

Some of the possibilities for dealing with these situations are quite decorative, while others are unnoticeable. Many decorative bind offs have added stitches to form tiny picots. The additional stitches make the edge stretchier, so they are good choices when you want a flexible edge with a bit more excitement.

Yarn-Over Bind Off

Adding yarn overs between stitches as you bind off makes the edge twice as long as it would be otherwise, so there's plenty of room for it to stretch. If the edge is too stretchy, adjust the amount of stretch by working the yarn overs after every second or third stitch. Setup by knitting 1 stitch.

Yo (one knit stitch is already on needle).

Pass the knit stitch over the yo.

K1, then pass the yo over the knit stitch.

Repeat steps 1–3 to end of round.

Sewn Bind Off

The Sewn Bind Off allows you to adjust the stretch. Work it tightly, and it will hardly stretch at all. Work it loosely and it will stretch to the limit of the knitting below it. It's particularly useful for the cuff of toe-up socks or the bottom of top-down hats. This is the one bind off that has no chain and creates no noticeable ridge, so it's great for understated edges.

Cut the yarn about twice as long as the circumference of your knitting. Thread through a yarn needle and use it to sew through the stitches. Hold the knitting in your left hand and sew with your right.

❶ **Insert the yarn needle** through two stitches from right to left and pull the yarn through.

❷ **Insert the yarn needle** through the first stitch again, but going from left to right. Pull the yarn through and slip that stitch off the knitting needle.

❸ **Repeat these two steps** until you have only one stitch left on the needle. Work once more from right to left through this last stitch, then right to left through the first stitch you bound off.

❹ **Now work one last time** from right to left through the stitch still on the needle. This seems backwards, but it looks better this way. Take the last stitch off the needle. Pull the yarn through to the wrong side and weave it in.

Either side of this bind off could be the "right" side. You'll need to decide which you prefer. If you are left-handed, just reverse the directions in order to sew with your left hand. So in step 1, you'll work through two stitches from left to right and in step 2 you'll work through one stitch from right to left.

Picot Bind Off

This is a decorative bind off that adds little bumps ("picots") to the edge of the fabric. The Picot Bind Off lends itself nicely to variations in size. You can make the points larger by casting on more stitches, but remember that you'll also need to bind off more stitches to compensate. You can also change the distance between picots by binding off more or fewer stitches.

Setup. Bind off 1 or 2 stitches at the beginning of the round.

1 **Slip the stitch** on the right needle back onto the left needle.

2 **Cast on 2 stitches** using the Knitted Cast On (page 302).

3 **Bind off 4 or 5 stitches** (including the 2 you just cast on).

Repeat these three steps until all stitches have been bound off. At the end of the round, you may need to adjust the number of stitches between picots to make the spacing look even. Join the beginning and end of the bind off so it looks continuous (see Making the Bind Off Look Continuous, pages 56–57).

Finished picot edge

Crown Picot Bind Off

This exuberant bind off makes large loops of picots that ruffle around the edge. It's great for a cuff or neckline embellishment, and it's very stretchy. Like the Picot Bind Off (at left), the "crowns" of the picots can be made larger or smaller by varying the number of picots made in step 2. You can also change the distance between the crowns by binding off more or fewer stitches in step 4.

❶ Cast on 2 stitches using the Knitted Cast On (page 302). Bind off 2 stitches. This forms a little bump or picot. Slip the remaining stitch on the right needle back to the left needle.

picot

❷ Repeat step 1 three more times, making a chain of four picots. The last time, leave the remaining stitch on the right needle.

❸ Knit the next stitch and pass the remaining stitch of the picot over it, binding it off.

❹ Bind off 2 more stitches. Slip the remaining stitch back to the left needle.

Repeat these four steps until all the stitches are bound off. At the end of the round, you may need to adjust the number of stitches between crowns to make it look consistent. Join the end of the round to the beginning of the round to make it look continuous (see Making the Bind Off Look Continuous, pages 56–57).

Finished crown picot edge

Tubular Bind Off

The edge of the Tubular Bind Off lacks the characteristic ridge associated with most bind-off techniques. It matches the edge of the Tubular Cast On (pages 18–19) perfectly, making it an excellent choice when you want the beginning and end of a project to be identical. And, it integrates flawlessly with K1, P1 ribbing.

Setup. Cut the yarn, leaving a tail about three times the circumference of the knitting plus about 6" (15 cm), and thread it through a yarn needle. If this is too long to work with comfortably, start with a shorter length and begin a new piece of yarn when it runs out. If you've been working in K1, P1 ribbing, start with a knit stitch. If the first stitch on your needle is a purl, either work one more stitch before binding off, or begin working the Tubular Bind Off with steps 3 and 4.

❶ **Insert the tip** of the yarn needle knitwise into first stitch and slip it off the needle.

❷ **Insert the yarn needle** purlwise into the third stitch and pull yarn through.

❸ **Insert the yarn needle** purlwise into the second stitch and slip it off the needle.

❹ **Bring the needle and yarn around** to the back of the knitting, and insert the yarn needle knitwise into the fourth stitch. Pull yarn through.

You've bound off two stitches and have worked into the first two stitches that remain. These will be stitches number 1 and 2 as you work through the instructions again. Repeat these four steps until all stitches have been bound off. As you become familiar with the process, you'll be able to merge these steps into two smooth movements, working steps 1 and 2 together and steps 3 and 4 together.

At the end of round, the first two stitches bound off at the beginning of round will serve as stitches three and four in the instructions. When there are two stitches remaining on the left needle, slip them temporarily onto the yarn needle. Pick up the first two stitches from the beginning of the round on the left needle ❺. Slip the stitches from the yarn needle back onto the knitting needle. Repeat the instructions once more and take all the stitches off the needle ❻.

first 2 stitches last 2 stitches

❺

❻

Completed bind off

For a true tubular edge, work circular tubular knitting for a few rounds before you finish off the edge: If you've been working K1, P1 ribbing, before cutting the yarn and working the Tubular Bind Off, work the following two rounds twice. Be sure to work your slipped stitches loosely so the edge doesn't suddenly become tight.

Round 1: Knit the knit stitches and slip the purl stitches purlwise with the yarn in front,

Round 2: Purl the purl stitches and slip the knit stitches purlwise with the yarn in back.

True tubular edge

For a more substantial tubular edge, one that produces a full hem or casing and integrates well with stockinette or any pattern stitch, first double the number of stitches by working a Make 1 (M1) with the working yarn before every stitch (or you may find it easier to work a yarn over before every stitch, and then twist it into an M1 by working into the back of it on the following round). Work tubular knitting (repeating the two rounds above) for as long as you like. Finally, work the Tubular Bind Off to finish the edge.

Tubular bind off with hem or casing

A TUBULAR BIND OFF VARIATION

If you find the steps described on the preceding pages confusing or difficult to remember, you may slip the stitches alternately onto two needles, with the first stitch on the front needle, the second stitch on the back needle, the third stitch on the front needle, and so on . If you have been working in K1, P1 rib, then the knit stitches should be on the front needle and the purl stitches on the back needle. You can accomplish this most easily by taking the needle out of the stitches completely. The knit stitches will naturally spring out to the front and the purl stitches to the back. Slip one needle back into the knit stitches and a second needle into the purl stitches .

If you're working on double-pointed needles, then it's easiest to rearrange and bind off one needle full of stitches at a time. If you're working on a circular needle, you can transfer all the stitches to two empty circular needles before beginning to bind off or you can slip groups of stitches onto two double-pointed needles as you work **C**.

A Slip stitches alternately onto two needles.

B You can remove K1, P1 ribbed stitches from needle so that they spring alternately to back and front.

C With stitches on two double points, begin to work Kitchener stitch.

Shifting the stitches to two needles also makes it easier to maintain consistent tension, so if your Tubular Bind Off looks sloppy done the conventional way, this may be the solution.

Work Kitchener stitch (pages 70–74) to join the stitches on the two needles  .

At the end of the round, the first two stitches you worked into at the beginning of the round (steps 1 and 2) will serve as the second stitch on the front and back needles (steps 4 and 6). It can be difficult to figure out how to work them once they're off the needles, but if you slip them back onto the needle it's much clearer **E**.

Kitchener stitch in progress to bind off stitches

first 2 stitches

last 2 stitches

At end of round, slip first 2 stitches back onto needles.

Hems

Just like at the cast on, you can make flat, double-thickness borders at the bound-off edge. This can be used to advantage when you want the beginning and end of what you're making to match, such as the Side-to-Side Sweater (pages 287–301). Hems are also useful if you need a casing for a drawstring or elastic.

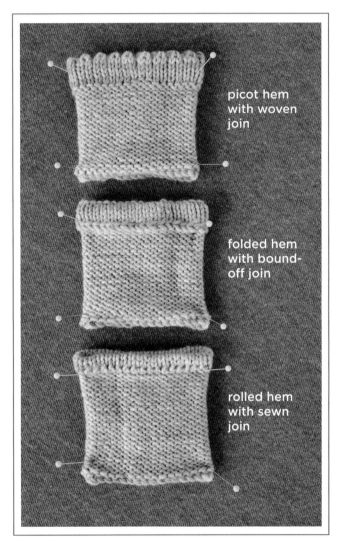

picot hem with woven join

folded hem with bound-off join

rolled hem with sewn join

❶ **Work in stockinette,** K1, P1 ribbing, K2, P2 ribbing, or some other not-too-bulky pattern stitch, to the edge of the knitting. Purl one or two rounds to make a fold line, repeat (K2tog, yo) around to make a picot edge, or do nothing to make a rolled edge. To disguise the jog where the ends of the purl rounds or the picots are discontinuous, see Disguising the "Jog" in single pattern rounds (page 95). Before working the inner layer (step 2), decrease a few stitches, switch to smaller needles, or change to thinner yarn to prevent bulging. ❷ **Continue in stockinette** until the hem is as deep as desired. Cut the yarn leaving a long tail and thread it through a yarn needle. Start with a tail that's as long as possible, but short enough so that it's easy to sew with. Begin a new piece of yarn if it runs out. There are several ways to join the hem to the inside of the knitting.

Sewn Join

For a sewn join, sew the live stitches to the back of the fabric, working once under a strand on the back of the fabric for each stitch on the needle. The purl side of the fabric  is made up of interlocking "smiles" and "frowns." To ensure that the hem is attached straight, sew into the "frown" just before the column of stitches that aligns with the next stitch on the needle. Overcast (rather than sewing a straight running stitch) and work loosely so that the sewing will stretch along with the knitting.

Bound-Off Join

If you prefer knitting to sewing, you may make a bound-off join by picking up strands on the back of the fabric and knitting them together with each live stitch as you bind off. Slip 1 knitwise from the left needle, insert the tip of the right needle under  a "smile" in the same column as the stitch you are binding off, then wrap the yarn and knit the smile and the stitch together. Finally, lift the stitch waiting on the right needle over and off the needle as you normally do when binding off.

Woven Join

The neatest finish of all, however, combines Kitchener stitch with duplicate stitch:

1 Insert the yarn needle knitwise into the first stitch on the needle and slide it off the knitting needle.

2 Insert the yarn needle purlwise into the second stitch, leaving it on the knitting needle, and pull the yarn through.

3 Duplicate stitch the top of the stitch in the fabric where you want to join the hem, working up through one "smile" bump.

4 Sew down through the next "smile" to form the curved top of the stitch.

Be careful to work straight across one row on the back, or your hem will be crooked. Repeat these four steps until you've worked all the way around.

TIPS

If you have trouble identifying the stitches that should be matched up, which is especially difficult in dark or fuzzy fibers, use contrasting crochet cotton to create a guide before you begin to sew. Using a yarn or tapestry needle, pull one strand of crochet cotton through every tenth stitch along the row on the back of the fabric where you'll be sewing. Using a second strand, pull the crochet cotton through every tenth stitch on the needle. When you sew the two layers together, you'll be able to see clearly that your stitches and rows are properly aligned.

If you find it difficult to work consistently into a single round of stitches, use a very thin circular needle or a set of thin double-pointed needles to pick up the stitches all the way around, then work the Three-Needle Bind Off (page 69) or Kitchener (pages 70–74) to join the two layers.

CLOSED BIND OFFS

Like closed cast ons, closed bind offs leave no opening. They are used for the centers of hats, the tips of mittens, and the toes of socks. They can also be used to join the bottom of a bag, or to join the beginning and end of a piece of knitting. Like open bind offs, there are times when they should be stretchy and other times when they should be supportive, so I've provided instructions for a variety below.

Closed Center Bind Off

Anything that ends in the center, like the crown of a hat, the tip of a thumb, or a round-toed sock, should be finished off with as little bulk as possible, so a regular bind off is not a good idea.

❶ **When you have decreased** to the center of the project, cut the yarn and thread it into a yarn needle. Slip the needle purlwise into all the remaining stitches, and draw the yarn through. You can slip one stitch at a time, or several. If there are more than three or four stitches, it's a good idea to pull the yarn through half of the stitches and then do the other half. This makes it easier to pull the yarn through without tangling it.

❷ **The stitches will frequently look loose.** You can tighten them up by changing to smaller needles for the final round or fill them up with more yarn by running the yarn through all the stitches a second time. Or do both!

❸ **Take the yarn through the center** of the circle of stitches and weave it in on the inside.

Three-Needle Bind Off

The Three-Needle Bind Off makes a straight seam and is used most often to close the shoulders of vests or sweaters, the bottoms of bags, and sometimes the tops of hats. While knitting wisdom decrees that the toe of a sock should be finished off seamlessly using Kitchener stitch, many knitters find that the Three-Needle Bind Off is easier to execute and just as comfortable on their feet, even though it leaves a noticeable seam. The Three-Needle Bind Off stretches only a little, making it the perfect support when you want a seam to be flexible but to retain its shape.

Because it's a bind off, this forms a chained seam. If you want to hide the seam on the inside of the knitting, turn the piece inside out by pushing the knitting through between the needles before binding off so that the right sides of the fabric are facing each other.

❶ **Setup.** Divide the stitches in half.

If you are working on double-pointed needles, put half on one needle and half on a second needle.

If you are working on a circular needle, find the halfway point and pull a loop of the cable through between the stitches at this point.

If you are working on two circular needles or the Magic Loop, your stitches should already be divided in half, but check to make sure before binding off. Slide the knitting up onto both needle points.

❷ **Using a third needle** or an unused point of one of the circular needles, knit the first stitch on the front needle together with the first stitch on the back needle.

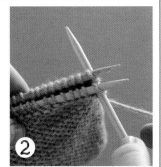

Divide stitches in half between two needles or needle points.

Knit first stitch on each needle together.

❸ **Knit together** the next stitch on each needle, one from the front and one from the back.

❹ **Pass the right-hand stitch** over the left-hand stitch and off the needle, binding off as usual.

Knit next two stitches on each needle together.

Pass right-hand stitch over left-hand stitch and off needle.

❺ **Repeat** steps 3 and 4 until all stitches have been bound off. If you started with an odd number of stitches, you'll have one lonely stitch with no partner at the end. Just work it singly to finish off the seam.

TROUBLE-SHOOTING THREE-NEEDLE BIND OFF

If you started with an even number of stitches but have an extra stitch left over at the end, you either dropped a stitch somewhere along the seam, or you forgot to knit two stitches together at some point. This can be quite noticeable from the right side, so turn your knitting right-side out to look for the problem. If there's a dropped stitch, you'll need to either unravel the bind off back to that point and do it over, or run a piece of yarn through that stitch and weave it in on either side to prevent it from unraveling. If there's a single stitch bound off rather than two stitches knit together, you can leave it as is unless you find it unsightly.

Kitchener Stitch

Kitchener stitch, also known as grafting or weaving, is used to join knitting seamlessly by sewing in a new row of stitches. In circular knitting, it is used most often to finish off the traditional flat toe of a sock or the tip of a mitten. It's also useful for joining endless tubes to make cowls or headbands, and for making a seamless join at the top of a hat.

Setup. The knitting should be right side out (the wrong sides of fabric should be facing each other). Cut the working yarn to a comfortable length for sewing and thread it onto a yarn needle. If you run out of yarn, just start a new piece when it's too short to sew with comfortably and weave the ends in on the inside later. Divide the stitches in half and arrange as described for Three-Needle Bind Off (page 69). The working yarn should be hanging from the right end of the needles.

❶ Insert the yarn needle into the first stitch on the front needle as if to purl and leave the stitch on the knitting needle. Pull up the slack in the yarn.

❷ Insert the yarn needle into the first stitch on the back needle as if to knit. Leave the stitch on the knitting needle, and pull up the slack in the yarn.

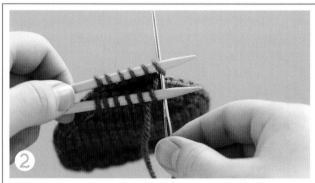

❸ Insert the yarn needle into the first stitch on the front needle as if to knit and slip the stitch off the knitting needle. Don't pull the yarn through yet!

KITCHENER MANTRA

Once you get going, here's a short version you can use to keep track of what you're doing:

• Front: knit off, purl on, pull yarn.

• Back: purl off, knit on, pull yarn.

   Tip: It may help you to think of this as making a "frown" on the front needle (first you lead the yarn up with the needle, then down, making a crescent like a frown) and as making a "smile" on the back needle (first you lead the yarn down with the needle, then up, making a crescent facing the other way, like a smile).

❹ Insert the yarn needle into the next stitch on the front needle as if to purl and leave the stitch on the knitting needle. Pull up the slack in the yarn.

❺ Insert the yarn needle into the first stitch on the back needle, as if to purl, and slip the stitch off the knitting needle, but don't pull the yarn through.

❻ Insert the yarn needle into the next stitch on the back needle as if to knit. Leave it on the knitting needle, and pull up the slack in the yarn.
Repeat steps 3–6 until all stitches have been worked.

❼ Work once more into just the last stitch on the front and on the back, pull the yarn through the very last stitch and weave in the end on the inside.

TIPS FOR PERFECT KITCHENER

• Usually the yarn will be attached to the knitting on the back needle, but it won't always be possible to set things up this way. If the yarn is attached to the front needle, work step 2, then step 1 to get started. This will make you sew into the back, then into the front. Proceed to work steps 5 and 6 (back needle). Now you can repeat steps 3 through 6 until you get to the end.

• Always work with the yarn under the tips of the knitting needles so that the yarn you are sewing with won't be confused with knitted stitches.

• Always wait until you've gone through the second stitch on the needle before you pull the yarn through. Not only is this faster, it prevents errors because you are less likely to accidentally skip sewing through the second stitch.

Kitchener for Mirror-Image Knitters

The instructions on the preceding pages assume that you are right-handed and working across the knitting from right to left, in the same direction that we knit. If you are a left-handed knitter and you knit in the opposite direction (from left to right across the knitting), you are a "mirror image" knitter. Just follow the right-handed directions but hold the needles pointing to the left. If you need to refer to a picture, hold it up to a mirror and you'll see exactly what your Kitchener stitch should look like.

Kitchener for Left-Handed Knitters

Even if you knit in the normal direction (from right to left), if you are left-handed you probably find it difficult to sew from right to left. Turn your knitting around so that the yarn hangs at the left edge. Of course, when working from left to right, the terms *knitwise* and *purlwise* are very confusing, because they are only meaningful when working in the opposite direction. The photos below illustrate the difference. Once you understand that purlwise is "from the side away from you" and knitwise is "from the side facing you," you can follow the directions on the preceding pages.

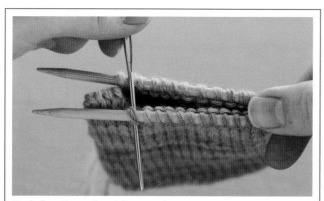

Purlwise: From the side away from you

Knitwise: From the side toward you

Alternative Approaches to Kitchener

Removing the Needles before Working Kitchener

Sometimes Kitchener stitch is confusing because it's difficult to see what you're doing with the knitting in two layers on your needles. You can take the knitting off the needles and see if it's easier that way. If you're worried about the fabric unraveling, here are some suggestions.

Working Kitchener with stitches off needle

• Let the knitting sit for several days before taking it off the needles. If you want to begin working sooner, steam it lightly or dampen it and let it dry before taking it off the needles.
• Slip just a few stitches off the needles at a time.
• Run a piece of crochet cotton through all the stitches to secure them, then remove it when you're done.

"Sock Toe Chimneys"

This method comes from designer, teacher, and author Lucy Neatby, who developed it for closing off sock toes. It can also be used on other small tubes.

1 Set up. Knit a few rounds with contrasting yarn to hold the stitches in place, then bind off the contrasting section. The contrasting rounds prevent the knitting from unraveling, and they also provide a guide to follow while joining.

2 Tuck the contrasting rows inside and use a matching piece of yarn (shown here in gold for clarity). Leave half of the yarn dangling, and sew under two strands beginning at the center of the opening.

3 Sew under two strands on the opposite side.

4 Sew back into the same spot you came out of on the first side, and under two strands.

5 Continue alternating sides until you get to the end of the opening, and sew just once into the last stitch on each side.

6 Turn and use the other half of the yarn to sew across to the other end of the opening.

7 Turn inside out, unravel the contrasting chimney, and use the tails to neaten up the corners as you weave them in.

Debbie New's Method

Designer, teacher, and author Debbie New worked out another novel method, leaving the stitches on the thin cable of a circular needle and working from the purl side.

❶ **With the yarn attached** at the end of one needle, work once through the first stitch on both needles. If the yarn is attached to the back layer, work first through the front and vice versa.

❷ **Whichever direction you came out** on the first pass, work through the next stitch on the same needle and then through the last stitch you worked on the other needle

❸ **Turn your yarn needle around** and repeat step 2 in the opposite direction. Always work underneath the cable.

❹ **When you've worked through** all of the stitches, slide the needles out.

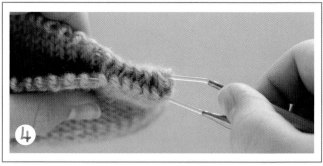

If this is confusing, work a swatch in stockinette with one row of a contrast color Ⓐ. Fold it at this row with the purl side out and you'll see the same structure you're working across the two needles. Practice by sewing with a different contrasting yarn along the path of the single-row stripe Ⓑ.

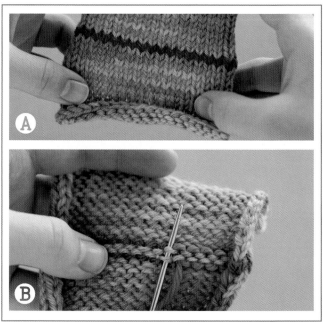

WORKING KITCHENER IN THE ROUND

Sometimes you'll want to work Kitchener stitch in the round, for instance, to join two ends or two layers of a piece of circular knitting. Work the Kitchener just as described above. To make the join appear continuous at the point where the end of round meets the beginning of round, follow the instructions for ending Tubular Bind Off (page 63).

ENDS, EDGES, AND BORDERS

Even if what you make is seamless, you still need to weave in your ends, pick up stitches, add borders, and make minor adjustments when finishing your projects. There are a few considerations you should keep in mind while you're knitting and when you're putting on the finishing touches.

Weaving In Ends as You Go

As with flat knitting, you can just weave in the ends on the back of the fabric when the knitting is finished, or you can weave in the ends as you knit. (For instructions on weaving as you go, see Stranded Knitting Basics, pages 206–209.) Keep in mind, however, that you're always going the same direction in circular knitting. This means that all the ends are woven in the same direction. Several problems result from this phenomenon. If all the ends are woven in at color changes at the beginning of round, the fabric will be thicker to the left of this point. The tail of the new ball of yarn will also be woven back on itself, which causes distortions in the fabric. To avoid these problems, begin weaving in the tail of the new yarn for a few stitches before you need to use it, then weave in the tail of the old yarn after you make the change to the new ball. You can also weave in the old yarn as you knit, but leave the tail from the new ball hanging to weave in later. Note that none of these techniques for weaving as you go work unless you're knitting at least some of the stitches. In other words, you can't use the techniques when you're purling.

ANOTHER WAY TO WEAVE IN AS YOU GO

Weave in the new ball one stitch to the right each time you approach the end of the round. When you're one stitch from the end of round, lay the tail of the new ball over the right needle. Knit under it. On each subsequent round, stop a stitch or two earlier and knit under the tail again. Repeat this six or seven times, then stretch the fabric and trim the end. This makes a very nice diagonal weave, but it is surprisingly difficult to execute because it's so easy to just knit past this point.

On subsequent rounds, stop a stitch or two earlier and knit under tail again, weaving tail in diagonally on back (shown inside out for clarity).

MANAGING EDGES

If you're working circularly, you'll need to worry about edge stitches only in sections of your project that are flat. For example, a sweater may be knit circularly up to the underarms, and then flat from the underarms to the shoulders, like the V-Neck Vest in chapter 10 (pages 252–261). Just as in flat knitting, how you treat the edge stitches can make it easier to pick up stitches later on if you need to add a border or another section of a garment such as a sleeve. Here's what I recommend:

• If the project is worked in garter stitch or a pattern stitch based on garter stitch (where right and wrong side rows are mostly knitted), you have two choices. You can knit the first and last stitch of every row, which will leave a little bump at the end of each ridge of garter stitch, or you can slip the first stitch knitwise and purl the last stitch, which will make a neat chained edge. Slipped stitch edges are best used for an exposed edge, the heel flap of a sock, or where a section of garter stitch will be added to the side of another piece of garter stitch. The slipped stitch edge makes it easy to pick up one stitch for every two rows of garter stitch, which is the perfect proportion for these situations. In all other cases, it's best to knit the first and last stitch of every row.

• If the project is worked in stockinette or a pattern stitch based on stockinette (where the right side is mostly knit and the wrong side is mostly purl), then keep the edge stitches in stockinette.

• Work any shaping at least one stitch away from the edge. This leaves a smooth edge so it's easy to pick up stitches consistently. See the V-Neck Vest and the Side-to-Side Sweater, pages 287–301, for examples of where to place increases and decreases.

MIND THE GAP

There's always a gap or unevenness of some sort at the beginning and end of the round at the cast-on edge and the bound-off edge. In the sections on each of these techniques (for cast ons, see chapter 1, Getting Started; for bind offs, see pages 57–65), I've provided tips for making them look continuous, but you may find that the join at the cast on is still noticeable. Camouflage this by working a figure 8 of yarn as you begin to weave in the tail from the cast on. Here's how: Bring the tail across the beginning/end of round and sew through the fabric from the back just above the cast-on edge **Ⓐ**. Bring the tail across to the other side of the beginning/end of round and sew through the fabric from the back again **Ⓑ**. If it looks even now, stop and weave the end in on the wrong side **Ⓒ**. Otherwise, repeat step A and possibly step B again before finishing off.

Ⓐ Bring tail across beginning/end, and sew through from back just above cast-on edge.

Ⓑ Bring tail across other side of beginning/end, and sew through from back again.

Ⓒ Repeat steps A and B if necessary.

Completed

PICKING UP STITCHES

Even in circular knitting, you need to pick up stitches to add borders and embellishments, to work sleeves down from armhole to cuff, and to provide a foundation for bindings, which are handy for hiding ends and messy edges. (See pages 297–298, for a variety of examples.) Picking up around a circular opening or edge is identical to picking up along the edge of flat knitting, but here are a few details to keep in mind.

• **Using a flexible circular needle** is usually the easiest way to pick up stitches. When picking up around a very small opening where the end of the circular needle is too long to work easily, however, use a set of double-pointed needles, two circular needles, or the Magic Loop.

• **Begin picking up at the point** where it will be least noticeable, such as the underarm or a seam (for example, the shoulder seam of a sweater when working the neck border). Avoid beginning at the center front. The one exception to this is beginning at the point of a V-neck, but only if you plan to work the neck border flat, crossing the ends and sewing them down at the center front (see pages 270–271).

• **Always use working yarn** to pick up and Knit (see appendix, pages 307–308).

• **Picking up the correct number of stitches** is critical to making borders or adding sections that don't ruffle or flare (too many stitches) or pull in too tightly (too few stitches). Pattern instructions almost always indicate either the total number of stitches or how many stitches to pick up in proportion to the number of rows (for example, 3 stitches for every 4 rows along the side of the fabric). If you don't have this information, here are a few guidelines:

Along the side of garter stitch, to add a garter stitch border or another section of garter stitch perpendicular to the original fabric, pick up one stitch for every two rows (which is the same as one stitch for every ridge).

Along the side of stockinette stitch, to add a ribbed border, use needles two sizes smaller than for the stockinette and pick up three stitches for every four rows of the stockinette. For a tighter, more supportive border, pick up two stitches for every three rows instead.

In other situations, such as adding a decorative border that's not ribbed to either garter or stockinette stitch; adding stockinette or garter stitch to a textured, lace, or stranded fabric; or any situation that's not described above, work out the ideal number as follows:

Work a swatch of the fabric you're planning to add and measure its stitch gauge. Next, measure the length of the edge where you want to attach the border and multiply to get the correct number of stitches. Adjust to get an even multiple of any pattern stitch. If you are adding a border that will be under tension, reduce the number you get by about 10 percent to allow for stretching. You may want to test out your calculations by picking up stitches on a swatch and adding to it before committing yourself to a full-sized garment.

Curved edges, such as armholes, neck openings, and the curved outer edges of shawls, present special challenges. To prevent flaring, you'll need the measurement for the outer edge of the border, not the inner edge where it's attached to the garment. For example, if you're planning to add a border 1"/2.5 cm wide, you'll need to measure a circle 1"/2.5 cm away from the actual edge of the garment. On a neck or armhole opening, this will be shorter than the edge of the garment; on a shawl, this will be longer.

Planning for Pattern Stitches

If you will be working ribbing or any other repeating pattern, pick up an even multiple of the pattern repeat. For K1, P1 ribbing, for example, you need an even number of stitches. For K2, P2, you need a multiple of four. If you find this difficult, then pick up as best you can and adjust by increasing or decreasing as necessary on the first round. If you get to the end of the first round and discover you have an extra stitch, check to make sure you worked the pattern correctly and recount your stitches. If you find that you do have an extra stitch, simply decrease at the end of the round and keep going in pattern. If there is more than one extra stitch, you'll need to unravel some of the round and spread the required decreases out so they aren't noticeable. The best location for this is a point where the edge makes a concave curve (like the back neck corners or the underarm corners), because the decreases will help fit the border or sleeve to the curve.

When you've picked up all the way around, don't turn; just keep going in the same direction to start working circularly — unless, of course, you want to make a flat border instead of a circular one.

CONVERTING FLAT TO CIRCULAR

You may be wondering whether everything can be knit circularly, and if so, why anyone would want to take the extra trouble to knit separate pieces and then sew them together. Although there are many obvious pluses to knitting circularly, there are also very good reasons why some projects don't translate well to circular knitting. Typically these have to do with structure and support, but some pattern stitches are surprisingly resistant to circular adaptation.

First consider the Pros and Cons (at right), which will help you decide whether the garment is likely to be successful if knit circularly. If you then decide to proceed with converting an existing pattern from flat to circular construction, the two major areas you must deal with are the pattern stitch and the overall instructions for the project. Pattern stitches must be converted to circular knitting, either by rewriting the instructions or by charting. Both of these techniques are discussed in detail, with a wide range of examples, beginning on page 82. Once you've determined that you can successfully work the pattern stitches circularly, you'll need to revise the instructions for the project as a whole. You must consider the order and direction of construction as well as finishing details, and make clear notes of your plans for circular knitting. This process is discussed in Converting Garment Instructions from Flat to Circular (page 99).

PROS AND CONS OF CIRCULAR VS. FLAT KNITTING

Five Reasons to Knit Circularly

1 No sewing. Any part of the garment that's knit circularly is seamless, so there's no sewing up.

2 No purling. If you are working in stockinette stitch, then there's no purling (and we all know how much some knitters hate to purl).

3 Matching lengths. Circular knitting guarantees that the front and back are the same length, so you don't have to count rows or measure to be consistent.

4 Matching horizontal stripes and patterns. If you're working colored stripes or textured patterns, circular knitting ensures that the stripes and patterns match, back to front and side to side.

5 Yarn management. If there's any chance that you'll run out of one color, working circularly means that you don't end up in a situation where you've included that color in the back, but run out before you can knit the matching front.

Five Reasons to Knit Flat

1 Pattern stitches. While all pattern stitches can be converted to be worked in circular knitting, some are much more difficult or time consuming when worked circularly. Others, like cables, can be difficult to work consistently, because the pattern rows are easier to keep track of when there are both right-side and wrong-side rows. In these cases, you may prefer to work them flat.

2 Intarsia. The color technique of working separate areas with separate yarn supplies, called intarsia, can only be worked flat. There are several ways to incorporate intarsia into circular knitting, such as joining the fabric into a round so that no seams are required, while continuing to work the color-patterned areas back and forth. All of these require more effort than simply working the intarsia pattern flat and then sewing seams. One alternative is to convert the intarsia pattern to a stranded pattern so that it can be easily worked circularly with fewer yarn supplies, but this is not practicable with all designs.

3 Support. A knitted bag, for example, holds its shape better if there are sewn seams to support it. A heavy sweater, especially if it's made of anything but wool, tends to stretch in length if there are no seams.

4 Bias. Some yarns are over- or under-twisted, and items knitted from them tend to spiral without seams to stabilize them. This may not be apparent with a strongly horizontal pattern, but if there is vertical ribbing or cables, it may become noticeably diagonal.

5 Fit. Tailored garments, with fitted armholes and sleeve caps, can be made circularly, but they require short-row shaping, which is a bit more complicated than shaping flat garment pieces. Without seams to support them, fitted circular garments may still stretch in length and end up not fitting properly. For this reason, simply shaped garments made from wool or a wool-blend yarn, knit firmly enough so that the fabric holds its shape, are your best bet for circular construction. On the other hand, short-row shaping used for shoulders or for bust darts can be just as easily incorporated into circular garments as into flat garments. Keep in mind, if your primary reason for choosing knitting in the round is to avoid purling, short-row shaping will always require you to work back and forth; if you are working in stockinette, half of the rows will be purled.

KNITTING FROM CHARTS

Charts make it easy to work pattern stitches flat or circularly, without having to rewrite the instructions in words. Charts of pattern stitches are laid out in a grid, with one square representing each stitch. They portray textured pattern stitches using individual symbols for the various stitch manipulations, such as purls and slipped stitches. For a complete list of the symbols used in this book and their meanings, see page 310.

When representing flat knitting, charts usually show a single pattern repeat plus any additional stitches that serve to center the pattern on the fabric. In circular knitting there are usually no centering stitches because, assuming that the stitch count is a multiple of the pattern repeat, the pattern will repeat around endlessly. The repeating section of the chart is usually indicated by a wide bracket across the bottom or heavy vertical lines on each side of the repeat. If there are no special markings, check for supporting text instructions that clarify which stitches are in the repeating section of the pattern.

Each horizontal row of a chart represents a row of your knitting. Each square across the row represents an individual stitch. Because the first row hangs at the bottom of your knitting, the first row of a chart is the bottom row.

Occasionally wrong-side rows do not appear on a chart at all. This is sometimes done to reduce the size of large lace charts. In this case, the right-side rows are the pattern rows and the wrong-side rows (that do not appear) are simply purled or the stitches are worked "as established," knitting the knits and purling the purls. If wrong-side rows are omitted from the chart, it will say so in the instructions.

Working Charts Circularly

If you are working circularly, work the pattern repeatedly until you get to the end of the round. Then, move up one row on the chart and continue to follow it from right to left, working the pattern repeat in the new row until you again reach the end of the round. Always read from right to left and always move up one row in the chart each time you begin a new round.

Working Charts Flat

If you are working flat, read the right-side rows from right to left, just as for circular knitting. Work any edge stitches at the beginning of the row, work the pattern repeat across, and end with any edge stitches at the end of the row. Turn your knitting. When you work the next row across the wrong side of your knitting, you must read across the next higher row of the chart in the opposite direction, from left to right. First work any edge stitches at the left edge of the chart, then work the pattern repeat across, and finish by working any edge stitches at the right edge of the chart. Continue moving up one row on the chart each time you complete a row of your knitting. Be sure to read the right-side rows from right to left and the wrong-side rows from left to right. Whenever you are working on the wrong side, you must also remember that knits and purls are reversed on the wrong-side rows.

Chart Symbols

Knits are usually shown as an empty square. On right-side rows, knit these stitches. On wrong-side rows, purl them (so that when you turn to the right side they look like knits). The symbol key usually provides guidance such as "knit on the right side, purl on the wrong side." Purls are usually shown as dashes, shaded squares, or dots. On right-side rows, purl these stitches. On wrong-side rows, knit them (so that when you turn to the right side they look like purls).

Symbols for common stitch manipulations are listed on page 310 in the appendix.

If the pattern has a different number of stitches on some rows, you may see a black or dark gray square mysteriously labeled "no stitch." This seeming contradiction means that, while there's a place holder in the chart for a stitch that has disappeared or will appear on a subsequent row, there's currently no corresponding stitch on your needle. When you come to "no stitch" in the chart, ignore that square on the chart, skip to the next square on the chart that represents a real stitch, and continue working with the next stitch on your needle.

Pattern Stitches: Converting Flat to Circular

It's important to be able to work a pattern stitch identically both flat and circularly, because many projects have flat sections as well as circular sections. For example, if you make a bag, you can knit the body of the bag circularly, but the flap is normally just one layer thick, so it would be knit flat. Vests and sweaters (unless you plan to cut the armholes and neck open later) are usually constructed circularly below the underarms, then the fronts and backs are worked separately (flat) up to the shoulders. In both of these cases, if the same pattern stitch is used in both flat and circular sections, you need to make them look identical.

Converting Stockinette Stitch

The simplest example of a pattern stitch that must be converted from flat to circular is stockinette stitch. When you are working flat, stockinette is a two-row pattern:

Row 1 (right side): Knit.

Row 2 (wrong side): Purl.

To make stockinette in flat knitting, you must purl on the wrong side. In circular knitting, the right side is always facing you and you never work on the wrong side; therefore, you never have to purl. Circular stockinette stitch is a one-round pattern:

Round 1 (and all other rounds): Knit.

One of the difficulties you may face is that your knitted stitches are looser or tighter than your purled stitches. (See my discussion of this in relation to gauge, Making Circular Swatches, page 52.) If your gauge changes between flat and circular knitting, it affects the finished size of your project. If your project has some sections that are worked flat and others that are worked circularly, then the gauge may vary from section to section. Not only does this affect the size, it affects the appearance. With every round knitted, all the rounds will look identical. When you switch to flat knitting and begin purling the wrong side rows, any variation in tension between knitting and purling makes alternate rows look looser or tighter (see photo above). When working patterns that combine knits and purls on the same rows or rounds, the gauge may not change noticeably, but the appearance will. If you see that columns of knit stitches look irregular after changing to flat knitting, it is prob-

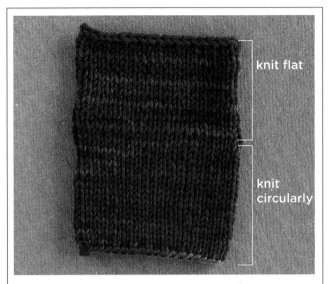

Need to adjust? If your flat knitting looks inconsistent, like the top half of this swatch, then you need to figure out whether the purls are looser or tighter than your knits, and adjust your tension to make them identical.

ably because they are alternately tighter and looser when they are knitted and then purled on subsequent rows. To determine if you will have this problem, you'll need to make both circular and flat swatches for any project that requires you to use both techniques.

• **To make your purls tighter,** wrap the yarn an extra time around one of your fingers, be conscious of purling firmly, and form the new stitches on the tapered tip of the needle.

• **To make your purls looser,** reduce the number of wraps around your fingers (if this is the way you tension your yarn), slide each new stitch down onto the straight shaft of the needle, and lift that needle up after the stitch is formed to loosen it a bit.

• **Change needle size.** You may simply be able to use a larger or smaller needle for the purled rows while continuing to use the normal needle size for the knit rows. If you have a set of interchangeable circular needles, you can put a larger point on one end of a circular needle and a smaller point on the other, which may be all you need to do to bring the stitches into sync.

• **Knit backwards.** Another solution, for some knitters, is to knit backward rather than turning and purling. Because everyone's knitting is very individual, you'll need to experiment to discover what works best for you.

MAKING YOUR OWN CHARTS

When the pattern stitch you plan to use isn't charted, you can create your own chart. Use graph paper with a fairly large grid (about 5 stitches per inch). Have a copy of standard chart symbols handy.

① Draw a rectangle on the graph paper with as many squares across as the pattern repeat plus the edge stitches and as many squares high as the number of rows. Sometimes you'll need to make the chart wider, charting two or three pattern repeats across in order to fully represent the pattern.

② Following the written instructions, stitch by stitch, work across each row, from bottom to top within the rectangle, filling in the symbols. On right-side rows, work from right to left and on wrong-side rows work from left to right.

③ For ease in working circularly, mark the pattern repeat with a bracket or heavy vertical lines.

④ Test your chart by knitting from it, both flat and circularly.

If you find that you need to make charts frequently, you may want to invest in one of the charting software programs now available. If you are comfortable working with MS Excel, MS Word, or other spread sheet or word-processing programs that support tables, you can also use them to create charts. A quick Internet search turns up numerous postings and hints on how to do this.

Converting Knit-Purl Patterns

K2, P2 Ribbing

Notice that the flat instructions below include two extra edge stitches so that there is a knit rib at both edges on the right side of the fabric. In the circular instructions, there are no edge stitches so the ribbed pattern repeats continuously around.

K2, P2 RIBBING KNIT FLAT

Cast on a multiple of 4 stitches plus 2.
Row 1 (right side): *K2, P2; repeat from * across, ending K2.
Row 2 (wrong side): P2, *K2, P2; repeat from * across.
Repeat these 2 rows for pattern.

K2, P2 RIBBING KNIT CIRCULARLY

Cast on a multiple of 4 stitches.
Round 1: *K2, P2; repeat from * around.
Repeat this round for pattern.

Beaded Rib

Damask Diamonds

In Beaded Rib, there are two pattern rows, and they are essentially the same in both flat and circular knitting, except that the edge stitch is absent from the circular instructions. Other knit/purl pattern stitches, such as Damask Diamonds (right), are not quite so simple to adapt to circular knitting from flat instructions.

BEADED RIB KNIT FLAT

Cast on an odd number of stitches.
Row 1 (right side): Knit across.
Row 2 (wrong side): P1, *K1, P1; repeat from * across.
Repeat these 2 rows for pattern.

BEADED RIB KNIT CIRCULARLY

Cast on an even number of stitches.
Round 1: Knit around.
Round 2: *K1, P1; repeat from * around.
Repeat these 2 rounds for pattern.

Unlike the narrower, simpler pattern stitches at left, Damask Diamonds isn't symmetrical, so there's more effort involved in rewriting the instructions for circular knitting.

To make the pattern repeat seamlessly in the round, you must make several adjustments when you convert the flat instructions to circular:

• Because there is no edge stitch, cast on one stitch fewer, delete the first column at the right side of the chart, and delete the first stitch from the text of the right-side (odd-numbered) rows and the last stitch from the text of the wrong-side (even-numbered) rows.

• Because wrong-side (even-numbered) rows are worked in the opposite direction, rewrite the text directions for these rows so that the stitches are worked in the opposite order.

• Because wrong-side rows are worked on the right side, reverse all the knits and purls in the text directions.

After you've completed these three steps, you'll have perfect instructions for working circularly. Rewriting instructions can be quite time consuming, however, and it's easy to make mistakes. Becoming adept at reading charts means that you can skip rewriting the text entirely, and delete just the one column from the chart.

DAMASK DIAMONDS KNIT FLAT

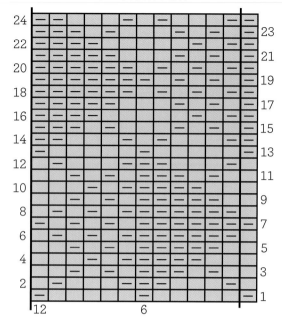

DAMASK DIAMONDS KNIT CIRCULARLY

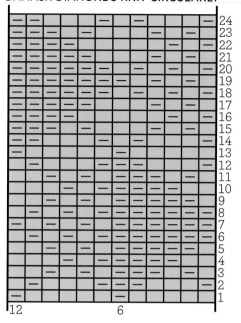

Cast on a multiple of 12 stitches plus 1.

Row 1 (right side): P1, *K5, P1; repeat from *.

Row 2: *P1, K1, P3, K3, P3, K1; repeat from * ending P1.

Row 3: K1, *K1, P1, K1, P3, (K1, P1) twice, K2; repeat from *.

Row 4: *P3, K1, P1, K5, P2; repeat from *, ending P1.

Row 5: K1, *K1, P5, (K1, P1) twice, K2; repeat from *.

Row 6: *(P1, K1) twice, P1, K7; repeat from * ending P1.

Row 7: P1, *P6, (K1, P1) three times; repeat from *.

Row 8: *(P1, K1) twice, P1, K7; repeat from * ending P1.

Row 9: K1, *K1, P5, (K1, P1) twice, K2; repeat from *.

Row 10: *P3, K1, P1, K5, P2; repeat from * ending P1.

Row 11: K1, *K1, P1, K1, P3, (K1, P1) twice, K2; repeat from *.

Row 12: *P1, K1, P3, K3, P3, K1; repeat from * ending P1.

Row 13: P1, *K5, P1; repeat from *.

Row 14: *K2, P3, K1, P1, K1, P3, K1; repeat from * ending K1.

Row 15: P1, *(K1, P1) twice, K3, P1, K1, P3; repeat from *.

Row 16: *K4, P5, K1, P1, K1; repeat from * ending K1.

Row 17: P1, *(K1, P1) twice, K3, P5; repeat from *.

Row 18: *K6, (P1, K1) three times; repeat from * ending K1.

Row 19: P1, *(K1, P1) twice, K1, P7; repeat from *.

Row 20: *K6, (P1, K1) three times; repeat from * ending K1.

Row 21: P1, *(K1, P1) twice, K3, P5; repeat from *.

Row 22: *K4, P5, K1, P1, K1; repeat from * ending K1.

Row 23: P1, *(K1, P1) twice, K3, P1, K1, P3; repeat from *.

Row 24: *K2, P3, K1, P1, K1, P3, K1; repeat from * ending K1.

Repeat these 24 rows for pattern.

Cast on a multiple of 12 stitches.

Round 1: *K5, P1; repeat from *.

Round 2: *P1, K3, P3, K3, P1, K1; repeat from *.

Round 3: *K1, P1, K1, P3, (K1, P1) twice, K2; repeat from *.

Round 4: *K2, P5, K1, P1, K3; repeat from *.

Round 5: *K1, P5, (K1, P1) twice, K2; repeat from *.

Round 6: *P7, (K1, P1) twice, K1; repeat from *.

Round 7: *P6, (K1, P1) three times; repeat from *.

Round 8: *P7, (K1, P1) twice, K1; repeat from *.

Round 9: *K1, P5, (K1, P1) twice, K2; repeat from *.

Round 10: *K2, P5, K1, P1, K3; repeat from *.

Round 11: *K1, P1, K1, P3, (K1, P1) twice, K2; repeat from *.

Round 12: *P1, K3, P3, K3, P1, K1; repeat from *.

Round 13: *K5, P1; repeat from *.

Round 14: *P1, K3, P1, K1, P1, K3, P2; repeat from *.

Round 15: *(K1, P1) twice, K3, P1, K1, P3; repeat from *.

Round 16: *P1, K1, P1, K5, P4; repeat from *.

Round 17: *(K1, P1) twice, K3, P5; repeat from *.

Round 18: *(P1, K1) three times, P6; repeat from *.

Round 19: *(K1, P1) twice, K1, P7; repeat from *.

Round 20: *(P1, K1) three times, P6; repeat from *.

Round 21: *(K1, P1) twice, K3, P5; repeat from *.

Round 22: *P1, K1, P1, K5, P4; repeat from *.

Round 23: *(K1, P1) twice, K3, P1, K1, P3; repeat from *.

Round 24: *P1, K3, P1, K1, P1, K3, P2; repeat from *.

Repeat these 24 rounds for pattern.

Converting Knit-Below Patterns

Shaker Rib

In the flat version of Shaker Rib, the first two stitches of each row are worked simply as knit stitches, which avoids having to execute a knit below (see page 307) in the very first stitch of the row. There is only one pattern row, making it fully reversible.

The circular version, on the other hand, requires two different pattern rounds. The first round is identical to Row 1 of the flat pattern, except that there is no K2 at the beginning of the round; this means that the pattern repeats endlessly across the beginning/end of the round. Round 2 must do all of the work to reverse the pattern, using the technique of purling below on alternate stitches.

SHAKER RIB KNIT FLAT

Cast on an even number of stitches and knit 1 row.
Row 1: K1, *K1, K below; repeat from * across, ending K1.
Repeat Row 1 for pattern.

SHAKER RIB KNIT CIRCULARLY

Cast on an even number of stitches and knit 1 round.
Round 1: *K below, K1; repeat from * around.
Round 2: *P1, P below; repeat from * around.
Repeat Rounds 1 and 2 for pattern.

Converting Slipped-Stitch Patterns

Slipped Honeycomb

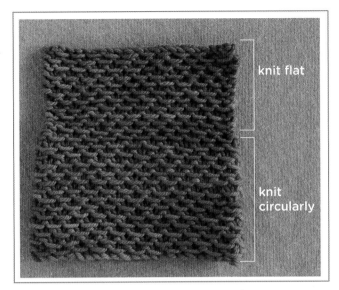

When you work this pattern flat, you always knit the right-side rows and work the pattern rows on the wrong side. When you turn back to the right side at the end of each pattern row, you can see the longer strands created by the holding yarn in back while slipping stitches; this is what produces the pattern. *When you work this pattern in the round,* the right-side rows are the same as flat knitting (knit around). The pattern rows must be reversed, however, and you alternate purling and slipping stitches with the yarn held in front, so that the longer strands are visible as you work circularly.

The actual slipping of the stitches is the same in both cases — always slip the stitch purlwise. The position of the yarn (always on the right side of the fabric) is the same as well. What's different about working circularly is that the right side is facing you.

SLIPPED HONEYCOMB KNIT FLAT

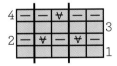

Cast on an odd number of stitches.
Row 1 (right side): Knit.
Row 2: K1, *Slip 1 purlwise wyib, K1; repeat from *.
Row 3: Knit.
Row 4: K1, *K1, Slip 1 purlwise wyib; repeat from * until 2 stitches remain, K2.
Repeat these 4 rows for pattern.

Cast on an even number of stitches.
Round 1: Knit.
Round 2: *P1, slip 1 purlwise wyif; repeat from * around.
Round 3: Knit.
Round 4: *Slip 1 purlwise wyif, P1; repeat from * around.
Repeat these 4 rounds for pattern.

Converting Cables

Cabled patterns are usually based on ribbing, with the cables crossing the stitches in the knit ribs. When worked flat, cables are almost always crossed on the right-side rows. On wrong-side rows, you continue to work the ribbing (knitting the knits and purling the purls). These conventions make it very easy to convert instructions for cables from flat to circular knitting. The instructions for right-side rows don't need to be rewritten, and the instructions for wrong-side rows are all "work in ribbing as established."

The challenge when working cables circularly is that it can be difficult to see what row you're on in your knitting. In flat knitting, you can tell you're on a right side row and be sure that it's the correct row to cross the cable. In circular knitting, all of the rows are on the right side, and it's easy to cross a cable one round too early or too late, so count your rounds carefully.

To make it easier to count the rounds, you can work the purled ribs as garter stitch, knitting and purling on alternate rounds (for an example, see the Cable and Gusset Mitten, pages 230–233). Or take advantage of the fact that you can cross the cables easily on any round, and cross them every five or seven rounds (for example) if that looks best to you.

Cable with Purled Ribs

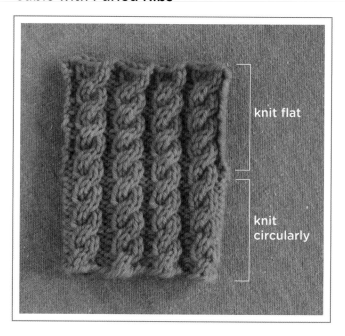

knit flat

knit circularly

CABLE WITH PURLED RIBS KNIT FLAT

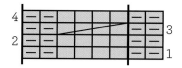

Cast on a multiple of 6 stitches plus 2.
Row 1 (right side): P2, *K4, P2; repeat from *.
Row 2: *K2, P4; repeat from *, ending K2.
Row 3: P2, *slip 2 to cable needle, hold in back of work, K2, K2 from cable needle, P2; repeat from *.
Row 4: *K2, P4; repeat from *, ending K2.
Repeat these 4 rows for pattern.

CABLE WITH PURLED RIBS KNIT CIRCULARLY

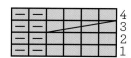

Cast on a multiple of 6 stitches.
Rounds 1 and 2: *K4, P2; repeat from *.
Round 3: *Slip 2 to cable needle, hold in back of work, K2, K2 from cable needle, P2; repeat from *.
Round 4: *K4, P2; repeat from *.
Repeat these 4 rounds for pattern.

Converting Single Decreases

Single decreases include K2tog, P2tog, ssk, and ssp. You'll see from the next two patterns, Turkish Stitch and Faggoting Stitch, that K2tog reverses to P2tog and ssk reverses to ssp. You rarely find pattern stitches with an ssk on a wrong-side row, which is a good thing because ssp is tiresome to work. (For instructions on how to work all of these, see Decreases, in the appendix.)

Turkish Stitch

Like Shaker Rib (page 87), Turkish Stitch is a fully reversible pattern, with only one row when worked flat. To convert it to circular knitting, you must substitute P2tog for K2tog on Round 2. Notice that yarn overs are worked the same on both rounds. But also notice that the circular chart and instructions include an edge stitch, which is very unusual. Because there is a yarn over at the end of Round 2, followed immediately by another yarn over at the beginning of Round 1, a single seam stitch separates the two. Because the pattern stitch is based on garter stitch (where every row is knitted), in the circular version it looks best if the seam stitch is knitted on the knit rounds and purled on the purl rounds.

TURKISH STITCH KNIT FLAT

Cast on an even number of stitches.
Row 1: K1, *yo, K2tog; repeat from * across, ending K1. Repeat this row for pattern.

TURKISH STITCH KNIT CIRCULARLY

Cast on an odd number of stitches.
Round 1: K1, *yo, K2tog; repeat from * around.
Round 2: P1, *P2tog, yo; repeat from * around.
Repeat these 2 rounds for pattern.

Faggoting Stitch

Like Turkish Stitch, circular Faggoting Stitch requires a seam stitch to separate the yarn over at the end of Round 2 from the yarn over at the beginning of Round 1.

FAGGOTING STITCH KNIT FLAT

Cast on an even number of stitches.
Row 1: K1, *yo, ssk; repeat from *, ending K1.
Repeat this row for pattern.

FAGGOTING STITCH KNIT CIRCULARLY

Cast on an odd number of stitches.
Round 1: K1, *yo, ssk; repeat from *.
Round 2: P1, *ssp, yo; repeat from *.
Repeat these 2 rounds for pattern.

Open Star Stitch

From top to bottom, worked in flat knitting Ⓐ, worked circularly the "easy" way Ⓑ, and a perfect match worked circularly Ⓒ. Notice the diagonal quality of the original pattern and how square the center section B is in comparison.

More complex lace patterns frequently have pattern rows on the right side alternating with plain purled rows on the wrong side. It's easy to convert these to circular knitting because the pattern rows are worked identically, and the plain rows are simply knitted instead of purled. When there are pattern rows on the wrong side — especially when they involve double decreases or passing a stitch over another stitch — it's much more difficult to convert them to circular knitting.

In the case of Open Star Stitch, the pattern rows are both wrong-side rows. You can convert to circular knitting by replacing the knits with purls, and by working the pattern in the opposite order across the row, but it's not so easy to convert the special stitch manipulation where the first of the three knit stitches is passed over the other two knit stitches and off the needle. Because of the stitch manipulations involved, this pattern is not easily understood by charting, so no chart has been included.

To work flat:
Cast on a multiple of 3 stitches.
Row 1 (wrong side): K1, *K3, pass the first knit stitch over the other two and off the needle, yo; repeat from * across, ending K2.
Row 2: Knit.
Row 3: K2, *yo, K3, pass the first knit stitch over the other two and off the needle; repeat from * across, ending K1.
Row 4: Knit.
Repeat these 4 rows for pattern.

To work circularly:
When you work Open Star Stitch circularly, the stitch that's passed over goes in the opposite direction compared to the flat version. This is fine if you are only going to work the pattern stitch circularly. If you have sections of flat and circular knitting in the same garment, however, they won't match. There are three different ways to work the stitch manipulation: one easy way that results in stitches that slant the wrong way, a "perfect" one that is difficult to execute, and, finally, one that is perfect *and* easy.

If you are working on double-pointed needles, two circular needles or Magic Loop, you may need to pass a stitch over stitches that fall on two different needles. To do this, see Making Shift, page 42.

The easiest conversion, but one that causes the stitch passed over to slant the wrong way.
Cast on a multiple of 3 stitches.
Round 1: P2, *yo, P3, pass the first purl stitch over the other 2 and off the needle; repeat from * around, ending P1.
Round 2: Knit.
Round 3: P1, *P3, pass the first purl stitch over the other 2 and off the needle, yo; repeat from * around, ending P2.
Round 4: Knit.
Repeat these 4 rounds for pattern.

Following these directions will produce a noticeable solid seam-like area at the beginning/end of round. You can make the pattern look continuous by modifying Rounds 1 and 3 as follows:

At the end of Round 1, when 1 stitch remains, yo, P1, then slip the first 2 stitches of the round from the left needle to the right needle purlwise, pass the third stitch on the right-hand needle over the 2 slipped stitches and off the needle, slip the same 2 stitches back to the left-hand needle. The beginning of round is between the two needle points.

At the beginning of Round 3, work P1, yo, then begin the pattern repeat. Work the end of the round as written, then slip the first stitch of the round from the left needle to the right needle purlwise, pass the third stitch on the right-hand needle over the last 2 stitches and off the needle. Do not slip any stitches back to the left-hand needle. The beginning of round is between the two needle points.

A "perfect" but painful conversion.
To truly reverse this pattern so the circular version exactly duplicates the flat version, a more complicated manipulation is required. Since all the slipping can be tedious and time consuming, you might want to consider whether it's worth the effort.

Cast on a multiple of 3 stitches.

Round 1: P2, *yo, P3, slip 3 purlwise back to the left needle, pass the third stitch from the end over the other 2 and off the needle, slip 2 purlwise back to the right needle; repeat from * around, ending P1.

Round 2: Knit.

Round 3: P1, *P3, slip 3 purlwise back to the left needle, pass the third stitch from the end over the other 2 and off the needle, slip 2 purlwise back to the right needle, yo; repeat from * around, ending P2.

Round 4: Knit.

Repeat these 4 rounds for pattern.

As in the "easy" version above, these directions will produce a noticeable solid area at the beginning/end of round. Following basically the same procedure, you can make the pattern look continuous.

At the end of Round 1, when 1 stitch remains, yo, P1, then slip the stitch you just worked from the left needle to the right needle purlwise, pass the third stitch on the left-hand needle over 2 stitches and off the needle. Do not slip any stitches back to the right-hand needle. The beginning of round is between the two needle points.

At the beginning of Round 3, work P1, yo, then begin the pattern repeat. Work the end of the round as written, then slip the last two stitches you worked from the right needle to the left needle purlwise. Pass the third stitch on the left-hand needle over the 2 stitches and off the needle. Slip 2 stitches from the left-hand needle back to the right-hand needle purlwise. The beginning of round is between the two needle points.

Perfect and easy.
Work this pattern inside out! Rounds 1 and 3 are worked identically to the flat instructions, and Rounds 2 and 4 are purled. Like all the other examples, following the directions exactly will make a solid area at the beginning/end of round and you can make it look continuous using the same approach.

Round 1: At the beginning of round, work K1, yo, then begin the pattern repeat. End the round as written. Slip the first stitch of the round from the left needle to the right needle purlwise and pass the third stitch on the right-hand needle over and off the tip of the needle. Do not slip any stitches back to the left needle. The beginning of round is between the two needle points.

Round 3: When 1 stitch remains at the end of the round, work yo, K1. Slip 2 stitches at the beginning of the round from the left needle to the right needle purlwise and pass the third stitch on the right-hand needle over and off the tip of the needle. Slip 2 stitches purlwise back to the left needle. The beginning of round is between the two needle points.

Converting Double Decreases

Double decreases, such as K3tog, P3tog, sk2p, and s2kp2 decrease 3 stitches down to just 1 stitch. These can be more difficult to reverse for circular knitting than single decreases. Luckily, it is rare that you really need to reverse them. I attempted to find a pattern stitch to use as an example but found none. Instead, all of the double decreases that fell on a wrong-side row were worked using P3tog, which is the equivalent of working K3tog on the right side. This just goes to show how clever knitters have always been — they don't make things any more difficult for themselves than is absolutely necessary.

If you do encounter a situation where double decreases are worked on both the wrong- and right-side rows, and they need to match each other or to slant in specific directions, here's how to do it: when you convert the pattern stitch for circular knitting choose the decrease to use based on whether you need a knitted or a purled stitch, which way it should slant, and how easy it is to execute. For example, while you can work a complicated left-slanting decrease on the reverse stockinette side, it's much easier to work a simple P3tog to match a K3tog, and let the decreases slant to the right instead of to the left. See A Study in Possibilities (below) to better understand these considerations.

A Study in Possibilities

While the knit sides of both swatches are shown, to compare the effects of these double decreases, the decreases were worked on the knit side in the left swatch and on the purl side in the right swatch.

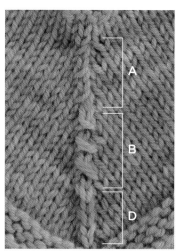

Knit-side decreases

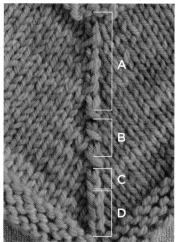

Purl-side decreases

Knit 3 together (K3tog) on the knit side and purl 3 together (P3tog) on the purl side match each other exactly, making a layered, right-slanting double decrease (Ⓐ left and right).

Finding an exact purl-side match for the left-leaning slip 1 knitwise-K2tog-psso (Ⓑ left) is, however, much more difficult. The best match is achieved by working the following (Ⓑ right):

- Purl 2 together.
- Slip 1 knitwise to the right needle.
- Slip 2 purlwise back to the left needle.
- Pass the left stitch over the right stitch and off the needle.
- Slip 1 purlwise to the right needle.

As you can see, it's hardly worth the effort!

Alternatively, you can achieve almost the same thing by working P2tog, slip 1 purlwise to the left needle, pass the left stitch over the right stitch and off the needle, slip 1 purlwise to the right needle (Ⓒ right). This approach results in the top stitch being twisted, which is unnoticeable in dark or textured yarn.

The centered double decrease at the bottom of both swatches is made on the knit side by working slip 2 together knitwise-K1-psso. The purl side requires a bit more effort: slip 1 knitwise-slip 1 knitwise-slip 2 together knitwise to the left needle-P3tog (Ⓓ left and right).

English Mesh Lace

6-stitch repeat

Cast on a multiple of 6 stitches plus 7

Row 1 (wrong side) and all odd-numbered rows: Purl.

Row 2: K1, yo, *ssk, K1, K2tog, yo, K1, yo; repeat from * until 5 stitches remain, ssk, K1, K2tog, yo, K1.

Row 4: K1, yo, *K1, sk2p, (K1, yo) twice; repeat from * until 5 stitches remain, K1, sk2p, K1, yo, K1.

Row 6: K1, K2tog, yo, K1, yo, *ssk, K1, K2tog, yo, K1, yo; repeat from * until 2 stitches remain, ssk, K1.

Row 8: K2tog, (K1, yo) twice, *K1, sk2p (K1, yo) twice; repeat from * until 2 stitches remain, K1, ssk.

Repeat these 8 rows for pattern.

This lace pattern is really only 4 rows long; Rows 5–8 are the same as Rows 1–4, but offset by 3 stitches. When a pattern repeats like this, shifted so that the key elements fall halfway between where they appeared on the previous repeat, it's called a half drop. In flat knitting, the half drop is centered by working single decreases at both edges, where there's not room for the double decrease used elsewhere in the fabric. This occurs in English Mesh Lace on Row 8. When you convert a pattern like this to circular knitting, you could retain the single decreases on both sides of the beginning and end of round, but it's preferable to omit the edge stitches and replace the two single decreases with a double decrease that falls across the beginning/end of round so that the pattern looks seamless, which is how it's handled in Round 8 of the circular version.

ENGLISH MESH LACE KNIT CIRCULARLY

Cast on a multiple of 6 stitches

Round 1 and all odd-numbered rounds: Knit.

Round 2: *Yo, ssk, K1, K2tog, yo, K1; repeat from * around.

Round 4: *Yo, K1, sk2p, K1, yo, K1; repeat from * around.

Round 6: *K2tog, yo, K1, yo, ssk, K1; repeat from * around.

Round 8: Sl 1 purlwise with yarn in back,*(K1, yo) twice, K1, sk2p; repeat from * completing the final sk2p by using the slipped first stitch of the round.

Repeat these 8 rounds for pattern.

Converting Increases

Just as with decreases, there will be times when you'll need to find a corresponding increase to work on the reverse side of the fabric when converting pattern stitches. The photos and descriptions here walk you through the possibilities. (For instructions on working all of these, see the appendix.)

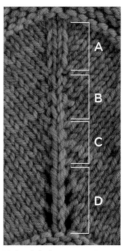

Knit-side increases · Purl-side increases

Single Increases

Compare the single increases in the two swatches from top to bottom: the increases in the left swatch were worked on the knit side; the increases in the right swatch were worked on the purl side.

Ⓐ Row below. Work these increases by knitting into the top of the stitch from the row below. Doing this *before* working the next stitch on the needle results in a right-slanting increase; working it *after* the stitch results in a left-slanting increase. These can be duplicated exactly on the purl side by purling into the top of the stitch on the row below.

Ⓑ Knit-into-the-front-and-back (Kfb). To work the equivalent of Kfb on the purl side, purl into the stitch (leaving it on the needle), then take the needle to the back and purl into the back of the stitch (Pfb).

Ⓒ Make 1 (M1). M1s made with the working yarn are identical on the knit or the purl side of the fabric. To reverse an M1 made by lifting the strand between two stitches on the row below, work identically to a knitted M1, but purl instead of knitting. You may insert the needle under the strand from either front to back or back to front, but when you purl it, take care to work into the front or the back as needed to insure that it twists. If you are working M1 increases in symmetrical pairs, pay attention to which way you twist it when you make it, so that the second stitch of the pair is a mirror image of its mate.

Ⓓ Yarn overs do not need to be reversed — they are the same on both sides of the fabric.

Knit and purl in a single stitch (not shown). If the instructions call for you to knit and purl into a single stitch (such as a yarn over from the previous row), it may look just fine if you don't bother to reverse it. If it does make an esthetic difference, however, simply purl into the stitch first, then knit.

Double Increases

The double increases in the left swatch were worked on the knit side; those in the right swatch were worked on the purl side.

Ⓐ K-P-K into next stitch: reverses to P-K-P into next stitch.

Ⓑ K-yo-K into next stitch: reverses to P-yo-P into next stitch. It is slightly smoother than K-P-K.

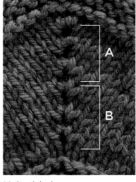

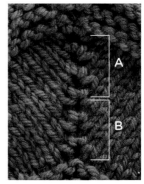

Knit-side increases · Purl-side increases

Disguising the "Jog"

In flat knitting, you can perfectly match pattern stitches and stripes at the seams when you join pieces together. One of the drawbacks of circular knitting is that some patterns cannot be matched perfectly at the beginning/ end of the round. There are, however, techniques to disguise the jog or stair-step effect that is integral to circular knitting.

The "jog" is the place where the pattern is noticeably discontinuous when you begin a new round. When you change to a new round of a pattern stitch, you'll notice that it no longer lines up. If you've just changed colors, you'll notice the beginning of the new color. The jog is caused by the fact that circular knitting is really a spiral, where each round lies above the previous one. Most of the tube doesn't appear to be spiraling: only where one round ends and the next begins is its true structure apparent.

There are several ways to make the jog less apparent. Which you choose will depend on the situation.

It's easy to see the line up the center of this swatch where the garter stitch changes from knit to purl and back again at the beginning/end of round.

Pattern Stitches without the Jog

Pattern stitches are usually a problem only when the pattern is horizontal.

• **Vertical patterns.** If your total number of stitches in a vertical pattern (such as ribbing or cables) is an exact multiple of the pattern repeat, the piece should look seamless.

knit flat

knit circularly

Ribbing pattern appears seamless because stitch count is multiple of pattern repeat.

Striped pattern appears seamless because stitch count is multiple of pattern repeat.

• **Patterns that reverse on every round.** Patterns like Seed Stitch and the two-color checkerboard known as Salt and Pepper can be forced to repeat seamlessly by adjusting the number of stitches. If you work them on an even number of stitches, the jog is obvious; if you add or subtract one stitch to make the total odd, they repeat joglessly.

Seed stitch, on odd number above (seamless) **Ⓐ** and even number of stitches below purled ridge (noticeable beginning/end of round at center) **Ⓑ**.

• **Strongly horizontal patterns.** It's not quite as easy to disguise the point where the end of one round meets the beginning of the next if the pattern is strongly horizontal.

Single pattern rounds. If there is just one round to be dealt with, for example one ridge of purl stitches, a round of eyelets, or a round of picots, work the single round, then slip the first stitch of the following round. This will pull the first stitch of the pattern round up next to the last stitch.

Two-round patterns. For patterns with a two-round repeat (garter stitch, for instance), you can use Helix Knitting (see pages 128–129) to hide the jog. Use one ball of yarn for the knit rounds and a second ball of yarn for the purl rounds. The jog will be apparent only at the bottom and top edges. (See the Jogless Garter Stitch Hat, pages 139–141, for an example)

Patterns more than two rounds long. If you have a horizontal pattern more than two rounds long, the most efficient solution is to introduce seam stitches. These are a small number of stitches at the beginning of the round that are worked in stockinette, garter, or some other simple pattern stitch. They serve to separate the beginning and end of the round of more complex patterns so that their misalignment is not so noticeable. On a hat or sock, you might want just one set of seam stitches at the beginning/end of round. Sweaters and vests, however, will be symmetrical if you introduce a second set of seam stitches halfway around.

Seam stitches. At the bottom of this swatch **Ⓑ**, double garter stitch shows a distinct jog that is disguised in the top half **Ⓐ** by seam stitches.

Stripes without the Stair Step

Single-round and multiround stripes present their own special problems, too. Carrying the yarn from stripe to stripe distorts the stitches at the color changes, and while knotting the new color to the old color eliminates the distortion, the jog is still evident (see photos below).

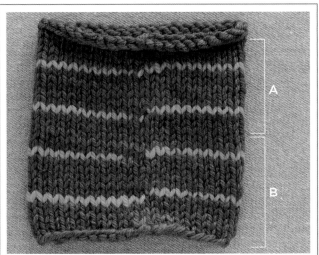

Carrying yarn from stripe to stripe distorts stitches at color changes (bottom two stripes) **B**; knotting new color to old color eliminates distortion but jog still apparent (top two stripes) **A**.

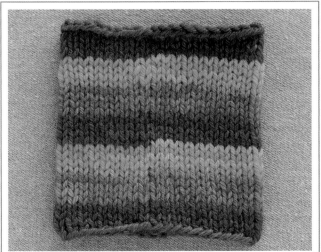

Knotting new color to old color in multiround stripes makes it obvious where each color change occurs.

• **Multiround stripes.** For stripes with more than one round of each color, here are three ways to camouflage the jog when you change colors.

• Knit below on the first stitch of the second round, and then work duplicate stitch **A**. (See Knit Below in the Appendix, page 307.)

• Slip the first stitch of the second round, and then work duplicate stitch **B**.

• Just work duplicate stitch **C**.

In my experience, slipping the first stitch of the second round of a color produces the best results. To do this, cut the yarn when you change colors. Knit the first round in the new color. When you come to the first stitch of the second round, slip it purlwise with the yarn in back. Continue knitting the rest of the stripe as usual. Do this each time you change to a new color. When the knitting is complete, use duplicate stitch to pull the color into alignment exactly as described on page 98 for single-round stripes.

If your knitting is very tight, however, slipping stitches to disguise the color change will make it even tighter. Try knitting into the stitch on the round below instead of slipping, because this makes the knitting a tiny bit looser. Choose between the two options based on what looks best to you.

These same techniques can also be used to disguise the jog in stranded color patterns, especially when there is a change in the background color.

• **Duplicate stitch disguise.** Single-round stripes can be made to look continuous only if you cut the yarns at both the beginning and end of the round at every color change: Leave 4"–6" (10–15 cm) tails, long enough to sew with easily. When you have finished the project, turn it inside out and duplicate stitch these ends across the end of the round, directly behind the stitches of the same color. As you work, take care to adjust the tension of the stitches attached to the tails so they are the same size as their neighbors. The photo below shows how to proceed. (For more on duplicate stitch, see Duplicate Stitch, Purl Side in the appendix, page 307.)

If you change and cut colors every round, you won't be doing circular knitting at all; you'll actually create a flat piece with loads of ends to join when you weave them in. Helix Knitting (pages 128–129) offers another method of working single-round stripes, without cutting the yarn.

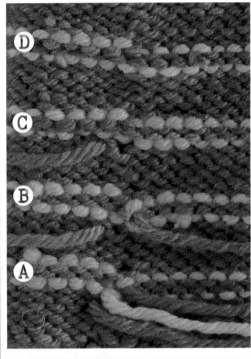

Step 1 Ⓐ. Duplicate stitch the contrast color from right to left across the end of the round behind stitches of the same color (one orange strand woven in, three strands left to go).

Step 2 Ⓑ. Duplicate stitch the contrast color from left to right across the end of the round behind stitches of the same color (two orange strands woven in, two burgundy strands to go).

Step 3 Ⓒ. Duplicate stitch the main color from right to left above the stripe (one burgundy strand left to go).

Step 4 Ⓓ. Duplicate stitch the main color from left to right below the stripe (all strands woven in).

Finished Ⓔ. The ends of the single-round stripes in the finished knitting line up when you take the time to do this.

CONVERTING GARMENT INSTRUCTIONS FROM FLAT TO CIRCULAR

All instructions can be reworked so that any garment can be constructed circularly. For some highly tailored or less-conventional garment structures, it may be more difficult to make them circularly, which you'll discover when you try to figure out how to do it. For almost every conventional sweater, however, following the seven steps below will let you plan for their seamless fabrication.

❶ **Review the instructions.** First read through the original pattern and make sure you understand it, including all shaping and finishing.

❷ **Convert the pattern stitches.** Convert any pattern stitches to circular knitting, as described earlier in Pattern Stitches: Converting Flat to Circular (page 83). Be sure to practice them and to check your gauge in circular knitting. If there is a colored or textured pattern stitch, the beginning/end of round will probably be noticeable, but you can take steps to disguise it (see Disguising the "Jog," pages 95–98). Practice this in your circular swatch. Also practice and check the gauge in flat knitting if it will be required in the garment.

❸ **Determine the beginning of the round.** Decide where the beginning of the round will be (usually a side seam for a pullover). Will there be a noticeable jog? If so, put the beginning/end of round where it will be least apparent. Will the first half of the round be the back or the front? Does it matter, or are back and front the same up to the underarms?

❹ **Decide the order of construction.** The circular architecture diagrams illustrate various ways sweaters can be constructed (for bottom-up construction, see below; for top-down construction, see the next page). Pick one that looks the most like the garment you plan to make, then decide whether you prefer to work from the bottom up or the top down. Pattern revisions are simpler if you work in the same direction as the original flat garment. Also decide whether the sleeves will be picked up and knit down, knit from the bottom up and joined to the body at a yoke, or sewn on later. If the pattern stitch can be turned upside down without looking bad, then you can avoid seaming by picking

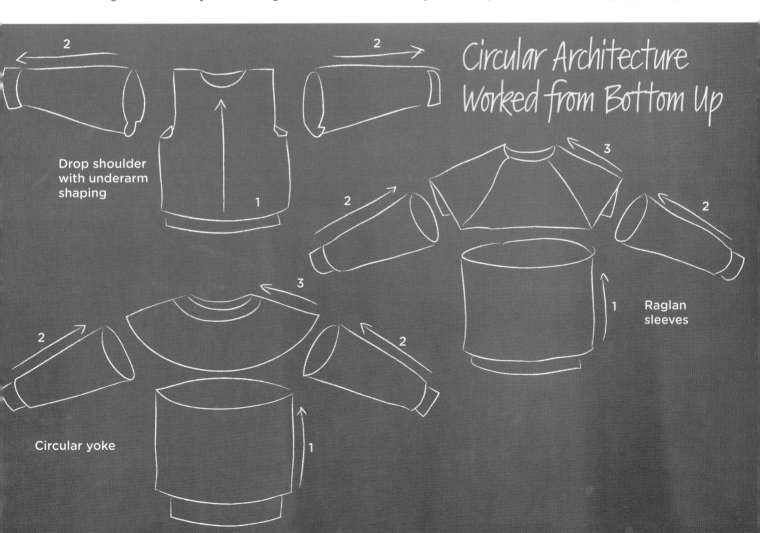

Circular Architecture Worked from Bottom Up

Drop shoulder with underarm shaping

Circular yoke

Raglan sleeves

up the stitches for the sleeves around the armholes and working circularly down to the cuff. This is easiest if you're making a sleeve that doesn't have sleeve cap shaping, but it's possible to introduce short rows to shape a simple sleeve cap, if desired (see Sleeve and Armhole Options, pages 260–261).

5 Plan the finishing details. If there are shoulder seams, do you want to sew them together or use the Three-Needle Bind Off to join them? If they are sloped, plan ahead and work short rows for the shaping rather than binding off so that you can then use the Three-Needle Bind Off (page 69) to join the seam (see Sloped Shoulder Shaping in the V-Neck Vest, page 259). Or, plan to bind off to shape the shoulders, then sew them together as usual. Do you want to knit the neck border as part of the body, or do you prefer to pick up stitches and add it later? Keep in mind that if there is neck shaping, it's most easily worked flat, which means completing the neck and adding the border later.

6 Rewrite garment instructions. Rewrite the instructions in rounds rather than rows. For example, a round includes the whole front plus the whole back. If a close fit is important, or the yarn is bulky, decide whether you need to delete seam stitches from the total stitch count. At a gauge of 5 stitches per inch (2 stitches/cm), the 4 stitches that would be lost to the side seams are equal to ⁴/₅ of an inch (2 cm). Will a garment this much bigger in circumference still fit okay? In sport-weight yarn, the difference is smaller, but in bulkier yarn, at 2½ stitches per inch (1 stitch/cm), the garment would be 1⅗" (4 cm) bigger around. Would this be too big? If you think so, then deduct two stitches from the back and two stitches from the front (one at each edge) to allow for the lack of seams. As you rewrite the instructions, be sure to put them in the order of construction for your garment. For an example of how to rewrite the instructions, see pages 102–103.

7 Draw it. Sketch a simple schematic for your sweater like the one shown for the circular sweater at the far right, including stitch counts for each stage, shaping details, and arrows indicating the direction of knitting.

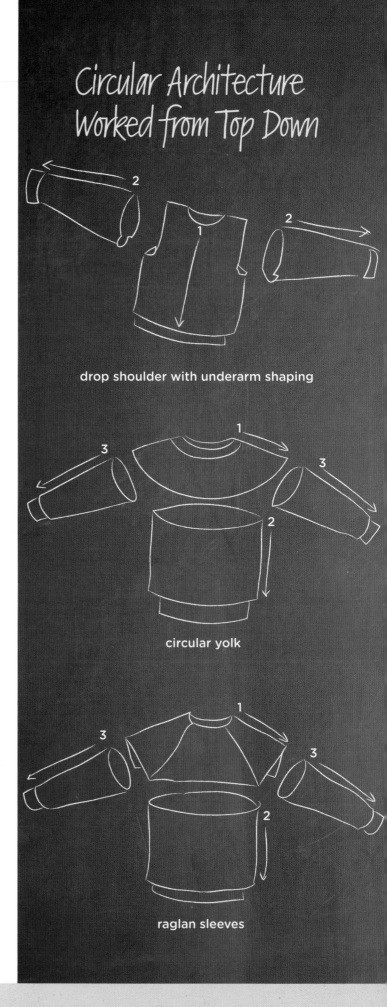

Circular Architecture Worked from Top Down

drop shoulder with underarm shaping

circular yolk

raglan sleeves

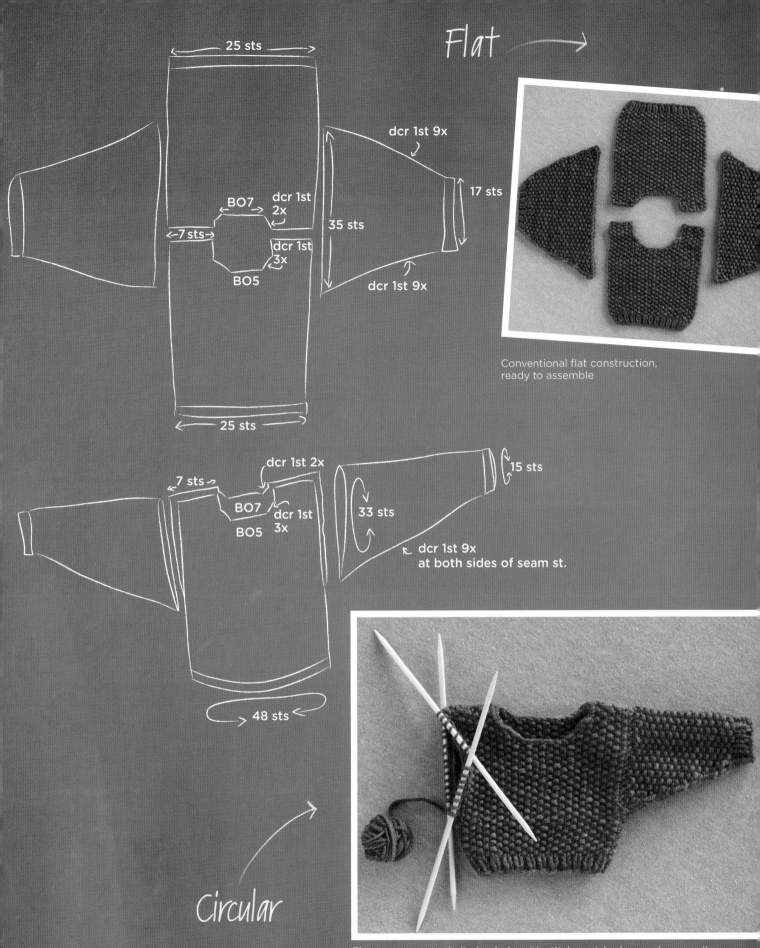

Flat

25 sts

dcr 1st 9x

17 sts

BO7   dcr 1st 2x

7 sts

35 sts

dcr 1st 3x

BO5

dcr 1st 9x

25 sts

Conventional flat construction, ready to assemble

dcr 1st 2x

15 sts

7 sts

BO7   dcr 1st 3x

33 sts

BO5

dcr 1st 9x at both sides of seam st.

48 sts

Circular

The same sweater knit circularly, with stitches picked up and on needles ready to work second sleeve.

CASE STUDY: CONVERTING A BASIC DROP-SHOULDER SWEATER FROM FLAT TO CIRCULAR

Original Flat Instructions	Your New Circular Instructions
Cast on 90 stitches for back.	**Cast on 176 stitches for back and front.** Note: This is (90×2) – 4 seam stitches. Make sure the number you cast on is an even multiple of the rib pattern. Join beginning and end of round.
Work ribbing.	**Work ribbing.**
Increase 10 stitches evenly spaced across (100 stitches).	**Increase 20 stitches** evenly spaced around (196 stitches).
Work back and forth until back is desired length to underarm.	**If desired, indicate side "seams,"** by placing markers at the beginning of the round and at the halfway point. Work circularly until body is desired length to underarm. Note: If you are working a pattern stitch, end with what would be a wrong-side row if you were working flat, so that you can begin the next step on a right-side row.
For flat knitting, the garment continues without shaping until back is desired length to the shoulder.	**Divide your tube in half.** Begin working the back flat between the armholes. On the first row, increase 1 stitch at each end of the row. These will disappear to the inside of the garment when the sleeves are attached. Work just the back stitches and leave the front stitches hanging on the cable of your circular needle, until the back is desired length to the shoulder. If you find it annoying or confusing to leave the front stitches on the needle, you may transfer them to a second circular needle or to a piece of waste yarn until you are ready to work with them.
Bind off.	**Cut the yarn and leave the stitches** for the back hanging on the cable of your circular needle, transfer them to a second circular needle, or place them on a piece of waste yarn.
Cast on 90 stitches for front. Work the front same as back up to the neck opening.	**You've already worked the front up to the underarms.** Attach the yarn to the front and begin working with a right-side row. On the first row, increase one stitch at the beginning and end of the row. Complete the front between the armholes up to the neck opening.
Bind off stitches at center front for neck opening. Shape neck opening. Work until front is the same length as back to shoulder.	**Work neck shaping and up to the shoulder** exactly as called for in the flat instructions.
Bind off both shoulders.	**Turn knitting inside out** and join front to back across first shoulder using Three-Needle Bind Off, bind off stitches for back neck, and join front to back across second shoulder using Three-Needle Bind Off.

To make the sweater seamless, you'll want to pick up for the sleeves around the armholes and knit down, but the pattern is written to knit from the bottom up, so rewrite the instructions, reversing the shaping. To do this, start with the maximum number of stitches at the top, then decrease as you progress rather than increasing. End with the minimum number of stitches at the cuff.

Original Flat Sleeve Instructions from the Bottom Up	Your New Circular Sleeve Instructions from the Top Down
Cast on 30 stitches for sleeve. Work cuff.	**Pick up 58 stitches** around armhole for sleeve, beginning and ending at the bottom of the armhole opening. Mark the "seam" at center of underarm by placing a marker at beginning of round. *Note:* 60 stitches minus 2 seam stitches = 58.
Work in pattern, increasing one stitch at each edge every fourth row until there are 60 stitches.	**Work circularly.** To make "seam" stitches always knit the stitch on either side of the marker, even if you are working a pattern stitch on the sleeve. Work a decrease round every fourth round until 28 stitches remain. **Decrease Round:** K1, ssk, work in pattern until 3 stitches remain before marker, K2tog, K1. **Work cuff.**
Bind off.	**Bind off loosely.**
Finishing: **Sew front to back** at one shoulder seam. **Beginning at open shoulder** pick up stitches across neck opening. Work neck ribbing flat until desired length, then bind off. **Sew front to back** at other shoulder seam. **Sew sleeve seam** and side seams.	**Pick up stitches around neck.** Work neck ribbing circularly, adjusting stitch count so that the ribbing repeats seamlessly, then bind off.

chapter 5

STARTING WITH A TUBE

One of the lovely things about knitting is that even the simplest projects can be knockouts. And in circular knitting, you can make an incredible number of things from a simple tube using plain stockinette or a very easy pattern stitch and minimal finishing. The projects in this chapter fall into this category. They include a scarf, headbands, a hat, and a bag — all made from perfectly straight tubes. Many require no finishing at all, and there are absolutely no seams to be sewn. These qualities make them not only a pleasure to work but also the perfect starting point for those unfamiliar with circular knitting.

In this chapter I also introduce a few techniques that are extremely useful when working circular projects: I-cord for the bag strap, a large buttonhole for the thumb of the fingerless glove, tubular knitting to make a flat potholder, Three-Needle Bind Off to join a seam while binding off, and Provisional Cast Ons used in combination with Kitchener stitch to join seamlessly. All of the projects are sized as small as possible, so you can learn the techniques, complete them quickly, and move on to more exciting knitting.

For simplicity's sake, I have used just one yarn for each of the projects in this chapter, but there's no reason you can't introduce colored stripes or stripes of textured yarns wherever you like, as long as all the yarns for a project knit up at the same gauge. These projects are a perfect place to experiment with color and yarn variations, so give your creativity free expression.

The projects in this chapter are a quick exploration of just a few things you can make from simple knitted tubes, but I've barely scratched the surface. Once you're familiar with circular knitting, you can use the skills you've learned from these beginning projects to make anything you like. Take a look at More Project Ideas (pages 118 and 121) for inspiration.

In the chapters that follow, we'll build on these basic tubes, adding shaping to make the crowns of hats, the bottoms of bags, and garments that fit. We'll explore how pattern stitches and colorwork are integrated into circular knitting and practice more advanced finishing techniques. In the meantime, have fun with these simple introductions to knitting in the round.

Reversible Seamless Scarf

This classic scarf is just a flattened tube, which makes it fully reversible. The colors in the hand-painted yarn spiral up the scarf in attractive diagonals. The fringe at both ends keeps them from curling and joins the two layers together.

For Project Shown You Need

YARN	Lorna's Laces Shepherd Sport (100% superwash wool, 200 yds/2.6 oz)
YARN AMOUNT	400 yds/366 m Bittersweet (630), including fringe
GAUGE	22 stitches = 4" (10 cm) in stockinette stitch
NEEDLE SIZE	US 7 (4.5 mm). Match the project's gauge if you want finished measurements to match pattern instructions. The needle size selected should produce a loose, stretchy fabric.
NEEDLE TYPES (any of the following)	12" (30 cm) circular needle Two circular needles 16" (40 cm) or longer 47" (120 cm) circular needle or longer for Magic Loop Set of four or five double-pointed needles at least 5" (13 cm) long
OTHER SUPPLIES	Stitch marker, 6" (15 cm) square of stiff cardboard, crochet hook (about size I/5.5 mm)
FINISHED SIZE	4¼" (11 cm) wide × 2 yds (1.8 m) long including fringe

New Technique Used
- Cutting and attaching fringe

Knitting the Scarf

- Wind off and set aside 27 yds (25 m) of yarn to be used for fringe.

- Cast on 48 stitches, leaving a tail at least 6" (15 cm) long. It doesn't matter what this cast on looks like, because it will be covered by the fringe, but it's important that it be loose enough so that the edge doesn't pull in.

- Place marker and join the beginning and end of the cast on, being careful not to twist it (see Off to a Good Start: Casting On and Joining, page 13).

- Knit until scarf is 63" (160 cm) long, the length you want, or until you run out of yarn.

- Bind off loosely, so that the end of the scarf doesn't pull in. Cut the yarn, leaving a tail at least 6" (15 cm) long.

Cutting and Applying the Fringe

- **Cutting the yarn.** Wrap all the yarn for the fringes around the cardboard. It should go around at least 78 times. Be sure to begin and end the wrapping at the same edge of the cardboard. Trim the end of the yarn even with this edge. Using a sharp pair of scissors, cut the yarn along this same edge.

- **Applying the fringe.** Working with three strands at a time, fold the yarn in half and use a crochet hook to pull the folded end through both layers of fabric at the end of the scarf. Tuck the cut ends through the loop formed and pull tight to secure the fringe. Attach 13 of these fringes evenly spaced across one end of the scarf. (This will be about every 2 stitches.)

- **Flatten the whole length** of the scarf neatly to make sure it's not twisted. You may want to block the scarf gently at this point to make it behave itself (see Blocking, page 302). Apply fringe to other end, pull the cast-on and bind-off tails into the fringe closest to them and trim the ends so they are even.

Wrapping the yarn for fringe

Using a crochet hook to attach the fringe, three strands at a time

REVERSIBLE SEAMLESS SCARF

Any Size, Any Yarn

Work a circular gauge swatch and measure to find the number of stitches per inch or per centimeter. Decide how wide you want your scarf to be and double this measurement to get the circumference. Multiply the stitches per inch or centimeter by the circumference to get the total number of stitches. Cast on this number of stitches, join the beginning and end of round, and work until the scarf is as long as you like.

Don't want to do the math or the gauge swatch? Set aside yarn for the fringes (you'll need more for a wider scarf). Take a short circular needle (12"/30 cm or 16"/40 cm) and cast on just enough stitches to go all the way around. Count the number of stitches so you'll be able to tell later whether you've dropped or added any. Join the beginning and end of round and begin working circularly. After a couple of inches, take a good look at the fabric. If it looks and feels good, then just keep going. But if it's too loose or too wide, start over with a thinner needle so that it's just right; if it's too tight or too narrow, try a thicker needle.

Optional "Seams"

You can make what appear to be seams at both edges of the scarf by placing a second marker exactly halfway around, opposite the beginning of round. Every other round, when one stitch remains before each marker, slip the stitch purlwise. On other rounds, just knit these stitches, as usual. The edges of the scarf will automatically fold at the columns of slipped stitches, and it's easy to see whether the scarf is twisted before you apply the fringe. If you like, you can purl the "seam" stitches instead of slipping.

Easy Ribbed Headband

Because of their small size, head-bands are some of the quickest projects to make. It's important that the edges don't curl and that the headband be elastic so it stays securely in place. The tremendous elasticity of K2, P2 ribbing makes it perfect for this project: it stretches to an amazing length, and yet it still stays snug.

For Project Shown You Need

YARN	Lorna's Laces Bullfrogs and Butterflies (85% wool/15% mohair, 190 yds/4 oz)
YARN AMOUNT	80 yds/73 m Pink Blossom (1ns)
GAUGE	16 stitches = 4″ (10 cm) in K2, P2 ribbing when stretched (see Measuring Gauge in Ribbing, see page 112)
NEEDLE SIZE	US 8 (5 mm). Match the project's gauge if you want finished measurements to match pattern instructions.
NEEDLE TYPES (any of the following)	16″ (40 cm) circular needle Two circular needles 20″ (50 cm) or longer 47″ (120 cm) circular needle or longer for Magic Loop Set of five double-pointed needles at least 7″ (18 cm) long
OTHER SUPPLIES	Stitch marker, yarn needle
FINISHED SIZE	Relaxed, the headband will be about 13″ (33 cm) around × 4½″ (11 cm) wide. It will stretch easily to 23″ (58 cm) in circumference with a width of about 3½″ (9 cm)

New Techniques Used

- Measuring gauge in ribbing
- Binding off in pattern

Knitting the Headband

- Cast on 92 stitches. This project requires a stretchy cast on, but it's important that it look nice and neat, so I recommend the Long-Tail Cast On (pages 302–303). To ensure that it's stretchy, spread your stitches out a bit on the needle while casting on. Place marker and join the beginning and end of the cast on, being careful not to twist it (see Off to a Good Start: Casting On and Joining, page 13).

- Work in K2, P2 ribbing until the headband measures 4" (10 cm) from cast on.

- Bind off loosely in K2, P2 ribbing (that is, knit the knit stitches and purl the purl stitches as you come to them while binding off).

- Weave in ends on the inside, making the cast-on edge look even (see Mind the Gap, page 76) and the bind off look continuous (see pages 56–57). Since the headband is reversible, choose whichever side looks best to you as the "right side," and weave the ends in on the other side, or weave them in using duplicate stitch (see page 305) so they don't show on either side.

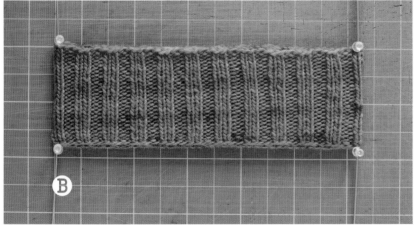

Testing the stretch. This headband is only about 13" (33 cm) around without stretching Ⓐ. But it stretches easily to more than 23" (58 cm) Ⓑ. Notice how much narrower it becomes when you stretch it.

To find the number of stitches per inch (or per centimeter) in the yarn you've chosen, work a gauge swatch in K2, P2 ribbing, then measure the width while stretching gently.

To determine the circumference needed for the finished headband, measure around your head, from the forehead over the ears and around the lower back. Multiply your stitches per inch by this measurement to get the total number of stitches you'll need. This number must be a multiple of four to make the ribbing pattern repeat properly, so round up or down to the nearest multiple of four. For example, if you calculate that you need 74 stitches, you can use either 72 or 76. Cast on this number of stitches and work as described in the instructions at left until the headband is the width you want when stretched to fit your head. Usually this will be 4"–6" (10–15 cm), which will end up as 3"–5" (7.5–12.5 cm) when worn.

MEASURING GAUGE IN RIBBING

It can be tricky to measure gauge accurately in ribbing because it's so very stretchy. K2, P2 ribbing in particular scrunches up so much when it's relaxed that you can't get an accurate measurement. The trick is to make sure that it stretches easily to the required gauge.

It doesn't matter if a ribbed swatch is worked flat or circularly because there are an equal number of knits and purls in the ribbing whichever way you work it. After you've worked about an inch (2.5 cm), stretch the swatch to make sure it stretches easily to the required width (a 20-stitch swatch at a gauge of 20 stitches per 4"/10 cm should stretch easily to 4"/10 cm). If it doesn't easily stretch this much, you'll need a thicker needle. If it stretches easily but looks loose, change to a thinner needle. When you stretch it, notice how much shorter it gets; keep working until the swatch is square when stretched to the correct width. This will give you an idea of how many rows there are in 4" (10 cm) under tension as well as verifying that the number of stitches matches the gauge.

Bind off loosely, wash the swatch and then block (see Blocking, page 302), stretching the swatch to the correct dimensions. Do you still like the ribbing? It should be stretched to show both the knit and the purl ribs, but it shouldn't be flattened out completely, and it should still be able to stretch more if needed. If you think it's too tight, try using a thicker needle.

Playful Pointed Hat

Hats are just tubes with one end open and the other end closed. The upper corners of this hat make two cute points when worn, but it folds completely flat when not in use. The points can be adorned with pom-poms, tassels, bells, braids, or yarn-wrapped rings.

For Project Shown You Need

YARN	Lorna's Laces Revelation (100% wool, 125 yds/4 oz)
YARN AMOUNT	110 yds/100 m Bold Red (11ns)
GAUGE	14 stitches = 4" (10 cm) in stockinette stitch
NEEDLE SIZE	US 10 (6 mm). Match the project's gauge if you want finished measurements to match pattern instructions.
NEEDLE TYPES (any of the following)	16" (40 cm) or 20" (50 cm) circular needle Two circular needles 24" (60 cm) or longer 47" (120 cm) circular needle or longer for Magic Loop Set of five double-pointed needles at least 7" (18 cm) long
OTHER SUPPLIES	Stitch marker; if working with just one circular needle, you'll need an additional needle the same size for working the Three-Needle Bind Off; yarn needle
FINISHED SIZE	20½" (52 cm) in circumference × 7½" (19 cm) in height with bottom edge curled up

New Technique Used

- Three-Needle Bind Off to join a seam

Any Size, Any Yarn

To determine the number of stitches you are getting per inch or per centimeter, work a circular gauge swatch in stockinette and measure. The fabric should be stretchy enough to wear comfortably as a hat, but stiff enough so the two points will stand up.

To determine the circumference of the finished hat, measure around your head, from the forehead, over the ears, and around the lower back. Usually hats are made 1–2" (2.5–5 cm) smaller than the head circumference, so that they cling and stay on, but you may prefer a larger hat that fits more loosely. Adjust your measurement accordingly. Multiply the stitches per inch in your gauge by this measurement to get the total number of stitches you need. This number must be even, so if you come up with an odd number, add 1.

Cast on this number of stitches and work until the hat is tall enough to cover the ears and reach to the crown of the head with the edge rolled up; usually this will be about 40 percent of the circumference. For example, on a hat 20" (51 cm) around, the height will probably be about 8" (20.5 cm). It's better to make the hat too long than too short, because the wearer can just roll up the edge. Follow the directions at the right to complete the hat.

Knitting the Hat

- Cast on 72 stitches using a stretchy cast on. Because of its stretchiness, I recommend the Knitted Cast On (see page 302). Even though it sometimes looks messy, it doesn't matter because the cast on will be hidden by the rolled edge.
- Join the beginning and end of the cast on, being careful not to twist it (see Off to a Good Start: Casting On and Joining, page 13).
- Place a marker to indicate the beginning/end of the round.
- Knit until the hat measures 9" (23 cm) from the cast-on edge with the edge unrolled, or the desired length to crown of head with the edge rolled up.
- When you get to the marker, remove it from the needle, and stop knitting.

Joining the Top of the Hat

- Prepare to work the Three-Needle Bind Off (see page 69) by pushing the knitting through the center of the needle to turn it inside out. (Right sides are now facing.)
- If you're using two circular needles or the Magic Loop, your knitting should already be divided evenly, with 36 stitches in each half. If you're working on double-pointed needles, put half the stitches on one needle and half on a second needle. If you're working on one circular needle, pull a loop of the cable through between the stitches exactly halfway around the hat before you start binding off.
- Join the top of the hat using the Three-Needle Bind Off. Using a yarn needle, weave in the tail on the inside. Weave in the cast-on tail along the cast-on edge.
- Embellish corners if desired.

TURNING A HAT INTO A BAG

A hat turned upside down becomes a bag — all you need to do is add a strap. Using two double-pointed needles, cast on 4 stitches leaving a 6" (15 cm) tail and work an I-cord to a length of about 47" (120 cm) when stretched, or to the desired length for a strap (see Basic I-Cord, page 50). Cut the yarn, leaving a 6" (15 cm) tail and pull through all 4 stitches. Use the tails to sew the strap to the inside of the bag, just below the rolled edge.

Heavenly Hand Warmers

Fingerless gloves, made from tubes with just a thumbhole, keep your hands warm but leave your fingers free for knitting, writing, or whatever else you need to do. Luxurious angora makes them unbelievably soft and warm.

For Project Shown You Need

YARN	Lorna's Laces Angel (70% angora/ 30% lambswool, 50 yds/½ oz)
YARN AMOUNT (for two hand warmers)	50 yds/46 m Berry (23ns)
GAUGE	18 stitches = 4" (10 cm) in stockinette stitch
NEEDLE SIZE	US 7 (4.5 mm) Match the project's gauge if you want finished measurements to match pattern instructions.
NEEDLE TYPES (any of the following)	Two circular needles 16" (40 cm) or longer 47" (120 cm) circular needle or longer for Magic Loop Set of four or five double-pointed needles at least 5" (13 cm) long
OTHER SUPPLIES	Stitch marker, yarn needle
FINISHED SIZE	7" (18 cm) circumference × 4¼" (11 cm) long

New Techniques Used

- Making a thumbhole
- Binding off in pattern

Any Size, Any Yarn

Don't bother to work a gauge swatch, because it would be as large around as the actual hand warmer. Instead calculate the number of stitches to cast on in this way:

- Get the circumference of your hand by measuring it around the middle; do not include your thumb.

- Estimate your stitch gauge by referring to the yarn label or allow about 6 stitches per inch (2.5 cm) in sport weight, 5 stitches per inch for worsted weight, or 4½ stitches in bulky-weight yarn.

- Get the number of stitches needed by multiplying the stitches per inch (or centimeter) by the measurement of the circumference of your hand.

You'll need an even number to accommodate the K1, P1 ribbing, so if you end up with an odd number, add 1.

Cast on this number of stitches and work in ribbing until the cuff is as long as you want. Slip the knitting over your hand to make sure it fits the way you want. If it's too big or too small, decide how many stitches you should have cast on, unravel, and start over with the new, correct number.

When the ribbed cuff is the length you want, change to stockinette stitch and work until the hand warmer is long enough to reach to the point where the crease forms between your thumb and your hand. At the end of the next round, bind off about 1¼" (3 cm) for the thumb opening. At the beginning of the following round, cast on the same number of stitches. (Binding off and casting on in K1, P1 rib will prevent the thumb opening from curling.)

Continue in stockinette until the piece is ½"–1" (1.3–2.5 cm) less than the total length you want.

Again work K1, P1 ribbing for the last ½"–1" (1.3–2.5 cm).

Bind off in K1, P1 ribbing and weave in the ends.

Hint: If you have a very small skein of yarn, divide it in half before beginning and use each half to make one hand warmer. This way, you won't make the first too large and run out of yarn for the second.

Knitting the Cuff and Hand

- Cast on 32 stitches, leaving at least a 6" (15 cm) tail. This needs to be a neat but stretchy cast on, so I recommend the Ribbed Cable Cast On (see page 303).

- Because the "right" side of the cast on is facing you, work one row of K1, P1 ribbing before joining, then join the beginning and end of the cast on, being careful not to twist it (see Off to a Good Start: Casting On and Joining, page 13).

- Place a marker to indicate the beginning/end of round.

- Work 2 rounds of K1, P1 ribbing.

- Work in stockinette stitch (knitting every round) until fabric measures 3" (7.5 cm) from cast on.

Making the Thumb Opening

- Work to 6 stitches before the end of the round. Bind off 6 stitches in K1, P1 ribbing (see Bind Offs: In Pattern, page 302). The ribbed bind off keeps the edge of the opening from curling.

- Knit the next round until you come to the gap where you bound off. Turn the knitting so the wrong side is facing you and cast on 6 stitches with the Ribbed Cable Cast On. Turn back so the right side is facing you again.

- Knit the next round until you come to the gap just before the stitches you cast on. To close the gap, pick up the long loose strand between the stitches, twist it and put it on your left needle. Knit this twisted loop together with the next stitch (see Casting On to Work in Progress, page 31).

Finishing the Top

- Knit 3 more rounds.

- Work 4 rounds in K1, P1 ribbing.

- Bind off loosely in K1, P1 ribbing.

- Use the cast-on tail to close up the gap from before you started working circularly (see Mind the Gap, page 76), then weave in the end on the inside. Use the bind-off tail to make the edge look continuous (see Making the Bind Off Look Continuous, pages 56–57), then weave in the end on the inside. If either end of the thumb opening looks messy or loose, weave the end over to that point and use it to neaten things up.

Endless Tube Headband

Here's a different approach to making a headband. Like the scarf at the beginning of the chapter, this headband is knit in a lengthwise tube, then flattened to make it reversible and double-thickness. Using a Provisional Cast On allows the end of the knitting to be attached seamlessly to the beginning. What you get is an endless, fully reversible tube.

For Project Shown You Need

YARN	Lorna's Laces Lion & Lamb (50% silk/ 50% wool, 205 yds/3½ oz)
YARN AMOUNT	120 yds/110 m Pink Blossom (1ns)
GAUGE	20 stitches = 4" (10 cm) in stockinette stitch
NEEDLE SIZE	US 8 (5 mm). Match the project's gauge if you want finished measurements to match pattern instructions.
NEEDLE TYPES (any of the following)	Two circular needles 16" (40 cm) or longer 47" (120 cm) circular needle or longer for Magic Loop plus a second circular needle on which to place the stitches when you remove the Provisional Cast On Set of four or five double-pointed needles at least 7" (18 cm) long
OTHER SUPPLIES	Small amount of waste yarn (1–2 yards/meters) for Provisional Cast On, stitch marker, yarn needle
FINISHED SIZE	4" (10 cm) wide × 21" (53 cm) in circumference

New Techniques Used

- Provisional Cast On (pages 303–304)
- Kitchener stitch (pages 70–74)

Any Size, Any Yarn

Don't bother to work a gauge swatch, because it would be as large around as the actual headband. Instead, calculate the number of stitches to cast on this way:

- Estimate your stitch gauge by referring to the yarn label or allow about 6 stitches per inch (2.5 cm) in sport weight, 5 stitches for worsted weight, or 4½ stitches in bulky-weight yarn.
- Decide how wide you want the headband to be, then double this measurement to get the circumference, since it will be a double thickness.
- Get the number of stitches needed by multiplying the estimated stitches per inch (or centimeter) by the circumference.

Cast on this number of stitches using a Provisional Cast On (see pages 303–304). After you've worked a few inches, check to see if it's the correct size and that the fabric is a little stretchy and not too thick so that it will be comfortable to wear. Knit until the headband is as long as you want, then remove the Provisional Cast On and use Kitchener stitch to join the two ends together as described at right.

MORE PROJECT IDEAS

There are lots more things you can make from simple tubes — you're only limited by your imagination! Here are just a few suggestions:

- Legwarmers or armwarmers worked in a stretchy rib so they don't fall down
- Soft stretchy cowls you can wear around your neck or pull up over your head as a hood to keep the cold out
- Big and little bags
- iPod or cell phone cases
- iPad, netbook, or laptop sleeves

Knitting the Tube

- Cast on 40 stitches using a Provisional Cast On (see pages 303–304).
- Place marker and join the beginning and end of the cast on, being careful not to twist it (see Off to a Good Start: Casting On and Joining, page 13).
- Knit until headband is 21" (53 cm) from cast on, or desired head circumference. At the end of the final round, knit the last two stitches together. Cut the yarn, leaving a 44" (112 cm) tail.

Joining the Tube

- *For double-pointed needles,* arrange the stitches so that the first half is on one needle and the second half (with one fewer stitch) is on a second needle, or slip them all to a circular needle.
- *For two circular needles,* slip all the stitches onto one needle. If the rigid needle point is too long to fit comfortably across half of the tube, pull a loop of the cable out at the halfway point so it will be easier to work with, just as if you'd been using the Magic Loop technique.
- *For Magic Loop,* your stitches are already set up correctly.
- Weave the tail at the cast on into the inside of the tube, at least a row away from the Provisional Cast On. Remove the Provisional Cast On and slip all the stitches onto a circular needle or onto two double-pointed needles (half on each), just as you did with the other end of the headband. Note that there will be one fewer stitch than you cast on.
- Arrange the headband so the beginning and end butt up against each other. Make sure the headband isn't twisted. If you kept track of your beginning/end of round as you worked and stopped knitting at the end of the round, the two ends should line up perfectly. Use Kitchener stitch (pages 70–74) to weave the two ends seamlessly together.

Tubular Potholder

This potholder exploits a method of knitting tubes on single-point needles in a double layer, called Tubular Knitting. Starting with a closed bottom and ending with a closed top eliminates the need to sew seams. There couldn't be an easier way to work a potholder.

New Techniques Used

- Tubular knitting
- Long-Tail Cast On
- Opening up tubular knitting
- Three-Needle Bind Off to join seam

For Project Shown You Need

YARN	Lorna's Laces Shepherd Bulky (100% superwash wool, 140 yds/4 oz)
YARN AMOUNT	92 yds/84 m Bold Red (11ns)
GAUGE	12 stitches = 4" (10 cm) in tubular knitting
NEEDLE SIZE	US 6 (4 mm). Match the project's gauge if you want finished measurements to match pattern instructions. Note: You'll notice that this is a very small needle size to use with bulky yarn. This is for two reasons. Tubular knitting, where stitches from the front half of the tube alternate on a single needle with stitches from the back half of the tube, results in a looser fabric than normal knitting worked in a single layer. Pot holders, to be functional, should be knit firmly to protect the cook from burns. Using a needle much smaller than usual ensures a tight, firm fabric. Even so, you may need to experiment with needle size more than usual while working your gauge swatch. Knitters who are very firm when slipping stitches may be able to use a thicker needle; knitters who slip loosely will need a thinner needle. It's not critical that you match the gauge exactly, but you do want a firm, dense fabric that will function safely as a pot holder.
NEEDLE TYPES (any of the following)	Pair of standard single-point (or straight) needles, at least 10" (25 cm) long 16" (40 cm) circular needle or longer
OTHER SUPPLIES	A third needle the same size to work the Three-Needle Bind Off, yarn needle or crochet hook Optional: Flameproof, melt-proof insulation (a good source is an ironing board cover), cut to about 7¾" (20 cm) square, or natural unspun wool or cotton — do not use polyester insulation, which will melt when exposed to high heat; a 16" (40 cm) circular needle the same size, to hold the stitches while inserting the insulation.
FINISHED SIZE	8" (20.5 cm) square

Setting Up the Knitting

- Cast on 34 stitches. You want a neat cast on, so I recommend the Long-Tail Cast On (pages 302–303).
- Double the stitch count by knitting into the front and back of every stitch to the end of the needle. (*68 stitches total*)

Knitting the Potholder Tubularly

- *Knit 1, bring the yarn to the front, slip 1 purlwise, bring the yarn to the back; repeat from *.
- Repeat this pattern on every row. Each time you work 2 rows you will have completed one full round. Continue to work in tubular knitting until potholder is square.

Finishing the Insulated Version

- To add the optional heat-resistant insulation, remove the knitting from the needle and place the stitches on a circular needle as follows: Starting with the stitches at the opposite end of the row from the working yarn, slip the first stitch to one point of the circular needle and the second stitch to the other point. Continue alternately slipping stitches to each point until you get to the beginning of the row.
- Insert the insulation into the pot holder.
- Work the Three-Needle Bind Off (page 69) to join the two layers. Cut the yarn and use a yarn needle or crochet hook to pull the ends to the inside.

Finishing the Non-Insulated Version

- Knit 2 stitches together all the way across while at the same time binding off. Pull the ends to the inside using a yarn needle or crochet hook.

TUBULAR POTHOLDER

Any Size, Any Yarn

Work a swatch in tubular knitting. Measure to determine the number of stitches per inch or centimeter. Decide how big you want the potholder or pad to be. Multiply the number of stitches per inch (or centimeter) by the measurement you want to get the total number of stitches.

Cast on this number of stitches, then double the number of stitches by increasing on the first row as described in the instructions at left. Work tubular knitting until it's as long as you like.

Follow the directions for finishing.

Note: If the potholder is wider than 8" (20.5 cm) across, you will need to use a longer circular needle as a stitch holder when opening the top to insert the insulation.

STILL MORE PROJECT IDEAS

Simple tubes can also be made into all kinds of delightful toys. Here are just a few suggestions to get you started.

- **Knitting a snowman.** Knit a small tube. Stuff it and pull the ends closed. Tie yarn around it to separate the head from the body, and embroider a face.

- **Knitting a cat (or other animal).** Begin with a closed straight-line cast on (see Closed Straight Cast Ons, pages 26–30) and knit a small tube. Stuff the tube before binding off, then pull the yarn tail through all the stitches to close the end (see Closed Center Bind Off, page 68). The square corners at the cast on will perk up to make ears. Tie yarn around to define the neck, add an I-cord tail, and embroider a face.

CARRYING ON WITH BAGS + HATS

As I said in the previous chapter, a bag is just a hat upside down, which is why this chapter is about both. The projects in this chapter explore a variety of shapings that sculpt simple tubes into hats and bags. The shapes include circles and octagons made from the center out and from the outside in, with and without I-cord finials. In two projects, I touch on the possibilities of textured and colored patterns: the Honeycomb Bag's slipped-stitch sides (see pages 133–135) and the Helix Hat's stripes (see pages 130–132). In later chapters, you'll find these same circles and octagons, as well as squares, triangles, and pentagons, integrated with more complex colorwork, textured patterns, and lace.

All of the bag projects are for small bags so that you can become familiar with the techniques and structures while doing a minimum of knitting. Likewise, the hats are designed for children or small adults, so they are sized like a hat you'd actually make, but they don't take forever to complete. All of the bags and hats, however, can be made any size you like once you understand how to shape them. A discussion following each project includes notes on making it any size, with any yarn. All of the projects also include tips on working them in the "other" direction (that is, from the top down or bottom up, the opposite of the original design of the project).

To give you experience with different types of shaping, you'll find bags and hats that are tapered, rounded, pointed, flat, or gathered. Some of the shapings are subtle, camouflaged by staggering the increases or decreases, while others are very obvious, highlighted by consistently lining up the increases or decreases. You'll also learn how to start with either a closed or open cast on and work in either direction (top down or bottom up).

DESIGNING YOUR OWN

A major consideration for bags is whether you want them to stretch or to hold their shape. Knitting, by its very nature, is stretchy; no matter what you do to prevent it, all knitting will stretch some. One option is to intentionally create a bag that you want to stretch, such as an open mesh market bag or wine bottle carrier. If you work flat, you can prevent some stretching by the judicious use of seams, which support the knitted fabric, but when knitting in the round, you may have no seams at all. Your best bet to control stretching, therefore, is to make a firm fabric, either by knitting on smaller needles than you might otherwise use with a particular yarn, or by incorporating a pattern stitch that prevents stretching.

When it comes to hats, the quality of the fabric is equally important. Hats that fit close to the head need to be stretchy enough to be comfortable, but firm enough that they don't fall off. Occasionally you'll want a hat that keeps its shape — one with a taller crown or a brim, for instance, that needs to be stiff, but then it will need to fit the head of the wearer more exactly because it can't stretch easily to fit. For a chart of standard head measurements, see the appendix for the website of the Craft Yarn Council.

Bubble Bag

This basic bag is cast on at the top, then increased gradually to round it. The bottom of the bag is gathered into a firm seam while binding off to minimize stretching. Simple I-cord straps show off the thick-and-thin nature of this yarn for a beaded effect that harmonizes with the bubble shape of the bag.

New Techniques Used

- Staggered increases
- Knitting together
- One-Over-Two Bind Off (page 57)
- I-cord for straps

For Project Shown You Need

YARN	Lorna's Laces Revelation (100% wool, 125 yds/4 oz)
YARN AMOUNT	90 yds/82 m Grapevine (3ns)
GAUGE	14 stitches = 4" (10 cm) in stockinette stitch
NEEDLE SIZE	US 10 (6 mm). Match the project's gauge if you want finished measurements to match pattern instructions.
NEEDLE TYPES (any of the first three options)	Two circular needles 16" (40 cm) or longer 47" (120 cm) circular needle or longer for Magic Loop Set of five double-pointed needles at least 7" (18 cm) long For straps, a pair of double-pointed needles
OTHER SUPPLIES	Stitch marker, yarn needle
FINISHED SIZE	19½"/49.5 cm in circumference at widest point × 8"/20.5 cm in height with edges curled up (not including straps)

STAGGERED VS. SWIRLED INCREASES

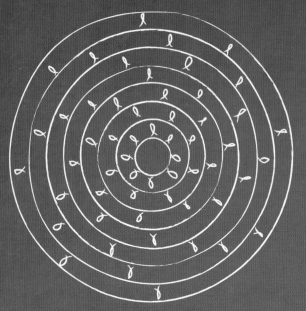

Swirled

Staggered

If you make the increases consistently at the same locations in the round, for example at the beginning of the round and then every second, third, or fourth stitch around, they will appear in an obvious swirled pattern. If you stagger the increases so they never line up from round to round as shown in the circular chart above, then they are far less noticeable. In garter stitch, the increases will disappear between the ridges. Staggering and aligning have exactly the same effect when decreasing: if they are aligned they'll be obvious, but if they are staggered, they'll be camouflaged.

Getting Started

- Cast on 40 stitches. A loose cast on is best, so I recommend the Knitted Cast On (page 302). Place marker and join the beginning and end of the cast on, being careful not to twist (see Off to a Good Start: Casting On and Joining, page 13).

Knitting the Bag

- Knit 5 rounds.
- Round 1: Knit, increasing 4 stitches evenly spaced around.
- Round 2: Knit.
- Repeat Rounds 1 and 2 until there are 68 stitches. On the increase rounds, stagger the increases from round to round so they never line up with the previous set of increases (see Staggered vs. Swirled Increases, at left).
- Continue working in stockinette until the bag is about 8" (20.5 cm) tall with the top edge unrolled.
- On the next round, reduce the number of stitches by working K2, *K2tog, K1; repeat from * around. (46 *stitches remain*)

Finishing the Bottom

- Turn the bag inside out by pushing the knitting through the center of the needle(s).
- *For two circular needles or the Magic Loop,* your knitting should already be divided with half in one section and half in the other. Double check to make sure you have 23 stitches in both halves and rearrange if necessary. If you are using the Magic Loop, you'll need one more needle for this step — a double-point that you can also use for the I-cord will work fine.
- *For double-pointed needles,* arrange the stitches so half are on one needle and half are on a second needle.
- Join the two sides of the bag together by knitting each

FOR A DIFFERENT LOOK, TRY THIS

- **Add a pattern stitch.** After you finish the increases, begin working a simple pattern stitch. You may need to adjust the number of stitches to an even multiple of the pattern repeat. Make your gauge swatch in the pattern stitch to determine the desired total number of stitches.
- **Use multiple colors.** Change colors to make stripes.

stitch on the front needle together with a stitch on the back needle (photo below). This is like working a Three-Needle Bind Off, except that you aren't binding off. Twenty-three stitches will remain, on a single needle.

- Turn and work the One-Over-Two Bind Off (page 57) across the remaining stitches.
- Cut the yarn and weave in the end on the inside of the bag. Weave the tail from the cast on along the top of the bag, where it will be hidden by the rolled edge.

Making the Straps

(make 2)

- Using a pair of double-pointed needles, cast on 4 stitches, leaving a tail about 6" (15 cm) long.
- Work in I-cord (pages 50–51) for 8" (20.5 cm).
- Cut yarn, leaving a tail about 6" (15 cm) long and pull through all 4 stitches.
- Flatten the bag along the bottom seam so that you can center the straps at the upper edge. Sew the straps to the inside of bag, directly opposite each other, just below the rolled top edge. The ends of each strap should be about 2" (5 cm) apart.

In the bag shown, the 4-stitch width of the I-cord coordinates with the thick-and-thin repeat of the yarn to make the cord alternately thicker and thinner. If your I-cord doesn't do this, it's because you knit at a different tension than I do. Change to a different size needle or try using 3 or 5 stitches to see if your results improve.

BUBBLE BAG

Working from the Bottom Up

You'll need to use either two circular needles or the Magic Loop because it's difficult, if not impossible, to get this started on double-pointed needles. To begin, calculate the number of stitches for the widest point as described at right. Divide this by three to determine the number of stitches to cast on. Firmly cast on this number of stitches using the Cable Cast On (page 302), then follow the directions for Cast On and Pick Up stitches (see page 28). You will double the number of stitches you cast on. Begin working circularly and increase to the correct number of stitches on the first round by working (K2, M1) repeated around. If this is not exactly the multiple of four you need, adjust the number of increases by one or two so that you do end up with a multiple of four. Work in stockinette until the bag is about half as tall as it is wide. Begin decreasing 4 stitches evenly spaced, every other round, being careful to stagger the decreases so they never line up with the previous set of decreases, until you are almost down to the same number of stitches you cast on. Bind off loosely. Make straps and attach the same as for top-down bag.

Any Size, Any Yarn

- Work a circular gauge swatch and measure to find the number of stitches per inch or per centimeter. If you don't want your bag to stretch out of shape, it needs to be worked firmly, so use smaller needles than you normally would with your yarn.
- Decide how big around you want your bag to be at the widest point (the middle of the bag).
- Multiply the stitches per inch or centimeter by this length and round to the nearest multiple of four to get the total number of stitches at the widest point. The top of the bag is smaller than this, with only 60 percent of the number of stitches at the widest point, so multiply this number of stitches by 0.6 to determine the number of stitches to cast on. Again, round to the nearest multiple of four.
- Cast on the number of stitches for the top of the bag and work in stockinette for 5 rounds. Begin increasing 4 stitches every other round as described in the instructions on page 126, until you reach the correct number of stitches for the widest part of the bag. Continue in stockinette stitch on these stitches until the bag is as tall as desired.
- Decrease about one-third of the stitches by working (K2tog, K1) repeated around. Make sure that you end up with an even number of stitches. If not, then skip the last decrease. Follow the instructions on pages 126–127 for joining the bottom seam and making and attaching the straps.

HELIX KNITTING

Helix knitting is a form of circular knitting that makes single-round stripes, where every color is used continuously and there is no jog at the beginning and end of rounds. You need to use a minimum of two colors. The maximum number of colors is dictated by how many balls of yarn you can stand to have attached to your work. The absolute maximum would be one ball of yarn for each stitch you cast on, but this is impractical in most human-size garments. To make wider stripes, use multiple balls of the same color. For example, three balls of black used one after the other will make a three-round stripe. The more balls of yarn you introduce, the greater the slant of the spiral stripes. Using just two colors in the body of a sweater, the angle of the spiral isn't noticeable. If you use more colors in something small like the thumb of a mitten, however, the angle of the spiral will be much steeper.

Open Cast On: Starting a Helix from the Edge

If you're starting at the bottom of a hat or the top of a bag, or if you're making a sweater, begin with an open cast on. When using just two colors, the easiest way to begin is with the Two-Color Long-Tail Cast On (page 303). Cast on whatever number of stitches you need and arrange them on your needle(s), but don't do anything to join the beginning and end of round. Take the color that was on your thumb (the bottom of the cast on) and knit the first round Ⓐ.

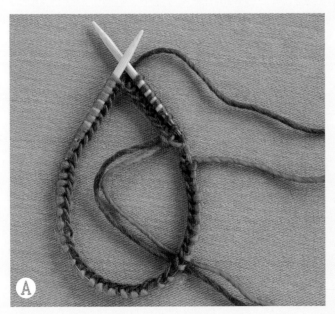

Closed Cast On: Starting a Helix from the Center

If you're starting from the top of a hat, the toe of a sock, or the tip of a mitten, you'll need to begin at the center as described in Closed Center Cast On #1 (page 22), but you'll be working alternately with two different yarns. Cast on and work the plain knit rounds with the first yarn and work the increase rounds with the second yarn.

The Jogless Garter Stitch Hat (page 139) requires you to begin at the center in garter stitch with two yarns, which is the same basic process, except that the plain rounds are purled rather than knitted. It can be confusing because both yarns are the same color, so detailed instructions for starting on either two circular needles or Magic Loop are provided here.

Using a circular needle and the Half-Hitch Cast On (page 302), cast on 8 stitches. Slide the stitches to the other end of the needle and turn so that the cast-on tail is closest to the point of the needle. Using the second ball of yarn, knit across, working an M1 increase after every stitch (16 stitches) Ⓑ.

Divide the stitches in half. For two circulars, place 8 stitches on each needle; for Magic Loop, place 8 on the first half and 8 on the second half. Arrange the needle(s) so the working yarns are attached at the back needle tip Ⓒ.

Using the *lower* working yarn (the one you used to cast on), purl across the front and then across the back to the end of the round. This joins the knitting into a round. Mark the beginning/end of round with a split marker D.

Starting with More Than Two Colors

The open and closed cast ons described assume you are working with just two colors. If you want to work with more colors, you can cast on with one color, then knit part of the first round with each of the other colors. For example, if you want to use three colors (red, yellow and blue), cast on with red. Tie the yellow to the red to join the round, then knit half of the first round with yellow. Change to blue and knit the other half of the round. This brings you back to the beginning of the round. You can use this same method to start with more colors: just cast on with one and then knit a portion of the first round with each of the others.

Working Helix Knitting

The basic rules of Helix Knitting are:
• Always work in the round.
• Always repeat the colors in the same order.
• Wherever there is another color attached, change colors.
• Do not twist or tighten the yarns when you change colors.

When you are working with two colors, you'll knit all the way around with one color, then knit all the way around with the second color. When you're working with more than two colors, you'll work a partial round until you reach the point where the next color is attached and then change colors.

Regardless of how many colors are involved, take care when you change not to twist the two yarns around each other and not to pull hard on the new color. Twisting or tightening will cause a noticeable difference in the fabric at the color change, spoiling the perfect helix E.

Binding Off in Helix Knitting

When working an open bind off, you can use just one color for the whole round or work a section in each of the colors as you come to them. When closing up the center of a hat, cut all the yarns and then pull the one that would come next in the color sequence through all the remaining stitches. If you need to end with a Three-Needle Bind Off (page 69), use the color that comes next in the sequence.

Helix Hat

This simple rolled-brim hat is made with alternating stripes of two balls of yarn. Using helix knitting means that there is no noticeable beginning or end of round — the stripes make a continuous double helix. Decreases are lined up at eight points to construct a classic rounded crown. Before you start, please read the instructions for Helix Knitting (see page 128–129).

New Techniques Used

- Helix knitting
- Open cast on in two colors
- Aligned decreases to shape a rounded crown

For Project Shown You Need

YARN	Lorna's Laces Bullfrogs and Butterflies (85% wool/15% mohair, 190 yds/4 oz)
YARN AMOUNT	70 yds/64 m each Grapevine (3ns) and Watercolor (18)
GAUGE	18 stitches = 4" (10 cm) in stockinette stitch
NEEDLE SIZE	US 8 (5 mm). Match the project's gauge if you want finished measurements to match pattern instructions.
NEEDLE TYPES (any of the following)	Circular needle 16" (40 cm) long (*Note:* When working the crown of the hat, a 16"/40 cm circular needle will be too long and you'll need to use one of the other options.) Two circular needles 20" (50 cm) or longer 47" (120 cm) circular needle or longer for Magic Loop Set of five double-pointed needles at least 7" (18 cm) long
OTHER SUPPLIES	Yarn needle
FINISHED SIZE	19½" (50 cm) in circumference × about 9" (23 cm) in height with bottom edge curled up

Knitting the Hat

- Cast on 88 stitches using the Two-Color Long-Tail Cast On (page 303) and both yarns. (See Open Cast On, page 128.)
- Work helix knitting in stockinette stitch with the two balls of yarn until hat is 9" (23 cm) tall.

Shaping the Crown

- Continue in helix knitting, but whenever you work a round with the multicolor yarn, decrease 8 stitches evenly spaced around the hat. When you work a round with the solid yarn, just knit. On your first decrease round, you'll work (K9, K2tog) repeatedly around. At the end of the round, there will be 80 stitches left. Each time you decrease, there will be 1 fewer knit stitch between the decreases, so the second time, you'll work (K8, K2tog), the third time you'll work (K7, K2tog), and so on. When you are down to about 64 or 56 stitches, the hat will be too small to work on a 16" (40 cm) circular needle, so switch to one of the other options. On your last decrease round, you'll work (K1, K2tog), and there will be only 16 stitches left.

Finishing

- Cut both strands of yarn, thread both of them through a yarn needle with a large eye, and pull both strands through all the remaining stitches. Go through the first few stitches a second time, pull up tightly, then pull the yarn to the inside of the hat and weave in the ends. Weave in the tails at the bottom along the cast-on edge, where they won't show when it's rolled up.

FOR A DIFFERENT LOOK, TRY THIS

- **I-cord stem.** Continue decreasing at crown until 8 stitches remain. K2tog all the way around so that only 4 stitches remain. Using both colors or a single color, work I-cord on these 4 stitches until the cord is the length you want. (For Basic I-Cord, see page 50; for two-color I-cord, see Striped I-Cord, page 229.) Cut the yarn and pull through the 4 I-cord stitches, then into the center of the cord to hide it. Trim the end or weave in on the inside of the crown.

- **Ribbed border.** If you prefer a hat that doesn't roll up, work K2, P2 ribbing with both colors in helix knitting for about an inch (2.5 cm) after casting on. Change to stockinette stitch and work until the hat measures 7" (18 cm) or desired length from cast on, then begin working crown shaping.

- **Fold up border.** Work garter stitch in both colors in helix knitting for 1" (2.5 cm) after casting on. Change to stockinette stitch and work until the hat measures 7" (18 cm) or desired length from the bottom edge with the band folded up, then begin crown shaping.

Working from the Top Down

Following the directions for Closed Cast On: Starting a Helix from the Center (page 128), cast on 8 stitches with the solid-color yarn, then work the first increase round using the multicolor yarn and working an M1 after every stitch (16 stitches). Continue using the solid yarn on the plain knit rounds and the multicolor yarn on the increase rounds until the hat is 88 stitches, or whatever size you like. Be sure to place your increases consistently to make the swirled crown of the hat. Work straight in helix knitting in stockinette stitch until the hat is as long as you like (allowing for the bottom edge to roll up), then bind off loosely. If you like, you can finish with a ribbed or garter stitch border as described in For a Different Look, Try This (page 131). You may bind off the whole round with a single ball of yarn or half with each ball of yarn.

Any Size, Any Yarn

- The easiest way to make the hat whatever size you like is to work from the top down (see Working from the Top Down, above), which allows you to increase until the hat is exactly the size you want without any prior planning. If you prefer starting from the bottom, however, estimate the stitch count by working a circular gauge swatch and measuring the swatch to determine the number of stitches per inch or centimeter. Multiply this number by the desired circumference to calculate the number of stitches to cast on.

- Cast on using both colors and the Two-Color Long-Tail Cast On. Work helix knitting in stockinette stitch until the hat is about 1½–2" (4–5 cm) shorter than desired finished length.

- When you are ready to begin the crown shaping, work 1 round, decreasing just enough so that you have a multiple of 8 stitches. Decrease 8 stitches every other round, placing the decreases consistently to make the swirled crown, and finish as described on page 131.

- The rolled bottom edge makes it easy to fit this hat in length, because it can be rolled higher or lower to suit the wearer.

Honeycomb Bag

Unlike the Bubble Bag (pages 125–127), the Honeycomb Bag starts with a closed cast on at the center bottom and is worked up from there. Drawstrings run through eyelets to close the bag and produce a ruffle, which is topped off with a decorative Picot Bind Off.

For Project Shown You Need

YARN	Lorna's Laces Shepherd Worsted (100% superwash wool, 225 yds/4 oz)
YARN AMOUNT	100 yds/92 m of Blackberry (4ns)
GAUGE	21 stitches = 4" (10 cm) in Slipped Honeycomb
NEEDLE SIZE	US 7 (4.5 mm). Match the project's gauge if you want finished measurements to match pattern instructions.
NEEDLE TYPES (any of the following)	Circular needle 16" (40 cm) long Two circular needles 20" (50 cm) or longer 47" (120 cm) circular needle or longer for Magic Loop Set of four or five double-pointed needles at least 7" (18 cm) long
OTHER SUPPLIES	Stitch marker, yarn needle
FINISHED SIZE	12¼" (31 cm) in circumference × 5¼ (13.5 cm) in height with upper edge curled

New Techniques Used

- Starting from the center
- Aligned increases to make a flat circle in stockinette
- Adding a pattern stitch
- Eyelets for drawstrings
- Picot Bind Off
- I-cord drawstrings

Getting Started

- Cast on 9 stitches, starting from the center bottom of the bag (see Closed Center Cast On #1, page 22). Use a marker to indicate beginning/end of round.
- Round 1: Knit around, increasing 9 stitches evenly spaced, aligning all the increases to form a swirl on the bottom of the bag (see Staggered vs. Swirled Increases, page 126). (I suggest using the M1 increase here.)
- Round 2: Knit.
- Repeat these 2 rounds until there are 63 stitches, ending with Round 1.
- *Note:* Since this is based on a multiple of 9 stitches, it fits very nicely on three double-pointed needles 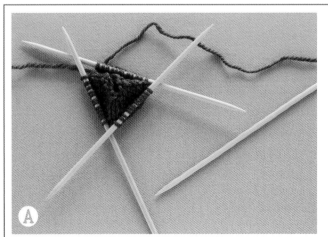.
- On the next round, knit around, increasing 1 stitch at end of round to obtain 64 stitches. You need a multiple of 8 to work the eyelets for the drawstring.

Working the Sides of the Bag

Work even on 64 stitches in Slipped Honeycomb:

- Round 1: *Slip 1 wyif, P1; repeat from * around.
- Round 2: Knit.
- Round 3: *P1, slip 1 wyif; repeat from * around.
- Round 4: Knit.

Repeat these 4 rounds for pattern. Continue to work even in Slipped Honeycomb until patterned section measures 4½" (11.5 cm).

Making Eyelets for the Drawstring

- Knit 2 rounds.
- Eyelet Round: *K2tog, yo, K2; repeat from * around.
- Knit 5 rounds.
- Bind off using Picot Bind Off (page 60). Use the tail at the end of the bind off to join it to the beginning of the bind off (see Making the Bind Off Look Continuous, pages 56–57).
- Use the cast-on tail to sew neatly through all the stitches at the cast on, closing the hole at the center bottom, then weave in ends on the wrong side.

Making and Inserting the Drawstrings

- Cast on 2 stitches and work I-cord until it measures 24" (61 cm) long. Cut yarn and pull end through both stitches to secure them. Using a yarn needle, pull tails of yarn to the inside of I-cord and trim any excess. Make a second cord identical to the first.
- Starting at the beginning/end of round, weave one cord in through the first hole and out through the second hole, then continue weaving in and out all the way around. Knot the two ends of this cord together. Starting at the opposite side of the bag, weave the second cord through the eyelets, following the same in-and-out path as the first. Continue all the way around and knot the ends of the second cord together .

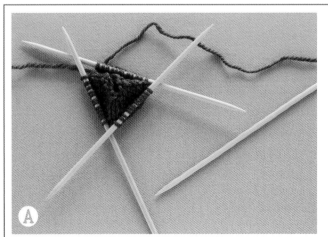

The 9-stitch multiple fits conveniently on three double points.

Weave two lengths of I-cord through the eyelets.

Working from the Top Down

- Work a circular gauge swatch in Slipped Honeycomb and measure to find the number of stitches you are getting per inch or per centimeter. Decide how big around you want your bag to be. Multiply the gauge per inch or centimeter by the circumference you want to get the total number of stitches for the cast on. Round to a multiple of 8 stitches. Cast on this number of stitches using the Channel Islands cast on (page 20). The tiny bumps along the edge of this cast on are a good substitute for the Picot Bind Off.

- Join beginning and end of round, and knit 5 rounds. Make eyelets as described above. Knit 2 rounds. Work in Slipped Honeycomb until bag is desired height. Work a knit round, decreasing to the nearest multiple of 9 stitches. Working in stockinette stitch, decrease 9 stitches evenly spaced, every other round, placing the decreases consistently so that they form a spiral on the bottom of the bag (see Staggered vs. Swirled Increases, page 126). Continue decreasing until 9 stitches remain. Cut yarn and pull tail through remaining stitches to secure. Weave in ends and make cords as described on page 134.

Any Size, Any Yarn

- Cast on 9 stitches at the center of the bottom. Work in stockinette stitch, increasing 9 stitches every other round until the circumference of the circle you've knitted is the size you want. Increasing 9 stitches every other round in stockinette stitch makes a nice, flat circle, every time.

- When the bottom of the bag is completed, if you don't have a multiple of 8 stitches, adjust by increasing or decreasing as needed on the last round of the bottom. Work in Slipped Honeycomb until the bag is 1" (2.5 cm) shorter than desired length. Work eyelets, drawstrings, and finishing as described on page 134. For a larger bag, you will probably want to make longer drawstrings.

FOR A DIFFERENT LOOK, TRY THIS

- **Market or wine-bottle bag.** Use a stretchy open lace stitch for the bag. Make it larger around for a market bag or smaller for a mesh wine-bottle bag.

- **Ruffled top.** *If working from the bottom up,* double the number of stitches at the top by increasing after every stitch as soon as the eyelets have been completed, then work as many rounds as you like before binding off. *If working from the top down,* cast on twice as many stitches, then cut them in half by working K2tog all the way around just before making the eyelets.

Beret

This beret is knit from the center of the crown out, beginning with a short, decorative I-cord. Decorative increases are used to shape the almost-flat top of the hat, then it's finished off with a very tailored, comfortable hem for the bottom band.

For Project Shown You Need

YARN	Lorna's Laces Shepherd Worsted (100% superwash wool, 225 yds/4 oz)
YARN AMOUNT	155 yds/142 m (about 2.5 oz) Grapevine (3ns)
GAUGE	20 stitches = 4" (10 cm) in stockinette stitch
NEEDLE SIZE	US 6 (4.0 mm). Match the project's gauge if you want finished measurements to match pattern instructions.
NEEDLE TYPES	The most straightforward way to make this hat is to begin with a pair of double-pointed needles for the I-cord and move up to a set of five double-pointed needles until the crown is about 16" (40.5 cm) in circumference. After the I-cord is complete, you may also work the hat using two circular needles at least 16" (40 cm) long or the Magic Loop using a needle 47" (120 cm) or longer. If you prefer, you may switch to a single 16" (40 cm) circular needle when the beret is large enough.
OTHER SUPPLIES	Eight split markers to indicate the increase points, plus one marker that looks different to indicate the beginning/end of round
FINISHED SIZE	18" (46 cm) in circumference at bottom band (stretches easily to fit up to 20"/51 cm); 29" (74 cm) in circumference at the widest point after blocking

New Techniques Used

- Starting from the center with I-cord
- Shaping an octagon using eight pairs of increases
- Double increases
- Binding off with a hem

Knitting the Beret

Review Closed Center Cast On #2 (page 25) before beginning. This will tell you how to arrange the stitches on your needles as you begin. Just keep in mind that the increases in this project are different from those used in the examples in chapter 1. Before you complete the bottom band of the hat, you may also want to look at Hems (pages 66–67).

- Using a pair of double-pointed needles, cast on 4 stitches and work I-cord for 1" (2.5 cm).

- If you will be using two circular needles or Magic Loop to work your beret, divide the stitches on the two needles (or two halves of the needle) so that 2 are on the front and 2 are on the back. If you will be using double-pointed needles, divide the stitches between 2 needles as you work Setup Round 1.

- Setup Round 1: *K1, M1 with the working yarn; repeat from * around. (*8 stitches total*)

- Setup Round 2: Knit around.

- Setup Round 3: K-yo-K into each stitch. (*24 stitches total*)

- On double-pointed needles, the stitches should now be arranged on four needles, with 6 stitches on each needle.

- Place a split marker in each of the 8 yarn overs (through the stitches themselves, not on the needles) to indicate the location of the increases. Mark the beginning of the round using a different kind of marker so that it is easily identifiable.

- Rounds 1–3: Knit around.

- Round 4: Knit around, working K-yo-K into each of the 8 marked stitches. At the end of round, move the increase markers up into the yarn overs on the needle. Each time you work Round 4, you'll have 16 additional stitches.

- Repeat Rounds 1–4 until you have 120 stitches.

- Remove the 8 increase markers.

- Work in stockinette stitch for about 2¾" (7 cm), or about 21 rounds, without increasing.

- Decrease the total number of stitches by 25 percent: *K2tog, K2; repeat from * around. (*90 stitches remain*)

- Continue working in stockinette for 11 more rounds (about 1¼"/3 cm).

- Purl 1 round. This is the fold line for the hem that forms the bottom band.

- Knit 10 more rounds.

- Join the live stitches to the top round of the border  (A). (See Hems, pages 66–67.)

- Weave in the ends on the inside, hiding the cast-on tail inside the I-cord.

FOR A BETTER FIT

- **For a more secure band.** Encasing a length of elastic within the hem that serves as the bottom band will help the band hold its shape and grip the head better. Cut a length of 1" (2.5 cm) elastic 1" (2.5 cm) longer than the circumference of the band. About 2" (5 cm) before completing the hem join, run the elastic through the section of the band already joined. (To make it easier to feed the elastic, fasten a large safety pin to the forward end.) Overlap the ends 1" (2.5 cm), making sure that the elastic is not twisted. Sew the ends together using a sewing needle and thread, then finish joining the hem.

- Block by soaking the hat, rolling it in a towel to remove excess moisture, and placing it over a plate that is about 9¼" (23.5 cm) in diameter (B). Make sure the hat is centered and smoothed out on the plate. Balance the plate on a smaller-diameter bowl or cup, and arrange the band so it hangs down neatly around the bowl and is neither loose nor stretched (C).

Completed, showing live stitches joined to top round of border

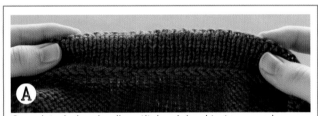

Hat centered on plate

Plate balanced on a cup

Working from the Bottom Up

To determine the number of stitches needed for the cast on, make a circular swatch in stockinette stitch, and measure your stitches and rounds per inch or centimeter. Decide the circumference you want for the bottom band. This should be 1"–2" (2.5–5 cm) smaller than the head circumference, so that it will cling without falling off. Multiply this measurement by your stitch gauge.

Bottom band. Use a Provisional Cast On (pages 303–304) to cast on this number of stitches. Work circularly for about 1¼" (3 cm). Purl 1 round and then knit exactly the same number of rounds as you worked before the purl round. Join the two layers (see Hems, pages 66–67).

Sides. Increase the total number of stitches by 33 percent. You can do this by working (K3, M1) repeated around, or by working (K2, Kfb) repeated around. You will need a multiple of 8 stitches when it comes time to shape the crown, so plan for this when you increase and try to come out with the correct number. If it's not quite right, adjust on the following round by increasing a few stitches. Work even in stockinette for about 2¾" (7 cm).

Shape crown. Mark eight decrease points, equidistant around the hat, by placing a split marker in each of the stitches.

If you are working on double-pointed needles, there will be two markers on each of your four needles. If you are working on two circular needles or Magic Loop, there will be four decrease points in each half of the hat. In all cases, place the decrease points so that they are centered on each needle, with the same number of stitches between the closest decrease point and the end of the needle. This is just for convenience, so you won't need to transfer stitches between needles to work the decreases.

To work a decrease round, *knit until 1 stitch remains before the marked stitch, work s2kp2 to make a neat centered double decrease (see page 305); repeat from *, knit to end of round. Work the decreases every fourth round.

Stem. When you get to the center of the crown, you'll have 8 or 16 stitches left. Remove all the markers. Knit 2 together around until you have just 4 stitches. Work I-cord for an inch (2.5 cm), cut the yarn, and pull it through all the remaining stitches. Weave in the ends.

Any Size, Any Yarn

The bottom band should be 1"–2" (2.5–5 cm) less than the head circumference of the wearer. To estimate the beret's largest circumference where it blouses out, add 33 percent to the bottom band measurement. Work as directed on page 137 until the circumference is the desired size. There are several ways to determine when it's big enough:

• Spread the hat out on a long circular needle or two, or put it on a length of yarn, so that it can lie flat, then measure around the circumference.

• Measure from the center to the needle, multiply by 2 to get the diameter, then by 3.14 to calculate the circumference.

• Measure a straight section of the stockinette to determine your number of stitches per inch or centimeter, multiply this by the desired circumference to calculate the number of stitches you should have. Count your stitches to ensure that the two numbers agree.

Work even in stockinette for about 2¾" (7 cm). At this point you will need to decrease quickly down to the desired size of the bottom band. Decrease by working (K2tog, K2) all the way around.

Before continuing, verify that the hat is the size you want. If you have not already done so, determine your gauge by measuring the stitches per inch or centimeter in a straight section of the hat, multiply this by the desired length of the bottom band to calculate the number of stitches you need and make sure you are close to the right number. If you need to adjust, do it now before working the bottom band.

Jogless Garter Stitch Hat

This hat is a variation on the helix knitting used in the Helix Hat on pages 130–132. In this case, rather than working with colored stripes, the same color is alternated in knit and purl rounds to make seamless garter stitch in the round. In this project you'll practice beginning at the center of the crown using two strands of yarn and increasing to shape the crown.

New Techniques Used

- Jogless garter stitch using helix knitting
- Starting from the center in helix knitting
- Shaping a flat crown in garter stitch

For Project Shown You Need

YARN	Lorna's Laces Shepherd Bulky (100% superwash wool, 140 yds/ 4 oz)
YARN AMOUNT	121 yds/111 m of Cedar (7ns)
GAUGE	14 stitches = 4" (10 cm) in garter stitch
NEEDLE SIZE	US 10 (6 mm). Match the project's gauge if you want finished measurements to match pattern instructions.
NEEDLE TYPES (any of the following)	Two circular needles 16" (40 cm) or longer 47" (118 cm) circular needle or longer for Magic Loop Optional: 16" (40 cm) circular needle to use when the hat is large enough
OTHER SUPPLIES	Split marker, yarn needle
FINISHED SIZE	18" (46 cm) in circumference × 9" (23 cm) in height

FINDING YOUR WAY AROUND

How can you tell whether your increases are correct? On two circular needles or Magic Loop, half the stitches should be in the front and half in the back at the end of each increase round.

How can you tell which round you're on? If there are horizontal bumps immediately below the needle all the way around, then you've just finished purling Round 2 and should knit and increase on Round 1.

FOR A DIFFERENT LOOK, TRY THIS

- **For a pillbox hat.** Make the sides shorter.
- **For a basket.** Knitted more firmly or worked in a stiffer fiber that will stand up on its own, this shape makes an excellent basket when turned upside down. You can also knit a strand of craft wire along with wool to achieve the same effect.
- **For color interest.** Alternate strands of two different colors, either solid or variegated, for a completely different look.

Getting Started

Before you begin, you may want to review Helix Knitting (pages 128–129).

- Cast on 8 stitches exactly as described in Closed Cast On: Starting a Helix from the Center (page 128).
- Increase to 16 stitches and work the first purl round as described in those instructions.

Increasing for the Crown

- Round 1: Using the lower strand, knit around, increasing 8 stitches evenly spaced.
- Round 2: Using the lower strand, purl around.
- Repeat these 2 rounds, staggering the increases so they never line up with the previous set of increases (see Staggered vs. Swirled Increases, page 126) until there are 64 stitches. The crown will grow larger with each increase round. Move the marker up closer to the needles as the crown grows to help keep track of the beginning/end of round.
- When there are 64 stitches, it will be big enough to place on a single 16" (40 cm) circular needle, which will make working the sides simpler and quicker, so you may want to shift your knitting onto the single short needle. The easiest way is to purl all the stitches onto the needle when working Round 2 after your final increases.

Working the Sides

- Round 1: Using the lower strand, knit.
- Round 2: Using the lower strand, purl.
- Repeat Rounds 1 and 2 until the hat is 7" (18 cm) tall.

Finishing

- Stop after having worked a Round 1. On the next round, purl 32 stitches; drop the yarn. If you're working on a single circular needle, either conventionally or Magic Loop, slip 32 stitches purlwise. You'll be back at the beginning/end of round. If you're working on two circular needles, just turn the knitting so that you're back at the beginning/end of round. Using the yarn attached at this point, bind off 32 stitches loosely in knitting. You'll be at the halfway point of the round. Pick up the other strand of yarn waiting for you at this point, and bind off the rest of the round loosely in knitting. Make the bind off continuous (see Making the Bind Off Look Continuous, pages 56–57).
- Use a yarn needle and the cast-on tail to sew through each stitch of the cast on and close up the hole at the center of the crown. Decide which side of the hat you want to be the outside and weave in ends on the inside. If there is any looseness in the increase round immediately after the cast on, tighten it up on the inside while weaving in the ends.

Working from the Bottom Up

Cast 32 stitches onto a 16″ (40 cm) circular needle using the Knitted Cast On (page 302). Using a second ball of yarn (or the other end of a center-pull ball), cast on 32 more stitches. There is no need to start this second strand with a slipknot — just knit the first stitch with the new strand through the last stitch made with the old strand. Join the beginning and end of round, making sure the cast on isn't twisted around the needle, and knit 32 stitches with the second strand of yarn. The first strand of yarn will be attached at this point. Mark it as the beginning of round and purl 1 round using the lower strand of yarn.

Round 1: With the lower strand, knit.

Round 2: With the lower strand, purl.

Repeat Rounds 1 and 2 until hat is 7″ (18 cm) tall, ending with Round 2.

Round 1: With the lower strand, knit around, decreasing 8 stitches evenly spaced.
Round 2: With the lower strand, purl.

Repeat Rounds 1 and 2 and stagger the decreases (see Staggered vs. Swirled Increases, page 126) until 8 stitches remain.

Cut both strands of yarn leaving 4″–6″ (10–15 cm) tails. Use a yarn needle to pull the upper strand of yarn through all the remaining stitches. Decide which side is the outside of your hat and weave in the ends on the inside.

Any Size, Any Yarn

From the top down. Continue to increase every other round until the hat is as big around as you like. If the size you want isn't an even multiple of 8, adjust for this on your final increase round. Work even in jogless garter stitch until the hat is as tall as you like. Bind off and finish as described on page 140.

From the bottom up. To estimate the number of cast-on stitches, make a circular gauge swatch, measure it, and multiply the number of stitches per inch (or centimeter) by the desired circumference of the hat. Cast on and work the sides as described above for the bottom-up version of the hat. On the first decrease round, decrease to an even multiple of 8 stitches, then continue shaping the crown as for the bottom-up hat.

Little Hats

These three little hats are intended to fill in a few of the gaps left by the larger projects. They demonstrate additional variations in crown shaping and band or brim details.

Picot-Band Hat

Witch's Hat

Ruffle-Top Hat

Knitting the Hats

The hats shown were all made using Lorna's Laces Bullfrogs and Butterflies (85% wool/15% mohair, 190 yds/4 oz) and US size 8 double-pointed needles. If you absolutely detest double-pointed needles, you can certainly use two circular needles or the Magic Loop, but you still will probably find it more comfortable to use double points for the I-cord that begins the top of each hat. (See Closed Center Cast On #2, page 25, for complete instructions.)

One of the beauties of top-down construction, as you may already have gathered from the other projects in

this chapter, is that you can so easily make your project any size you like just by continuing to increase until you reach the desired circumference. Use whatever yarn you like and whatever size needles are appropriate for that yarn. The gauge really doesn't matter because you'll increase to whatever size you like, regardless of gauge. What is important is that you adjust the needle size to make a fabric you like — not too stretchy or too tight. You can quickly test out ideas for hat shaping and embellishments by making tiny hats like the ones pictured.

Witch's Hat

- Cast on 3 stitches using double-pointed needles and work I-cord (see pages 50–51) for 1" (2.5 cm).

Shaping the Crown

- Knit around, working an M1 with the working yarn at the end of every round. Think back to the Honeycomb Bag bottom (pages 133–135) or the Helix Hat crown (pages 130–132), where a definite swirl formed when increases or decreases were aligned with those on the earlier rounds. With a single increase per round in this hat, you get just one line of increases swirling continuously around the hat.
- As the hat grows wider, divide the knitting between two, then three needles (or move to two circulars or Magic Loop).
- Stop whenever the hat is big enough, and the stitch count is a multiple of 8.

Shaping the Brim

Note: The flat circular brim is shaped identically to the circular top of the Jogless Garter Stitch Hat (pages 139–141).

- Round 1: Purl.
- Round 2: Knit around, increasing 8 stitches evenly spaced and taking care to stagger the increases on subsequent rounds.
- Repeat Rounds 1 and 2 until the brim is as wide as you like.
- In the little hat shown, the brim is only one layer thick; it was bound off at the outer edge. To keep the brim from flopping on a larger hat, make it more rigid by working a second layer. To make the second layer, reverse the process, decreasing 8 stitches on each knit round until you are back to the original number of stitches. Sew down the live stitches on the inside of the hat where it meets the brim, or knit the inner edge of the brim to the hat as you bind off (for details, see Hems, pages 66–67).
- As soon as it's large enough to fit a human head, the top of this hat will tend to flop because knitting is soft. If you want it to stand up, especially in larger sizes, use bulky yarn or a double strand of worsted weight and knit it very firmly on much smaller needles than usual. You will probably still need to stuff the top of the hat to force it to stand up. You could also loosely knit a very oversized hat and felt it in the washing machine, but you'll have to experiment with the shrinkage factor to be sure the resulting hat will fit.

Ruffle-Top Hat

Opposite in concept to the slow increase that builds the pointy Witch's Hat, the ruffly crown of this hat is created by making the increases as quickly as possible.

- Cast on 2 stitches using double-pointed needles and work I-cord for 1" (2.5 cm).
- Double the number of stitches every other round by making an M1 with the working yarn after every stitch. Keep doing this until the hat is almost as big around as you like. You'll be surprised how quickly it grows; in fact, it's easy to make it too big. When it gets up to 64 stitches, do a reality check because it's a rare head that needs 132 stitches to reach around it, unless the yarn is very fine! It's best to plan ahead, making a gauge swatch and calculating the desired number of stitches before you begin. On the last round, increase just enough stitches to reach the size you want.
- Work even until the hat is as tall as desired.

Variations for Bottom Edge

- **Rolled edge** (not shown). Work an additional inch (2.5 cm) or so in stockinette and then bind off loosely.
- **Conventional ribbed band** (not shown). Work an inch (2.5 cm) or so of K1, P1 or K2, P2 ribbing.
- **"Flip-up" garter stitch band** (shown in purple). Work an extra 4 to 6 rounds in stockinette stitch, then alternate rounds of knit and rounds of purl until the band is as wide as you like. Bind off loosely on a knit round. The stockinette stitch above the garter stitch band will follow its nature and curl to the outside, forcing the band to flip up. The garter stitch section, also true to its nature, will be bigger around than the stockinette so will lie nicely outside the bottom of the hat.
- Sew the end of the I-cord down to make a loop.

Picot-Band Hat

Shown in multicolor, this decorative little hat is a variation on the Ruffle-Top Hat. They are made identically, except that this one begins with a short 4-stitch I-cord rather than a loop and is bound off with the Picot Bind Off (see page 60).

WRAPPING UP WITH SCARVES + SHAWLS

This chapter builds on the same shapes used in chapter 6 to construct the crowns of hats and the bottoms of bags. In those cases, it didn't really matter whether the shapes came out flat or slightly rounded, because they would stretch to accommodate whatever filled them. For things that must lie flat, however, the shaping needs to be more exact, taking into account the proportions of the pattern stitch: stockinette stitch, for example, is taller and narrower than garter stitch; lace patterns tend to be wider; cabled and slipped-stitch patterns are usually narrower.

To provide practice in the many approaches to knitting flat things circularly, the projects in this chapter are as varied as possible. Most of them are small, sample-size exercises just big enough to help you develop a thorough understanding of the required construction techniques, while taking a short amount of time to complete. There are, however, projects here that any knitter will find challenging. The Double Double Circular Shawl on pages 147–149 is constructed by doubling the number of stitches each time the diameter doubles, as is the Double Double Trellis Shawl on pages 150–152), which combines shaping with lace patterns. There is a circle with swirls of lace (Lacy Swirl Shawl, pages 153–157), and a circle transformed into a square (Lacy Square Shawl, pages 158–161) just by shifting the shaping to four corner points. Both of these projects provide experience in shaping while maintaining a lace pattern. And, there are projects like the Oval Placemat (pages 169–173), where you'll learn to stretch those circles and squares to make ovals and rectangles. Finally, you'll progress to more complicated shapes in the Potholder Collection (pages 174–183): triangles, pentagons, and octagons, with some lessons in how to control the appearance of your increases and decreases along the way.

A WORD ABOUT FABRICS

When working projects that absolutely must end up flat, it's important to work them fairly loosely. Their planar nature depends upon the fact that knitting stretches and compresses. If the fabric is too stiff, it will ruffle or buckle instead of behaving itself. This is most critical in the first two projects, the circular shawls that double in stitch count every time the diameter doubles.

One excellent way to test out your fabric is to make a very small shape with the same yarn, pattern stitch, and needles that you plan to use for the real thing. You can make sure you like the details such as the cast on, the type and placement of the increases and decreases, the integration of the pattern stitch, and the bind off. If you begin from the center and you like the results, this swatch could grow right into the full-size project.

If you plan to work from the outer edge toward the center, it still makes sense to work a small sample to serve as a trial run. There's nothing worse than working a very large piece beginning at the outer circumference and then realizing you could have improved the cast on, the outer border, or the transition from the border to the main pattern. You'll also learn your pattern stitches so that you may not even need to refer to the instructions or charts when you begin the real thing.

Double Double Circular Shawl

The basic concept for this shawl is that the number of stitches must double every time the diameter of the shawl has doubled. Working in stockinette, simply knit the plain rounds and work a yarn over after every stitch on the increase rounds. These occur less and less frequently as the shawl grows, because you work an increase round only when the shawl has doubled in diameter.

Featured Techniques

- Closed Center Cast On #1 (pages 22–24)
- Doubling the number of stitches when the number of rounds has doubled
- Seamless Seed Stitch in the round (see page 96)
- Picot Bind Off (see page 60)

For Project Shown You Need

YARN	Lorna's Laces Helen's Lace (50% silk/50% wool, 1250 yds/4 oz)
YARN AMOUNT	160 yds/146 m (about ½ oz) Sage (43ns)
GAUGE	15 stitches = 4" (10 cm) in stockinette stitch
NEEDLE SIZE	US 10½ (6.5 mm). Match the project's gauge if you want finished measurements to match pattern instructions.
NEEDLE TYPES	Set of double-pointed needles, two circular needles (16"/40 cm or longer), or 47" (118 cm) circular needle (or longer) for Magic Loop to begin the shawl. If you're working on double-pointed needles, use a set of four or of five — whichever you prefer. Switch to a single circular needle when the shawl grows large enough to work comfortably. With such fine yarn, you can fit a very large number of stitches onto the needle(s), but a longer needle lets you lay the shawl out flat to get a better idea of how it looks. You can even move to two circular needles to accommodate the larger circumference as it grows.
OTHER SUPPLIES	Stitch marker (optional)
FINISHED SIZE	About 20" (51 cm) in diameter

This is the simplest of all circular structures, but it works only if knit loosely so that each band between the increase rounds can stretch to lie flat. If it's knit tightly, what you'll have is a series of ruffles (which, of course, you can do intentionally). Because it's worked in stockinette, the edges will curl if you don't take preventive measures. A border of Seed Stitch at the outer edge prevents this, and the Picot Bind Off completes the decorative edge.

Knitting the Shawl Center

- Rounds 1–2: Cast on 9 stitches using the Long-Tail Cast On (pages 302–303) and leaving at least a 6" (15 cm) tail (see Closed Center Cast On #1, pages 22–24). Join beginning and end of round, being careful not to twist the stitches. Mark the beginning of round using a marker or the cast-on tail (see Using Markers in Circular Knitting, pages 42–43).

- The cast on counts as 2 rounds: The thumb strand of the Long-Tail Cast On makes half hitches across the bottom edge and the index finger strand makes a second round of knitted stitches.

- Round 3: Knit.
- Round 4: When you work Round 4, you will have worked twice as many rounds as when you cast on, so it's time to increase. To do this, *K1, yo; repeat from * around. (*18 stitches, double the number you cast on*)
- Rounds 5–7: Knit.
- Round 8: When you work Round 8, you will have worked twice as may rounds as the last time you increased (on Round 4). Increase again, just as you did on Round 4. (*36 stitches, double the stitch count on the previous round*)
- Rounds 9–15: Knit.
- Round 16: Again, on Round 16, you'll have worked twice as many rounds as the last time you increased (on Round 8). Increase again, just as you did on Rounds 4 and 8. (*72 stitches, double the stitch count on the previous round*)
- Rounds 17–31: Knit.
- Round 32: Once again, you've doubled the number of rounds, so increase again. (*144 stitches, double the stitch count on the previous round*)
- Rounds 33–63: Knit.
- Round 64: The diameter of the shawl has doubled, so it's time to increase again. (*288 stitches, double the stitch count on the previous round*)

Working the Border

- Setup: *K1, P1; repeat from * around, ending with an M1. (*289 stitches*) *Note:* You need an odd number of stitches so that the Seed Stitch border repeats continuously from round to round.
- Round 1: P1, *K1, P1; repeat from * around.
- Round 2: K1, *P1, K1; repeat from * around.
- Repeat Rounds 1 and 2 once more.
- Bind off using Picot Bind Off (page 60). Cut yarn and make beginning and end of bind off continuous as described on pages 56–57.
- Use the cast-on tail to disguise any gap where the cast on is joined at the center of the shawl, then weave in the end behind a solid area of stockinette stitch.

Blocking the Shawl

- Wash and squeeze gently, and then roll in a towel to remove excess moisture. Lay the shawl out, stretching a bit so that it lies flat. It's not practical to stretch and pin each point of the Picot Bind Off, but pat it out flat and straighten out the points so they look neat and even all the way around.

Any Size, Any Yarn

For a larger size. To make a full-size shawl, instead of working the border when you get to 288 stitches, work 63 more rounds and then double the number of stitches again to 576 stitches. You can continue until the shawl is as large as you like, doubling the number of stitches each time the shawl doubles in diameter, but it's really not practical to count so many rounds. Instead, you can either measure the diameter of the shawl or fold the fabric toward the center along the most recent line of increases to see if the outermost band is as wide as the rest of the shawl to the center. Each section of plain knitting should be twice as long as the previous section, plus one round. You may want to stop short of the full width of the final section. If you do, *don't* double the number of stitches before working the Seed Stitch border. When the shawl is as big as you like, add the border and bind off.

For a different yarn. This shawl doesn't work if the fabric is firm and holds its shape. Instead of lying flat and draping nicely once it's blocked, a stiff, firm fabric will make a series of concentric ruffles. To create the very loose, soft fabric required, no matter what yarn you use, select a much larger needle size than usual for that particular yarn. Start at the center exactly as directed and continue until the shawl is the size you want or until your yarn runs out.

For a Different Look, Try This

- Make a garter stitch border rather than Seed Stitch by alternating knit and purl rounds.

- Work a band of lace as a decorative border. To keep it from curling, choose a pattern stitch that is either based on ribbing (that is, it has knit and purl stitches on every round) or based on garter stitch (alternate rounds mostly knit and mostly purled).

Double Double Trellis Shawl

This shawl is a variation on the Double Double Circular Shawl (pages 147–149). The two begin identically, but this one integrates patterned bands between plain stockinette bands. Varying the pattern stitch affects the gauge of each band. It's important to work loosely and not to vary the gauge too much, or the shawl won't be smoothly shaped. Because of the changes in gauge of the knitting, the placement of increase rounds is dictated by the measurements of the shawl rather than the row count. It's easy to tell when to increase. Fold the outer band of fabric toward the center along the line formed by the last round of increases. When the outer band reaches the center of the hole at the cast on, it's time to increase. Of course you can also measure the shawl: when the distance from the center to the last increase round is the same as the distance from that increase round to the needle, it's time to increase again.

For Project Shown You Need

YARN	Lorna's Laces Helen's Lace (50% silk/50% wool, 1250 yards/4 oz)
YARN AMOUNT	313 yds/286 m (about 1 oz) Sage (43ns)
GAUGE	15 stitches = 4″ (10 cm) in stockinette stitch
NEEDLE SIZE	US 10½ (6.5 mm). Match the project's gauge if you want finished measurements to match pattern instructions.
NEEDLE TYPES	Set of double-pointed needles, two circular needles (16″/40 cm or longer), or 47″ (118 cm) circular needle (or longer) for Magic Loop to begin the shawl. If you're working on double-pointed needles, use a set of four or of five — whichever you prefer.
	Switch to a single circular needle when the shawl grows large enough to work comfortably. With such fine yarn, you can fit a very large number of stitches onto the needle(s), but a longer needle lets you lay the shawl out flat to get a better idea of how it looks. You can even move to two circular needles to accommodate the larger circumference as it grows.
OTHER SUPPLIES	Stitch marker (optional)
FINISHED SIZE	About 27″ (68.5 cm) in diameter

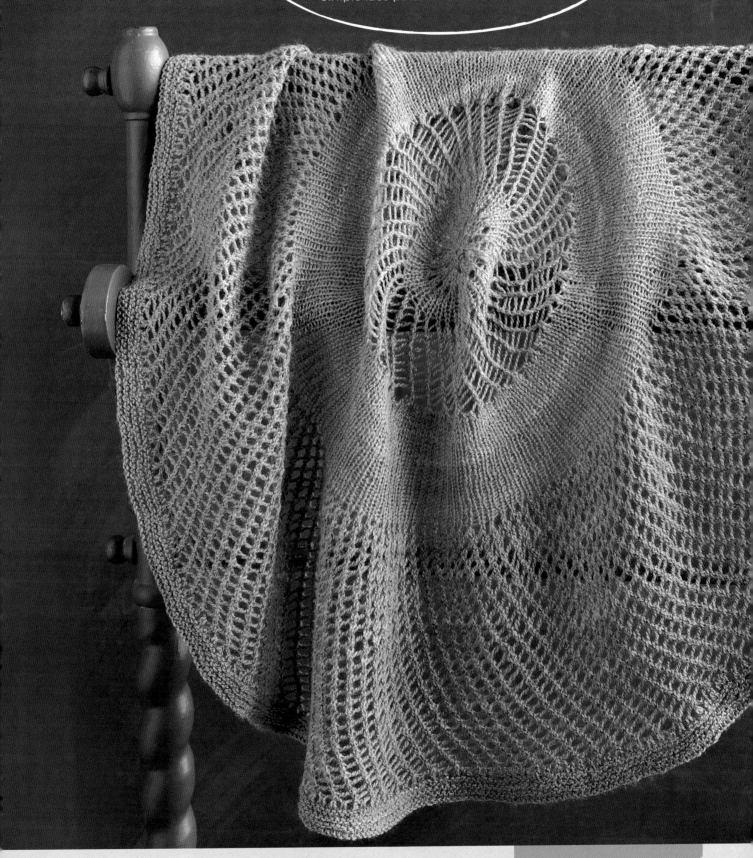

Featured Techniques

- Closed Center Cast On #1 (pages 22–24)
- Doubling the number of stitches when the diameter doubles based on measurement
- Simple lace patterns in the round

Double Double Trellis Shawl

Knitting the Shawl Center

- Work identically to the Double Double Circular Shawl (page 148) from the cast on until you have 72 stitches.

Working Band 1

Band 1 is a delicate trellis formed as follows:

- Pattern Round: *K2tog, yo; repeat from * around.
- Repeat Pattern Round until the diameter of the shawl has doubled.
- Increase Round: *K1, yo; repeat from * around. (*144 stitches, double the stitch count on the previous band*)

Working Band 2

- Knit around until the diameter of the shawl has doubled.
- Increase Round: *K1, yo; repeat from * around. (*288 stitches, double the stitch count on the previous round*)

Working Band 3

Band 3 is a more substantial trellis, made by alternating plain knit rounds with rounds of the pattern stitch in Band 1.

- Round 1: Knit.
- Round 2: *K2tog, yo; repeat from * around.
- Repeat Rounds 1 and 2 until the shawl has once again doubled in diameter, ending with Round 1.
- Increase Round: *K1, yo; repeat from * around. (*576 stitches, double the stitch count on the previous round*)

Working the Garter Stitch Border

- Round 1: Knit.
- Round 2: Purl.
- Rounds 3–6: Repeat Rounds 1 and 2. For a wider border, you may keep repeating these two rounds.
- Round 7: Knit
- Bind off loosely on a purl round, or turn the shawl over and bind off from the wrong side in knitting. Use the tails to close up the gap at the cast on and at the bind off when you weave them in.

CAN I START FROM THE PERIMETER?

This shaping isn't practical for working from the outer circumference to the center. Casting on hundreds of stitches and then joining them without twisting can be a challenge, but the real difficulty is that you can't tell when to halve the number of stitches.

DOUBLE DOUBLE TRELLIS SHAWL

Any Size, Any Yarn

Double the stitches each time the diameter has doubled until the shawl is as big as you like. You can also vary the pattern bands any way you like. Like the plain Double Double Circular Shawl, this shawl doesn't work if the fabric is too firm. To create a loose, stretchy fabric so that it won't form a series of ruffles, no matter what yarn you use, select a much larger needle size than usual for that particular yarn.

Lacy Swirl Shawl

Yet another way to shape a circular shawl, but this time beginning at the outer edge. Decreases at eight points on alternate rounds form wedges that swirl to the center. The Channel Islands Cast On at the outer edge is both decorative and functional: it makes tiny beads all along the outer edge and stretches beautifully. The border is a chevron pattern whose increases and decreases create points along the outer edge. The simple Lace Rib pattern that makes up the main body of the shawl must be continued even when it is being eaten away by the decreases, so this shawl serves as a tutorial on maintaining a pattern stitch while working shaping.

For Project Shown You Need

YARN	Lorna's Laces Fisherman (100% wool, 500 yds/8 oz)
YARN AMOUNT	150 yds/137 m (about 1½ oz) Aqua (13ns)
GAUGE	14 stitches = 4" (10 cm) in Lace Rib pattern
NEEDLE SIZE	US 10½ (6.5 mm). Match the project's gauge if you want finished measurements to match pattern instructions.
NEEDLE TYPES (any of the following)	47" (120 cm) circular. Use conventionally at the outer edge of the shawl, then switch to Magic Loop when the center becomes too small to work comfortably on the long needle.
	Two long circular needles. These are especially helpful at the cast on so you can spread out the stitches to make sure they aren't twisted; they can be used all the way to the center.
	If you don't like using the Magic Loop or two circular needles as the stitches dwindle, you can change to a shorter circular needle and then to a set of five double-pointed needles for center of the shawl.
OTHER SUPPLIES	Eight split markers (one should be a different color or style to mark the beginning/end of round), yarn needle
FINISHED SIZE	About 13½" (34 cm) in diameter

Featured Techniques

- Channel Islands Cast On (page 20)
- Chevron pattern to make a pointed border
- Aligned decreases to form a swirl (page 126)
- Maintaining pattern stitch while decreasing

Before You Begin

Work a gauge swatch, not because it's necessary to exactly match the specified gauge, but in order both to learn the Lace Rib pattern and to make sure you like the fabric you are creating. If it seems too loose, use a smaller needle; if it seems too tight, change to a bigger needle.

To make a circular swatch in Lace Rib, cast on a multiple of 4 stitches, join the beginning and end of round, being careful not to twist the stitches, and work as follows:

- Rounds 1 and 2: *P1, K3; repeat from * around.

- Round 3: *P1, yo, sk2p, yo; repeat from * around.
- Round 4: Repeat Round 1.
- Repeat these 4 rounds for pattern. When you have learned the pattern stitch, are sure you like the fabric, and have checked to see if your gauge is somewhere in the neighborhood specified on page 153, you're ready to start on your sample shawl.

Getting Started

- Using Channel Islands Cast On (page 20), cast 192 stitches onto circular needle. Joining the beginning and end of round without twisting can be quite

challenging with this many stitches (and even more so when confronted with enough stitches for a full-size shawl). If you find it difficult, instead of joining the beginning and end of round, turn and knit 1 row, which takes the place of Round 1 of the border pattern. At the end of this row, join the beginning and end of round, being very careful not to twist the cast on around the needle, and begin with Round 2 of the border.

Knitting the Border

Note: The border pattern is worked on a multiple of 8 stitches. Also, see Border Chart on page 156.

- Round 1: Purl.
- Round 2: *P1, yo, K2, sk2p, K2, yo; repeat from * around.
- Round 3: Purl.
- Round 4: Repeat Round 2.
- Round 5: *P1, K7; repeat from * around.
- Round 6: Repeat Round 2.
- Round 7: Repeat Round 5.

- Round 8 (decrease round): *P1, yo, K2tog, sk2p, ssk, yo; repeat from * around. This reduces each pattern repeat from 8 stitches to 6. (*144 stitches remain*)
- Round 9: *P1, K5; repeat from * around.
- Round 10 (decrease round): *P1, K1, sk2p, K1; repeat from * around. This reduces each pattern repeat from 6 stitches to 4. (*96 stitches remain*)

Knitting the Lace Rib Swirl

- Setup: Place eight markers on the needle, with the first at the beginning/end of round and the others after every 12 stitches. Use a different color or style marker for the beginning/end of round. Refer to Preparing to Work the Lace Rib Swirl below for a discussion of how to maintain the pattern stitch while decreasing. Also, see Swirl Chart, page 156.
- Round 1: *P1, K3; repeat from * around.
- Round 2 (decrease round): *Work in P1, K3 ribbing as established until 2 stitches remain before the next marker, K2tog; repeat from * around. (*8 stitches decreased*)

PREPARING TO WORK THE LACE RIB SWIRL

In the main section of the shawl, several things are going on at the same time, and it may be confusing when you first begin. I'm discussing each of them in depth here to make it easier for you to understand as you continue with this project, and so that you can see how to handle decreasing while working in pattern in future projects.

- **Establishing the pattern.** You are already familiar with the Lace Rib pattern from having made your gauge swatch. Now you'll work it on the shawl itself, but you'll need to decrease to shape the shawl at the same time.

- **Changing number of stitches.** As you work, your decreases eat up stitches of the Lace Rib pattern, one at a time, so after each decrease round, you'll find a different number of stitches in the last pattern repeat before each marker. If possible, work these in pattern. How do you do this?

  - **On Lace Rib Rounds 1, 2, and 4,** maintain the ribbing, matching the knits and purls from the previous round.

  - **On Lace Rib Round 3,** if you have enough stitches to work the whole pattern repeat before the marker, do so. When there are fewer stitches, try to work half of the lace pattern.

When you work only half of the pattern, you work a yarn over and a single decrease. If the decrease falls on the last two stitches before the marker, work K2tog instead of ssk to match the other decreases in that column of stitches. This means that sometimes, when there are enough stitches, you'll work P1, yo, sk2p, yo, K1 just before the marker and other times you'll work P1, yo, K2tog before the marker. The round-by-round instructions tell you exactly what to do in each case, but notice what's going on here, so that you can maintain patterns around decreases in other projects. If you like working from charts, you may find the chart for the beginning of the shawl and the center section easier to follow than the verbal instructions and, for other projects, you may find charting the pattern with the decreases makes it much easier to plan and to knit.

- **Shaping.** Decrease every other round on the 2 stitches immediately before each marker. Always work K2tog on these stitches, regardless of where they fall in the Lace Rib pattern. So that there's less to keep track of, the decrease rounds are always on the ribbed rounds of Lace Rib, never on Round 3, which is the lace pattern round.

- Round 3: *Repeat (P1, yo, sk2p, yo) until 3 stitches remain before marker, P1, yo, K2tog; repeat from * around. Note that the K2tog continues the column of decreases you worked on previous rounds.
- Round 4: Repeat Round 2. (*8 stitches decreased*)
- Round 5: *Work in P1, K3 ribbing as established until 2 stitches remain before marker, P1, K1; repeat from * around.
- Round 6: Repeat Round 2 (decrease round). (*8 stitches decreased*)
- Round 7: *Repeat (P1, yo, sk2p, yo) until 1 stitch remains before marker, K1; repeat from * around.
- Round 8: Repeat Round 2 (decrease round). (*8 stitches decreased*)
- Repeat Rounds 1–8 once more (*32 stitches remain*). When the piece becomes too small to work easily with the circular needle, see the notes at Needle Types (page 153) for hints on changing to other needles if desired.

Knitting the Shawl Center

With only 4 stitches remaining between markers in each of the eight sections, it's no longer possible to work full repeats of the Lace Rib pattern. In the few remaining rounds, your goal is to decrease until only 8 stitches remain, to craft an attractive center that continues in the lace pattern as long as possible, and to maintain unbroken columns of K2tog shaping swirling to the center — all at the same time. Also, see Center Chart, below.

- Round 1: *P1, K3; repeat from * around, removing all of the markers except the one at the beginning/end of round.
- Round 2 (decrease round): *P1, K1, K2tog; repeat from * around. (*24 stitches remain*)
- Round 3: *P1, yo, K2tog; repeat from * around. You've worked half of the lace pattern on the available stitches and the K2tog extends the column of decreases.
- Round 4 (decrease round): *P1, K2tog; repeat from * around. When working each K2tog, the yarn over from the previous round is knit together with the following stitch. (*16 stitches remain*)
- Round 5: *P1, K1; repeat from * around. This maintains the ribbed pattern.
- Round 6 (decrease round): K2tog 8 times. This final round continues the swirl of decreases to the center of the shawl. (*8 stitches remain*)
- Cut the yarn and pull through the 8 remaining stitches, then pull to the inside and weave in behind a solid section of the fabric. Use the cast-on tail to join the beginning and end of the cast on evenly and then weave it in, too.

Unless you knit very, very loosely, the center of this shawl will pop up a bit until it's been blocked. To block, wash it gently by hand, roll it in a towel to remove excess moisture, then lay it out flat, stretching just enough so that the lace pattern opens up. Make sure all the points around the edge are pulled out neatly and leave it to dry.

Border Chart

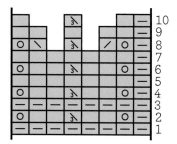

Starts with an 8-stitch repeat and ends with a 4-stitch repeat

Swirl Chart

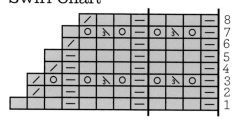

Center Chart

Starts with a 4-stitch repeat and ends with a 1-stitch repeat

Any Size, Any Yarn

Choose a fairly large needle size for your yarn. The resulting fabric should be soft and stretchy. The bigger the needles, the lacier the shawl. Work a gauge swatch in Lace Rib, wash and block under tension to open up the lace. Measure to find the number of stitches per inch or centimeter. Decide on the desired diameter of your finished shawl, then multiply this measurement by π (3.14) to determine the circumference of the shawl. Multiply this number by your gauge. Then, because the number of stitches is reduced by half when the pointed border is completed, double that result and you'll have the approximate number of stitches for your cast on.

The border pattern requires a multiple of 8 stitches, and in order to work the decreases, you must have eight identical sections. Since 8 × 8 = 64, you need a multiple of 64 stitches. Round the number of stitches that you estimated for your cast on to the nearest multiple of 64. If you are about halfway between multiples, then round down, because the pointed edge adds about 2" (5 cm) to the diameter of the shawl.

For example, I decided a 13" (33 cm) shawl would be large enough to explore all the techniques and concepts in this project. I worked a circular swatch in Lace Rib and determined that my gauge, when slightly stretched (as the shawl will be after blocking), was 3½ stitches per inch (1.4 stitches per centimeter). The chart below illustrates how I figured out how many stitches to cast on.

If you use a different yarn, substitute your own gauge in Lace Rib for the 3½ stitches/inch and 1.4 stitches/cm used in the example.

	Inches	Centimeters
Diameter	13"	33 cm
Adjust for width of 2" (5 cm) border on both sides of shawl: subtract 4" (10 cm)	9"	23 cm
Circumference = 3.14 × diameter not including border	28.3"	72 cm
Stitches for Lace Rib = circumference times gauge (3½ sts/inch or 1.4 sts/cm)	99 sts	101 sts
Stitches for border = stitches for Lace Rib × 2	198 sts	202 sts
Round to nearest multiple of 64	192 sts	192 sts

WORKING FROM THE CENTER OUT

Use the same technique as for the Lacy Square Shawl, pages 158–161, starting with 8 stitches. Place eight markers, one after each stitch. Every other round, increase 1 stitch before each marker. This will make eight wedge-shaped sections, with the new stitches added at the end of each section. As soon as there are 4 stitches in each section, you can start working in the Lace Rib pattern. As you add more stitches, maintain them in the K3, P1 base pattern. Every time there are 4 additional stitches, you can work another repeat of the pattern in each section. Keep working until the shawl has a diameter about 4" (10 cm) less than the final desired size. Keep in mind that the shawl will be stretched larger when you block it. You can measure the number of rounds per inch or centimeter on your swatch and multiply to calculate the number of rounds to reach the desired finished size before the border.

Work the outer border like the Lacy Square Shawl, or substitute a more pointed chevron pattern at the outer edge.

Lacy Square Shawl

Like the Lacy Swirl Shawl on pages 153–157, the pattern stitch in this square shawl is Lace Rib. Unlike the Lacy Swirl Shawl, however, the square version of the shawl starts at the center, which means you don't have the challenge of joining the beginning and end of the cast on without twisting. Shaping is done using pairs of yarn overs at four points to create corners. Additional repeats of the lace pattern must be introduced as each of the four sections of the shawl grows wider.

For Project Shown You Need

YARN	Lorna's Laces Fisherman (100% wool, 500 yds/8 oz)
YARN AMOUNT	500 yds/457m Mint (25ns)
GAUGE	14 stitches = 4" (10 cm) in Lace Rib
NEEDLE SIZE	US 10½ (6.5 mm). Match the project's gauge if you want finished measurements to match pattern instructions.
NEEDLE TYPES	Begin with a set of four double-pointed needles, two circular needles, or a circular needle long enough to work the Magic Loop. As the shawl grows larger, you can work on either one or two circular needles. I prefer to work on two long circular needles, because I can use the same needles throughout, and I find it easier to see the shape of the shawl as I work.
OTHER SUPPLIES	Four split markers (one marker should be different to indicate the beginning/end of round), yarn needle
FINISHED SIZE	About 25" (63.5 cm) square

Featured Techniques

- Closed Center Cast On #1 (pages 22–24)
- Paired increases at corner points to make a square
- Maintaining pattern stitch while increasing
- Making the transition to the outer border

Before You Begin

First work a gauge swatch to learn the Lace Rib pattern and to make sure you like the fabric it creates. See Lacy Swirl Shawl: Before You Begin (page 154) for instructions. Wash and block the swatch under tension to open up the lace. Measure to find the number of stitches per inch or centimeter.

Working the Center of the Shawl

This section of the shawl begins with just 8 stitches; 4 of them are the corner stitches. As you work out from the center, you establish the increase pattern (a yarn over on either side of each corner stitch, every other round) as well as the Lace Rib pattern, beginning with the P1, K3 ribbing that's its base and then, when there are enough stitches, the yarn overs and corresponding double decrease that creates the lace.

Note that I have taken care to center the pattern stitch in each of the four sections of the square, and to keep all of the sections identical to each other. Sometimes there are enough stitches in each section to work full repeats of the pattern stitch, but most of the time there is a partial repeat of the pattern at the beginning and end of each section. Any extra stitches at the beginning and end of a section are maintained in the rib pattern (P1, K3) that forms the base for Lace Rib.

- Starting from the center, loosely cast on 8 stitches using the Long-Tail Cast On (pages 302–303). Place markers in the first, third, fifth, and seventh stitches (see Using Markers in Circular Knitting: Split markers, pages 42–43). Note: The total stitch counts provided below apply only the first time you work these twelve rounds.
- Round 1: *Knit marked stitch, yo, K1, yo; repeat from * around. (*16 stitches total*)
- Round 2: Knit.
- Round 3: *Knit marked stitch, yo, knit to next marked stitch, yo; repeat from *around. (*24 stitches total*)
- Round 4: *Knit marked stitch, P1, K3, P1; repeat from * around.
- Round 5: *Knit marked stitch, yo, P1, (yo, sk2p, yo, P1); repeat section within parentheses to next marked stitch, yo; repeat from * around. (*32 stitches total*)
- Round 6: *Beginning with marked stitch, K2, P1, (K3, P1); repeat section within parentheses until 1 stitch remains before marked stitch, K1; repeat from * around.

- Round 7: *Knit marked stitch, yo, K1, P1, (K3, P1); repeat section within parentheses until 1 stitch remains before marked stitch, K1, yo; repeat from * around. (*40 stitches total*)
- Round 8: *Beginning with marked stitch, (K3, P1); repeat section within parentheses until 2 stitches remain before marked stitch, K2; repeat from* around.
- Round 9: *Knit marked stitch, yo, K2, P1, (yo, sk2p, yo, P1); repeat section within parentheses until 2 stitches remain before marked stitch, K2, yo; repeat from * around. (*48 stitches total*)
- Round 10: *Knit marked stitch, work in K3, P1 pattern as established until 3 stitches remain before next marked stitch, K3; repeat from * around.
- Round 11: *Knit marked stitch, yo, work in K3, P1 pattern as established until 3 stitches remain before next marked stitch, K3, yo; repeat from * around. (*56 stitches total*)

Lacy Square Shawl Center Chart

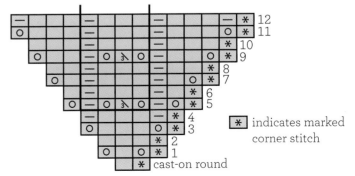

[*] indicates marked corner stitch

- Round 12: *Knit marked stitch, P1, (K3, P1); repeat section within parentheses to next marked stitch; repeat from * around.
- Repeat Rounds 5–12 until shawl is desired size, ending with Round 6. There will be a multiple of 8 stitches in each of the four marked sections. The stitch count at this point is important in order to make the transition to the outer border. The sample shown has 64 stitches on each side (256 stitches total) and is 19½" (49.5 cm) in width, excluding the border.

Setting Up for the Border

The border is a version of the traditional Old Shale pattern, with a 12-stitch repeat. Because it's a wavy pattern, it requires more stitches in width than the Lace Rib it will be attached to, so you must begin by increasing the number of stitches. You also need more stitches at each corner so that the border turns the corners without cupping. You will add these extra stitches in increase rounds before beginning the border pattern. See also Border Chart, page 161.

- Transition Round 1 (increase round): *K-yo-K in marked stitch, K-yo-K in next stitch, [(K1, yo) four times, K4]; repeat section within brackets until 6 stitches remain before next marked stitch, (K1, yo) four times, K1, K-yo-K in next stitch; repeat from * around. At the end of round, knit 1 more stitch (the first of the 3 stitches worked into the marked stitch at the beginning of this round). You've added 6 stitches at each corner and 4 stitches to each pattern repeat across the four sides. Shift your markers so that they are in the yarn overs at the center of each of the four marked corner stitches.
- Transition Round 2: Purl.
- Transition Round 3 (increase round): *K-yo-K in marked stitch, K2, K-yo-K in next stitch, knit until 3 stitches remain before next marked stitch, K-yo-K in next stitch, K2; repeat from * around. At the end of round, knit 1 more stitch (the first of the 3 stitches worked into the marked stitch at the beginning of this round). You've added 6 more stitches at each corner. Shift your markers again so that they are in the yarn over at the center of the marked stitch.

Note: The instructions don't refer to the marked stitches again, but they may help you stay oriented. The border pattern repeats evenly on all four sides, so a pattern repeat begins at each marked stitch. You should always have a multiple of 12 stitches in each of the four sections.

Working the Border Pattern

- Round 1: *(K1, yo) twice, K2tog four times, (K1, yo) twice; repeat from * around.
- Round 2: Purl.
- Round 3: Knit.
- Rounds 4–7: Work Rounds 1–3 a second time, then work Round 1 a third time.
- Bind off loosely in purl (or turn to wrong side and bind off loosely in knit). Use the cast-on tail to join the beginning and end of the cast on evenly and weave the ends in behind a solid section of the fabric. See Making the Bind Off Look Continous (pages 56–57).

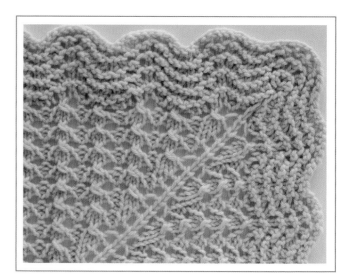

Border Chart

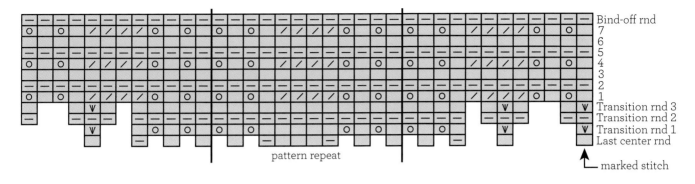

pattern repeat

Bind-off rnd
7
6
5
4
3
2
1
Transition rnd 3
Transition rnd 2
Transition rnd 1
Last center rnd

marked stitch

CENTER OUT OR PERIMETER IN?

You can make any shape starting from the center and increasing or starting from the outer edge and decreasing. Each method has its benefits.

Starting from the center is the simplest way to make a shape any size you like, because you just keep working until it's as big as you like, then bind off. Unfortunately, it can be very fiddly to start with just a few stitches at the center (see Closed Center Cast Ons, pages 22–25) and it can be difficult to establish a pattern stitch as the fabric grows. You also must be careful to bind off loosely or end with a stretchy border, or the edge of your knitting may curl up. If you want to add a decorative border or bind off, then you can do so to finish off a project worked from the center out.

Starting from the outer edge requires you to work a gauge swatch and calculate the correct number of stitches to cast on. Then you must cast on and join them without twisting, which can be challenging on a large shawl or blanket, where there could potentially be thousands of stitches. On the positive side, starting out with all your stitches, you can begin with a decorative cast on, and it's easier to establish a pattern because you can start with the correct multiple of stitches and then maintain the pattern as you decrease toward the center.

Mitered Rectangle Scarf

This scarf is worked in garter stitch from the center out, alternating rounds of two colors in helix knitting. The rectangular shape expands on the idea of a mitered square. The long center section of the scarf is worked straight while two corners of a square are created at each end. Using two colors of yarn makes it easy to keep track of which pattern round you're on. The first color is used to cast on and to work the knitted increase rounds. The second color is used on the purl rounds. An advantage of using two colors is that helix knitting hides the beginning and end of round so there is no jog to be disguised, except where both yarns end at the bind off. You should be comfortable working on two circular needles before attempting this project.

For Project Shown You Need

YARN	Lorna's Laces Fisherman (100% wool, 500 yds/8 oz)
YARN AMOUNT	95 yds/87 m (about 1½ oz/43 g) in each of two colors, Aqua (13ns) and Brick (38ns) (*Note:* In photo, Aqua is color 1 and Brick is color 2.)
GAUGE	18 stitches = 4" (10 cm) in garter stitch
NEEDLE SIZE	US 7 (4.5 mm). Match the project's gauge if you want finished measurements to match pattern instructions.
NEEDLE TYPES	Two circular needles, 36" (90 cm) or longer. *Note:* 47"/120 cm needles may be most comfortable to work with throughout the project, and they allow you to lay it flat to admire it as you work.
OTHER SUPPLIES	Four split markers, yarn needle
FINISHED SIZE	44" × 4" (112 × 10 cm)

Featured Techniques

- Starting from a closed straight cast on at the center, using the Turkish Cast On (pages 29–30)
- Working on two circular needles (pages 44–45)
- Helix knitting (pages 128–129)
- Double increases to make mitered corners

Setting Up

- Using color 1 and two circular needles, anchor the yarn to the lower needle with a slipknot or overhand knot. Cast on 360 stitches (180 wraps) using the Turkish Cast On (pages 29–30).
- Still using color 1, knit across the top needle.
- With color 2, slip the knot securing the tail of color 1, then purl all the way around.
- Unravel the knot that anchors the cast-on tail. Secure the two tails by knotting them loosely together. Place a split marker in the first and last stitch on each needle. (See Using Markers in Circular Knitting: Split markers, pages 42–43.) What you have now is a narrow, unwieldy snake of knitting suspended between two needles. But take heart: the hardest part of the whole project is now behind you!

Working the Scarf

- Round 1: Using color 1, knit around, working K-yo-K into each of the 4 marked stitches.
- Round 2: Using color 2, purl around.
- Repeat Rounds 1 and 2 until the scarf is 4" (10 cm) wide. Move the markers up closer to the needles as the scarf grows. Always place the marker in the center stitch of the double increase. To avoid collapsing the last stitch of the previous round, be careful not to pull too hard on the new yarn when you change colors. (See Helix Knitting, pages 128–129.)
- When the scarf is 4" (10 cm) wide, complete Round 1, then stop 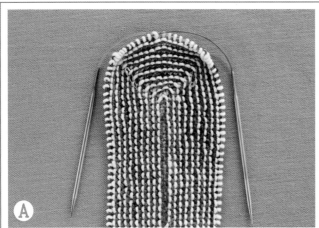.

Finishing

- Using color 2, purl to the first marked stitch. Slip the stitches you just purled back to the left needle point.
- Using color 1, knit to the first marked stitch. Cut color 1, leaving a tail long enough to weave in (**B**). This moves the working yarns to a corner before beginning the bind off, because it's easier to disguise the end of the bind off at a corner than along a straight edge.
- Use color 2 to bind off in purl. Note: Although I frequently advocate turning around and binding off in knitting from the opposite side on some projects, that's a bad idea in this one because it creates an extra row that is difficult to disguise at the corner. For an alternative way to bind off in purl, see An Easier Way, page 165.
- When you finish binding off the first needle, there will be a few stitches at the beginning of the round still on it. If this is annoying, slip them to the far end of the second needle so that you can discard the first needle. They will be waiting for you when you come to the end of the bind off.
- Weave in the ends, using the tails at the outer edge to even up the corner where the bind off ends. If there are loose stitches at the center where each color begins, tighten them up before weaving in the cast-on tails.
- When the scarf is complete, the ends will splay out just a bit. Block gently to make it a perfect rectangle.

Round 1 completed prior to bind off

Scarf ready to bind off

Any Size, Any Yarn

Make a swatch in garter stitch and determine your gauge in inches or centimeters. Decide how long and how wide you want your scarf. Calculate the length of the center cast on by subtracting the desired width from the desired length. Follow the formulas in the chart below for details.

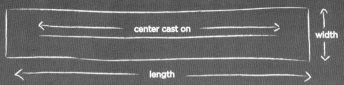

	In Inches	In Centimeters
Step 1: Subtract width from length to find center length.	44" – 4" = 40"	112 cm – 10 cm = 102 cm
Step 2: Multiply center length by gauge.	40 × 4.5 = 180 sts	102 × 1.8 = 183.6 sts
Step 3: Round to an even number.	180 sts	184 sts

Follow the directions in Setting Up and in Working the Scarf on page 164, but cast on the number of stitches you calculated for your own scarf. Keep working until the scarf is the width you want, ending with Round 1. Follow the directions under Finishing (page 164) to bind off.

AN EASIER WAY

If you hate binding off in purl, try this alternative: Purl the first stitch, then follow the illustrated steps:

1 Insert right needle into first stitch on left needle (as if you were going to purl, but don't). Insert left needle into first stitch on right needle, with point in back of right needle.

2 Wrap yarn around front needle point.

3 Purl the two stitches together.

Repeat steps A–C until all stitches have been bound off.

Working from the Outside In

After you've determined your gauge and the measurements of the scarf you want, calculate the perimeter of the scarf this way.

	In Inches	In Centimeters
Step 1: Add the length and width, and then multiply by 2 to find perimeter.	$(44'' + 4'') \times 2 = 96''$	$(112 \text{ cm} + 10 \text{ cm}) \times 2 = 244 \text{ cm}$
Step 2: Multiply perimeter by gauge.	$96'' \times 4.5 = 432 \text{ sts}$	$244 \text{ cm} \times 1.8 = 439 \text{ sts}$
Step 3: Round to an even number.	432 sts	438 or 440 sts

Using color 1, cast on the number of stitches you calculated on a very long circular needle (at least 47"/120 cm). To place your markers correctly, you need to know how many stitches make up the width of your scarf, so multiply the width by the gauge to get that number.

	In Inches	In Centimeters
Step 1: Multiply width by gauge.	$4'' \times 4.5 \text{ sts} = 18 \text{ sts}$	$10 \text{ cm} \times 1.8 \text{ sts} = 18 \text{ sts}$
Step 2: Round up to an odd number if necessary.	19 sts	19 sts

Starting at the beginning of round, count across the number of stitches in the width, and place a marker in that stitch. In the example, the width is 19 stitches, so place the marker in the 19th stitch. (See Using Markers in Circular Knitting: Split markers, pages 42–43.) Next, find the point exactly halfway between the beginning and end of round, and place a marker in the last stitch before the halfway point. From this point, count across the number of stitches in the width and place a marker in that stitch. In the example, this is the 19th stitch. Finally, place a marker in the last stitch of the round. You should end up with an even number of stitches between the markers for the two short ends of the scarf (18 stitches in the example). The number of stitches between the markers for each of the two long sides should also equal each other.

Alternate knit and purl rounds, working a double decrease at each of the corners on the knit rounds as follows:

Round 1: Using color 2, purl.

Round 2: *Using color 1, knit until 1 stitch remains before each marked stitch, s2kp2; repeat from * around. When you reach the end of round, work the first stitch of the following round as part of your double decrease. (*8 stitches decreased*)

Repeat these 2 rounds until no stitches remain between the markers at each end. This means you've reached the center of the scarf. Remove the markers and use either Kitchener stitch (pages 70–74) or Three-Needle Bind Off (page 69) to join the center seam.

Round Potholder

This round potholder is a throw-back to the Jogless Garter Stitch Hat on pages 139–141. It has exactly the same shaping: 8 stitches are increased or decreased every other round in garter stitch to make a circle. The hat starts from the center and increases to the outer edge. In this pot holder, you work the same structure, but start at the circumference and decrease down to the center. This serves as preparation for the Oval Placemat (pages 169–173), which consists of two half circles (the curved ends) with a rectangle in the middle.

Featured Technique

- Staggered decreases in garter stitch to make a circle

For Project Shown You Need

YARN	Lorna's Laces Swirl Chunky (83% merino/17% silk, 120 yds/4 oz)
YARN AMOUNT	about 30 yds/27m Aqua (13ns)
GAUGE	14 stitches = 4" (10 cm) in garter stitch
NEEDLE SIZE	US 10 (6 mm). Match the project's gauge if you want finished measurements to match pattern instructions.
NEEDLE TYPES (any of the following)	16" (40 cm) circular needle (*Note:* As you approach the center, the 16"/40 cm circular needle will be too long to continue working comfortably, and you must change to one of the other options below.) Two circular needles 16" (40 cm) or longer 47" (120 cm) circular needle for Magic Loop Set of five double-pointed needles
OTHER SUPPLIES	Stitch marker, yarn needle, 1" ring for hanging (optional)
FINISHED SIZE	6" (15 cm) in diameter

Knitting the Potholder

- Cast on 80 stitches loosely. Place marker and join beginning and end of round, being careful not to twist the cast-on row (see Off to a Good Start: Casting On and Joining, page 13).
- Round 1 (decrease round): Knit, decreasing 8 stitches evenly spaced around.
- Round 2: Purl.
- Repeat Rounds 1 and 2, being careful to stagger the decreases whenever you work Round 1 (for how to position the decreases, see Staggered vs. Swirled Increases, page 126). When you get down to 8 stitches, work 1 last purl round.
- Cut the yarn and pull it through the remaining stitches, then weave it in on the back. Use the cast-on tail to disguise any gap where the cast on was joined on the first round, then weave it in on the back. (See Mind the Gap, page 76.) If knit very firmly, the center may protrude. If this happens, unravel the final purled round, then pull the yarn back through the 8 stitches and finish off.
- Sew on ring for hanging, if desired.

ROUND POTHOLDER

Any Size, Any Yarn

Work a gauge swatch in garter stitch and measure the stitches per inch or centimeter. Decide how wide you want your pot holder to be (the diameter), then multiply this by π (3.14) to get the circumference of the circle. Multiply the circumference by the gauge to find how many stitches to cast on, then round this number to the nearest multiple of 8. This gives you the correct number of stitches to cast on. Follow the directions above to decrease down to the center of the circle.

Working from the Center Out

Cast on 8 stitches at the center (See Closed Center Cast On #1, pages 22–24).

Round 1: Knit around, increasing 8 stitches evenly spaced around.

Round 2: Purl.

Repeat these 2 rounds, staggering the increases on Round 1 each time you work it, until the circle is as big as you like.

End with Round 1. Bind off loosely in purl, or turn to the other side and bind off in knitting.

Oval Placemat

An oval can be made by splitting a circle (see Round Potholder, pages 167–168) into two halves, and then placing a rectangle or square between them. The outer edge of this placemat is worked in noncurling garter stitch, so the shaping of this border is identical to the pot holder, with 8 stitches decreased every other round. Half the decreases are made at one end for one semicircle and half at the other end. The placemat's center is worked in stockinette stitch. Because stockinette stitches are taller and narrower than garter stitches, the decreases must happen a little more quickly to keep the center flat: they are still worked every other round, but alternating 8 stitches with 10 stitches per round, divided between the two ends.

New Technique Used

- Staggered decreases to make half circles (see Staggered vs. Swirled Increases, page 126)
- Changes in rate of decrease for stockinette versus garter stitch
- Kitchener stitch to close the center seam (pages 70–74)

For Project Shown You Need

YARN	Lorna's Laces Shepherd Worsted (100% superwash wool, 225 yds/3½ oz (100 g)
YARN AMOUNT	180 yds/165 m (about 2.8 oz/80 g) Sage (43ns)
GAUGE	20 stitches = 4" (10 cm) in stockinette stitch
NEEDLE SIZE	US 8 (5 mm). Match the project's gauge if you want finished measurements to match pattern instructions.
NEEDLE TYPES	36" (90 cm) circular needle A second circular needle the same size (but any length) to work the center of the placemat
OTHER SUPPLIES	Four split markers, yarn needle
FINISHED SIZE	12" (30.5 cm) wide × 17" (43 cm) long

Setting Up

I recommend the Cable Cast On (page 302) for a neat edge. You could also use the Long-Tail Cast On (pages 302–303), but you'll need to allow a tail long enough to cast on 238 stitches. To avoid a too-tight cast on, which causes the edge to curl up, use a larger needle just for the cast on, if you wish.

- Cast on 238 stitches.
- Place the first marker after 25 stitches, the second after the next 94 stitches, the third after another 25 stitches, and the fourth after 94 stitches at the end of round.
- Join beginning and end of round, being careful not to twist the stitches (see Off to a Good Start: Casting On and Joining, page 13). The two sections with 25 stitches each are the straight edges along the top and bottom of the placemat; these sections remain at 25 stitches throughout the project. The two sections with 94 stitches are the curved ends of the placemat. All the decreases are worked in these sections; this shapes the curves, so you will gradually have fewer and fewer stitches in these sections, until you get down to just 4 stitches at both ends of the center line of the placemat.

To prevent confusion, you may want to color code your markers, using two of one color for the first and second markers and two of a different color for the third and fourth markers. This signals you to keep your decreases in an area that falls between two markers of the same color **A**.

Knitting the Garter Stitch Border

Be sure to stagger the decreases whenever you work Round 1, so the decreases never line up with the previous set of decreases (see Round Potholder, pages 167–168, and Staggered vs. Swirled Increases, page 126).

- Round 1 (decrease round): Knit to first marker; continue knitting between the first and second markers, decreasing 4 stitches evenly spaced; knit to the third marker; continue knitting between the third and fourth markers, decreasing 4 stitches evenly spaced. (*8 stitches decreased*)
- Round 2: Purl.
- Work Rounds 1 and 2 a total of five times. (*198 stitches remain*)

Knitting the Stockinette Stitch Center

Because stockinette stitches are taller and narrower than garter stitches, the rate of decrease needs to change so that the center of the placemat lies flat. To decrease just a little faster, you decrease 5 stitches in the curved sections on Round 1 (below) but still decrease 4 stitches in the curved sections on Round 3. Again, remember to stagger the decreases on Rounds 1 and 3 so they don't line up with the previous round of decreases. This becomes impossible as you near the center, but do your best until then.

- Round 1: Knit to first marker; continue knitting between the first and second marker, decreasing

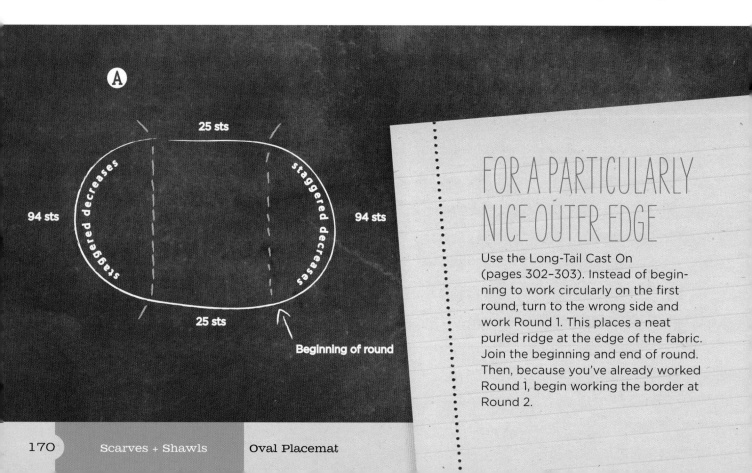

A

25 sts

staggered decreases

staggered decreases

94 sts

94 sts

25 sts

Beginning of round

FOR A PARTICULARLY NICE OUTER EDGE

Use the Long-Tail Cast On (pages 302–303). Instead of beginning to work circularly on the first round, turn to the wrong side and work Round 1. This places a neat purled ridge at the edge of the fabric. Join the beginning and end of round. Then, because you've already worked Round 1, begin working the border at Round 2.

5 stitches evenly spaced; knit to third marker; continue knitting between the third and fourth marker, decreasing 5 stitches evenly spaced. (*10 stitches decreased*)

- Round 2: Knit.
- Round 3: Knit to first marker; continue knitting between the first and second markers, decreasing 4 stitches evenly spaced; knit to the third marker; continue knitting between the third and fourth markers, decreasing 4 stitches evenly spaced. (*8 stitches decreased*)
- Round 4: Knit.
- Repeat Rounds 1–4 until you can no longer work comfortably on the 36" (90 cm) needle.
- Divide the knitting so that the first two sections (from beginning of round to the second marker) are on one circular needle and the second two sections (from the second marker to the end of round) are on a second circular needle **B**.
- Continue to work Rounds 1–4, remembering that the second marker falls at the end of the first needle and the fourth marker falls at the end of the second needle.
- Stop when 9 stitches or fewer remain in the curved sections. If you've followed the directions perfectly, there should be 6 stitches remaining in each of the curved sections, but it's easy to get off by a stitch or two. If you did, don't worry about it.
- On the next round, decrease so that there are 4 stitches remaining in each of the curved sections.

- Lay the placemat out flat, patting it into shape. Uncurl the knitting at the center to see how close the two needles come together without distorting the fabric. You're going to knit 2 more rounds, and then work Kitchener stitch (pages 70–74) along the very center, so allow for 5 rows of knitting between the two needles. If it looks like the two needles are more than 5 rows apart, knit 1 more round before continuing.

Working the Final Shaping

- *K2tog, knit until 2 stitches remain before the first marker, K2tog, remove marker, K2tog twice; repeat from * on second needle. (*25 stitches remain on each needle*)
- Knit until 3 stitches remain at the end of the first needle. Move these stitches to the beginning of the second needle. Working now on the second needle, knit until 3 stitches remain at the end of the second needle. Move these stitches to the beginning of the first needle. Cut the yarn, leaving a tail about 30" (76 cm) long .
- Using a yarn needle, pull the tail through the first 4 stitches on the first needle **C**.
- Work Kitchener stitch to join the stitches on the two needles together until all the stitches on the first needle have been worked and 4 stitches remain on the second needle. Slide these stitches to the other end of the second needle and pull the yarn through all of them. Weave in the ends on the wrong side.

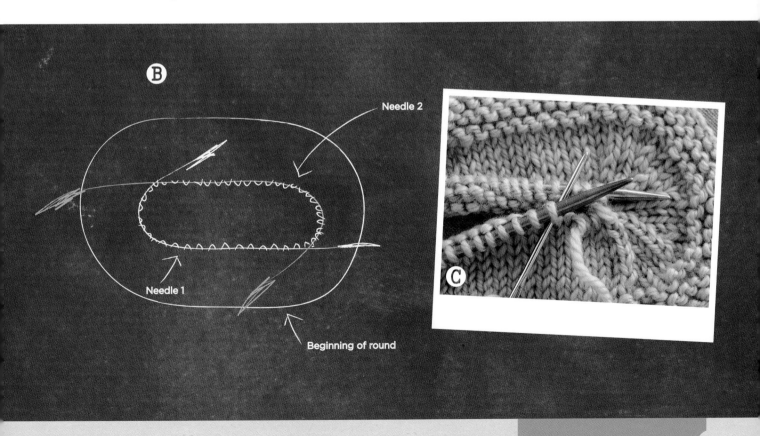

B

Needle 2

Needle 1

Beginning of round

C

Any Size, Any Yarn

Make a gauge swatch in stockinette stitch, because it makes up most of the placemat. If you want to make a placemat that is mostly or all garter stitch, then make your gauge swatch in garter stitch instead. The fabric for the placemat needs to be stretchy; if you make it too firm it will not lie flat. Determine the stitches per inch or centimeter. Decide how big you want your placemat to be — you'll need to know length and width. The width determines the diameter of the half circles that form both the ends. Using the total length and the diameter of the half circles, you can then figure out how wide the rectangular section between the two half circles will be. (See diagram at right.)

Calculate the circumference of your oval this way:

Circumference = 2 × (length – width) + (π × width).

Multiply the circumference by your gauge to get the number of stitches to cast on. You must have an even number of stitches. Let's take the example of the placemat in the project on page 169. It is 12″ × 17″ (30.5 × 43 cm), and the gauge is 5 stitches to the inch (about 2 stitches to the centimeter) in stockinette stitch, which makes up most of the placemat.

	In Inches	In Centimeters
Step 1: Calculate circumference based on length and width.	2 × (17″–12″) + (3.14 × 12) = 47.68	2 × (43 – 30.5) + (3.14 × 30.5) = 120.77
Step 2: Multiply by gauge to get cast-on stitches.	47.68 × 5 = 238.4 sts	120.77 × 1.97 = 237.9 sts
Step 3: Round to an even number.	238 sts	238 sts

You also need to know how many stitches are in the semicircular sections and how many stitches are in the rectangular section between the two curved ends. The length of the straight center section is equal to the length minus the width, so calculate this and then multiply it by the gauge.

	In Inches	In Centimeters
Step 1: Calculate center section.	17″ – 12″ = 5″	43 cm – 30.5 cm = 12.5 cm
Step 2: Multiply by gauge to get center stitches.	5 × 5 = 25 sts	12.5 × 2 = 1.97 = 24.625 sts
Step 3: Round to a whole number of stitches, if necessary.	25 sts	25 sts

Based on this calculation, set aside two sections of 25 stitches for the straight center of the placemat, and divide the remaining stitches equally between the two curved sections. Calculate how many stitches should be in each curved section as follows:

Cast-on stitches ÷ 2 – center stitches = curved stitches

Example: 238 ÷ 2 – 25 = 94.

There should be 94 stitches in each of the curved sections. The diagram for the placemat on the next page shows how these stitch counts relate to the structure of the placemat.

The 25 stitches for the center rectangle are worked with no decreases. The remaining 94 stitches are decreased to form each curved end.

Once you have cast on and placed your markers to delineate each section, follow the general directions beginning with Knitting the Garter Stitch Border (page 170) to shape your oval. If you are making a placemat with a garter stitch border, decrease 4 stitches at each end every other round in garter stitch until the border is as wide as you like, then begin decreasing as described in Knitting the Stockinette Stitch Center on pages 170–171. If you are making a placemat that is all garter stitch, then continue decreasing 4 stitches at each end of the oval every other round until there are fewer than 9 stitches left between the markers. In both cases, complete the placemat by following the instructions in Working the Final Shaping, page 171, but if you are working in garter stitch to the center, take care to continue alternating knit and purl rounds.

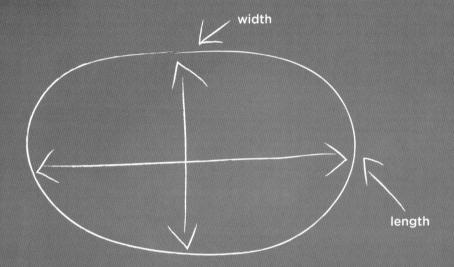

Working from the Center Out

This is the same method of construction used for the Mitered Rectangle Scarf (pages 162–166), except that the corner increases are spread out to make the ends rounded instead of square.

Using a closed cast on, such as the Turkish cast on (pages 29–30), and two circular needles, cast on the stitches needed for the center rectangle plus 4 more. The example on page 172 would require 29 wraps, to make the 25 stitches on each side of the center, plus the additional 4 stitches, for a total of 58 stitches. Place markers 4 stitches from the far end of each needle (no markers at the beginning of the needles). Work circularly in stockinette stitch, reversing the shaping of the Oval Placemat as follows:

Round 1: Knit around, increasing 4 stitches between the marker and the end of each needle.

Round 2: Knit.

Round 3: Knit around, increasing 5 stitches between the marker and the end of each needle.

Round 4: Knit.

Repeat these 4 rounds until the oval is as big as you like before the border. Be sure to stagger the increases (see Staggered vs. Swirled Increases, page 126).

Begin working in garter stitch, purling the plain rounds and increasing 4 stitches at each curved end on the knit rounds, as follows:

Garter Stitch Round 1: Knit around, increasing 4 stitches between the marker and the end of each needle.

Garter Stitch Round 2: Purl.

Repeat these 2 rounds until the border is the width you like, then bind off loosely on a purl round. Weave in the ends, using the bind-off tail to make the beginning and end of the bind off look continuous (pages 56–57).

group of three small shapes that make up the Potholder Collection provides practice in making other shapes: octagons, triangles, and pentagons, all beginning at the outer edge. For an example of an octagon worked from the center out, see the Beret (pages 136–138). Each of the three pot holders demonstrates a different method of decreasing, so you can see the varying effects of working pairs of decreases versus double decreases and of maintaining the corner stitches in stockinette versus garter stitch.

For Project Shown You Need

YARN	Lorna's Laces Swirl Chunky (83% merino/17% silk, 120 yds/4 oz)
YARN AMOUNT	About 30 yds/27 m Aqua (13ns) for each pot holder
GAUGE	14 stitches = 4" (10 cm) in garter stitch
NEEDLE SIZE	US 10 (6 mm). Match the project's gauge if you want finished measurements to match pattern instructions.
NEEDLE TYPES	To begin, a 16" (40 cm) circular needle.
	As you approach the center, the needle will be too long to work on comfortably; change to two circular needles 16" (40 cm) or longer, a circular needle at least 47" (120 cm) long for Magic Loop, or a set of four or five double-pointed needles.
	See the instructions for each pot holder for notes on the best way to set up the project on the needles.
OTHER SUPPLIES	Markers for corners (some projects require split markers), yarn needle
FINISHED SIZE	Octagon 6" (15 cm) in diameter; Triangle 7¼" (18.5 cm) in height; Pentagon 6½" (16.5 cm) in height

DESIGNING WITH FLAT SHAPES

Creating projects based on the shapes of the items in this chapter is a great pleasure and can be incredibly inspiring. Used individually, they can be made any size, from a coaster to a king-size blanket, but you can also incorporate them anywhere you need a flat area. This could be the center of a sweater front or back, the top of a hat, or the bottom of a bag. You can also make many small repetitions of a shape and create whole projects from these tiny modules. A single large circle, square, or triangle can be used at a neckline as a collar and become the focal point of the whole sweater, or if stiff enough, it could be the brim of a hat, like the Witch's Hat on pages 142–143.

Octagon Potholder

The only difference between an octagon and a circle is that the decreases must be lined up to create the eight corners, rather than staggered around the circle. This project uses two mirror-image decreases at each corner, because single decreases make a swirled circle rather than an octagon (see photo of Helix Hat crown, pages 126 and 130). The advantage of working a pair of decreases, rather than a double decrease, is that you never have to slip stitches from one needle to another to work them. Placing the decreases in columns of stockinette stitch, with one on either side of the beginning/end of round, effectively disguises the jog that you'd see in garter stitch. Working two decreases at eight corners, however, means that you are decreasing 16 stitches on each decrease round, which is twice as many as we worked every other round to make a circle. To prevent the decreasing from happening too fast, making the pot holder ruffle, we'll work them every fourth round instead of every second round.

New Techniques Used

- Decreases at eight points every fourth round to form an octagon
- Paired single decreases
- Columns of decreases maintained in stockinette stitch

Notes on Needles

If you choose to use double-pointed needles, this project is most easily and most logically worked with a set of five.

Knitting the Octagon

- Setup: Cast on 80 stitches. Join beginning and end of round being careful not to twist the stitches (see Off to a Good Start: Casting On and Joining, page 13). Place markers at the beginning/end of round and after every 10 stitches. If you work on a set of double-pointed needles, divide the stitches evenly among four needles, with 20 stitches per needle, and place only four markers, one at the center of each needle. The ends of the needles serve to orient you in place of other markers. If you work on two circular needles or Magic Loop, you can dispense with markers at the beginning of round and the halfway point.

- Round 1 (decrease round): *Ssk, knit until 2 stitches remain before next marker (or end of needle), K2tog; repeat from * around. (*16 stitches decreased*)

- Round 2: Purl around, knitting the stitches before and after each marker.

- Round 3: Knit.

- Round 4: Repeat Round 2.

- Repeat these 4 rounds until 16 stitches remain, ending with Round 1. You can remove all the markers now.

- Knit 2 rounds.

- Final decrease round: There are no stitches between decreases: *Ssk, K2tog; repeat from * around. (*8 stitches remain*)

- Cut the yarn and pull through all the stitches. Weave in ends, using the tail at the cast on to make it look continuous (see Mind the Gap, page 76).

Depending on how firmly you knit, the center of the octagon may pop out. To fix this, unravel the last two rounds (the final decrease round and the preceding knit round), put the 16 stitches back on the needles, rework just the final decrease round, and finish off.

THE FINISHING TOUCH: A SPECIAL EDGE

You can add anything you like at the outer edge: fringes, beads, picked-up borders, and I-cord or an edging that is either worked as a bind off or applied as you go are all excellent choices. Select a pattern stitch with an equal number of knits and purls to prevent the edge from curling.

Any Size, Any Yarn

If you want to get started without any preliminary planning, follow the directions for Working from the Center Out, below. If you prefer to begin at the outer edge and work toward the center, first figure out the measurement of the perimeter, then multiply that number by the gauge to find the number of stitches to cast on. You can calculate the circumference of a circle with the same diameter as your octagon. Decide how wide you want it to be (the diameter). Multiply this by π (3.14), then multiply that by the gauge. Round this to the nearest multiple of 8; generally it's best to round up so the pot holder doesn't come out too small. The example below assumes a gauge of 4 stitches/inch (1.6 stitches/cm) and a diameter of 6″ (15.2 cm)

	In Inches	In Centimeters
Step 1: Multiply width (or diameter) by π	6″ × 3.14 = 18.84″	15.2 cm × 3.14 = 47.73 cm
Step 2: Multiply perimeter by gauge.	18.84″ × 4 = 75.36″	47.73 cm × 1.6 = 76.37 sts
Step 3: Round up to a multiple of 8.	80 sts	80 sts

Working from the Center Out

- Cast on 8 stitches (see Closed Center Cast On #1, pages 22–24). On the first round, work an M1 increase with the working yarn after every stitch, adding 8 stitches for a total of 16. Place markers at the beginning/end of round and between every 2 stitches. You may use the needle ends as substitutes for some of these, as described on the previous page.

- Round 1: *K1, M1L, knit until 1 stitch remains before marker (or end of needle), M1R, slip marker (if there is one); repeat from * around. (*16 stitches increased*)

- Round 2: Purl, knitting the stitches before and after each marker.

- Round 3: Knit.

- Round 4: Repeat Round 2.

- Work Rounds 1–4 until the octagon is as big as you like. End with Round 1, then bind off in purl, or turn over and bind off on the wrong side in knitting. Weave in ends, using the cast-on tail to close the hole at the center.

Triangle Potholder

The whole triangle is worked in garter stitch, so the columns of stitches where decreases occur are hidden by the garter stitch ridges. The shape's structure is still clear, however, thanks to the grain of the garter stitch, which bends at each corner. Reversing the decreases (that is, working ssk or ssp before the corner and K2tog or P2tog after it) makes a sharper corner. Before beginning, check the Appendix to make sure you know how to do all the decreases correctly (pages 304–305).

Featured Techniques

- Working pairs of decreases at three points on 2 out of 3 rounds to form a triangle
- Paired single decreases
- Decreasing on purl rounds
- Columns of decreases maintained in garter stitch

Notes on Needles

If you choose to use a set of double-pointed needles, this project is most easily and most logically worked with the stitches divided equally among three needles. The decreases fall conveniently at the beginning and end of each needle, so no markers are required, except perhaps one to indicate beginning/end of round.

Knitting the Triangle

- Cast on 84 stitches and divide equally among three double-pointed needles (28 stitches per needle). The ends of the needles serve to mark the corners, where the decreases will take place. You may also use two circular needles or Magic Loop. In that case, divide the stitches in half on the two needles or front and back of the Magic Loop. Place a marker 28 stitches from the beginning of round and 28 stitches from the end of round to indicate where the corner decreases will be placed. (see Off to a Good Start: Casting On and Joining, page 13).

The decrease pattern required to make a triangle in garter stitch may be a little confusing at first. What you are doing is decreasing on 2 out of every 3 rounds, and at the same time alternating knit and purl rounds to make garter stitch. This means that sometimes you decrease on knit rounds and sometimes on purl rounds. This is easy to understand when laid out in a table.

	Pattern Round	Decrease Round
Round 1	Knit	Knitted decreases
Round 2	Purl	Purled decreases
Round 3	Knit	
Round 4	Purl	Purled decreases
Round 5	Knit	Knitted decreases
Round 6	Purl	

- Round 1: *K2tog, knit until 2 stitches remain at end of needle (on double-pointed needles) or before marker (on circular needles), ssk; repeat from * around. (*6 stitches decreased*)
- Round 2: *P2tog, purl until 2 stitches remain at end of needle (on double-pointed needles) or before marker (on circular needles), ssp; repeat from * around. (*6 stitches decreased*)
- Round 3: Knit.
- Round 4: Repeat Round 2.
- Round 5: Repeat Round 1.
- Round 6: Purl.
- Repeat these 6 rounds until 6 stitches remain.

On double-points, 2 stitches remain on each needle, so you may want to put 4 on one needle and 2 on the other for stability. On circular needles, 3 stitches remain in each half. Cut yarn and pull through all stitches. Weave in the ends, using the cast-on tail to make the cast on look continuous (see Mind the Gap, page 76).

Any Size, Any Yarn

If you don't want to do any planning, follow the instructions below for making a triangle from the center out. If you want to start at the outer edge, begin by calculating the perimeter of the triangle. Decide first how wide you want the triangle to be, measured from one corner to the center of the opposite side, as shown by the arrow in the drawing at right. This is what mathematicians call the "altitude," but you can think of it as the "height." Multiply this number by 3.5 to get the perimeter. (I could explain why this works for equilateral triangles, but that would involve the Pythagorean theorem, cosigns, and square roots, and we don't really want to go there right now!) Multiply the perimeter by your gauge and then round that to the nearest multiple of 6 to find the number of stitches to cast on. In the example below, the height of the pot holder is 7" (18 cm) and the gauge is 3½ stitches/inch (1.38 stitches/cm). Cast on the number of stitches you calculated, mark the three corners, and then follow the directions above.

	In Inches	In Centimeters
Step 1: Multiply height by 3.5 to get perimeter.	7" × 3.5 = 24.5"	18 cm × 3.5 = 63 cm
Step 2: Multiply perimeter by gauge.	24.5" × 3.5 = 85.75	63 cm × 1.38 = 86.94
Step 3: Round to multiple of 6.	84 sts	84 sts

Working from the Center Out

Cast on 6 stitches at the center. Begin as described for Closed Center Cast On #1, pages 22–24, but increase 6 stitches instead of 8 on each increase round, as described below.

Place a split marker in every other stitch to mark the three corners (see Using Markers in Circular Knitting: Split markers, pages 42–43).

Round 1: Knit around, working K-yo-k into each marked stitch. (*6 stitches increased*)

Round 2: Purl around, working P-yo-P into each marked stitch. (*6 stitches increased*)

Round 3: Knit.

Round 4: Repeat Round 2.

Round 5: Repeat Round 1.

Round 6: Purl.

Repeat these 6 rounds until the triangle is as big as you like.

End with one of the knit rounds, then bind off in purl or turn over to the "wrong" side and bind off in knitting. Weave in the ends using the bind-off tail to make the beginning and end of the bind off continuous (see pages 56–57).

Pentagon Potholder

Working a column of knit stitches at each corner and incorporating double decreases into these for shaping results in a very different look from the garter stitch corners of the triangle or the paired decreases of the octagon: the corners are more pointed and more clearly defined. In order to work the double decreases without constantly shifting stitches between needles, it's important to place the decreases at the center of needles, rather than at the ends. This entails some rearrangement of the stitches to set things up properly as you begin the first round.

Project Notes

- This pattern uses a centered double decrease (s2kp2) at each corner. Before you begin, review this decrease in the appendix to ensure you are working it correctly. The center stitch must be on top — not leaning to either side.

New Techniques Used

- Working single corner stitches in stockinette on a garter stitch background
- Working double decreases at five points to form a pentagon
- Spreading out the decrease rounds so none fall on purl rounds

Notes on Needles

- It is easiest by far to begin this project on a 16" (40 cm) circular needle, and then switch to double points, two circulars, or Magic Loop as soon as the pentagon becomes too small to work easily on the single circular needle.

- Like the Triangle Potholder (pages 178–179), making a pentagon requires that you integrate the decreases with the garter stitch pattern. In this case, you need to work the decreases on 2 rounds out of every 5. To avoid making decreases on purl rounds, I've spread the decrease plan out so that they fall on 4 rounds out of every 10, allowing you to work all of them on knit rounds (see chart below). Notice that there are no decreases on Round 9. If you mistakenly decrease on Round 9, you'll reduce the number of stitches too quickly and the pot holder will ruffle.

- At the beginning of Round 1, the 2 stitches you slip for the decrease are *always* the last stitch of the round (still on the left needle point) and the first stitch of the round. On the very first round, the decrease joins the beginning and end of round (see photo **B** at right). To prepare for this, I tell you to slip that stitch to the left-hand needle after you've cast on and placed the required markers. On subsequent rounds, the decrease creates a seam stitch that hides the jog at the beginning and end of round.

	Pattern Round	Decrease Round
Round 1	Knit	Decrease
Round 2	Purl, knitting the corner stitches	
Round 3	Knit	Decrease
Round 4	Purl, knitting the corner stitches	
Round 5	Knit	Decrease
Round 6	Purl, knitting the corner stitches	
Round 7	Knit	Decrease
Round 8	Purl, knitting the corner stitches	
Round 9	Knit	
Round 10	Purl, knitting the corner stitches	

Setting Up for Knitting the Pentagon

- Cast on 85 stitches. Place a marker in the first stitch of the round and every 17th stitch thereafter. Use a different kind of marker for the beginning of round so it's easy to tell when you start a new round. Once you get going, the corners should be easy to see, since they're in stockinette stitch, but if you find it at all difficult to identify the corner stitches, move the markers up closer to the needles as the pentagon grows. (See Using Markers in Circular Knitting: Split markers, pages 42–43.)

- Slip the last stitch you cast on from the right needle point to the left needle point to join the beginning and

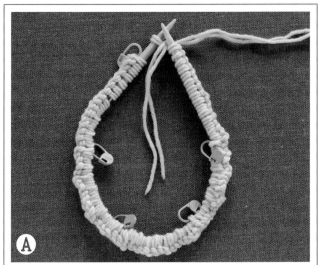

Slip last cast-on stitch to left needle point in preparation for s2Kp2 at beginning of Round 1.

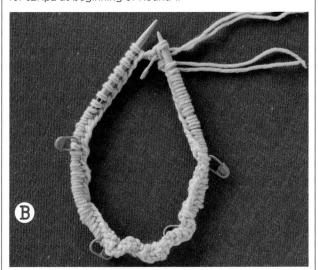

The first decrease on Round 1 joins beginning and end of round.

Double points. One-fifth of stitches are on one needle and two-fifths are on each of the other needles. There is an equal number of stitches between corner stitch and both ends of each needle.

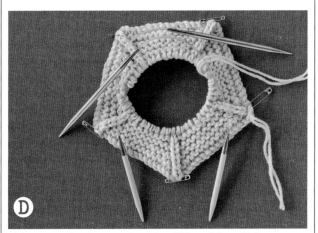

Using two circular needles. Two-fifths of the stitches are on one needle and three-fifths are on the other needle. Again, there is an equal number of stitches between the corner stitch and both ends of each needle. For Magic Loop, set up the stitches on the two halves of the needle just as they are shown on the two circular needles.

end of round **A**. Note that samples were worked with a double strand of yarn.

Knitting the Pentagon

- Round 1: *S2kp2 **B**, knit until 1 stitch remains before next marked stitch; repeat from *; K1, which brings you to the end of round. (*10 stitches decreased*)
- Round 2: *Knit the marked stitch, purl until you reach the next marked stitch; repeat from *, stopping 1 stitch before the end of round.
- Rounds 3–8: Repeat Rounds 1 and 2 three more times, purling the last stitch of Round 8.
- Round 9: Knit.
- Round 10: Repeat Round 2.
- Repeat these 10 rounds until the pentagon becomes too small to work easily on the single circular needle, which will happen when you complete your third or fourth decrease round.

- Move the knitting onto three double-pointed needles **C**, two circular needles **D**, or Magic Loop. Make sure you place an equal number of stitches between the ends of the needles and the decreases as shown. This ensures that you don't have the annoyance of slipping stitches back and forth between needles to work the decreases. As you work, remember that the end of round is NOT at the end of a needle.
- Continue working Rounds 1–10 until 15 stitches remain, ending with an even-numbered round. On the next round, work s2kp2 five times. (*5 stitches remain*) If working on double points, you may want to consolidate your knitting onto just two needles at this time.
- If the center still seems to be open, knit 1 more round. If it protrudes or looks bumpy, unravel this last round before securing the stitches.
- Cut the yarn and pull through the remaining stitches. Weave in ends.

Any Size, Any Yarn

The simplest way to make a pentagon (or any other shape) any size you like is to start from the center, as described at right. To start at the center, you first must calculate the perimeter of your pentagon. Luckily, since knitting stretches, you can just calculate the circumference of a circle the same width as your pentagon and go from there. Multiply the width by π (3.14), then multiply this by your gauge to get the number of stitches for the circumference. You'll need a multiple of 10 stitches plus 5, but the double decreases (s2kp2) tend to pull the knitting tighter, so the pentagon will be a little smaller than expected; therefore, round up to the next larger multiple of 10 plus 5. This example assumes a diameter of 7″ (18 cm) and a gauge of 3½ stitches/inch (1.4 stitches per cm). Cast on the number of stitches you calculate and mark the 5 corners (place a marker in the first stitch of the round, and then in 4 other stitches, equally spaced around). Follow the directions on pages 180–181 for shaping the pentagon.

	In Inches	In Centimeters
Step 1: Multiply width by π to get circumference.	7″ × 3.14 = 21.98″	18 cm × 3.14 = 56.52
Step 2: Multiply circumference by gauge	21.98″ × 3.5 = 76.9 sts	56.52 cm × 1.4 = 79.128 sts
Step 3: Round up to a multiple of 10 plus 5.	85 sts	85 sts

Working from the Center Out

Needles: You may use a set of double-pointed needles, two circulars or Magic Loop.

Cast on 5 stitches. Begin as described for Closed Center Cast On #1, pages 22–24), but increase 10 stitches instead of 8 on each increase round, as in Round 2 below.

> On double points, place 2 stitches on the first needle and 3 on the second needle; after you increase the first or second time, shift one-third of the stitches on the second needle to a third needle.

> On two circular needles (or Magic Loop), place 2 stitches on the first needle (or first half of the needle) and 3 on the second needle (or half of the needle). There's no need to rearrange the stitches at all as your pot holder grows.

Set up round, work K-yo-K into every stitch. (*15 stitches*)

Place a marker in the yarn over at the center of each increase.

Round 1: Purl around, knitting the marked stitches.

Round 2: Knit around, working K-yo-K into each marked stitch. (*10 stitches increased*)

If it becomes difficult to identify the center yarn over at the corners as the knitting grows, move the markers up closer to the needles, being careful to place them in the center yarn over of the increases.

Rounds 3–8: Repeat Rounds 1 and 2 three more times.

Round 9: Repeat Round 1.

Round 10: Knit.

Repeat these 10 rounds until the pentagon is as large as you like, ending with a knit round. Bind off in purl, or turn to the wrong side and bind off in knitting.

Weave in the ends using the bind-off tail to make the beginning and end of the bind off continuous (see pages 56–57). Use the cast-on tail to close the center hole (see page 24).

STEPPING UP TO SOCKS

Socks are just tubes with one open end, one shaped end, and a heel added somewhere in between. In this chapter we'll explore different ways to construct these small projects and how to use our needles most efficiently.

The sock projects are designed to teach you:
• How to work from the top down or the toe up
• Toe shapings — star, round, and flat
• How to add heels — conventional, "afterthought," and "forethought"
• Heel shapings — common, plus those shaped like round and flat toes
• Stranded knitting

Note that in order to present projects that are quick to work, the socks are all small in scale — just big enough to give you a chance to get used to the techniques they are intended to teach. Because they are not sized to fit anyone in particular, it's assumed that you'll make only one of each as a practical lesson in construction; therefore, the yarn amounts are given for just one. If you want to make a pair, you'll need twice as much yarn.

At the end of the projects is a discussion of how to design your own, touching on fabric quality, fit, and integrating pattern stitches with shaping.

MAKING ARRANGEMENTS

As with other knitted tubes, you can arrange the stitches for socks on your needles in many ways, but because of the need to line heels up with toes when making socks, some arrangements are more efficient than others. For instance, you can organize the stitches so that the needles help you keep track of which part of the sock (front or back, top or bottom) you're working. There are situations, however, where you may want to arrange the stitches on your needles differently.

Double-Pointed Needles

You need a set of at least four double points. Place all the stitches for the front of the leg (which are also the stitches for the top of the foot) on one needle. This is usually half of the stitches. Divide the remaining stitches between two needles for the back/bottom of the sock. This way, you can always tell what section of the sock you're working on.

Stitches arranged on three double points. The front stitches are all on one needle.

If you prefer using a set of five double-pointed needles, set it up just as you would on three needles, at left, but divide the stitches for the front/top of the sock between two needles as you did the back/bottom. A quarter of the stitches will be on each needle.

Stitches arranged on four double points. Front and back stitches are each divided between two needles.

The beginning of round can fall either at the center back/bottom of the foot or at one side. If you are designing your own sock, do whatever makes sense to you. If you're following someone else's instructions, make sure you know where the designer thinks the beginning of round is so that you stay oriented.

Two Circular Needles

When using two circular needles, place the front/top half of the stitches on one needle and the back/bottom half on the other. The beginning of round is at one side of the sock. Ⓐ

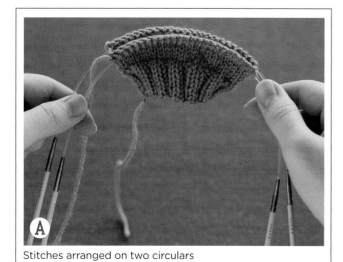

Ⓐ Stitches arranged on two circulars

Magic Loop

Just as for two circular needles, place half the stitches on the back of the Magic Loop and half on the front. The beginning of round is at one side of the sock. Ⓑ

Ⓑ Stitches arranged for Magic Loop

Breaking the Rules

As with all knitting, the instructions given for needles are not rules, but guidelines that won't always apply. Here are some examples:

• **Gussets.** While working the gusset section of a sock, you temporarily have far more stitches on the bottom than on the top. Even if you arrange the stitches during the rest of the sock on three double-pointed needles, you may want to put them on four until the gusset decreases are completed.

• **Pattern stitches.** When working the patterned leg of a sock, you may find it easiest to work if you arrange things so that each needle or each half of the Magic Loop holds a full pattern repeat. If there is a pattern stitch on the top of the foot, but the bottom of the foot is plain, you may have a different number of stitches for the top than you do for the bottom. When this is the case, divide the sock by section, with the top stitches separated from the bottom stitches, even if the number of stitches isn't equal.

• **Proper setup for heel and toe.** If you have rearranged the stitches for any reason, make sure the stitches are once again divided properly between the needles before beginning to work the heel or the toe.

Afterthought Heel Sock

The simplest of socks, the Afterthought Heel Sock is a perfect introduction to the art of sock making. It is knit from the cuff down, ignoring the heel entirely. To finish off the tube, the "star" toe is shaped with four equidistant decreases, making a shape similar to the crown of a hat.

When the body and toe of the sock have been completed, the "afterthought" heel is added in a separate step. The shaping for this heel is actually borrowed from a method for shaping the toe, known as the "round" toe. The star toe is too pointed to substitute for a heel, but the round toe adapts admirably. This sock gives you practice with both shapings.

Tube, before adding the heel

For Project Shown You Need

YARN	Lorna's Laces Shepherd Worsted (100% superwash wool, 225 yards/4 oz)
YARN AMOUNT (for one sock)	56 yds/51 m Turquoise (22ns), MC; and 10 yds/9 m Grapevine (3ns), CC
GAUGE	22 stitches = 4" (10 cm) in stockinette stitch
NEEDLE SIZE	US 6 (4 mm). Match the project's gauge if you want finished measurements to match pattern instructions.
NEEDLE TYPES (any of the following)	Set of four or five double-pointed needles Two circulars 16" (40 cm) or longer 47" (120 cm) circular needle or longer for Magic Loop
OTHER SUPPLIES	Stitch marker for beginning/end of round (optional)
FINISHED SIZE	Length of foot 6½" (16.5 cm), length of leg above heel 4¼" (11 cm), circumference 6½" (16.5 cm)

New Techniques Used

- Star toe
- Cutting and unraveling for an "afterthought" heel
- Round heel/toe

Knitting the Leg

- Using MC, cast on 36 stitches. Because you'll be working in K1, P1 ribbing, the Ribbed Cable Cast On (page 303) is an excellent choice.
- Arrange the stitches as described in Making Arrangements, page 187. Turn and join the beginning and end of round, being careful not to twist (see Off to a Good Start: Casting On and Joining, page 13).
- Work in K1, P1 ribbing for 1" (2.5 cm).
- Work in stockinette stitch for 7½" (19 cm).

Working the Star Toe

Make sure your stitches are still correctly arranged on the needles; otherwise it will be difficult to work the toe decreases.

- Round 1 (decrease round): *K7, K2tog; repeat from * around. (*4 stitches decreased*)
- Round 2: Knit.
- Repeat Rounds 1 and 2, continuing to decrease 4 stitches, evenly spaced, every other round. On each subsequent decrease round there is 1 fewer stitch between the decreases.
- When 8 stitches remain, cut the yarn, leaving a 6" (15 cm) tail and pull it through all the stitches. Pull to the inside and weave in. Use the tail at the cast on to make it look continuous, then weave in on the inside (see Mind the Gap, page 76).

CREATING THE AFTERTHOUGHT HEEL OPENING

Decide where you want the center of your heel to be. I made mine halfway down the sock and lined it up with one of the columns of decreases at the toe. Using a pair of sharp-pointed scissors, snip the top of just one stitch at the center of the heel 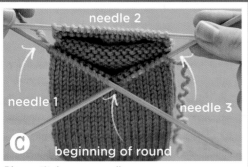.

Using the tip of a knitting or yarn needle, gently pull the yarn out a half stitch at a time, until you've unraveled at least one-fourth of the sock's stitches. This should be an even number; in this project, a quarter would be 9 stitches, so unravel one more to make 10. Unravel the same number of stitches in the opposite direction .

Above the opening (toward the cuff of the sock), 20 stitches are now waiting to be picked up. Slip them onto a needle. If you find it hard to do this, use a thinner needle and transfer them to the correct size as you knit around.

There are only 19 stitches below the opening (toward the toe). This is normal: you haven't lost a stitch somewhere. When you pick up across the bottom of a row of stitches, you always end up with 1 fewer or 1 more stitch. On the first round, you will increase 1 stitch at the center of the sole to replace the "missing" stitch. For now, slip these stitches onto a second needle, or if you're working Magic Loop, onto the other half of the loop. If you're using double-pointed needles, slip half of these stitches onto a third needle. Since there's an odd number of stitches, divide them so that the needle on the left has 1 more stitch than the needle on the right .

You're ready to start working around with the contrasting yarn (CC) and shaping the heel. One of the problems with this type of heel, however, is that gaps always form at the two corners of the opening. Also, it's traditional to work an afterthought heel on the same number of stitches as are used for the circumference of the sock; however, the heel fits much better if it's a little larger than this. You can address both of these concerns by picking up a few extra stitches where the gaps form, so that's what you do on the first round.

Snip top of one stitch at heel center.

Unravel about ¼ total stitches on each side of center.

Place stitches on needles.

Starting the Afterthought Heel on Double-Pointed Needles

- Setup: Follow the instructions in Creating the Afterthought Heel Opening on page 190 to get the heel stitches onto the needles. The beginning of round is now at the bottom of the foot, between the bottom two needles. This ensures that the jog at the beginning and end of round is hidden on the bottom of the foot.

- Knitting the First Round: Using a fourth needle and CC, and starting at the center bottom of the heel, knit across Needle 1, then pick up and knit 2 stitches at the beginning of the gap that forms at the corner of the heel opening Ⓐ.

- Using an empty needle, pick up and knit 2 stitches along the second half of the gap Ⓑ.

- Using the same needle, knit all the way across Needle 2 (these are the stitches for the back of the heel, attached to the top of the sock), and then pick up and knit up 2 stitches at the beginning of the gap at the corner of the opening Ⓒ.

- Using an empty needle, pick up and knit 2 stitches along the second half of the gap Ⓓ.

- Continuing with the same needle, knit all the way across Needle 3, then increase 1 so that Needles 1 and 3 have the same number of stitches Ⓔ. If you prefer, you may arrange the heel with a quarter of the stitches on each of four needles Ⓕ. (48 stitches total)

Ⓓ Pick up 2 more stitches at gap.

Ⓔ Knit across and increase 1 stitch at end of round.

Ⓕ Stitches evenly divided among four double points

Ⓐ Pick up 2 stitches at gap.

Ⓑ Pick up and knit 2 stitches along other half of gap.

Ⓒ Knit across back of heel and pick up 2 stitches.

Starting the Afterthought Heel on Two Circulars or the Magic Loop

- Setup: Follow the instructions in Creating the Afterthought Heel Opening on page 190. The beginning of the round is the beginning of the needle with 20 stitches.

- Knitting the First Round: *Using CC, pick up and knit 2 stitches at the corner gap before the first stitch of the round, knit across this half of the heel, then pick up and knit 2 more stitches at the next gap; repeat from * for the second half of the round, but also increase 1 stitch at the center of the needle. Make sure that the stitches are divided equally between the two halves of the sock before shaping the heel Ⓐ and Ⓑ. (*48 stitches total*)

Completing the Round Heel

(all needle types)

- Decrease Round 1: *K4, K2tog; repeat around. (*8 stitches decreased*)

- Knit 4 rounds even.

- Decrease Round 2: *K3, K2tog; repeat around. (*8 stitches decreased*)

- Knit 3 rounds even.

- Continue decreasing this way, working 1 fewer stitch between decreases on each decrease round and one fewer round between decrease rounds until just 16 stitches remain. See Round Heels and Toes Dissected (opposite) for details.

- Final Decrease Round: Work K2tog around. (*8 stitches remain*)

- Cut the yarn, leaving a 4"–6" (10–15 cm) tail. Pull it through all the remaining stitches, then weave it in on the inside.

There will be holes at the corners of the heel: Use the tails of yarn that were unraveled to close these up as you weave them in. When you do this, try to imitate the architecture of a knitted stitch, looping up and down from row to row, to close up the gap. Weave in any other ends. Your sock is complete.

Stitches divided on two circulars

Stitches divided for Magic Loop

ROUND HEELS AND TOES DISSECTED

The shaping for a round heel or toe is very similar to that for a round hat crown. In fact, you can make a lovely hat using this shaping! To construct a round heel follow these two basic rules:

- You must have a multiple of 8 stitches, because whenever you work a decrease round, you decrease 8 stitches evenly spaced.

- However many plain knit stitches there were between the decreases, knit that many rounds even before working the next decrease round. This means that the decrease rounds will be closer and closer together as you reach the center of the heel.

For example, if you begin the heel with 64 stitches, to decrease 8 stitches evenly spaced you work (K6, K2tog) repeated around and end up with 56 stitches. Note that there are 6 knit stitches between each decrease. This means that you work 6 plain knit rounds before the next decrease round. When you work the second decrease round, you again decrease 8 stitches evenly spaced, but there is one fewer stitch between decreases. You therefore work (K5, K2tog) repeated around and have 48 stitches remaining. You just worked 5 knit stitches between the decreases, so you knit 5 plain rounds before decreasing again. Continue working decreases in this same progression, with one fewer round between each decrease round and one fewer stitch between each K2tog on each decrease round.

To reverse the shaping so you can use it for the beginning of a toe-up sock, first cast on 8 stitches at the center (see Closed Center Cast On #1, pages 22–24). On the first round, work (K1, M1) repeated around. You'll add 8 stitches for a total of 16. Work 2 rounds even before working the following increase round. On the next increase round, work (K2, M1) repeated around. You'll add 8 more stitches for a total of 24. Knit 3 rounds, then increase by working (K3, M1) repeated around. You'll add another 8 stitches for a total of 32. You can always tell how many rounds to work before increasing again by adding 1 to the number of stitches between increases on the previous increase round. Keep increasing this way until the sock is big enough around for the foot.

FORETHOUGHT HEEL

If you can't stand to cut your knitting, but you like the idea of adding the heel last, you can make a "forethought" heel, instead of an afterthought one. At the point where the heel opening will be, knit a strand of waste yarn across the heel stitches. Remove it when you're ready to knit the heel. Keep the following details in mind:

• The waste yarn should be the same thickness as the working yarn.

• If there is any pattern stitch on the sock, the heel should be centered on that pattern stitch.

• For a round heel, the opening should use at least half of the stitches of the sock and must be a multiple of 4 stitches wide (to give you the required 8-stitch multiple).

Note: You can also use the flat toe shaping for a heel (see Flat Toe Dissected for instructions, page 204). In that case, the opening needs to be an even number of stitches wide.

Based on these considerations, decide how many stitches there will be in the heel opening and where they'll be positioned in relation to any pattern stitch. You might want to place markers at both ends if you think you'll get confused.

Work around the sock to the point where the heel opening will begin. Cut your working yarn leaving a tail about 6" (15 cm) long. Using waste yarn and leaving a tail about the same length, knit across the stitches for the heel opening. Cut this yarn and leave another tail the same length **Ⓐ**. You'll use the two tails of the working yarn later to close up the gaps that form at the corners of the heel. Begin using the working yarn again, leaving a tail about the same length and continuing any pattern stitch on the top of the foot. The sole of the foot is usually worked in plain stockinette so that it's smooth and comfortable to wear.

Continue working until the leg, foot, and toe are all finished **Ⓑ**.

When you're ready to add the heel, pick out the waste yarn **Ⓒ**.

Put the "live" stitches on needles exactly as described in Creating the Afterthought Heel Opening on page 190, then complete either a round heel or a flat toe (see Round Heels and Toes Dissected on page 193 and Flat Toe Dissected on page 204). The resulting heel may look out of proportion until the sock is either blocked or on a foot, especially if a large area of the sock is ribbed.

Ⓐ Top of foot knit in working yarn; heel knit in waste yarn

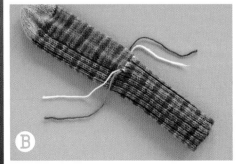

Ⓑ Leg, foot, and toe completed

Ⓒ Removing waste yarn

Anatomy of a Sock

The conventional sock begins at the top and has what's known as a common heel. This consists of the heel flap, the heel turning, and gussets. When the foot is the desired length, the sock is finished off with a flat toe. The common heel strikes fear into the hearts of many knitters, which is why the introductory After-thought Heel Sock (page 189) features an alternative. The fact is, however, that the common heel really does fit better than other heels, so it's best to overcome your fear. If you follow the directions below, it will all turn out just fine.

Each structural section of this sock is worked in a different color, for clarity. Although I don't tell you to do so, each time you change colors, you can knot the ends of the yarn together for greater security. The leg of this sock is very short. I'm assuming that you already know how to knit a tube, so there's no need to practice by making the leg longer before moving on to the excitement of shaping the heel.

For Project Shown You Need

YARN	Lorna's Laces Shepherd Sport (100% superwash wool, 200 yds/2.6 oz)
YARN AMOUNT (for one sock)	26 yds/24 m Pond Blue (5ns); 13 yds/12 m Turquoise (22ns); 16 yds/15 m Sunshine (40ns); and 3 yds/3 m Douglas Fir (6ns)
GAUGE	29 stitches = 4" (10 cm) in stockinette stitch
NEEDLE SIZE	US 3 (3.25 mm). Match the project's gauge if you want finished measurements to match pattern instructions.
NEEDLE TYPES (any of the following)	Set of four or five double-pointed needles / Two circular needles 16" (40 cm) or longer / Circular needle 47" (120 cm) or longer for Magic Loop
OTHER SUPPLIES	Stitch marker for beginning/end of round (optional), yarn needle
FINISHED SIZE	Length of foot 6¾"(17 cm), length of leg above heel 1¾" (4.5 cm), circumference 7½" (19 cm)

New Techniques Used

- Common heel, with heel flap, heel turning, and gussets
- Flat toe
- Kitchener stitch

Knitting the Cuff and Leg

- Setup: Using Pond Blue, cast on 48 stitches. Arrange the stitches on your needles as described in Making Arrangements on page 187. If you are using a set of four double-pointed needles, it's best to put the first 24 stitches of the round on one needle and divide the last 24 stitches between two needles.
- Work in K2, P2 ribbing for 1" (2.5 cm).
- Knit around (stockinette stitch) for ¾" (2 cm).
- Cut the yarn, leaving a 4" (10 cm) tail to weave in later. (See photos at right for working with each kind of needle.)

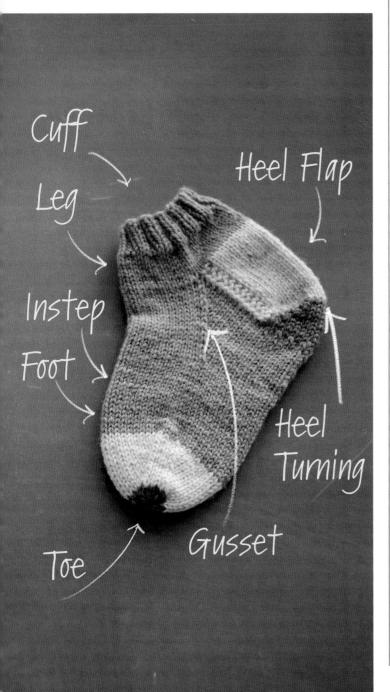

Cuff
Leg
Heel Flap
Instep
Foot
Heel Turning
Gusset
Toe

Ready to Start the Heel Flap

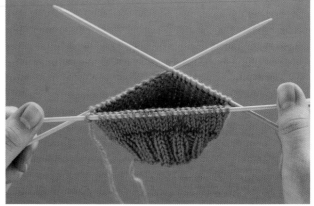

On 3 double points

On 4 double points

On 2 circulars

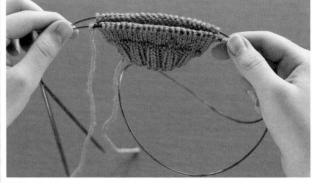

With Magic Loop

Working the Heel Flap

- Setup: For double-pointed needles, place the 24 stitches for the back of the sock on one needle. Work only on these stitches for the heel flap; the other stitches wait on their needle until needed again. For circular needles, you already have 24 stitches on each needle or each half of the Magic Loop; work the heel flap on just one of these 24-stitch halves.

- Row 1 (right side): Using Sunshine, slip 1 knitwise, knit until 1 stitch remains on the needle, P1, turn.
- Row 2 (wrong side): Slip 1 knitwise, K2, purl until 3 stitches remain on the needle, K2, P1, turn.
- Repeat Rows 1 and 2 until the heel flap has as many rows as it does stitches: 24 stitches and 24 rows.
- Cut Sunshine, leaving a tail 4" (10 cm) long to weave in later.

HEEL FLAP DISSECTED

The heel flap is the section that goes straight down the back of the heel, and it's normally worked on half of the stitches. Before working the heel flap, make sure that half of your stitches for the back (or bottom) of the sock are on one needle. If you are working with a set of five double points, you'll combine the stitches from two needles onto one needle. If you're using other types of needles, the stitches should already be in the correct arrangement. Regardless of what kind of needles you're using, the other half of the stitches just sit on their needle(s), waiting for you to complete the heel flap and heel turning.

You'll knit the heel flap flat, back and forth, turning at the end of each row, and working only the heel stitches. Before you get started, here's a step-by-step look at how the heel flap is constructed.

- Slip the first stitch of every row, because this makes it easy to pick up stitches along the edge later on.
- Work the next 2 stitches in garter stitch (which means you knit them on every row). The garter stitch prevents curling (making it easier to pick up stitches later), and because garter stitch is shorter than stockinette, it makes the sides of the heel flap curve in, providing a better fit.
- Work the center section of the heel flap in stockinette, knitting the right-side rows and purling the wrong-side rows.
- Work 2 more stitches in garter at the end of each row to match the beginning of the row.
- Purl the last stitch, because this makes the slipped stitches form a beautiful chained edge.

The photos below show the completed heel flap on double-pointed needles Ⓐ, two circular needles Ⓑ, and the Magic Loop Ⓒ.

The completed heel flap normally has the same number of rows as stitches. Follow the directions above to make your heel flap. It's easy to count the edge stitches: just count the garter ridges along the edge. Two rows make each ridge, so when you have half as many ridges as you do stitches, the heel flap is done. Be sure to end with a wrong-side row.

Ⓐ On double points

Ⓑ On 2 circulars

Ⓒ With Magic Loop

VARIATIONS ON A HEEL FLAP

Like everything else in knitting, there are traditionally many ways to make a heel flap. The one I give instructions for is from Elizabeth Zimmermann's *Knitting Without Tears*. When you make your own socks, experiment to refine your heel flaps with the details you prefer.

- Decide which stitches will compose the heel flap based on the pattern stitch of the leg. If there's a noticeable color or pattern change at the beginning or end of round, you may want to place it to the right of the flap on one sock and to the left on the other sock in the pair. Then, wear the socks with the color change hidden on the inside of your ankle.

- Slip the first stitch purlwise and knit the last stitch (as opposed to slipping the first stitch knitwise and purling the final stitch, as in my directions).

- Omit the garter stitch edges and work the whole width in stockinette stitch

- Reinforce the heel flap, making it thicker and tighter by slipping every other stitch on the knit rows. Never slip the last stitch of the row.

- Work your heel flap in pattern to match or complement the rest of the sock. If the pattern stitch changes the proportion of the stitches to rows, you'll need to adjust the number of rows in your heel flap so that it is approximately square before working the heel turning. The number of rows in the heel flap will dictate how many stitches you can pick up in the gussets.

Turning the Heel

For photos and an explanation of this process, refer to Heel Turning Dissected on the facing page.

- Setup Row 1 (right side): Using Douglas Fir, Slip 1 purlwise wyib, K13, ssk, K1, turn.

- Setup Row 2 (wrong side): Slip 1 purlwise wyif, P5, P2tog, P1, turn.

- Row 1: Slip 1 purlwise wyib, knit until 1 stitch remains before the gap, ssk, K1, turn.

- Row 2: Slip 1 purlwise wyif, purl until 1 stitch remains before the gap P2tog, P1, turn.

- Repeat Rows 1 and 2 until you've worked out to the edges of the heel flap. On the last 2 rows there will not be enough stitches to work the final K1 or P1; just turn after the decrease. (*14 stitches remain*)

- Cut the Douglas Fir yarn, leaving a 4" (10 cm) tail to be woven in later.

Heel turning complete

HEEL TURNING OPTIONS

- If you find that the slipped stitch at the beginning of each row looks loose, slip it knitwise rather than purlwise. When you work it on the following row, it will twist and tighten up.

- On larger socks, knit in fine yarns, with many stitches in the heel flap, you may want to begin the turning by working 3 or 4 stitches past the center of the flap, rather than 2 as specified in these directions.

- On smaller socks worked in thick yarn, which have fewer stitches in the heel flap, you may want to begin the turning by working just 1 stitch past the center.

HEEL TURNING DISSECTED

The heel turning is a tiny wedge-shaped section at the bottom of the heel. It cuts off what would otherwise be a lump of excess sock fabric inside your shoe. To turn the heel, you'll add short rows to the end of the completed heel flap, working partway across the flap and then turning around and working back. You will also work decreases and slipped stitches each time you turn to prevent holes from forming and to smooth the transition at the end of each short row. Every time you work across, you'll work a few more stitches, until you're once again working across the entire heel flap. The process begins this way:

• On the right side, knit across until you're 2 stitches past the center of the flap, then ssk , knit one more stitch, and turn so the wrong side is facing you.

• Now you're on the wrong side. With the yarn in front, because you will be purling across, slip the first stitch purlwise (the same stitch you knitted just before turning), purl until you're 2 stitches past the center of the flap, then purl 2 together, purl one more stitch 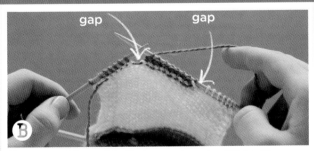 and turn so the right side is facing you again.

A On right side, knit 2 stitches past center, ssk, K1.

B On wrong side, purl 2 stitches past center, P2tog, P1.

At this point there are two gaps: one where you turned on the knit row and one where you turned at the end of the purl row. Make sure you have the same number of stitches between the gap and the end of the needle on each side of the heel. If they aren't equal, your heel will be off-center. To complete the heel turning, here's what you do:

C On right side, knit to 1 stitch before gap.

D Ssk to close gap.

E On wrong side, P2tog to close gap, P1..

• On the right-side rows, with the yarn in back because you'll be knitting, slip the first stitch purlwise, knit until 1 stitch remains before the gap where you turned on the previous row. The gap is clearly visible between the Douglas Fir stitch and the first Sunshine stitch on the left needle **C**. Work an ssk to close the gap **D**, knit one more stitch and turn to the wrong side.

• On the wrong side rows, slip the first stitch purlwise, purl until 1 stitch remains before the gap. Purl 2 together to close the gap, purl one more stitch **E**, and turn back to the right side.

Keep working right-side and wrong-side short rows, which will get longer and longer until you've worked all the way out to both edges. Depending on the number of stitches you started with, there may not be enough stitches to work the final K1 and P1 at the end of the last two rows. Don't worry about this; just turn after the decrease and work the next row. When the turning is completed, you have fewer stitches than you started out with and a nice little cup that fits your heel.

Picking Up for the Gussets

Please refer to the detailed explanation in Gusset Pickup Dissected at right for specifics of working with each type of needle.

- Setup: You ended the heel flap with a wrong-side row; now turn to work your first round of the gussets on the right side.
- Using Turquoise, knit across the bottom of the heel, pick up and knit 12 stitches along the first side of the heel flap, pick up and knit 1 or 2 stitches at the corner, knit across the 24 front stitches, pick up and knit 1 or 2 stitches at the corner, and pick up and knit 12 stitches along the second side of the heel flap. (*64 to 66 stitches total*)
- If you are using double-pointed needles, be sure to rearrange the heel and gusset stitches so that they are divided evenly between two needles, with the beginning of round at the center of the heel, as described in Gusset Pickup Dissected at right.
- From this point to the end of the sock, you once again work circularly.

GUSSET PICKUP DISSECTED

To start the gussets, you work across the bottom of the heel flap, pick up stitches along one side of the heel flap, work across the front of the sock, pick up stitches along the second side of the heel flap, and end up back where you started, ready to begin working circularly again. Ideally, you'll have picked up the same number of stitches along both sides of the heel flap, but if you're off by one, don't worry about it. Exactly how you accomplish this is a little different depending on what type of needles you're using. First, knit across the bottom of the heel.

- **With double-pointed needles.** Use an empty needle to pick up and knit 1 stitch in each of the Sunshine slipped stitches along the edge of the flap Ⓐ.
- **With circular needles.** Continue using the same needle to pick up and knit these stitches. It can be difficult to work around the corner. To make it easier, push the heel stitches onto the cable of the needle, and then bend the point of the needle around to pick up along the side of the heel flap Ⓑ.

Picking up along edge of heel flap with double points

Picking up along edge of heel flap with circular (heel stitches on cable)

When you reach the end of the Sunshine slipped stitches, there is a gap where the flap joins the front of the sock, so pick up an extra stitch or two at this corner in the Pond Blue stitches.

- **With double-pointed needles.** The picked-up stitches stay on the needle used to pick them up.

- **With circular needles.** The picked-up stitches share the needle with the existing heel stitches. Slide all the picked-up stitches down onto the cable to join them.

Work across the front of the sock (the Pond Blue stitches).

- **With four double-pointed needles.** Use an empty needle to knit across the front of the sock.

- **With five double-pointed needles.** Using empty needles, knit across both the needles holding the front stitches of the sock. When you are done, the front stitches should still be divided between two needles.

- **With two circular needles.** Knit the front stitches onto the needle they are already on . Push these stitches onto the cable of their needle.

- **With Magic Loop.** Slide the front stitches up onto the point at their end of the needle, and work across them with the other needle point 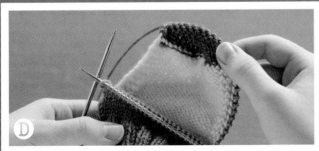. Push these stitches onto the cable of their needle.

Now, pick up stitches along the other side of the heel flap: first pick up and knit a stitch or two in the Pond Blue stitches at the gap (to match the ones you picked up on the opposite side), then pick up and knit one stitch in each of the Sunshine slipped stitches along the edge of the heel flap.

- **With four or five double-pointed needles.** Use an empty needle to pick up along the second side of the flap , and then use the same needle to knit across half of the stitches at the bottom of the heel. Slip the other half of these stitches onto the needle that's already holding the stitches along the other side of the heel flap. The heel and gusset stitches are now divided evenly between two needles.

- **With two circular needles.** Pick up along the side of the heel flap using the needle holding the heel stitches. Using the same needle, knit to the end of the needle. All the heel and gusset stitches (both sides and the bottom of the heel) are on this one needle, and all the front stitches are on the other needle .

- **With Magic Loop.** Pick up the stitches along the side of the heel flap, then knit across the rest of the heel and gusset stitches. All the heel and gusset stitches are on one section of the needle, and all the front stitches are on the other section of the needle.

See Gusset Decreases Dissected (pages 202–203) for photos of this stage on each type of needles.

Knitting across front on 2 circulars

After knitting across front with Magic Loop

Ready to pick up along second side of heel with double points

Picking up along second side of heel with 2 circulars

Working the Gusset Decreases

See detailed discussion in Gusset Decreases Dissected (at right)

With double-pointed needles:

- Round 1: Knit until 2 stitches remain of the first gusset, K2tog; knit across the top of the foot; ssk (on the first two stitches of the gusset); knit to end of round.
- Round 2: Knit.

With circular needles:

- Round 1: Knit across top of foot, ssk, knit until 2 stitches remain before end of the round, K2tog.
- Round 2: Knit.

All needles:

- Repeat Rounds 1 and 2 until 48 stitches remain (the number you started with at the beginning of the sock).
- Cut the Turquoise yarn, leaving a 4" (10 cm) tail to be woven in later.

Gussets completed on 3 double points

Gussets completed on 2 circulars

Gussets completed with Magic Loop

GUSSET DECREASES DISSECTED

Even without counting your stitches, it's obvious that there are now many more on the heel-and-gusset side of the sock than there were before. This is good, because it allows extra space in the heel so the sock will fit comfortably. You'll need to decrease the number of stitches before you get down to the instep, however, or the foot of the sock will be baggy. The gusset decreases taper the sock gradually, making a neat triangular inset at the two corners where the heel flap meets the foot.

You'll alternate decrease rounds (decreasing 1 stitch on both sides of the sock where each gusset meets the instep stitches) with plain rounds of knitting, until you've gotten back down to the original number of stitches. The decrease rounds are described for each type of needle below.

- **With four or five double-pointed needles.** The beginning of round is at the center of the heel **Ⓐ**, between the two heel needles. On the decrease rounds, knit across the first needle until 2 stitches remain, K2tog, then knit across the top of the foot. At the beginning of the last needle (holding the second side of the heel), ssk, then knit to the end of the needle.

needle 1

Ⓐ

Ready to start gussets on 3 double points. (On 4 double points, divide heel and gusset as shown, and divide stitches for front between two needles.)

- **With circular needles.** The beginning/end of round is at one side, and the round starts with the top of the foot (with 2 circulars, **B**; for Magic Loop, **C**). On the decrease rounds, knit across top of foot (on the first needle/first half of the loop). On the second needle/half of the loop, ssk, knit until 2 stitches remain before the end of round, K2tog.

Ready to start gussets on 2 circulars

Ready to start gussets with Magic Loop

If you have an extra stitch on one side of the heel flap, just decrease once more only on that side to get the correct stitch count. Depending on the pattern stitch on your sock, or your personal preference, you can shift the decreases one or two stitches away from the end of the needle. If you tend to have loose stitches where the needles meet, this problem may be exacerbated when you decrease at the very end of the needle. Shifting the decrease a stitch or two from the end of the needle may help get rid of the gap.

Working the Foot

The foot of the sock is a relaxing break between completing the heel and shaping the toe.

- Using Pond Blue, work stockinette stitch for 1¾" (4.5 cm). Cut the yarn, leaving a 4" (10 cm) tail to be woven in later.

Working the Flat Toe and Finishing the Sock

Refer to Flat Toe Dissected (page 204) for a detailed explanation of the process.

Use Sunshine to work the first section of the toe.

With double-pointed needles:

- Round 1 (decrease round): Beginning at the center bottom, knit until 3 stitches remain at the edge of the sole, K2tog, K1. On the top of the toe, K1, ssk, knit until 3 stitches remain at the other edge of the top, K2tog, K1. At the beginning of sole stitches, K1, ssk, knit to the end of the round. (4 stitches decreased)
- Round 2: Knit around.

With circular needles:

- Round 1 (decrease round): Beginning with the top of the foot, *K1, ssk, knit until 3 stitches remain on the top of the foot, K2tog, K1; repeat from * on the sole stitches. (4 stitches decreased)
- Round 2. Knit around.

All needles:

- Repeat Rounds 1 and 2 until 24 stitches remain (12 on the top and 12 on the sole). Cut Sunshine, leaving a 4" (10 cm) tail to weave in later.
- Using Douglas Fir, repeat just Round 1 until 12 stitches remain (6 on the top and 6 on the sole).

With double-pointed needles:

- Using the last needle of the round, knit across the rest of the sole stitches, so that all the sole stitches are on one needle. If the top stitches are divided between two needles, slip them all onto one. See photo below.

All needles:

- Cut the yarn leaving a 12" (30 cm tail). Use Kitchener stitch (see pages 70–74) to join the top and bottom stitches to each other. Pull the yarn through to the inside of the sock. Turn the sock inside out and weave in all the ends.

Toe decreases completed and ready for Kitchener stitch

FLAT TOE DISSECTED

Flat toes are worked in three steps:

1. Decrease half the stitches at a rate of 4 stitches *every other* round.

2. Decrease half the remaining stitches at a rate of 4 stitches *every* round.

3. Join the remaining stitches seamlessly using Kitchener stitch.

What makes the toe flat is the placement of the decreases, which are worked at both edges of the top of the toe and both edges of the bottom of the toe.

Before beginning the decreases, make sure your stitches are arranged properly on your needle(s).

• **With four double-pointed needles.** The top half of the foot is on one needle, and the bottom half is equally divided between two needles.

• **With five double-pointed needles.** The top half of the foot is equally divided between two needles, and the bottom half is equally divided between two needles. As the toe becomes smaller, however, you will probably want to shift the top stitches onto a single needle.

• **With two circulars.** The top half is on one, and the bottom half is on the other.

• **With Magic Loop.** The top half of the foot is on one half of the loop, and the bottom half of the foot is on the other half of the loop.

It's very important that the toe line up exactly with the heel. If you're off, even by a few stitches, the foot will be twisted. Before you start decreasing, therefore, make sure that the front stitches where the heel flap begins line up exactly with the top stitches at the toe. They should, unless you shifted stitches between needles for some reason after the heel was completed.

Directions for the decrease rounds differ slightly for double-pointed versus circular needles, because the beginning of round falls at the bottom of the foot for double points and just before the top half for circulars. To make the columns of decreases run parallel to the edge of the toe, you'll work SSK at the beginning of each half and K2tog at the end of each half.

You'll work the decreases every other round until half of the stitches remain. Then you'll work the decreases every round until half the remaining stitches have been decreased away.

To complete the toe, the few remaining stitches will be arranged with the top stitches on one needle and the bottom stitches on second needle. You'll join them using Kitchener stitch (pages 70–74).

FLAT TOE FINESSE

For a perfect fit. This toe is easily modified to fit anyone. To make a more pointed toe, work more of the alternate-round decreases and fewer of the every-round decreases. To make a blunter toe, work more every-round decreases and fewer alternate-round decreases.

Using this shaping for a heel. The flat toe can also be used as a heel. Make either an afterthought or forethought heel opening. Be sure to pick up an even number of stitches around the opening, then work the flat toe shaping to fill in the heel.

Using this shaping for toe-up socks. The flat toe is also easy to reverse to work from the toe up. Start with a closed straight-line cast on (pages 26–30). Which cast on you choose depends on which you like best and what kind of needles you're using. The Turkish Cast On (pages 29–30) is the most straightforward, but it's easier to work on circulars than on double points. If you're using double-pointed needles, a better choice would be either Double Your Stitches (pages 26–27) or Cast On and Pick Up (page 28). Cast on about an inch of stitches. Increase at both edges of the top and bottom every round until the sock is half the desired circumference. Continue increasing every other round until the sock is big enough to fit the foot. If you're using the M1 increase, place the increases 1 stitch away from the edges of the toe top and bottom. If you're using the Kfb increase, work it in the first stitch and the next to last stitch of the top and bottom. Because it makes a bump that looks like a purl following the stitch you worked, this places the bump one stitch in from each edge, so it looks symmetrical.

Post mortem: Toes versus Heels

In rapid succession you've been introduced to the star toe, the round heel and toe, the common heel, and the flat toe (which can also be used as a heel shaping). All of them can be reversed and knit either from the toe up or the top down, just as you can knit a hat from the bottom up or from the crown down. Let's do a quick review of their characteristics and uses.

Star toe. Easy to work, with four decreases or increases every other round, but pointed, so it's only good as a toe. If your feet are pointy, this shaping will fit you best.

Flat toe and heel. This shaping started out life as a toe, but it makes a very nice heel with noticeable diagonal shaping. It is a little more complex to work than the star toe. You can control how pointed or blunt the toe is by adjusting the frequency of the decreases. Beginning a sock at the toe with this shaping requires a closed straight-line cast on, while ending with a flat toe requires Kitchener stitch. See Flat Toe Dissected and Flat Toe Finesse (both opposite) for shaping details, in both directions.

Round heel and toe. This shaping also started out life as a toe, but it is so nicely rounded that it makes a beautiful, well-fitting heel as well. It's easy to work but probably the most complicated of the three to explain. It produces a very round toe, so if your feet are pointy, it might not fit you as well as the star toe. See Round Heels and Toes Dissected (page 193) for shaping details, in both directions.

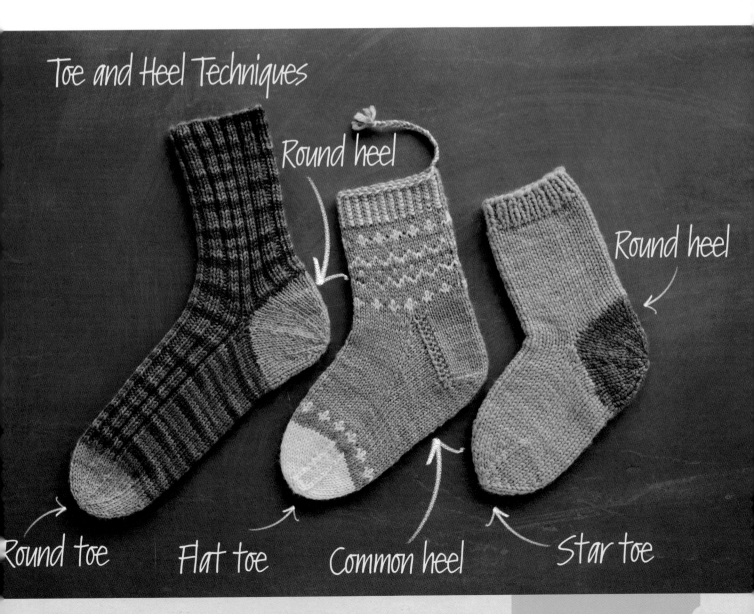

Toe and Heel Techniques

Round heel

Round heel

Round toe   Flat toe   Common heel   Star toe

STRANDED KNITTING BASICS

The next sock we'll make uses a technique known as *stranded* knitting. Stranded knitting is named for the strands that are carried across the back of the fabric when more than one color is used repeatedly on the same round. It is particularly suited to circular knitting because all the stitches are usually knitted and you're always working in the same direction, on the right side of the fabric. You can see the pattern clearly, rather than having to work half the time on the purl side. With no wrong-side rows, there's no need to ever read charts in the opposite direction. The color patterns worked in stranded knitting are almost always represented in charts, so you should be comfortable working from charts before you try to make a garment using this technique.

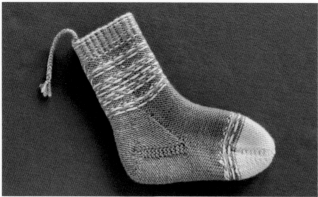

The strands of "stranded knitting" are obvious on the inside of the sock.

How to Read a Color Chart

Charts are always read from bottom to top. When you're working on the right side of the fabric (which you are almost always doing in circular knitting), you work from right to left across the chart, the same direction you work across your knitting. Begin reading the chart from the bottom right-hand corner and move across to the left. If you are a mirror-image knitter, who works from left to right across the row, then read from left to right instead.

In the example at right, the background color (Pond Blue in this sock) is represented by the blank squares. The pattern or foreground color (Sunshine) is represented by the Xs. Reading across the bottom row of squares, this means you knit the first stitch with Pond Blue, the second stitch

chart

		X		21
	X	X	X	20
		X		19
				18
				17
				16
X				15
	X		X	14
		X		13
				12
X				11
				10
		X		9
	X		X	8
X				7
				6
				5
				4
		X		3
	X	X	X	2
		X		1

with Sunshine, and then the next 2 stitches with Pond Blue. The chart is only 4 stitches wide, which is the repeat, so you know you are to repeat the same 4 stitches until you get to the end of the round.

When the round is complete, shift up to the second row of squares. Reading it from right to left, knit the first 3 stitches with Sunshine, and the fourth with Pond Blue, then repeat this pattern all the way around. Continue up the chart until you've completed all 21 rounds.

Note that the charted pattern used as an example here looks the same whether it's right-side up or upside down, so you can reverse the direction of the knitting with no problem. When knitting a pattern that has a noticeable top and bottom, if you are working from the top down instead of the bottom up, turn the chart upside down before you start knitting.

How to Hold the Yarn

You can hold the yarn any way that is comfortable for you, but it's best if you find a way to hold both strands of yarn all the time. This saves time and prevents frustration, because you don't need to drop one yarn and find the other one every time you change colors. It also results in more even tension throughout your knitting.

If you can knit (or learn to knit) with the yarn in either hand, then two-hand two-color knitting is your best bet. Instructions for both styles of knitting are in the appendix (see Knit Stitch, page 307). Hold one yarn in each hand and then knit the correct color as needed Ⓐ. You can also hold both yarns in your left hand Ⓑ. Try to keep the two strands separated on your index finger. Be careful as you work to pick just the strand you need with the tip of your right needle. The other option is to hold both yarns in your right hand Ⓒ. Keep them both on the index finger, slightly separated, and wrap whichever one you need

Ⓐ Holding one yarn in each hand

B

Holding both yarns in left hand

C

Holding both yarns in right hand

around the needle as you make each stitch. You can also drop each one off the index finger when it is not in use, but keep it tensioned against the palm of your hand.

Yarn Position — No Twisting!

However you hold your yarn, it's important that you avoid twisting the two strands around each other. When working with two hands, hold the same color in the same hand all the time. If you're holding both yarns in one hand, make sure that the colors stay in the same position all the time. You can tell that you're twisting the colors if the strands leading to the balls of yarn become twisted around each other. If you're doing it right, the working yarns should never become twisted.

There are two reasons for doing this. First, it's really annoying to have to stop and untwist your yarns all the time. The second, more important reason is that the appearance of the patterned fabric changes if you switch the colors. The stitches tilt just a bit every time you twist, with the result that they look uneven. The height of the stitch also varies, making one color look more predominant than the other. When this changes in the course of a garment, it is quite noticeable.

Weaving In Strands

You really shouldn't go too far without working a color, because you end up carrying a long strand across the back. This makes it hard to work the stitches evenly, and the strands may be so long that fingers and toes get caught in them when you try to put the garment on. If there are more than about 5 stitches in one color, weave the strand of the unused color into the back of the fabric. There's still no need to twist the strands, though.

If you're working with both yarns in one hand, catch the unused yarn in the back of a stitch this way: Insert your right needle into the stitch and lay the unused strand of yarn across the tip of the needle **D** **E**. Knit or pick the color in use, pulling it under the unused strand and through the stitch **F**.

If you're working with one yarn in each hand and the working yarn is in your right hand, lay the left strand over the needle and knit under it with the right strand, exactly the same method that's used when both yarns are held in the same hand.

D

Yarn in right hand, step 1: Put the unused blue strand over the needle, ready to knit with yellow.

E

Yarn in left hand, step 1, with unused blue strand over needle, ready to knit with yellow.

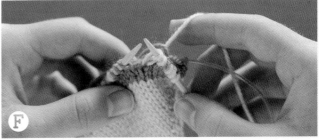

F

Yarn in right hand, step 2: Stitch knitted under the blue, using the yellow.

To weave in a strand when the working yarn is in your left hand and the unused yarn is in your right, insert the right needle tip through the first stitch on the left needle and wrap the unused yarn around the needle. Wrap the working yarn around the needle in the same direction **G**. Unwrap the unused yarn **H**. Pull the working yarn through the stitch and finish knitting it **I**.

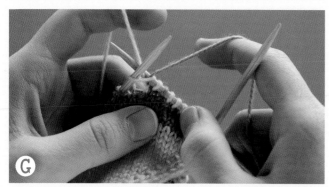

One color in each hand; unused yarn (blue) and working yarn (yellow) both wrapped around needle

Blue unwrapped and yellow ready to knit

Stitch knitted with yellow

You can weave in the strands this way as often as every other stitch, but doing it so frequently changes the quality of the fabric significantly, making it less stretchy and dimpling the surface slightly. To avoid this, catch each strand only once, near the center. Also avoid securing strands in the same column of stitches on every round because it becomes quite noticeable. Instead, catch the strand a stitch to the left or right on subsequent rounds.

If you realize later that you've forgotten to secure a long strand this way, then on the next round just insert your right needle into the stitch you want to knit, near the center of the loose strand, make sure the tip of the needle is under the loose strand, then knit the stitch, pulling the working yarn under the strand and through the stitch.

Gauge Swatches in Stranded Knitting

Stranded stockinette stitch is usually tighter than one-color stockinette stitch because of the strands running across the back of the knitting. If you plan to combine sections of each in one garment, you should work a gauge swatch for each. To make the gauge of the two different fabrics match, you can use a smaller needle for the one-color areas and a larger needle for the stranded sections.

Tension

If you're unhappy with the results of your stranded knitting, it may be because the tension is too loose or too tight. If the tension is too loose, single stitches knitted in a color may look very poofy. If the tension is too tight, the tube you're knitting gets smaller and smaller and the knitting looks puckered. To achieve the correct tension, always smooth the stitches on the right-hand needle before knitting the first stitch in a new color. They should be spread out so that the fabric below is smooth but not stretched.

A possible cause of tight stranding in a larger tube, like a sweater, is having too much fabric crammed onto too short a needle. Choose a circular needle or set of double-points that allows the garment to be spread almost flat where it meets the needle.

If you're making a small tube that persists in getting tighter, turn it inside out to force the strands to run around outside the circumference of the tube. If the fabric itself is too loose, strands on the back may show through. Correct this by using smaller needles to make a tighter fabric.

Knitting with the inside out

Corrugated Ribbing

Two-color ribbing can be the crowning touch of a stranded garment, but it's time consuming to make. K2, P2 ribbing takes less time than K1, P1, because there are half as many color changes, so consider it as a more efficient alternative. To work Corrugated Ribbing, work the knit stitches in one color Ⓐ. Bring the other color to the front between the needle points and work the purl stitches in the other color Ⓑ. Take this color to the back again after purling.

Ⓐ
Knitting with blue

Ⓑ
Purling with yellow

Blocking

All stranded knitting, no matter how neatly knit, looks uneven until it is blocked under a bit of tension. After knitting, wash your project gently, squeeze the water out, and roll in a towel to remove excess moisture. Use sock blockers, blocking wires Ⓐ, or a woolly board Ⓑ to stretch the knitting gently while it dries.

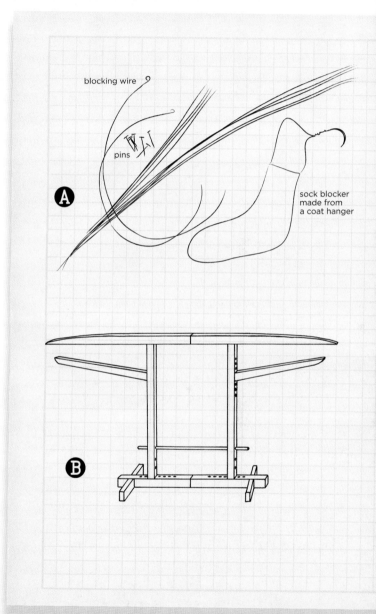

Toe-Up Stranded Sock

New Techniques Used

- Closed Straight Cast On
- Flat toe, worked from the toe up
- Stranded knitting
- Common heel, worked from the sole up
- Corrugated ribbing

All of the projects so far have been for socks knit from the top down, but you can also knit socks from the toe up. Working from the toe up lets you make the sock any size you like — just increase for the toe until the circumference is big enough to fit the foot, and then work straight until it's time to add the heel.

You can make any sock from the toe up. To make a simple sock with a round toe and after- or forethought heel, start as you would a hat knit from the top down and follow an increase plan that reverses the decrease plan for the original toe. Work the sock straight up to the top and add an afterthought or forethought heel.

You can also make a conventional sock, with a flat toe and common heel, from the toe up, which is the approach this project takes. You start with a Closed Straight Cast On. Form the toe by increasing until the sock is the desired circumference for the foot, then knit the foot even to the heel. Add a common heel (it's upside down, but it works just fine) and then knit straight up to the top of the sock.

This toe-up sock also serves as a lesson in stranded knitting. Even though this sock may look complicated, all the shaped areas are worked in a single color. The straight sections are patterned so you don't get bored making yet another plain tube. If you are unfamiliar with stranded knitting, see Stranded Knitting Basics (pages 206–209). You can try out the stranded techniques ahead of time, or just jump right in and start stranding while you're making the sock.

Top Down →

Toe Up →

For Project Shown You Need

YARN	Lorna's Laces Shepherd Sport (100% superwash wool, 200 yds/2.6 oz)
YARN AMOUNT (for one sock)	Yarn Amount for One Sock: 66 yds/60 m Pond Blue (5ns) and 25 yds/23 m Sunshine (40ns)
GAUGE	29 stitches = 4" (10 cm) in stockinette stitch
NEEDLE SIZE	US 3 (3.25 mm). Match the project's gauge if you want finished measurements to match pattern instructions.
NEEDLE TYPES (any of the following)	Set of four or five double-pointed needles Two circular needles 16" (40 cm) or longer 47" (120 cm) circular needle or longer for Magic Loop
OTHER SUPPLIES	Stitch marker for beginning/end of round (optional)
FINISHED SIZE	Length of foot 7" (18 cm); length of leg above heel 4" (10 cm); circumference 7½" (19 cm)

Starting from the Toe

- Setup: Using Sunshine and a Straight-Line Closed Cast On (see Closed Straight Cast Ons, pages 26–30), cast on a total of 12 stitches (6 for the top of the toe and 6 for the bottom). The beginning of round is at one side of the knitting, just before the stitches for the bottom of the toe.
- *For double-pointed needles,* the top stitches are on one needle and the bottom stitches are divided between two needles. If you'd rather use a set of five needles, wait until it grows a little larger before dividing the top stitches between two needles.
- *For circular needles,* the top stitches are on one needle or one half of the Magic Loop and the bottom stitches are on the other.
- Increase Round: *Kfb, knit until 2 stitches remain on the bottom of the toe, Kfb, K1; repeat from * on the top stitches. (*4 stitches increased*)
- Repeat the Increase Round until there are 24 stitches (12 on the top and 12 on the bottom).
- Now begin increasing on alternate rounds (work a plain round after each increase round) until you have 48 stitches.

This completes the toe.

Changing Color for the Foot

Because it's best to make the color change where it won't be visible, continue knitting with Sunshine to the center of the sole and then start the new color. *With circular needles,* this is in the middle of a needle/section of a needle. *With double points,* this is between two needles.

You can cut the Sunshine yarn at this point, leaving a 4" (10 cm) tail to weave in later, or you can leave it attached in order to use it again in a few rounds. Cutting the yarn provides tails that you can use to neaten up the jog at the color change (see Disguising the Jog: Stripes Without the Stair Step, pages 97–98). Carrying the yarn three rounds until it is needed again looks a little uneven, but this is hidden on the sole and you have two fewer tails to weave in.

Working the Foot

- Using Pond Blue, knit 3 rounds, stopping again at the center of the sole.
- Work the first 3 rounds of the Stranded Sock Chart using Pond Blue as the background color and Sunshine for the pattern. End the last round at the center of the sole.
- Cut Sunshine, leaving a 4" (10 cm) tail to weave in later.
- Continue knitting with Pond Blue until the sock measures 1½" (4 cm) from the diamond pattern (in Sunshine).

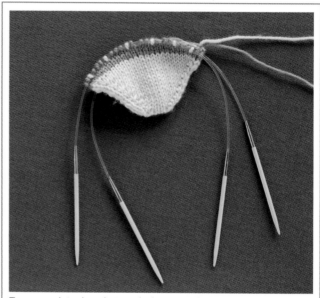

Toe completed and stranded pattern begun on 2 circulars

Stranded Sock Chart

		X		21
	X	X	X	20
		X		19
				18
				17
				16
X				15
	X		X	14
		X		13
				12
X				11
				10
		X		9
	X		X	8
X				7
				6
				5
				4
		X		3
	X	X	X	2
		X		1

☐ MC (Pond Blue)

☒ CC (Sunshine)

Working the Heel and Leg

- Continue working with Pond Blue. Follow the directions in Anatomy of a Sock starting with Working the Heel Flap (page 197), and continuing through Working the Gusset Decreases (page 202).
- When you're back down to 48 stitches, work 3 plain rounds in Pond Blue, and stop at the center back of the sock.
- Work all 21 rounds of the Stranded Sock Chart (opposite page) using Pond Blue for the background and Sunshine for the pattern.
- When you've completed the chart, you may cut the Sunshine yarn, leaving a 4" (10 cm) tail to weave in later, or you may carry the yarn up to the corrugated ribbing without cutting.
- Work 3 more rounds in Pond Blue, ending at the center back of the sock.

Working the Corrugated Ribbing and Finishing

- Round 1: *K1 Pond Blue, K1 Sunshine; repeat from * around. (By knitting with Sunshine on this first round, you make a clean transition to the purled stitches in the ribbing.)
- Rounds 2–7: *K1 Pond Blue, P1 Sunshine; repeat from * around. End at the center back of the sock.
- Bind off in knit, working the Pond Blue stitches with Pond Blue and the Sunshine stitches with Sunshine. The chain is made by binding off alternate colors and rolls to the outside of the sock, looking like a braid.
- Cut both yarns, leaving 6" (15 cm) tails. Cut a piece of each color 12" (30.5 cm) long. At the beginning of round, pull the cut strands through the edge of the ribbing, letting all the ends hang down. Including the bind-off tails, there are now six strands of yarn. Use them in pairs to make a braid any length you like. Tie just one or two of the strands around the others to secure the end of the braid and then trim.
- Weave in all ends on the inside.

TOP-DOWN STRANDED SOCK

Working from the Top Down

To make this same sock in the opposite direction, cast on the 48 stitches for the top of the leg, using both colors and the Alternating-Color Long-Tail Cast On (page 303) or the Alternating-Color Cable Cast On (page 302). Leave 6" (15 cm) tails to braid later. Work seven rounds in Corrugated Ribbing using both colors. Knit three rounds in background color. Work all of the Stranded Sock Chart, using both colors. Cut the pattern color. Using the background color knit three rounds, then make a common heel. After the gussets are completed, continue knitting with background color for 1½" (4 cm). Using both colors, work Rounds 1–3 of Stranded Sock Chart. Knit 3 rounds in background color, then cut it. Using pattern color, make a flat toe. See Anatomy of a Sock (pages 195–205) for common heel and flat toe instructions.

DESIGNING YOUR OWN SOCKS

Sock Fabric

Socks must be rather firmly knit or they will wear out quickly. If you are using sock-weight yarn, start with the suggested needle size and adjust smaller or larger to get a fabric you like. It should still stretch some but be nice and opaque (not loose and stringy) when not under tension. For yarns other than sock yarn, it's a good idea to begin with needles two sizes smaller than whatever is recommended for a normal garment. For practical purposes, keep in mind that even worsted-weight socks are thick enough that they usually can't be worn comfortably with shoes, so stick to sport-weight and sock-weight yarns unless you're planning on thick socks to fit inside boots or to wear around the house.

Pattern Stitches

The sock projects in this chapter are, for the most part, worked in stockinette stitch. This is for clarity in the photos and to make them a little easier to knit, since they are intended to be learning tools.

Ribbing (especially K2, P2 or K3, P3) is good for the legs of socks, because it clings and prevents the socks from falling down. It's also a good idea to continue the ribbing right down the top of the foot to the toe, because it helps the sock fit closely at the instep. At the same time, keep the heel and sole of the sock in stockinette so they are smooth and comfortable to walk on. You can see this in the sock with the Forethought Heel (page 194), which has a ribbed leg and ribbed top of the foot.

You can also introduce lace, cables, or other pattern stitches in the leg and top of the foot. Make sure that the fabric still stretches enough to pull easily over the heel and to be worn comfortably at the calf.

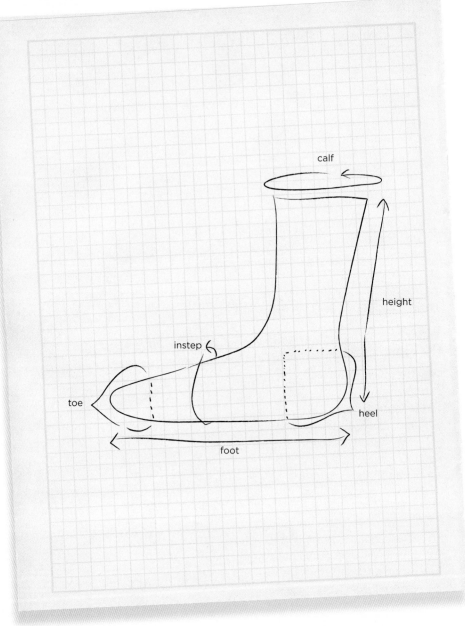

Sizing and Gauge

Before starting a sock, the key measurements you need are around the leg at the top of the sock and around the instep of the foot. The sock needs to fit around the instep without being loose, but it also needs to stretch enough to fit comfortably around the leg or calf at the top. There is one other important fitting measurement: the length of the foot. And, of course, you need to know how tall you'd like your sock to be. You control both the length of the foot and the height as you knit.

When you're starting from the top, there's really no point in knitting a separate gauge swatch, because it would be about as big as the sock is around. Just cast on what you think will be the right number of stitches for the top of the sock and work a couple of inches. Try it on. This is easiest if the sock is on circular needles. If you're working with double points, transfer the knitting to a circular needle or a piece of yarn temporarily while checking the fit. It should fit closely around the instep and stretch comfortably to fit where you want the top of the sock to fall. If it fits and you like the quality of the fabric, keep working. If not, adjust the number of stitches or the needle size and try again. When the sock is as tall as you like, to the top of the heel, work the heel. Keep an eye on the length after the heel, stop short of the full foot length to allow for the toe, then add the toe.

When you're starting from the toe, make whatever toe you like and continue enlarging it until it's big enough to fit the foot. As you work, evaluate the fabric; if it's too tight or too loose, start over with a different size needle. Once you've built a toe you like, start working straight to make the foot. Remember to stop before you reach the heel to allow for the extra length the heel will add.

Whether you are working top-down or toe-up, if you're making "afterthought" heels, then you don't need to worry about the heel position until later, and then you can position it exactly where it needs to be.

Heels, Toes, and Calves

As you learned in the sock projects above, heels and toes are usually the only shaped parts of socks, and their shaping depends entirely on proportions. Just make the heels and toes of your socks based on the general proportions given in the project instructions in this chapter and they should come out the right size.

If you make a very tall sock (for example, a knee sock), the leg needs to be either very stretchy ribbing or shaped in order to fit at the widest part of the calf as well as at the ankle. Taper the top of the leg so that there are more stitches at the calf than at the heel. This shaping is best worked along the back "seam line" of the sock, the same way that sweater sleeves are tapered (for sleeve shaping, see Circular Yoked Sweater: Working the Sleeves, pages 276–277, and Top-Down Raglan Sleeve Sweater: Working the Sleeves, page 284).

Reinforcement

The heels, soles, and toes of socks get a lot of abuse, rubbing against the inside of shoes and against the floor. You can extend the life of your socks by using sock yarn that has nylon already blended with it as reinforcement, you can knit an additional thread of woolly nylon or fine wool yarn along with the working yarn in areas where abrasion can be expected, or you can make the fabric thicker and tougher by using slipped stitches and color patterns.

For example, a traditional method of reinforcing the heel of a sock is to slip every other stitch on the right-side rows of the heel flap, which tightens and thickens the flap quite nicely. I personally don't do this because I don't like the way it affects the fit of the heel. If you're working stranded knitting, making a Salt and Pepper pattern (a single-stitch checkerboard of two colors) or working single-stitch vertical stripes on the heel, sole, and toe also creates a thick resilient fabric.

When working a sock on two circular needles, you can use a smaller needle just for the sole stitches, which will make a denser, longer-wearing fabric without any additional supplies or special pattern stitches.

Mittens and socks are really very much alike.
They both start as simple tubes with a shaped end which forms the toe of the foot and the tip of the hand. The difference is that socks have heels, mittens have thumbs, and gloves, naturally, have fingers. Mitten tips can be made like any of the toes described for socks in the previoius chapter: star, round, or flat shapings all work just fine. For a pointier, more geometric fingertip, you can work it like a flat toe but continue alternating decrease rounds with plain rounds until you are ready to Kitchener stitch the tip.

Thumbs are just smaller tubes. You can work them any way you like: on double points, two circulars, or Magic Loop. Or work them as a wide I-cord, intentionally leaving short strands across the back of the tube that will be hooked up into an additional column of stitches before the thumb is finished off. Just like heels, thumbs can be made as "after-thoughts" or "forethoughts."

A different structure is used in tailored mittens and gloves: the thumb gusset. The gusset gradually tapers the hand between the base of the thumb and the cuff.

Gloves go one step further than mittens: they have four fingers in addition to the thumb, all of which are made exactly like thumbs. They fit best if the little finger and thumb are started at different levels from the center three fingers — take a close look at the structure of the human hand and you'll see why.

Arrange the stitches for mittens and gloves on needles just as for socks, putting half of the hand on one needle and half on the other for circulars and dividing by halves and quarters for double-pointed needles.

This keeps the back of the hand separate from the palm and ensures that the thumb is properly aligned with the fingertips.

The projects included here are designed to give you an introduction to both mittens and gloves, and to the various ways of attaching and working fingers and thumbs. At the same time, there are other skills you'll learn:

- Starting mittens from the cuff or the tip
- Starting gloves from the cuff or the fingers
- Making half- and full-fingered gloves
- Making after- and forethought thumbs
- Using wide I-cord for fingers and thumbs
- Integrating helix knitting into a garment
- Making increases while working a pattern stitch
- Working cables in circular knitting
- Making textured patterns using twined knitting
- Making jogless stripes
- Using tubular bind off for a stretchy, bulk-free edge
- Hemming a cuff

All of the mittens and gloves are sized relatively small (a child's large or adult small), so that they knit up as quickly as possible but are not so tiny they are difficult to manage. It is assumed that you will be working the projects to practice techniques, so yarn amounts are given for just one of each mitten or glove. If you want to make a pair sized as written, you'll need twice as much yarn. Instructions for making them any size you like are in Designing Your Own Gloves and Mittens (pages 246–247).

Afterthought Mitten

This mitten is knit identically to the first sock in chapter 8, the Afterthought Heel Sock (pages 189–192), but instead of adding a heel, you snip a stitch and add an afterthought thumb. Working it as an afterthought is just as easy as planning ahead for the thumb and lets you fit it to the wearer later if he or she is not around while you're knitting the hand.

New Techniques Used

- Star fingertip
- Cutting and unraveling for an "afterthought" thumb
- Adding the thumb

For Project Shown You Need

YARN	Lorna's Laces Shepherd Worsted (100% superwash wool, 225 yds/4 oz)
YARN AMOUNT (for one mitten)	56 yds/51 m Turquoise (22ns) and 10 yds/9 m Grapevine (3ns)
GAUGE	22 stitches = 4" (10 cm) in stockinette stitch
NEEDLE SIZE	US 6 (4 mm). Match the project's gauge if you want finished measurements to match pattern instructions.
NEEDLE TYPES (any of the following)	Set of four or five double-pointed needles Two circulars 16" (40 cm) or longer 47" (120 cm) circular needle or longer for Magic Loop
OTHER SUPPLIES	Stitch marker for beginning/end of round (optional); split marker, yarn needle
FINISHED SIZE	Length of hand (cuff to tip) 9½" (24 cm); length of hand above thumb 4" (10 cm); hand circumference 6½" (16.5 cm)

Knitting the Mitten

Follow the directions for the Afterthought Heel Sock (pages 189–192) until the star toe is finished.

Creating the Thumb

- Preparing the opening: Decide where you want the center of your thumb to be. Try the mitten on and mark 1 stitch at the spot where the thumb meets the hand of the wearer with a split marker **A**.
- Using a pair of sharp-pointed scissors, snip the top of the marked stitch **B**.
- Just as described for the Afterthought Heel Sock heel, gently pull the yarn out a half stitch at a time, until you've unraveled about a half inch (1.3 cm) worth of stitches (at the gauge for this project, that would be 3 stitches). Unravel the same number of stitches in the opposite direction **C**.

A
Mark thumb-hand juncture.

B
Snip top of marked stitch.

C
Unravel about ½″ on each side of snipped stitch.

- Above this opening (toward the tip of the mitten), 5 stitches are now waiting to be picked up. Slip them onto a needle (or onto the first half of the loop if you're working Magic Loop). Below the opening (toward the cuff), 6 stitches are waiting to be picked up. Slip these onto a second needle (or second half of loop) **D** **E** **F**.

D
Thumb stitches placed on double points

E
Thumb stitches placed on 2 circulars

F
Thumb stitches ready for Magic Loop

With double points:

- Using the contrasting yarn (Grapevine) and leaving a 6" (15 cm) tail, knit across the top of the opening (the needle with 5 stitches) **G**.
- Using an empty needle, pick up and knit 2 stitches along the gap and then knit half the stitches from the needle below the opening (3 stitches, for a total of 5 stitches) **H**.
- Using an empty needle, knit the remaining stitches from that needle (3 stitches), then pick up and knit 2 stitches along the gap (a total of 5 stitches) **I**.
- *You now have* 15 stitches divided among three needles. There are so few stitches on a thumb that it's really not practical to divide them among four needles, even if you normally prefer to work this way.

With circulars or Magic Loop:

- Using the contrasting yarn (Grapevine) and leaving a 6" (15 cm) tail, pick up and knit 1 stitch in the gap just before the first half of the thumb **J**.
- Knit across the first half of the thumb, then pick up and knit 1 stitch at the gap (7 or 8 stitches are now on this needle or first half of Magic Loop) **K**.
- With the second needle (second half of magic loop), pick up and knit 1 stitch in the gap just before the second half of the thumb, knit across the second half of the thumb, then pick up and knit 1 stitch at the gap (7 or 8 stitches are now on this needle/half of loop) **L**.

G Knit across top with contrasting yarn.

H Pick up 2 stitches at gap; knit half the stitches below the opening.

I Knit remaining stitches; pick up 2 stitches at gap.

2 Circulars	Magic Loop
 **J**	 **J**

Pick up 1 stitch at gap.

 **K**	 **K**

Knit across bottom of opening, then pick up 1 stitch at gap.

 **L**	 **L**

On second needle, or second half of needle, pick up 1 stitch at gap, knit across, pick up 1 stitch at gap.

- You now have a total of 15 stitches divided between two needles/halves of the Magic Loop.

All needles:

- Round 1: Because 15 stitches is just a bit too big for a mitten this size (although it might be perfect for a larger mitten), decrease 2 stitches on the first round at the points where you picked up extra stitches at the gaps.

  With double points:

  - Needle 1: Knit.
  - Needle 2: K2tog, knit to end of needle.
  - Needle 3: Knit until 2 stitches remain on the needle, K2tog. (*13 stitches remain*)

  With circulars:

  - * K2tog, knit to end of first needle/first half of loop; repeat from * on the second needle/half of loop. (*13 stitches remain*)

All needles:

- Knit around on the 13 thumb stitches until the thumb is long enough to fit the wearer (on a mitten this size, that's about 2¼" (6 cm).
- Last Round (decrease round): Repeat K2tog around, ending K1. (*7 stitches remain*)
- Cut the yarn, leaving a 4" (10 cm) tail.
- Pull the tail through all the remaining stitches to the inside of the thumb Ⓐ Ⓑ, and weave it in. Using the tails of yarn where you unraveled and started the thumb, close up any loose spots at the corners of the opening Ⓒ, then weave in the ends.

Ⓐ Running tail through on double points

Ⓑ Running tail through on circulars

Ⓒ Closing holes and weaving in ends

Tip-Down Textured Mitten

Like socks, hats, and bags, mittens can be started at the open end (the cuff) and knitted up or started at the closed end (the fingertip) and knitted down. Starting a mitten from the tip is done identically to starting a sock or a hat. For information on how to get started on various needle configurations, see Closed Center Cast On #1, pages 22–24.

For Project Shown You Need

YARN	Lorna's Laces Shepherd Bulky (100% superwash wool, 140 yds/4 oz)
YARN AMOUNT (for one mitten)	57 yds/52 m Sunshine (40ns) plus 13"/33 cm contrasting bulky-weight yarn to be used as waste yarn
GAUGE	16 stitches = 4" (10 cm) in Seed Stitch
NEEDLE SIZE	US 8 (5 mm). Match the project's gauge if you want finished measurements to match pattern instructions.
NEEDLE TYPES (any of the following)	Set of four or five double-pointed needles Two circular needles 16" (40 cm) or longer 47" (120 cm) or longer for Magic Loop For the I-cord thumb, a set of three double-pointed needles
OTHER SUPPLIES	Four stitch markers, crochet hook about the same size as the knitting needles, yarn needle
FINISHED SIZE	Length of hand (cuff to tip) 8¼" (21 cm); length of hand above thumb 4" (10 cm); hand circumference 8" (20.5 cm)

New Techniques Used

- Starting at the tip
- Round fingertip
- Increasing in Seed Stitch
- Adding waste yarn for a "forethought" thumb
- Removing waste yarn to add the thumb
- I-cord thumb
- Tubular Bind Off for K1, P1 ribbing

Project Overview

This mitten starts at the fingertip. You then add a simple pattern stitch (to practice increasing while maintaining the pattern), learn to make an I-cord thumb (which is less fiddly than using several double points, two circular needles, or Magic Loop), and finish off the bottom edge with stretchy, barely visible tubular bind off. There's a lot going on in this mitten, but it knits up fast in bulky-weight yarn.

Getting started. Some of the instructions are contrary to the recommendations I've made throughout the book: Instead of half hitches, you start at the center with the Long-Tail Cast On. You then knit into the front and back of stitches to increase instead of working M1s. In addition, the rounds have an odd number of stitches. This is all because the mitten is worked in Seed Stitch where knits and purls alternate. I selected the knit-front-back increase (Kfb), because knitting into the back looks like a purl stitch. Working a series of Kfbs sets up the first round of alternating knits and purls for the Seed Stitch pattern. To ensure that the first round doesn't become too tight to work, I chose the Long-Tail Cast On, because it really consists of two rounds: the Half-Hitch Cast On (from the thumb strand) with a round of knitting above it (from the finger strand). The extra round allows enough slack for the Kfbs on the first round to be worked without the knitting becoming too tight. Each round is an odd number of stitches so the Seed Stitch pattern repeats seamlessly around (see Disguising the "Jog," pages 95–96).

Shaping the tip. To shape the round tip of the mitten, you increase 8 stitches every fourth round. This is the same shaping as the star fingertip, which increases 4 stitches every other round, but the After-thought Mitten is significantly pointier than the rounded tip of this mitten. This is because the After-thought Mitten is worked in stockinette, which is taller in proportion to its width than Seed Stitch.

Instead of spacing the 8 increases evenly around, they are placed together in four pairs. Seed Stitch has a 2-stitch pattern repeat. By increasing 2 stitches at a time, a whole new pattern repeat is added, which makes the Seed Stitch pattern look as continuous as possible.

Working seed stitch. In Rounds 1 through 3, you work K1, P1 continuously around, and because you have an odd number of stitches, you continuously knit the purl stitches and purl the knit stitches, without any need

to know where the end of the round is until you've gone around three times and are ready to work Round 4.

Working the thumb. Before you begin working the thumb, you may want to review Wider I-Cord (page 51). Because the thumb is worked in stockinette rather than Seed Stitch, it tends to be tighter than the rest of the mitten, so try to work loosely. If your thumb stitches are too tight, loosen them up by using needles one size larger.

Working the Fingertip and Hand

- Loosely cast on 8 stitches at the center using the Long-Tail Cast On (pages 302–303), see also Closed Center Cast On #1, pages 22–24.

- To make it easier to place the increases consistently, place markers at the beginning of round, after the second stitch, the fourth stitch, and the sixth stitch.

- Setup Round: Kfb around to the last stitch, K1. (*15 stitches*)

- Round 1: *P1, K1; repeat from * until 1 stitch remains at end of round, P1.

- Round 2: *K1, P1; repeat from * until 1 stitch remains at end of round, K1.

- Round 3: Repeat Round 1.

- Round 4: *Kfb twice, work (K1, P1) until you reach the next marker; repeat from *, ending the last repeat K1. (*23 stitches*)

- Rounds 5–8: Repeat Rounds 1–4. (*31 stitches*)

- Continue working in Seed Stitch (Rounds 1 and 2) without further increases until the mitten is 4" (10 cm) long.

- At the beginning of the next round, cut the yarn, leaving a 6" (15 cm) tail. Knit 5 stitches using the waste yarn, leaving similar-length tails. Rejoin the working yarn (leaving a 6"/15 cm tail) and work in Seed Stitch as established. When you come to the contrasting stitches at the beginning of the next round, knit across them, then continue in Seed Stitch. Knitting the waste yarn stitches makes them easier to remove when it's time to add the thumb. (See Fore-thought Heel, page 194.)

- Continue working in Seed Stitch until the mitten is 6½" (16.5 cm) long.

Working the Ribbed Cuff

- Round 1: K2tog, *P1, K1; repeat from * until 1 stitch remains, P1. (Decreasing 1 stitch and continuing to work [K1, P1] around results in ribbing instead of Seed Stitch.)
- Work in ribbing for 1¾" (4.5 cm).
- Cut the yarn, leaving a tail about 36" (91 cm) long.
- Work Tubular Bind Off (pages 62–65). *Note:* The general instructions for Tubular Bind Off assume that you're starting this bind off with a knit stitch, so if for some reason the first stitch at the beginning of your round is a purl stitch, purl that stitch and start the bind off with the following stitch.
- Weave in the end on the inside. Use the cast-on tail to close the small hole at the fingertip, pull it to the inside, and weave it in .

Completed mitten, with waste yarn in place for thumb

Working the I-Cord Thumb

- Setup: Remove the waste yarn (see Forethought Heel, page 194). Slip the 5 stitches above the opening onto one double-pointed needle and the 4 stitches below the opening onto a second double-pointed needle. Using just one double-pointed needle, pick up and knit 2 stitches at the first gap, knit all the stitches off the first needle, pick up and knit 2 stitches at the second gap, and knit all the stitches from the second needle. All 13 stitches are now crammed onto one needle .
- Do not turn. Pull the yarn across the back, then work around in I-cord, making two decreases as follows: *K3, K2tog; repeat from * once, K3. (*11 stitches remain*)
- Work I-cord, leaving short strands across the back, until the thumb is 2¼" (6 cm) long. See Wider I-Cord (page 51) for more information on working this way.

All thumb stitches on 1 needle

Closing the Gap

The column of loose strands along the back of the I-cord is transformed into a column of stitches with a crochet hook, as follows.

- Insert the crochet hook into the edge of the thumb hole (where you would normally pick up and knit a stitch), hook the lowest loose strand and pull it through the edge of the mitten .
- Continue hooking up stitches, pulling each strand through in succession, until you get to the top. When you get to the top, place the stitch on the end of the needle opposite where the yarn is attached 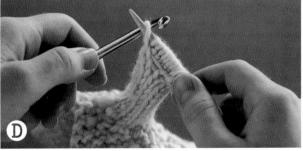. (*12 stitches*)
- With the right side of I-cord facing you, K2tog across. (*6 stitches*)
- Cut the yarn, leaving a tail 4" (10 cm) long, pull it through all the stitches, to the inside, and weave it in. Use the tails at the base of the thumb to close up any holes before you weave them in.

Hook up the lowest loose strand through the edge of the mitten.

Each strand hooked up in order to the top

Helix Half-Mitten

This truncated mitten is knit from the top down, which is easy because you begin with an open cast on and no shaping for the mitten tip. The Two-Color Long-Tail Cast On nicely integrates the two yarns from the very beginning and flows effortlessly into the helix striped pattern. Matching the predominant color in the hand-painted yarn with a solid color spreads out the contrasting lavender and yellow, making the variegations more subtle. This project is a lesson in another way to make a thumb opening with live stitches, and in integrating the thumb without interrupting the striped pattern. While working the thumb, you learn to make striped I-cord, and the whole project is topped off (actually, bottomed off) with the flamboyant Crown Picot Bind Off. Before you begin, I suggest that you familiarize yourself with Helix Knitting (pages 128–129).

For Project Shown You Need

YARN	Lorna's Laces Angel (70% angora/30% lambswool, 50 yds/½ oz)
YARN AMOUNT (for one hand warmer)	15 yds/14 m each Layette (303) and Natural (0ns)
GAUGE	18 stitches = 4" (10 cm) in stockinette stitch
NEEDLE SIZE	US 7 (4.5 mm). Match the project's gauge if you want finished measurements to match pattern instructions.
NEEDLE TYPES (any of the following)	Set of four or five double-pointed needles at least 5" (13 cm) long Two circular needles 16" (40 cm) or longer 47" (120 cm) circular needle or longer for Magic Loop Set of two double-pointed needles for thumb
OTHER SUPPLIES	Two safety pins or small stitch holders, stitch marker (optional)
FINISHED SIZE	7⅓" (18.5 cm) around × 6½" (16.25 cm) long

New Techniques Used

- Two-Color Long-Tail Cast On (page 303)
- Forethought thumb hole without waste yarn
- Maintaining a striped helix pattern in thumb (Helix Knitting, pages 128–129)
- Two-Color I-Cord (page 229)
- Making a partial thumb
- Crown Picot Bind Off (page 61)

Working the Top Border

- Setup: Cast on 33 stitches using Two-Color Long-Tail Cast On, with the Natural yarn on your thumb and the variegated Layette yarn on your index finger 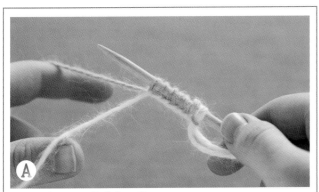.

Arrange the stitches on your needles any way you like. In order to avoid distorting the striped helix pattern, begin working in the round without doing anything special to join the beginning and end of the round; just make sure that the knitting isn't twisted when you begin working the first few rounds. You may want to mark the beginning and end of round with a stitch marker to avoid confusion.

- Round 1: With Natural, purl around.
- Round 2: With Layette, knit around.
- Repeat Rounds 1 and 2 once more. (*2 garter stitch ridges*)

Two-Color Long-Tail Cast On

Beginning the Hand

- Round 1: With Natural, knit around.
- Round 2: With Layette, knit around.
- Repeat Rounds 1 and 2 until mitten measures 2" (5 cm) from cast-on edge.

Creating the Thumb Hole

- Slip the first 5 stitches of the round onto a safety pin or small stitch holder .
- Using the correct color for this round and an empty needle, wrap the yarn around the needle five times 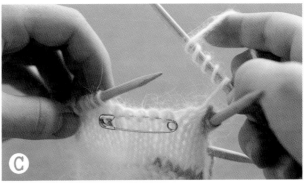. (You're starting the round with 5 yarn overs, which replace the stitches you placed on the safety pin.)
- Knit to the end of the round. The wraps are waiting for you at the beginning of the next round. Slide a second safety pin through the 4 loops that wrap below the needle, then close the safety pin 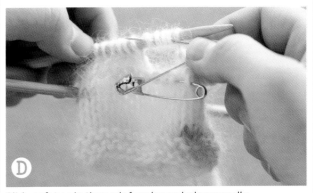.
- As you begin the next round, hold the safety pin below the needle while you knit the wraps. Be sure to use the correct color in the helix color sequence 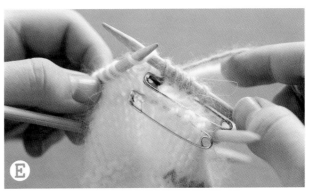.

Slip first 5 stitches to safety pin.

Wrap yarn around needle five times.

Slide safety pin through four loops below needle.

Knit the five wraps.

Completing the Hand

- Continue working in the striped pattern as established until mitten measures 5¾" (14.5 cm) from cast-on edge. Cut the yarn used on the last round, leaving a 4" (10 cm) tail.

Working the Cuff

- Work Crown Picot Bind Off (page 61) with the yarn that's still attached. (You shouldn't need to make any adjustments at the end of the bind off because you worked the mitten on 33 stitches, which is a multiple of 3.)
- Cut the yarn leaving a 6" (15 cm) tail. Use the tail to make the beginning and end of the bind off continuous (see Making the Bind Off Look Continuous, pages 56–57), then weave it in on the inside. Use the tails at the cast on to make the upper edge even at the beginning/end of round (see Mind the Gap, page 76), then weave them in on the inside.

Working the Thumb

Before you begin, refer to Two-Color I-Cord (facing page) and the instructions for making the thumb in the Tip-Down Textured Mitten (page 225).

- Slip the stitches from each safety pin or holder onto a separate double-pointed needle Ⓐ Ⓑ.

Ⓐ Completed mitten ready to work thumb

Ⓑ Slip stitches onto double points.

The stitches on one needle are Natural, and the stitches on the other needle are Layette. To maintain the established helix stripe pattern as you work across each needle on this first round, use the other color to work the stitches on the needle. (If the first stitches are Natural, start with Layette; if the first stitches are Layette, start with Natural. Because the multicolor Layette yarn contains lengths of the color Natural, you may not be able to tell which is which; don't worry — just use a different yarn for the stitches on each needle.

- Round 1: Using the color that's not already on the needle, pick up 2 stitches along the gap, then work across the first needle. Change to the other color and repeat for the second needle Ⓒ. (13 stitches)

Ⓒ Pick up 2 stitches at gap, work across first needle, change yarns and repeat for other needle.

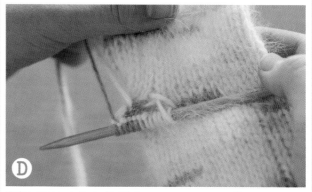

Ⓓ Knit across so that all stitches are on one needle.

- Using one of these two needles and its working yarn, knit across the other needle. All your stitches are now on one needle and both yarns are attached at the end of this needle Ⓓ.
- Pull the lower yarn across the back and begin working striped I-cord.

When you've worked a few rounds, you'll notice that there is no gap across the back of the cord. When you're working striped I-cord, guard against pulling too tightly, which makes the stitch at the end of the row noticeably tighter than the rest. As you work, check to see that the tension across the back of the tube is consistent and adjust (loosening or tightening) accordingly if it's not.

- Work in Two-Color I-Cord until the thumb is 1¼" (3 cm) long.
- Knit halfway across the next row, then work a purled bind off to the end of the row. This leaves half the stitches on the right needle and 1 stitch on the left needle. Cut the last color used, leaving a 4" (10 cm) tail. Bring the left needle around to the right with the single stitch still on it **E**.
- Work a purled bind off across the remaining stitches using the other color.
- Cut the yarn leaving a 4" (10 cm) tail. Use the tail to make the beginning and end of the bind off continuous, then weave in both tails on the inside. (See Making the Bind Off Look Continuous, pages 56–57.)
- Weave in the two tails at the base of the thumb, using them to close up any holes.

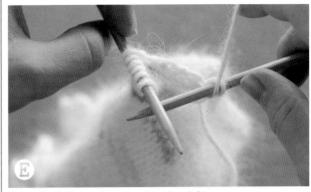

Bring the left needle around to the right.

- Blocking: The Crown Picot Bind Off tends to stand out like a tutu. This is caused by the natural tendency of the stockinette stitch to curl. You can fix this by gently blocking the bottom of the mitten where the bind off meets the cuff.

STRIPED I-CORD

Two-Color I-Cord. Using two double-pointed needles, cast on as many stitches as you like (3 to 8 work best) in the first color. Slide the stitches to the other end of the needle, and knit all the stitches with second color. *Do not turn. Slide the stitches to the other end of the needle and switch the needle to your left hand. Pull first color (used for the cast on) across the back, keeping it below the other strand of yarn. Be careful not to pull it too tight. Knit all the stitches. Repeat from *, alternating colors until the cord is as long as you like. Cut both yarns, and pull both through all the stitches to secure. Unlike single-color I-cord, there's no need to pull the yarn firmly across the back; in fact, avoid doing this because it will make a tight, unsightly column of stitches.

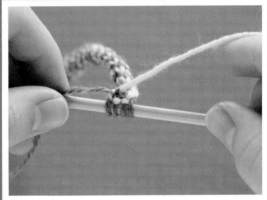

Striped I-cord

Many-Color I-Cord. Cast on the same number of stitches as you have colors of yarn; for example, to use four colors, cast on 4 stitches using the first color. *Slide the stitches to the other end of the needle. Knit across the 4 cast-on stitches using the second color, do not turn; repeat from * with each of the other two colors. Knot the tails of all the yarns together loosely to keep them organized and prevent you from knitting with them accidentally. From now on you will repeat the same four colors in the same order to make a 4-round pattern. Pull the next color in the sequence (the first time, this is the cast-on color) gently across the back of the cord *under* the other working yarns and knit across. Always take care to keep the knotted ends in front of the working yarn when you knit the I-cord, so they do not become entangled in the working yarns. This will be easier when the cord is a little longer. Continue to work each color in order until the cord is the desired length. Cut all the yarns and pull the one that would be used next through all the stitches to secure them. Because of the spiral effect of using so many colors, the ends of this cord are diagonal. (Instructions for making straight ends can be found in my previous book, *The Essential Guide to Color Knitting Techniques;* see appendix for more information).

Multicolored I-cord

Cable and Gusset Mitten

Up to this point in the chapter, the mitten projects have been straight tubes with just a hole for the thumb, making them easy to knit as well as able to fit either hand. This project introduces two new shapings: gussets (in which the mitten is tapered from thumb to cuff) and flat fingertips (which are almost identical to flat toes). You also get practice working a cable in circular knitting and learn a nifty trick for keeping track of which round you're on.

For Project Shown You Need

YARN	Lorna's Laces Swirl Chunky (83% merino wool/17% silk, 120 yds/4 oz)
YARN AMOUNT (for one mitten)	50 yds/46 m Firefly (54ns)
GAUGE	14 stitches = 4" (10 cm) in stockinette stitch
NEEDLE SIZE	US 10 (6 mm). Match the project's gauge if you want finished measurements to match pattern instructions.
NEEDLE TYPES (any of the following)	Set of four or five double-pointed needles at least 5" (13 cm) long Two circular needles 16" (40 cm) or longer 47" (120 cm) circular needle or longer for Magic Loop
OTHER SUPPLIES	Split markers, cable needle, small amount waste yarn
FINISHED SIZE	6½" (16.25 cm) around × 9" (23 cm) long

New Techniques Used

- Twisted Rib
- Thumb gusset
- Symmetrical increases
- Cable in the round
- Flat fingertip
- Kitchener stitch fingertip (pages 70–74)

Project Overview

Keeping track while working the hand. Before getting started, let's take a look at what's happening in the first eight rounds of the hand. First, you work every other round plain: all you have to do is knit. In between the plain rounds you work the cable pattern, consisting of 2 purl stitches on either side of the 6-stitch cable, which is crossed in Round 6. The purled stitches every other round make columns of garter stitch on both sides of the cable. This sets off the cable and gives you a quick way to figure out what round you're on. If the garter stitches were knitted on the previous round, then you now need to work a pattern round. If they were purled on the previous round, you just need to knit the current round. The garter ridges also make it easy to count the rounds. Starting from the bottom of the mitten, count each ridge as 2 rounds. Count "two-four-six-eight" repeatedly until you get up to the needle, and you'll know exactly where you are in the pattern repeat. One of the problems with making cables in circular ribbing is that it can be difficult to count the rounds, and it's easy to cross the cables a round too early or too late. The garter ridges solve this problem. Counting the garter ridges also helps you identify the gusset increase rounds: on Rounds 2 and 6 (that is, every fourth round), you work two increases, one on each side of the gusset.

Shaping the fingertip. With the flat toe shaping used for this mitten, you would normally have the option of working all the decreases on alternate rounds (which results in a longer more angular shape) or of working the second half of the decreases on every round (which results in a rounder fingertip). In this case, because the mitten is so bulky, there are really too few stitches and rounds to allow for the more complicated shaping, so we'll just work the decreases every other round.

Working the thumb. When there's a gusset, the thumb is still made essentially the same way as an afterthought or forethought thumb. The live stitches are placed on needles, stitches are picked up at the gap where the gusset meets the hand, and the thumb is worked up from there.

Working the Cuff

- Setup: Cast on 26 stitches. Place 14 on one needle for the first half of the round (the patterned back of the mitten), and place the remaining 12 on needle(s) for the second half of the round (the plain palm of the mitten). Join the beginning and end of round, being careful not to twist (see Off to a Good Start: Casting On and Joining, page 13). Mark the beginning and end of round (either with the tail or a split marker).
- Twisted Rib: *K1 through the back loop, P1; repeat from * around.
- Work Twisted Rib until the cuff measures 2" (5 cm) long.
- When you reach the end of the last round, place a marker on the needle, M1. (*27 stitches*)

Working the Hand

The first 14 stitches of the round are the back of the hand (where the cable is); the next 12 are the palm. The single stitch between the marker and the end of round is the beginning of the gusset, which grows wider as you work. The first time you work Round 2, there will only be 1 stitch between the two increases. Notice that you work a left-slanting M1 (M1L) on one side of the gusset and a right-slanting M1 (M1R) on the other side. These are mirror images of each other and make the two edges of the gusset look symmetrical.

- Rounds 1, 3, 5, and 7: Knit around.
- Round 2: K2, P2, K6, P2, knit to marker, slip marker, M1L, knit to end of round, M1R.
- Round 4: K2, P2, K6, P2, knit to end of round.
- Round 6: K2, P2, slip 3 to cable needle and hold in front, K3, K3 from cable needle, P2, knit to marker, slip marker, M1L, knit to end of round, M1R.
- Round 8: Repeat Round 4.
- Repeat Rounds 1–8 until there are 11 stitches in the gusset between the marker and the end of round, ending with an even-numbered round. The mitten should measure about 5½" (14 cm) from the cast on.
- Next Round: Work in pattern until you come to the marker. Remove marker from needle and place the gusset stitches on a piece of waste yarn 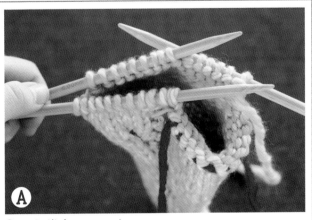. Retain the marker at the beginning/end of round. (*26 stitches remain*)

A Gusset stitches on waste yarn

Cable stitches rearranged to work tip decreases

Pull the working yarn across the gap and begin working the hand stitches.

- Fold the gusset to the outside of the mitten and pull the working yarn across the gap to begin working just the 26 hand stitches again  **B**.
- Work in pattern as established on these stitches, without any more increases, until the mitten measures about 8¼" (21 cm). Stop after completing Round 8.
- Place a second marker after 14 stitches to indicate where the back of the mitten ends and the palm begins.

Stitches on 2 needles ready for Kitchener stitch

Working the Flat Fingertip

- Round 1: Knit around.
- Round 2: *K1, ssk, work in pattern until 3 stitches remain before marker, K2tog, K1; repeat from * once more. (*22 stitches remain*)
- Repeat Rounds 1 and 2 once more, then knit 1 round. (*18 stitches remain*)

The cable pattern is decreased by 2 stitches on the next round so that the back and the palm have an equal number of stitches and the cable doesn't flare at the top of the mitten.

- Setup: Rearrange the 10 stitches for the back of the hand as follows so that the cable is already crossed. Slipping all the stitches purlwise and using an empty needle, slip 2 from the old needle to the new needle, slip 3 to cable needle and hold in front, slip 3 from the old needle to the new needle, slip 3 from the cable needle to the new needle, slip the remaining 2 stitches from the old needle to the new needle **C**.
- Next Round: (mitten back) K1, (ssk) twice, (K2tog) twice, K1; (palm) K1, ssk, K2, K2tog, K1. (*12 stitches remain: 6 on back and 6 on palm*)
- Cut the yarn leaving a tail about 12" (30.5 cm) long. Arrange the stitches so that the back stitches are all on one needle (or one half of the Magic Loop) and the palm stitches are on another. Join the back and palm stitches using Kitchener stitch (pages 70–74) **D**.

Working the Thumb

- Setup: Slip the 11 thumb stitches off the waste yarn and arrange on needles any way you like, with the beginning of round at the gap **E**.
- Using the working yarn, pick up and knit 1 stitch at the gap **F**.
- Knit around the live stitches. At the end of the round pick up and knit 1 more stitch at the gap **G**. (*13 stitches*)
- Next round: K2tog, knit until 2 stitches remain before end of round, ssk **H**. (*11 stitches remain*)
- Knit around until the thumb is 2¼" (5.5 cm) long, measured from the thumb crease.
- On the final round, K2tog around, ending K1. (*You've reduced the number of stitches by about half; 6 stitches remain*)
- Cut the yarn, leaving a tail about 4" (10 cm) long. Pull this through all the remaining stitches, to the inside of the thumb, and weave in. Use the tail at the base of the thumb to close any remaining holes before weaving it in.

E Thumb stitches on needles

F Pick up and knit 1 stitch at gap.

G At end of round, pick up and knit stitch at gap.

H Ready to work the thumb

GLOVES IN ALL DIRECTIONS

Gloves have hands and thumbs exactly like mittens, but gloves terminate in four fingers. The index, middle, and ring fingers are usually all the same circumference, but the little finger is a bit smaller and the thumb a bit bigger. Fingers are constructed exactly like thumbs. Preparation for adding the thumb is exactly the same for gloves as for mittens: you have your choice of afterthought, forethought, or gusset.

Look closely at your hand. Your little finger starts a fraction lower than your other three fingers. In gloves, this is accommodated by starting the little finger a few rounds below the other fingers. Each of the fingers is worked in turn, the same way that a thumb is made, so you can work them either as I-cord (see Wider I-Cord, page 51) or circularly on double-pointed needles, two circulars, or Magic Loop.

Like mittens, gloves can be worked from the cuff to the fingers or from the fingers down; you'll find one of each in the projects below. Finally, gloves can always be made with partial fingers and thumbs. If you don't want full fingers, then just bind off each digit at the desired length.

Twined-Cuff Glove

Twined knitting involves working alternate stitches with two different strands of yarn, twisting the two strands between every stitch. Before you begin this pattern, take a look at Twined Knitting Basics (pages 239–240). Twined knitting wears very well, which makes it good for cuffs, and it offers opportunities for subtle textured ornamentation. Because it can be time consuming to work, only the cuff of this glove is twined. The rest is in plain stockinette, so you can concentrate on learning the structure of a glove.

For Project Shown You Need

YARN	Black Water Abbey 2-ply Z-Twist Worsted (100% wool, 220 yds/4 oz)
YARN AMOUNT (for one glove)	60 yds/55 m Ecru
GAUGE	18 stitches = 4" (10 cm) in stockinette stitch
NEEDLE SIZE	US 7 (4.5 mm). Match the project's gauge if you want finished measurements to match pattern instructions.
NEEDLE TYPES (any of the following)	(Note: You may use any of the following, but note that the fingers are most easily worked on short double-pointed needles) Set of four or five double-pointed needles at least 4" (10 cm) long. Two circular needles 16" (40 cm) or longer 47" (120 cm) circular needle or longer for Magic Loop
OTHER SUPPLIES	Stitch markers (optional), waste yarn (three pieces about 12"/30.5 cm long), crochet hook about the same diameter as the knitting needles (optional), yarn needle
FINISHED SIZE	8" (20.5 cm) around × 8¼" (21 cm) long

New Techniques Used

- Twined knitting
- Right and left afterthought thumbs
- Setting aside stitches for each finger
- Starting the fingers and joining them to their neighbors

Getting Started

- Wind your yarn into a center pull ball.
- Cast on 36 stitches using both ends of the yarn and the Long-Tail Cast On, as described in Twined Knitting Basics (page 239).
- Arrange the stitches on needles any way you like. Join the beginning and end of round, if you like, by swapping the positions of the first and last stitch of the cast on, being careful not to twist the knitting (see Avoiding the Jog: Swap the First and Last Stitch, page 15. Other methods of joining make beginning the twined knitting more difficult. You may want to mark the beginning of round with a stitch marker to prevent confusion.

Working the Twined Cuff

Twined knitting can be much tighter than regular knitting, so be careful to work loosely or your cuff may be much too tight for the glove. If you find it difficult to work loosely enough, use needles one or two sizes larger than needed to obtain the correct gauge for the rest of the glove.

- Round 1: Work twined purling.
- Round 2: Work twined knitting.
- Rounds 3 and 4: Work Chain Path pattern (see page 240). Be sure to begin Round 3 with a knit stitch and Round 4 with a purl stitch.
- Rounds 5–7: Repeat Rounds 2–4.
- Round 8: Work twined knitting.
- Round 9: Work twined purling.
- Cut one of the strands of yarn, leaving a tail 4–6" (10–15 cm) long to weave in later. Continue in stockinette stitch with the other strand of yarn until the glove measures 4⅝" (11.5 cm) from the cast-on edge.

Reserving Stitches for Little Finger

- Next Round: Stop 4 stitches before end of round. Place the next 8 stitches (4 on each side of the end of round) on a piece of waste yarn. Do not cut the working yarn. (28 stitches remain)
- Rearrange the remaining stitches so that there are similar numbers on each needle
- Next 2 Rounds: Pull the working yarn across the gap where the stitches were removed, closing it, and continue working in stockinette. The glove should measure 5" (12.5 cm) from the cast-on edge.

Stitches reserved for little finger

Stitches reserved for ring and middle fingers

Reserving Stitches for Ring and Middle Fingers

- Next Round:
- K19.
- Place the next 4 stitches on a piece of waste yarn for the middle finger.
- Place the next 10 stitches on a second piece of waste yarn for the ring finger. (*5 stitches on each side of the end of round*)
- Place the next 4 stitches (which are also for the middle finger) on the first piece of waste yarn with the ones already there  (*8 stitches opposite each other on waste yarn; 10 stitches remain on needle*)
- Do not cut the working yarn.

Notes on Working the Fingers and Thumb

The instructions for working the fingers and thumb assume that you are using a set of double-pointed needles, but you may also work them on two circulars, Magic Loop, or as Wider I-cord. Rather than repeat all the details for all the possible configurations in the instructions for every finger, use these general guidelines.

For two circulars or Magic Loop: Work the first half of the finger with the first needle (or first half of the Magic Loop) and work the second half of the finger with the second needle (or second half of the loop).

For wider I-cord: Place all the stitches on one double-pointed needle, but pick up or cast on one fewer stitch at the end of the needle than specified in the directions. If you find it difficult to put all the stitches on one needle immediately, place them on two needles and then work them onto a single needle when you work the first round of I-cord. Before decreasing for the fingertip, use a crochet hook to hook up a column of stitches in the gap at the back of the cord. This replaces the missing stitch. (See Wider I-cord, page 51, and Tip-Down Textured Mitten, page 225, for details on working the cord and hooking up the additional stitch to close the gap at the back.)

Working the Index Finger

- Cast on 2 stitches next to the 10 stitches already on your needle using the Half-Hitch Cast On (page 302). (*12 stitches*)

- Rearrange the stitches on your needles as needed to make it comfortable to knit. Pull the yarn across the gap where stitches were removed for the other fingers and work circularly in stockinette stitch until the finger is 2¾" (7 cm) long.

- K2tog around, reducing the number of stitches by half.

- Cut the yarn, leaving a 4–6" (10–15 cm) tail to weave in later. Pull it through the 6 remaining stitches and then to the inside of the finger .

Index finger complete

Working the Middle Finger

- Setup: Holding the glove with the index finger to the left, slip the 4 stitches for the middle finger that are facing you from the waste yarn onto a needle. Join the yarn, leaving a 4–6" (10–15 cm) tail to weave in later. Knit across these 4 stitches, then pick up and knit 2 stitches along the base of the index finger . Slip the other 4 middle-finger stitches from the waste yarn onto a needle, making sure that the point is aimed toward the index finger. Knit across these 4 stitches, then cast on 2 stitches at the end of the needle. (*12 stitches*)

- Rearrange these stitches as needed to work comfortably 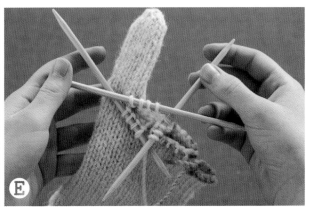, and work as for the index finger, making it 1 or 2 rounds longer. If the completed index finger gets in your way, turn it inside out and tuck it inside the glove.

Four stitches for middle finger slipped to needle and two picked up at base of index finger

Stitches for middle finger arranged on needles

Working the Ring Finger

- Setup: Slip the 10 stitches for the ring finger from the waste yarn onto needle(s).
- Starting at the gap with the right side of the finger facing you, join the yarn, leaving a tail to weave in later. Knit across these 10 stitches, then pick up and knit 2 stitches along the base of the middle finger. (*12 stitches*)
- Rearrange these stitches as needed to work comfortably and work as for index finger. If the completed fingers get in your way, turn them inside out and tuck them inside the glove.

Working the Little Finger

- Setup: Eight stitches remain for the little finger. Begin it as you began the ring finger. Place the 8 stitches on needle(s), knit across, and pick up 2 stitches at the base of the ring finger. (*10 stitches*)
- Rearrange these stitches as needed to work comfortably and work as for index finger until the little finger is 2" (5 cm) long.
- Finish as for the index finger.

Working the Thumb

- Lay the glove out flat with your hand on top and decide what row the thumb opening should be on. Make sure that the two sides are folded at the beginning of round (on one side of the little finger) and the middle of round (at the far side of the index finger). Use a split marker to mark the point where your thumb joins your hand

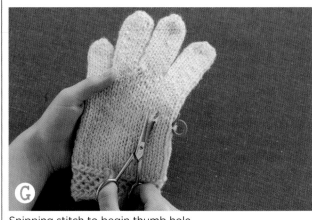

Snipping stitch to begin thumb hole

- Below the index finger, on the marked row, count 3 stitches in from the edge and carefully snip between this stitch and the next. If the index finger is on the left as you open the hole for the thumb, you'll have a left-hand glove. If the index finger is on the right as you do this, you'll have a right-hand glove
- Unravel 3 stitches in each direction from the snipped stitch and put the live stitches on needles.
- Make an afterthought thumb, 2¾" (7 cm) long, exactly as in the Afterthought Mitten (see pages 220–222).

Finishing

- Use the tails of yarn at the base of the fingers and thumb to close up any holes as you weave them in on the inside. Use the cast-on tails to make the cast-on edge look continuous (see Mind the Gap, page 76), and then weave them in on the inside.

Measuring and placing marker for thumb

TWINED KNITTING BASICS

Twined knitting is a Scandinavian variation on stranded knitting. In Swedish, it's called *tväänds-stickning,* which means "two-end knitting." Both the Swedish and English names are appropriate because the yarns are constantly twisted around each other (that is, "twined"), and when working in one color you use both ends of the same ball (that is, "two ends"). Twined knitting produces a tight, durable fabric quite unlike regular knitting. The right side of the fabric is flatter than normal knitting Ⓐ, while the wrong side has distinctive twisted ridges Ⓑ.

Ⓒ

S-twist, left; Z-twist, right

Ⓐ
chain path
crook stitch
twined knitting
purled round

Twined knitting swatch, right side

Ⓑ

Twined knitting swatch, wrong side

The yarn. Traditionally, the yarn used in twined knitting is a two-ply Z-twist, spun and plied in the opposite direction from the S-twist yarn that is the current standard for commercial yarns Ⓒ. If you must use an S-twist yarn, choose one that is loosely plied because working twined knitting adds twist.

Before working twined knitting, wind your yarn into a center-pull ball so that you can use both ends. Twined knitting is extremely difficult to work with the

yarns in the left hand, so if you don't normally knit with the yarn in your right hand, you should practice this skill before attempting twined knitting.

Casting on. There are many ways to cast on for twined knitting, but the important thing about all of them is that they are firm cast ons. The simplest, and not least effective, of the twined cast ons is to use both ends of the yarn and work the Long-Tail Cast On (pages 302–303), twisting the strands between each stitch. Here's how:
- Hold both yarn ends together and make a slipknot, leaving tails long enough to weave in later. Put the slipknot on your needle. Don't include the slipknot in your stitch count — it will be unraveled later.
- Place one strand connected to the ball over your index finger and the other over your thumb. Cast on 1 stitch, then switch the position of the two yarns. Take the yarn on the index finger down in front of the yarn on the thumb each time you twist Ⓓ.

When you've cast on all the stitches you need, arrange them on your needle(s) and take the slipknot off the needle. Don't unravel it yet: you need it to prevent the first cast-on stitch from becoming loose as you begin to work.

Working a twined knit. Working a knit stitch in twined knitting is identical to working any knit stitch, except that you twist the two strands of yarn between each stitch, and you knit with each strand

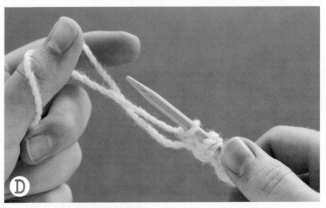

Ⓓ

Casting on for twined knitting

Working a twined knit

Working a twined purl

alternately. Always bring the strand you are about to use in front of the other strand **E**.

Working a twined purl. Twined purling is also very similar to regular purling. Bring both strands of yarn to the front before purling. Purl, alternating the two strands and twisting them between each stitch. You'll be twisting in the same direction as when knitting, but this can be confusing because the yarn is now in front of the needle. Hold the strands above the needle as you twist them and bring the one you are about to use in front of the other strand **F**.

Unwinding the yarn. Twisted yarn is just a fact of life in twined knitting. Because you're giving the two strands a half twist after each stitch, they constantly become plied around each other while you

work. When the twist is too tight to allow you to knit comfortably, stop and untwist the yarns. While the project is small, simply hold the yarn up and let the knitting and needles rotate in the air. When the project grows too large for this, secure the working yarn to the ball using a knitting needle and a couple of half hitches, and then let the ball untwist **G**.

Twined Pattern Stitches

Twined knitting can produce all kinds of lovely textured patterns. Crook Stitch and Chain Path are among the most pleasing and simplest to work.

Crook Stitch is a welcome break from twisting the yarn after every stitch. Bring one yarn to the front and leave the other yarn behind the fabric. Alternate stitches, knitting with the back yarn **H** and purling with the front yarn **I**. Never switch the position of the yarns. It's easiest to hold both yarns in the palm of your hand and slip your index finger underneath the one you need to use for the current stitch.

Chain Path is made by working two rounds of Crook Stitch. On the second round, work knit stitches above the purl stitches from the previous round and vice versa.

Binding off. Like casting on for twined knitting, binding off should be firm so that it doesn't flare. You can accomplish this by continuing to twine (that is, twist the yarn between each stitch and alternate yarns) as you bind off.

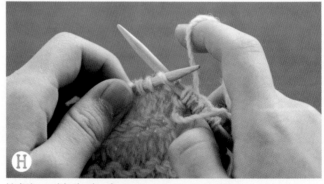

Knitting with the back yarn

Purling with the front yarn

Untwisting the working yarn

Half-Finger Glove

This last glove project is a bit of a *tour de force*, rounding out the mitten and glove techniques presented so far. It is knit from the fingers down. Each finger, including the thumb, is made separately with a different color. The fingers are then joined together to make the hand. We haven't tried a thumb gusset worked from the thumb down to the cuff, so this is a chance for you to see that it's a surprisingly simple construction. Finally, the bottom of the glove is embellished with a few stripes, giving you a chance to practice camouflaging the jog, and a neat contrast-color hem. I recommend working the fingers on double-points (either conventionally or as I-cord). The hand is most easily worked on two circulars; the beauty of this is that you can try on the glove at any point to check the fit or just to admire it as it progresses.

For Project Shown You Need

YARN	Lorna's Laces Shepherd Sport (100% superwash wool, 200 yds/ 2.6 oz)
YARN AMOUNT (for one glove)	4 yds/3.7 m Douglas Fir (6ns); 3 yds/2.7 m Natural (0ns); 6 yds/ 5.5 m Turquoise (22ns); 12 yds/11 m Firefly (54ns); 5 yds/4.6 m Sunshine (40ns); 32 yds/29 m Bittersweet (630)
GAUGE	24 stitches = 4" (10 cm) in stockinette stitch
NEEDLE SIZE	US 4 (3.5 mm). Match the project's gauge if you want finished measurements to match pattern instructions.
NEEDLE TYPES	For the fingers and thumb, a set of four double-pointed needles at least 4" (10 cm) long (*Note:* You can make the fingers any way you like — on a set of double points, as I-cord, on two circular needles, or Magic Loop — but for transferring them to the circular needles prior to joining them to the hand, double-pointed needles are by far the easiest tools.) For the hand, two circulars 16" (40 cm) or longer (*Note:* You could use one long circular needle for Magic Loop, but two circular needles give you more flexibility if you get disoriented or need to correct a mistake.)
OTHER SUPPLIES	About 64" (163 cm) crochet cotton cut into 8" (20.5 cm) lengths to use as stitch holders, yarn needle, stitch markers
FINISHED SIZE	7¾" (19.5 cm) circumference at knuckles × 5½" (14 cm) from base of fingers to cuff

New Techniques Used

- Fingers down to cuff
- Partial fingers and thumb
- Joining fingers to form hand
- Joining thumb and starting gusset
- Symmetrical gusset decreases
- Jogless stripes
- Hem

While the instructions call for different colors for all five fingers and the hand (to make it clear which one you're working with in the instructions), you can of course simplify things by making the whole glove in one color.

Working the Thumb

- Using Douglas Fir, cast on 18 stitches, leaving a 4–6" (10–15 cm) tail to weave in later; work circularly for 10 rounds. Cut the yarn, leaving a tail about 8" (20 cm). Place the stitches on a piece of crochet cotton. Weave in the cast-on tail on the inside of the thumb and trim off the excess. You could wait until later to weave in this end, but there will be many tails of yarn hanging down, so it is less confusing to get rid of the cast-on tails as you finish each finger, and it's actually easier to do it before they are attached to the hand.

Working the Little Finger

- Using Natural, cast on 14 stitches leaving a 4–6" (10–15 cm) tail to weave in later.
- Work circularly for 10 rounds.
- Cut the yarn, leaving a tail of about 8" (20.5 cm).
- Place the stitches on another length of crochet cotton.
- Weave in the cast-on tail on the inside of the finger, and trim.

Working the Index Finger

- Using Turquoise, cast on 16 stitches, leaving a 4–6" (10–15 cm) tail to weave in later.
- Work circularly for 12 rounds.
- Cut the yarn, leaving a tail of about 8" (20.5 cm).
- Place the last 2 stitches of the round on a piece of crochet cotton. Divide the remaining stitches between two double-pointed needles, with 7 stitches on each. (Half are for the back of the glove and half for the palm.)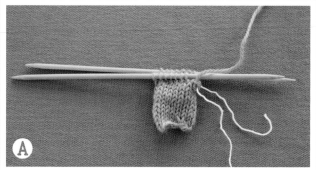
- Weave in the cast-on tail on the inside of the finger, and trim.
- Slip the 7 stitches from one double-point onto one circular needle and the other 7 onto the other circular needle 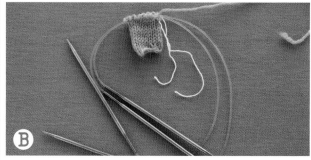. One of these circular needles will eventually hold all the stitches for the back of the hand and the other will hold all the stitches for the palm.

Working the Middle Finger

- Using Firefly, cast on and work as for index finger until you are ready to remove the stitches from the needle.
- Place the last 2 stitches of the round on another piece of crochet cotton.

A
Index finger on double points

B
Index finger on 2 circulars

C
Index and middle fingers on 2 circulars

- Place the next 6 stitches on one double-pointed needle.
- Place the next 2 stitches on another piece of crochet cotton.
- Place the last 6 stitches onto a second double-pointed needle.
- Like the index finger, the stitches on one needle are for the back of the glove and those on the other needle are for the palm. Hold the circular needles in one hand so that the tail attached to the index finger is toward the needle points you'll be using. Hold the double points in the other hand so that the tail attached to the middle finger is toward the needle points you'll be using. Slip the stitches from the front double point onto the front circular needle, then slip the stitches from the back double point to the back circular needle. When you're done, the two fingers should be on the circular needles with the two dangling tails next to each other 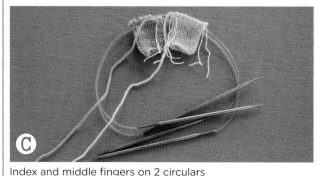.

Working the Ring Finger

- Using Sunshine, cast on and work as for index finger until you are ready to remove the stitches from the needle.
- Place the last 2 stitches of the round on another piece of crochet cotton.
- Arrange the remaining stitches so that 7 are on one double-pointed needle and 7 are on another.
- Hold the circular needles in one hand with the Firefly (green) middle finger closest to the needle points you plan to use. Hold the double points in the other hand with the tail closest to the needle points you plan to use. Slip the stitches to the front and back circular needles just as you did for the middle finger. When you're done, the ring finger's tail should be next to the middle finger **D**. (*40 stitches, 20 on each needle*)

Starting the Hand

- Using Bittersweet and beginning at the Sunshine (yellow) ring finger, knit 3 rounds, stopping 1 stitch before the end of the third round. Place the last stitch of the round and the first stitch of the next round on a piece of crochet cotton **E**. (*38 stitches, 19 on each needle*)

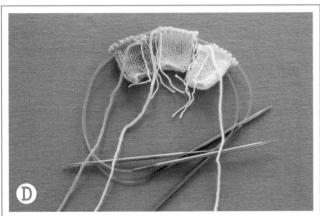

D

Index, middle, and ring fingers on 2 circulars

E

Ready to add little finger

F

Knitting across little finger

beginning of round

G

All fingers on 2 circulars

H

Checking length for thumb

Joining the Little Finger

- Setup: Slip a double-pointed needle through the first 6 stitches of the little finger; do this without removing the crochet cotton. Continuing to use Bittersweet and starting at the side of the little finger where the tail is attached, knit across these 6 stitches **F**.
- Leave the last 2 stitches of the little finger on the crochet cotton and slip the tip of the other circular needle through the next 6 stitches of the little finger **G**. The beginning of round is now at the outer edge of the little finger. (*50 stitches, 25 on each needle*)
- Round 1: Still using Bittersweet, knit around.
- Round 2 (decrease round): Decrease 4 stitches evenly spaced. Accomplish this by working *K2tog, K10, K2tog, K11; repeat from * once. (*46 stitches, 23 on each needle*)
- Rounds 3–11: Knit around.

This is an excellent point to stop and admire your handiwork and to make sure the glove is the correct length before adding the thumb **H**. If necessary, unravel a few rounds or add a few rounds until the hand is exactly the right length to the thumb.

Joining the Thumb

- On the next round, knit until 2 stitches remain at the end of the first needle. You are at the outer edge of the index finger. Remove the last 2 stitches from this needle and the first 2 from the other needle and place them on a piece of crochet cotton .

- Slip a double-pointed needle through the first 7 stitches of the thumb. (You should be able to do this without removing the crochet cotton.) Place a marker on the front circular needle. Beginning at the side of the thumb where the tail is attached, use Bittersweet and the front circular needle to knit across the 7 thumb stitches .

- Place a marker on the back circular needle. Leave the last 4 stitches of thumb on the crochet cotton and slip the other circular needle into the next 7 stitches .

Ⓘ Ready to add thumb

Ⓙ Knitting across thumb

Ⓚ All 5 fingers on needle

Working the Gusset

The beginning/end of round is now at the outer edge of the thumb. There are 56 stitches, 28 on each needle, which is too big to fit the wrist, so the gusset tapers the thumb until you get back down to 46 stitches for the hand.

- Still using Bittersweet, knit 1 round.

- Decrease Round: Knit until 2 stitches remain before the marker, K2tog, slip marker, knit around to the second marker (near the end of the other needle), slip marker, ssk, knit to end of round. Note that the K2tog decrease on one side of the gusset and the ssk decrease on the other side are mirror images of each other.

- Continue working in stockinette with Bittersweet, working the Decrease Round every fourth round until 46 stitches remain.

Working the Stripes

- Rounds 1–5: Using Bittersweet, knit around. Glove should measure about 4": (10 cm) from base of little finger to needle. As you work the stripes below, try out the methods for Stripes Without the Stair Step, discussed on pages 97–98.

- Rounds 6 and 7: Using Firefly, knit around.

- Round 8: Using Turquoise, knit around.

- Rounds 9 and 10: Using Sunshine, knit around.

- Rounds 11–15: Using Bittersweet, knit around.

- Round 16: Using Firefly, knit around.

Creating the Hem

Before you begin the hem, you may want to review Hems (pages 66–67).

- Round 1: Using Firefly, purl around.

- Rounds 2–8: Knit around.

- Cut yarn leaving a tail 1 yard (1 meter) long. Before joining the hem to the inside, weave in any ends from the last few stripes that will be encased in the hem. Use duplicate stitch on the purl side to disguise the jog (see Stripes Without the Stair Step, pages 97–98). Using a yarn needle, sew or weave the live stitches to the inside of the glove to finish the hem.

Finishing

- Weave in any remaining tails near the cuff, using duplicate stitch on the inside at the beginning/end of round to disguise the jog.

- Close up the holes at the base of the thumb and fingers as follows: At the base of each finger, there are 2 stitches on crochet cotton on each side of the opening. Slip each of these pairs of stitches onto separate double-pointed needles and remove the crochet cotton. (You can simply pull on it and it will come out.) There should be a tail of yarn connected to at least one of the sets of stitches on the needles. Using this tail, work Kitchener stitch (pages 70–74) to join the two sets of stitches, then close up any holes at either side before weaving in the tail on the wrong side.

- There are 4 stitches set aside on crochet cotton at the base of the thumb and the hand opposite it. Join them together exactly as you did for the fingers.

- Check for any remaining tails and weave them in.

Joining base of fingers with Kitchener stitch

Making This Glove with Full Fingers

Instructions follow for starting the fingers and thumb. As you finish each of them, place the stitches on crochet cotton and weave in the cast-on tail exactly as described for the half-finger version above. You may work the fingers on double-pointed needles, two circulars, or as I-cord (see Wider I-cord, page 51). You may also want to review Closed Center Cast On #1 (pages 22–24) before embarking on the ten fingers. Because there are so many increases in a small area, the best increase to use is an M1 with the working yarn.

Thumb

Setup: Cast on 6 stitches.

Round 1 (increase round): Knit around, increasing to double the number of stitches. (*12 stitches*)

Round 2 (increase round): Knit around, increasing 6 stitches evenly spaced around. (*18 stitches*)

Work even until the thumb is long enough to reach the thumb crease, where it will be joined to the hand.

Place all the stitches on a piece of crochet cotton.

Little Finger

Setup: Cast on 4 stitches.

Round 1 (increase round): Knit around, increasing to double the number of stitches. (*8 stitches*)

Round 2 (increase round): Knit around, increasing 6 stitches spaced around. (*14 stitches*)

Work even until the little finger is long enough to reach the hand, where it will be joined to the other fingers.

Place all the stitches on a piece of crochet cotton.

Other Three Fingers

Setup: Cast on 4 stitches.

Round 1 (increase round): Knit around, increasing to double the number of stitches. (*8 stitches*)

Round 2 (increase round): Knit around, increasing to again double the number of stitches. (*16 stitches*)

Work even until each finger is long enough to reach the hand.

Slip the stitches onto circular needles or crochet cotton as described for the Half-Finger Glove above. (See pages 242–243.)

Work the hand, including gusset shaping, stripes and hem, exactly as for the half-finger glove above. (See pages 243–245.)

DESIGNING YOUR OWN GLOVES OR MITTENS

Mittens and gloves can be made thick, stiff, and impervious to weather, or they can be loose and stretchy. The thicker and stiffer they are, the more carefully fitted they must be in order to be comfortable. Thick mittens also require the fingers, thumb, and hand to be a slightly larger circumference to allow for the thickness of the fabric. It's most fun to design mittens and gloves on the needles, trying them on for fit as you go. Since they knit up quickly, if something doesn't seem quite right, unravel a few rounds and adjust for it. Be careful to keep notes of what you do so that you can create a second mitten or glove to match.

The hands of mittens and gloves, with or without gussets, are sized identically. Measure around the hand below the fingers, excluding the thumb to find the circumference needed.

Estimate the number of stitches needed (a multiple of 4 or 8 is generally easiest to work with) at the usual gauge for the yarn you're using and start your mitten from the cuff. Unless your gauge is wildly off, it should be a reasonably good fit. Check as you begin the hand to see if the size seems accurate.

The following overview of mitten and glove construction assumes you are working from the cuff up to the fingertips.

Cuffs

If you want the cuff to be slightly tighter than the mitten, work it on needles one or two sizes smaller, or on 10 percent fewer stitches. Remember to change needle size or increase at the top of the cuff. For a cuff that doesn't curl up, use a noncurling pattern like ribbing or garter stitch.

Gussets and Thumb Openings

You can position the thumb centered at the beginning/end of round, or you can place it to one side of the beginning/end of round. If you have a pattern on the back of the hand or you place the thumb near the edge of the palm, be sure to position the two thumbs so that you end up with both a left and a right hand.

Afterthought thumb. Just work the hand and worry about positioning the thumb later.

Forethought thumb. Work in a piece of waste yarn where the thumb opening will be, or use safety pins to reserve stitches for the thumb. See Forethought Heel (page 194) and Helix Half-Mitten: Creating the Thumb Hole (page 227).

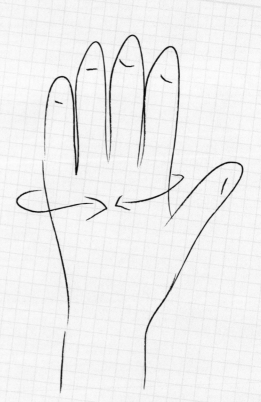

To find circumference, measure around your hand below fingers and excluding thumb.

Gusset. When you start the hand, increase 1 stitch at the end of round and put markers on both sides of this stitch. As you work, increase at each marker every fourth round (making sure that the increases are mirror images of each other) until you get to the point where you want the thumb opening. Place the thumb stitches on a piece of waste yarn and continue working the hand (see Cable and Gusset Mitten, pages 231–232).

Fingers

Work the hand up to the point where you need to divide the fingers or shape the tip. Before you separate the stitches for the fingers, you need to do a little planning. Remember that you need an equal number of stitches on the palm and the back side of each individual finger, and that the little finger should be a bit smaller and start a bit lower than the others. You also need to cast on or pick up a few stitches where each finger joins its neighbor. It's best to diagram this to get all the numbers right. Follow the general directions for the Twined-Cuff Glove (pages 235–238) on how to set aside stitches for each finger, adjusting the numbers to match your glove.

Beginning with the index finger, work the fingers in turn until they are the desired length. They can be either partial or full fingers. Remember to decrease about half of the stitches before closing off the ends of full fingers.

Mitten Tips

Use any of the mitten shapings found in this chapter:

Star tip. This is the easiest. Make sure you have a multiple of 4 stitches before you begin, then decrease 4 stitches evenly spaced every other round until 8 stitches remain, and finish off the tip. See Working the Star Toe (page 190).

Round tip. Decrease, if necessary, so that you have a multiple of 8 stitches, then make it identical to the round heel in the Afterthought Sock (see Round Heels and Toes Dissected, page 193).

Flat mitten tip. This requires an even number of stitches, so that the back and palm are symmetrical. It usually works out fine if you begin to shape the tip at about the last joint of the little finger. Follow the directions for Flat Toe Dissected (page 204). Keep an eye on the length as you work. If it seems to be coming out too long, switch to every-round decreases early. If it seems to be coming out too short, continue alternate-round decreases up to the tip. Be prepared, if these adjustments don't work, to unravel and work the shaping again to get it just right.

Thumbs

After the rest of the mitten or glove is complete, go back and add the thumb. How you do it depends on whether it will be built on an afterthought opening, a forethought opening, or a gusset.

Afterthought thumb: Take care to position the thumbs so that you make both a left and a right hand. Snip a stitch at the center of the intended thumb opening, unravel and place the stitches on needle(s). Follow the general directions for Afterthought Mitten: Creating the Thumb (pages 220–222) using your own stitch counts.

Forethought Thumb: Remove the waste yarn or stitch holders, place the stitches on needle(s) and add the thumb as for the Helix Half-Mitten (pages 228–229) or the Tip-Down Textured Mitten (page 225) using your own stitch counts.

Gusseted Thumb: Remove the waste yarn and place the stitches on needle(s). Follow the general directions for working the thumb in Cable and Gusset Mitten: Working the Thumb (page 233) using your own stitch counts.

Mittens and Gloves from the Tips Down

To make mittens and gloves in the opposite direction, reverse the process described above.

Mittens start from the tip exactly like socks from the toe up, then continue to the cuff, and the thumb is added later. Just as when making mittens from the cuff up, you have the options of afterthought, forethought, or gusseted thumbs. Afterthought and forethought thumbs are very straight forward: Make them exactly as if you were working in the opposite direction. For a gusseted thumb, make the thumb before beginning the fingertip and keep it in reserve. When you come to the point where the thumb should be attached, add it just as for the Half-Finger Glove (see Joining the Thumb, page 244). As you work the rest of the hand, decrease for the gusset (also on page 244). Add any kind of cuff you like at the bottom of the mitten.

With gloves, you must begin by creating all the fingers and the thumb; each of these is started like a tiny hat (see Closed Center Cast On #1, pages 22–24) and worked until they are the right length. The index, ring, and middle fingers are then joined, followed by the little finger, and finally by the thumb. Work the rest of the hand and whatever cuff you like. Detailed instructions for joining the fingers and thumb are given in the Half-Finger Glove (pages 243–244); follow these using your own stitch counts.

TOPPING OFF WITH VESTS + SWEATERS

Now that we've explored everything from straight tubes to socks and mittens, with flat scarves and shawls in between, it's time to move on to vests and sweaters. The five projects selected for this chapter are designed to provide you with as wide a range of circular construction techniques as possible. There's a basic vest, knit circularly from the bottom up to the underarms and then flat to the shoulders with a V-neck. One of the advantages of this method is that if you use Three-Needle Bind Off to join the shoulders, and work the neck and armhole borders circularly, there's no sewing up at all. The second project is a stranded V-necked vest, but this one is worked circularly throughout, with the introduction of steeks at the neck and armhole openings so that they can be cut open later. Two circular sweater structures follow the vests: one has a circular yoke, worked from the bottom up, and the other is a top-down raglan-sleeved sweater. The chapter culminates in a steeked, cuff-to-cuff sweater knit in one piece, with bindings to enclose the cut edges. One thing that all of these projects have in common is their small size. They all have a chest measurement between 16" (41 cm) and 20" (51 cm) — big enough to get plenty of practice, but small enough to finish quickly.

Designing Your Own

Obviously, there are a great many variations on circular sweaters and vests, very few of which could be included in this chapter. When you know how to work them circularly from the bottom up, the top down, or sideways, every garment can be converted from a flat version to a circular version. Refer to chapter 4, Converting Flat to Circular, page 78, for advice on how to do this, as well as how to avoid a few pitfalls.

Pattern stitches. Except for a little ribbing and garter stitch, the sweaters in this chapter are knit in stockinette so that you can concentrate on how they are made without worrying about maintaining a pattern stitch. Once you are comfortable constructing garments in the round, however, you can add any pattern stitches and embellishments you like. Explore the possibilities of integrating textured stitches, cables, lace, slipped stitches, and slipped-stitch color patterns into your circular sweaters. When you do so, keep in mind that small pattern stitches are much easier to accommodate than large ones and that the garment will be most easily worked on an even multiple of the pattern stitch. Where it's not possible to achieve the right size using even multiples of the pattern, use half panels of the pattern or introduce stockinette or Seed Stitch in the stitches directly below each underarm to enlarge the sweater so it does fit. If you're working a stranded color pattern, add a section of simple vertical stripes, salt and pepper, or 2-stitch blocks. On tapered sleeves you won't be able to work with an even multiple throughout, but be sure to center the pattern stitch from side to side so the sleeve doesn't look lopsided.

Fabric quality ("hand"). When designing a sweater, keep in mind the comfort of the wearer. You can knit a thick cabled pattern on tiny needles to get it down to a gauge that makes the sweater the correct size. If knit too tightly, however, the fabric will be stiff as a board and extremely uncomfortable to wear. Also avoid erring in the opposite extreme: knitting on very large needles to make a sweater bigger results in a loose fabric that easily stretches out of shape.

Stretching and structure. Sweaters that are knit all in one piece have a tendency to stretch out of shape because there are no seams to support them. Make sure that the borders have enough body to hold their shape and support the sweater. Avoid using non-wool fibers with no elasticity, because these generally stretch the most. Alternatively, design a garment that *must* stretch to be successful, such as a contour-hugging fitted sweater or a long loose coat that's intended to stretch in length. If you use non-wool fibers, try to go with thinner rather than thicker yarns; the thicker the yarn, the heavier it will be and the more it will stretch in length.

Trust your own judgment. Having issued so many dire warnings, I encourage you to ignore them all and to try whatever you are inspired to create. Whether you make detailed plans in advance or you design right on the needles, the results are sure to be either gratifying or educational. Above all, do not knit blindly. Stop frequently and look at your knitting. Ask yourself if it's working out as you planned. Is the fabric what you wanted? Is it coming out the shape you anticipated? Is the gauge correct? Do the colors and textures look and feel the way you envisioned? Have you planned the shaping so the borders are easy to pick up? As you answer these questions and act on the answers, your knitting may take you down unexpected paths.

V-Neck Vest

A basic seamless V-necked vest is the perfect introductory garment. You'll learn almost everything you need to know about shaping from this project. It is cast on at the bottom. To prevent the bottom band from stretching out of shape, it's worked on 10 percent fewer stitches than the body, on needles two sizes smaller, and in Twisted Rib. When the band is completed, knit around with a larger needle, increasing to add the missing 10 percent of the stitches. This is the easiest way to change needles — there's no need to slip stitches back and forth. Once the body is completed up to the underarms, the back and front are divided by binding off the stitches at both underarms. There's an easy trick for identifying the underarm stitches and marking them, so you don't need to count stitches while you're binding off. The back is completed first, because with only armhole shaping to be done, it's simpler than the front. The front is worked next, with the same armhole shaping as the back and the addition of the neck opening. There's no need to transfer any of the stitches to a holder, because the cable of the circular needle holds the front while you work the back, and vice versa. The simplified shape of this garment (no back neck shaping or shoulder shaping) allows you to focus on the major points of garment architecture and circular knitting techniques.

New Techniques Used

- Working neck, armhole, and bottom borders on fewer stitches, with smaller needles
- Changing to larger needles
- Binding off for underarms
- Working front and back separately
- Working both sides of the front at the same time with two balls of yarn
- Three-Needle Bind Off (page 69) to join shoulders
- Seamless circular borders
- Neck border mitered at center front

For Project Shown You Need

YARN	Lorna's Laces Shepherd Bulky (100% superwash wool, 140 yds/4 oz)
YARN AMOUNT	140 yds/128 m China Blue (41ns)
GAUGE	16½ stitches and 23 rounds = 4" (10 cm) in stockinette stitch
NEEDLE SIZE	US 10 (6 mm). Match the project's gauge if you want finished measurements to match pattern instructions.
NEEDLE TYPES	For body, 16" (40 cm) circular needle, plus extra needle for Three-Needle Bind Off For bottom border, 16" (40 cm) circular needle two sizes smaller than that used for body For armhole and neck borders, any of the following, two sizes smaller than needles used to work body: set of four or five double-point needles 7" (18 cm) or longer, a 12" (30 cm) circular needle, two circulars 16" (40 cm) or longer, or one circular needle 47" (120 cm) or longer for Magic Loop
OTHER SUPPLIES	Three split markers
FINISHED SIZE	19½" (48.5 cm) circumference and 10" (25 cm) long (shoulder to bottom)

Twisted Rib Pattern Stitch

- Round 1: *K1 through the back loop, P1; repeat from * around.
- Repeat Round 1 for pattern.

Working the Bottom Border

- Using smaller 16" (40 cm) circular needle, cast on 72 stitches. Join beginning and end of round being careful not to twist (see Off to a Good Start: Casting On and Joining, page 13). Mark the beginning/end of round.
- Work Twisted Rib until the piece measures 1" (2.5 cm).

Working the Body

- Using larger 16" (40 cm) circular needle, knit around, increasing 8 stitches evenly spaced. (*80 stitches*)
- Work even in stockinette until the piece measures 5½" (14 cm) from the cast on, stopping 3 stitches before the end of round. Remove the marker.

Binding Off at Underarms and Dividing Front and Back

To separate the back and front, you bind off the bottom of the armholes. The bound-off stitches are centered over the beginning/end of round and at the halfway point directly across the garment. You have 80 stitches on the needle. Six stitches are allocated to each of the underarms, leaving 68 stitches to be divided equally between the front and the back: 34 for each. The easiest way to ensure that the correct stitches are bound off is to place markers on the needle before beginning to bind off. First place a marker 6 stitches from the beginning of the left needle point. When you begin knitting again, you'll bind off these 6 stitches, then remove the marker from the needle, but don't do it yet! Count 34 stitches past this marker and place another marker on the needle to mark the beginning of the other underarm. Count 6 stitches past this marker and place a third marker on the needle. These are the 6 stitches that you'll bind off for the other underarm. Finally, count from this last marker to the end of the needle. There

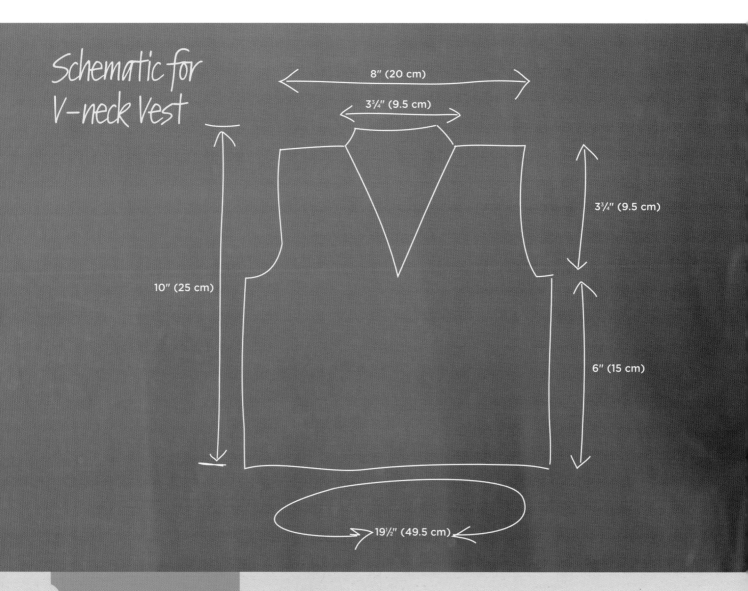

Schematic for V-neck Vest

8" (20 cm)

3¾" (9.5 cm)

3¾" (9.5 cm)

10" (25 cm)

6" (15 cm)

19½" (49.5 cm)

should be 34 stitches. If not, check the position of all the other markers and don't begin binding off until you have placed all of them correctly .

- Bind off the 6 stitches before the first marker. To bind off the last of these stitches you must remove the marker, knit the next stitch, and pass the sixth stitch over it.
- Knit to the second marker and remove it from the needle.
- Bind off the 6 stitches before the third marker. Once again, you'll have to remove the marker and knit 1 more stitch to bind off the sixth underarm stitch.
- Knit to the end of the round, where you won't be able to continue because of the gap created by the bound-off underarm stitches. The stitches you just finished knitting will be the back of the vest. Count them to make sure there are 34. The stitches on the opposite side of the needle, between the underarms, are for the front of the vest. Count them as well and make sure there are 34 . If either count is off, fix the problem before continuing.

Worked up to underarms (marked)

Underarms bound off

Shaping Back Armholes

The rest of the back is worked in flat, not circular, knitting. While you're working the back, the stitches for the front sit on the cable of the needle, patiently waiting for you to get back to them. If you find this annoying or it makes it difficult to measure the length of the back, you can slip the front stitches onto a separate circular needle. The next step is to decrease gradually at the armhole, to reduce the width of the back so it fits at the shoulders.

- Row 1 (wrong side): Turn and purl across.
- Row 2 (right side): K1, ssk, knit until 3 stitches remain, K2tog, K1. (*32 stitches remain*)
- Rows 3–6: Repeat Rows 1 and 2 twice. (*28 stitches remain*)
- Work even in stockinette stitch (knitting the right-side rows and purling the wrong-side rows) until the vest measures 10" (25 cm) from the cast on. Your last row should be a wrong-side row.
- Do not bind off. Cut the yarn, leaving a tail about 4" (10 cm) long to weave in later.

Shaping Front Armholes and Neck

You'll shape the front armholes exactly as you did the back, decreasing every other row three times. At the same time you'll divide the front in half to begin the neck and work decreases at the neck edges to shape the V. To shape the armhole edges, you will decrease 1 stitch at each armhole edge every other row, and for this vest, you'll shape the V-neck edges by decreasing every other row as well. You will need to use either two balls of yarn or two ends of a center-pull ball to work the two sections of the front. If you need to rewind your yarn to make this possible, do it now.

- Place a marker on the needle at the center of the front (17 stitches on each side of the center). Join one end/ball of yarn to the armhole edge of the front closest to the needle points, ready to work across on the wrong side.
- Row 1 (wrong side): Purl across the first half of the front. Change to the other ball/end of yarn and purl across the second half of the front.
- Row 2 (right side): *K1, ssk, knit until 3 stitches remain before the center marker, K2tog, K1. Drop the working yarn and use the second ball/end of yarn to repeat from * for the second half of the front. (*15 stitches remain in each half of the front*)
- Rows 3–6: Repeat Rows 1 and 2 two more times. (*11 stitches remain in each half of the front*)

After you've worked Row 1 the first time, it should be obvious where the center is, so remove the marker. The armhole shaping is now completed, but you will need to continue shaping the neck. To do this, on Rows 7–20 you'll stop decreasing at the armholes but continue to decrease at the neck edges.

- **Row 7:** (wrong side) Purl across the first half of the front. Change to the other ball/end of yarn and purl across the second half of the front.
- **Row 8:** (right side): Knit until 3 stitches remain before the center neck opening, K2tog, K1. Drop the working yarn and use the second ball/end of yarn. K1, ssk, knit to end of row.
- **Rows 9–20:** Repeat Rows 7 and 8 six more times. (*4 stitches remain in each half of the front*)

The shoulders may seem very narrow, but keep in mind that adding the neck border and the armhole border widens them significantly.

- Work even on both of the shoulders until the front is the same length as the back (about 5 more rows) **C**.

C

Back and front completed to shoulders

D

First shoulder joined with three-needle bind off

E

Second shoulder ready to join with three-needle bind off

F

Second shoulder joined

Joining the Shoulders

To set up for the Three-Needle Bind Off (page 69) that joins the shoulders, turn the vest inside out so that the chained seam of the bind off will be hidden on the inside.

- Bind off: Working from wherever you ended the final row of the fronts and using a third needle in the same size, work the Three-Needle Bind Off to join the 4 shoulder stitches of the front to the first 4 stitches of the back **D**. Do not cut yarn.
- Using the same yarn, continue binding off across the back neck, until just 4 stitches remain **E**.
- Join these last 4 stitches to the 4 stitches of the other front shoulder using the Three-Needle Bind Off.
- Cut both strands of working yarn, leaving ends about 4" (10 cm) long to weave in later. Turn the vest right side out **F**.

Working the Armhole Borders

Since a 16" (40 cm) needle is too long for the small armhole opening, use a set of double-pointed needles, a 12" (30 cm) circular needle, two circulars, or one long circular for the Magic Loop. If you find it difficult to pick up on the double points, you can use any length circular needle, then transfer the stitches to the double points before beginning to work on the border.

Because the armhole and neckline decreases were all worked a stitch away from the edge, you will see two straight columns of stitches that parallel the edge of the garment, making it easy to pick up stitches consistently. When picking up stitches, always insert your needle a whole stitch in from the edge, wrap the working yarn, and knit up a stitch through the fabric. For more details, see Picking Up Stitches, page 77, and Pick Up, pages 307–308.

- **Pickup Round:** Using the working yarn and needles two sizes smaller than those used to make the body, begin the pickup at the center of the underarm. Pick up and knit 1 stitch in each stitch across the bound-off stitches, and then 3 stitches for every 4 rows along the side of the armhole **G**. Continue until you get back to the beginning of the bound-off stitches, then pick up 1 stitch for each of them until you reach your starting point. Rearrange the stitches as necessary so you can work comfortably **H**. (*about 44 stitches*)

- Work Twisted Rib as for the bottom border. If you picked up an odd number of stitches, adjust for this when you reach the end of the first round by purling the last 2 stitches together. Continue in Twisted Rib until the border is ¾" (2 cm) wide.

- Bind off in pattern, remembering to knit into the back of the knit stitches as you bind off. Cut the yarn, leaving a tail about 4" (10 cm) long to weave in later. Use the tail to make the beginning and end of the bind off continuous (see pages 56–57).

- Repeat for the other armhole.

G Picking up border stitches at underarm

H Armhole pickup completed and on double points

I Stitches on left side of neck picked up

J Picking up strand at center front

K Knitting into back of strand

L Center stitch completed

Working the Neck Border

If you are a loose knitter, you may be able to work the neck border on a 16" (40 cm) circular needle. If it's not comfortable to do this, use a set of double points, a 12" (30 cm) circular needle, two circulars, or the Magic Loop. When you arrange the stitches, be sure to put at least 3 stitches on either side of the center V on one needle, so you can work the decreases for the mitered corner without transferring stitches between needles.

- Using a needle two sizes smaller than that used to make the body, start at the left shoulder seam and pick up 3 stitches for every 4 rows along the left side of the neck opening. Continue until you get to the center V **I**. (*about 20 stitches*)

- Work an M1 increase at the center, by first picking up the strand between the 2 stitches on each side of the V **J** and then knitting into the back of the strand on the needle **K** **L**. Mark this center stitch by placing a split marker in it.

- Continue up the other side of the V, taking care to pick up the first stitch in exactly the same row as you did the last stitch before the M1, so that the border is symmetrical (see photo below, right). Make sure you have the same number of stitches on this side as on the first side of the neck.
- Continue across the back of the neck, picking up about 17 stitches. You need an odd number across the back neck to make an even number of stitches total, so that the ribbed pattern can be centered properly. (about 58 stitches)

A centered double decrease (s2kp2) turns the corner neatly at the center front. If it is worked on every round, the neck border will pull in too quickly. If it's worked on alternate rounds, the border will flare. To achieve a happy medium, decrease on 2 rounds out of every 3, including the bind-off round. You must work the stitches immediately before and after the center decrease identically (either as knits or as purls) so that the pattern is symmetrical at the center front.

- Rounds 1 and 2: Work in Twisted Rib until 1 stitch remains before the marked center stitch. Notice whether you purled or knitted the stitch you just worked. Work s2kp2. Now work the following stitch exactly as you did the stitch before the decrease; if it was a knit, knit it through the back loop; if it was a purl, purl it.

- Round 3: Work in Twisted Rib as established, but do not decrease at the center front. Just knit the center stitch (but not through the back loop — this is not a twisted stitch).
- Bind-Off Round: Bind off in pattern, remembering to work into the back of the knit stitches. When 1 stitch remains before the marked center stitch, work the s2Kp2, and then bind off the stitch. Continue binding off in pattern to the end of the round.
- Cut the yarn and use the tail to make the beginning and end of round continuous (see pages 56–57).

Finishing
- Weave in all the ends on the inside.

Stitches on either side of the center should mirror each other.

V-NECK VEST
Any Size, Any Yarn

Work a circular gauge swatch to determine your stitches per inch (or cm) in stockinette. Decide how big around your vest should be, allowing "ease" so that it will fit comfortably over other clothing (see appendix for Craft Yarn Council website, which provides Garment Sizing Guidelines). Multiply the gauge by the desired circumference, and round that to a multiple of four.

Bottom border and body. So the bottom border will hold its shape, subtract 10 percent from this number to find the number of stitches to cast on. Work the border on needles two sizes smaller than the body. Change to the larger needles, increase to the correct number of stitches, and knit until the vest is the desired length to the underarm.

Armhole shaping. Figure out how wide you want the garment to be across the shoulders, and subtract the width of the armhole borders at both sides from this measurement. Multiply this times the gauge to find the number of stitches across the back at the shoulder. Double this number (to account for both the front and the back) and subtract it from the total body stitches on your needle. Divide this number by 4 to determine how many stitches to bind off at each underarm. Place markers to indicate the underarm bind offs as described in the instructions above, then bind them off on the next

round. Work back and forth across the back of the garment, decreasing 1 stitch at each armhole edge every right-side row until you get down to the desired number of stitches for the back at the shoulders.

V-Neck shaping. Figure out how wide you want the neck opening to be at the shoulders and multiply this by your gauge to find out the number of stitches. Divide this number in half to find the number of decreases on each side of the neck. Count the rows in the back from the armhole bind off up to the shoulder. Divide the number of rows by the number of neck decreases to find out how often to decrease. For example, if you need to decrease 11 times over 46 rows, 46 ÷ 11 = 4.2. You'll decrease at the neck edge every fourth row. Mark the center front and work the two sides of the front with separate balls of yarn. Remember as you start the V-neck shaping to also shape the underarms exactly as you did for the back. After the armhole decreases are completed, continue working the neck decreases. When the neck decreases are completed, work even until the front and back are the same length.

Finishing. Turn inside out. Join shoulders, bind off back neck, and work borders as described for V-Neck Vest above.

For a Different Look, Try This

Overlapping neck border. See Steeked V-Neck Vest (pages 264–272) for a neck border that is knit flat and then overlapped at the center front.

Back neck shaping. Bind off for the center back neck and then work the two back shoulders separately up to the shoulder seam, just as you did for the front. You need to plan ahead and start the back neck shaping at the right time to make the back and the front the same lengths. Also make sure you end up with the same number of stitches for all four shoulders. You can still use the Three-Needle Bind Off to join the shoulder seams, you just won't be able to continue across the back neck from one shoulder to the other because the back neck is already bound off. Back neck shaping is really an excellent idea because it significantly improves the fit of your vest. See Designing the Neck Opening (pages 262–263 for planning the neck opening.

Sloped shoulder shaping. You can work this conventionally, binding off groups of stitches to form a slope, or you can work short-row shaping. The advantage of short-row shaping is that you are still able to use the Three-Needle Bind Off to join the shoulder seams. How many fewer stitches should you work for each short row? That depends on how much slope you want. Figure out how tall you want the slope to be in rows and divide this by two. This gives you the number of short rows. Divide the number of stitches at the shoulder by the number of short rows, which gives you the *stitch increment*. The stitch increment is the number of stitches you leave unworked each time you turn at the end of a short row. The stitch increment probably won't be a whole number, so round it off and fudge a bit toward the end of the process. To work the shaping, start at the neck edge and work across until only the stitch increment remains unworked. Wrap-and-turn (see Short Rows in the Appendix, pages 308–309, for how to do this), then work all the way back to the neck edge and repeat the process, working one increment fewer stitches each time. For example, if you figured out that your stitch increment is 6, on the first short row you'd turn back leaving 6 stitches unworked; on the second short row you'd turn back leaving 12 stitches unworked, and so on, until all of the stitches are unworked. Finish up by working one row all the way across, picking up the wraps and knitting (or purling) them together with their stitch so that they fall to the back of the fabric.

SLEEVE AND ARMHOLE OPTIONS

The basic V-Neck Vest can easily be modified to serve as the body of a sweater. For the vest, the armholes are enlarged to allow for the addition of borders. In order to attach sleeves, the armholes must be smaller — the same size as the finished armhole including the border, so that the shoulder line falls at the wearer's shoulder Ⓐ. Alternatively, you can omit the armhole shaping altogether and make a basic T-shaped garment Ⓑ.

After you have joined the shoulders, use a circular needle to pick up and knit stitches all the way around the armhole (about 3 stitches for every 4 rows along the sides and 1 stitch for every stitch in bound-off sections). Knit the sleeve from the top down, referring to the directions for the Top-Down Raglan Sleeve Sweater, pages 280–285.

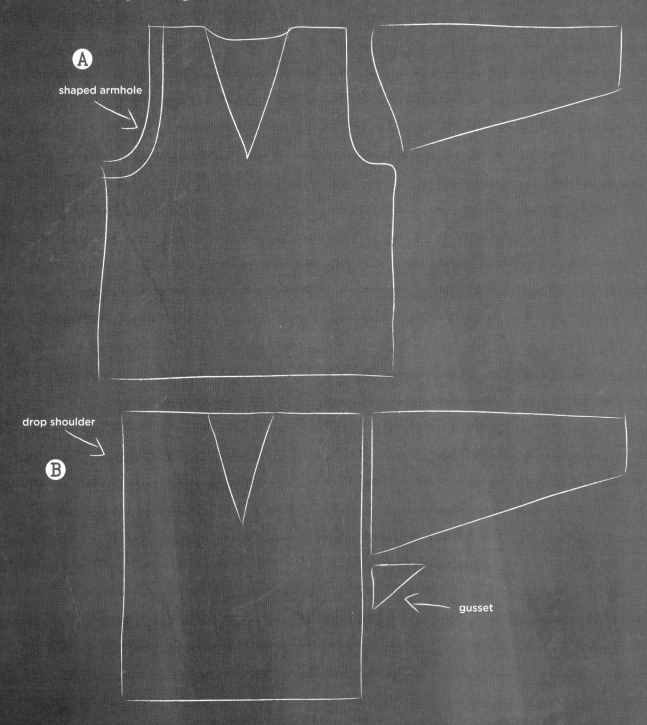

Ⓐ shaped armhole

Ⓑ drop shoulder

gusset

Gussets. If you're making a drop-shoulder T-shaped sweater, then you have the option of adding an underarm gusset to improve the fit. See the discussion of gussets in the Sleeve Variations for the Steeked V-Neck Vest, page 272. You must plan ahead for the gussets and add them at both sides of the body as you approach the underarm.

Sleeve Caps. If you prefer a shaped sleeve cap, create it using short rows as follows: After picking up stitches around the armhole, work around to the shoulder. Work a few stitches past the shoulder seam, then turn and work back to the same number of stitches on the other side of the shoulder seam. Turn again and continue working a few stitches further each time. If you have a shaped armhole, stop turning and working short rows when you reach the bound-off stitches at the underarm. If you are making a drop-shouldered, T-shaped sweater, keep working short rows until you reach the center of the underarm. In either case, work the sleeve circularly from this point down to the bottom cuff. (See the Top-Down Raglan Sleeve Sweater, pages 280–285, for a tapered top-down sleeve. For a complete description of working short rows, see the appendix, pages 308–309.)

How many additional stitches should you work for each short row? That depends on how high you want your sleeve cap to be and how many stitches there are in your armhole. Here's how you figure that out:

- Decide how tall you want the cap to be: for an adult sweater, this could be anywhere from 1" (2.5 cm) up. Measure the cap in sweaters you like the fit of to get an idea of how tall the sleeve cap should be.

- Measure the rows per inch (or centimeter) in your washed and blocked swatch and then multiply by the number of inches (or centimeters) in the sleeve cap. Divide this by two. This gives you the number of sets of short rows.

- If you're making a T, count the stitches all the way around the armhole. If you've got a shaped armhole, don't include the underarm bind off in your count.

- Divide the number of stitches around your armhole by the number of short rows: this is the number of additional stitches to work on each short row. It probably won't come out to be a whole number, so round it off and fudge a bit toward the end of the process.

Tapered Sleeves. To make a tapered sleeve exactly the right length, you first need to know how many stitches there are at the cuff just above the border, how many stitches there are at the underarm (the widest point), and how many rounds there are between these two points. Calculate all of these based on your gauge, then you can calculate how often to work decreases (or increases if you are working from the bottom up) to taper the sleeve.

Shaping rounds = (Stitches at underarm − Stitches at cuff) ÷ 2

Frequency = Rounds between cuff and underarm ÷ Shaping rounds

Here's an example, assuming you need 44 stitches at the cuff, 112 stitches at the underarm, and there are 140 rounds between the two.

- Shaping rounds = (112 − 44) ÷ 2 = 34. (If your calculation isn't a whole number, round up or down to get a whole number.) There will be 34 shaping rounds. On each you will decrease (or increase) 2 stitches, one on each side of the beginning/end of round.

- Divide the total number of rounds by the number of shaping rounds plus 1 to get the frequency. Frequency = 140 ÷ 35 = 4. (If your calculation isn't a whole number, round it up or down to get a whole number.) You will work shaping on every fourth round. Working 34 shaping rounds every fourth round will take only 136 rounds (34 × 4 = 136). Work 4 more rounds after the final shaping round to reach the desired length of 140 rounds. (If your calculation results in additional rounds to be worked to reach the required length, divide them between the top and bottom of the sleeve.)

DESIGNING THE NECK OPENING

Before designing a neck opening, you need to know how big the opening is. There are three measurements:

- The width at the shoulders Ⓐ
- The depth from the shoulder to the bottom of the front neck opening Ⓑ
- The depth from the shoulder to the bottom of the back neck opening Ⓒ

Using your gauge in rows and stitches per inch (or centimeter), multiply to figure out how many stitches or rows make up each of these measurements. For a sweater worked from the bottom up or top down, the width of the neck will be in stitches and the depth of each opening will be in rows Ⓓ. For a sweater worked from side to side, this will be reversed Ⓔ. The easiest way to get these measurements is to lay a sweater that fits out flat and measure it. Be sure to allow for any border that will be added after the sweater is completed. For example, if there will be a 1″ (2.5 cm) border all the way around, this means the width of the opening will need to be 2″ (5 cm) bigger and the depth of the front and the back will each need to be 1″ (2.5 cm) bigger, so that the opening will end up the right size with the border in place.

Once you know the number of stitches and rows, draw a rectangle that size on a piece of knitter's graph paper, which has rectangles in the proportions of the pattern stitch you will be using. For example, in stockinette stitch the stitches are wider than the rows are tall. The first example Ⓓ is a front that is 30 stitches wide by 21 rows deep paired with a back neck that is the same width but only 12 rows deep. To chart this yourself, you would draw a rectangle for the front that is 30 stitches wide by 21 rows deep, then sketch in a smooth curve across the bottom that looks like a reasonable neck shaping, and finally draw in the stair steps representing bind offs and decreases that most closely match the curve. Make sure that the shaping on each side is perfectly symmetrical. The back neck is charted the same way, but in a rectangle that's only 12 rows tall.

If you want to make a sideways sweater, then you need to chart the neck openings with the graph paper turned 90 degrees to match the direction you're knitting. The second example Ⓔ shows the same neck charted for sideways knitting. Note that with more rows across the neck and fewer stitches, the proportions come out the same as in Ⓓ.

When you knit the neck from your chart, first bind off all the stitches across the bottom of the opening. On subsequent rows, when there is more than one stitch to get rid of, bind off. When there is only one stitch, decrease it. If you are working a steek across the neck opening, it will be confusing, if not impossible, to work any bind offs after the first one, so rearrange the shaping so that they can all be worked one at a time as decreases.

To design a V-neck, the front measurement will be the depth to the point of the V. When you draw the front opening on graph paper, instead of drawing a curve, draw a diagonal line from the center point up to the corner of the neck.

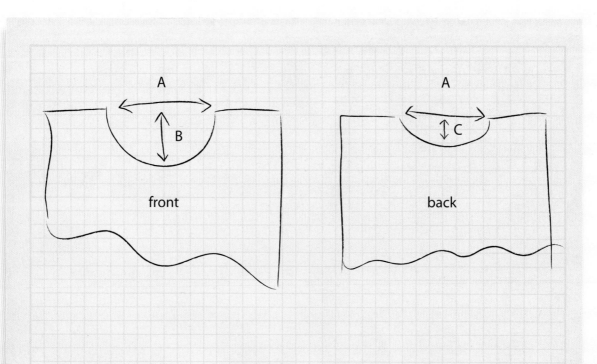

D Neck shaping for sweaters knit from the top or from the bottom

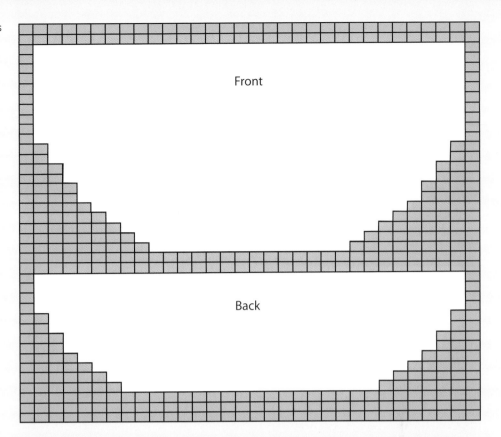

Front

Back

E Neck shaping for sweaters knit side to side

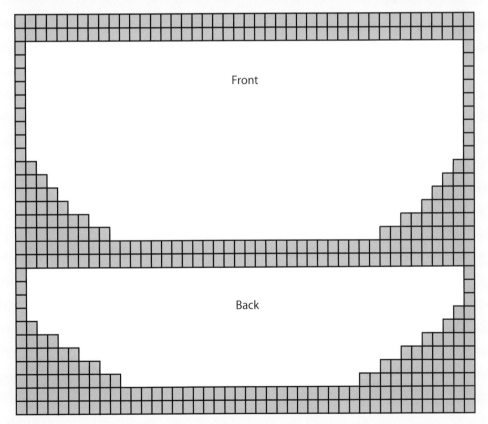

Front

Back

Steeked V-Neck Vest

This project builds on the V-Neck Vest (pages 252–259), which was knit circularly only up to the underarms, reverting to conventional flat shaping in the shoulder and neck areas, with no pattern stitch. This vest is knit circularly throughout, adding stranded color work and *steeks* that serve as bridges over the neck and armhole openings. Steeks are simply extra stitches that allow you to knit across the openings and to cut them open later. When working a pattern, this means that you never need to reverse it to work on the wrong side. When cut, the excess fabric in each steek rolls to the inside of the garment and becomes a seam allowance. To prevent the steeks from unraveling, they are sewn down after the borders are added.

New Techniques Used

- Stranded knitting (pages 206–209)
- Adding steeks and finishing them
- Overlapping front neck border

For Project Shown You Need

YARN	Lorna's Laces Shepherd Sport (100% superwash wool, 200 yards/ 2.6 oz)
YARN AMOUNT	110 yds/101 m Periwinkle (49ns); 40 yds/37 m China Blue (41ns); 10 yds/9 m Firefly (54ns); 8 yds/7 m Sunshine (40ns)
GAUGE	29 stitches and 34 rounds = 4" (10 cm) in stranded stockinette stitch
NEEDLE SIZE	US 4 (3.5 mm) needle(s) for body and US 3 (3.25 mm) needle(s) for borders. Match the project's gauge if you want finished measurements to match pattern instructions.
NEEDLE TYPES	*For body:* 16" (40 cm) circular needle plus one extra for Three-Needle Bind Off (the extra actually can be any length, any type) *For bottom border:* 16" (40 cm) circular needle one size smaller than that used for body *For armhole and neck borders:* a set of four or five double-point needles 7" (18 cm) or longer, a 12" (30 cm) circular needle, two circulars 16" (40 cm) or longer or one circular needle 47" (120 cm) or longer for Magic Loop
OTHER SUPPLIES	Stitch marker (optional), split marker, sharp sewing shears, sewing needle and thread or sewing machine, yarn needle
FINISHED SIZE	16¼" (41 cm) circumference × 9" (23 cm) length from shoulder to bottom

Except for the addition of color patterns and steeks, and the fact that you don't work any flat areas, this vest is identical in structure to the previous project. The proportions are a bit different from the first vest: longer and slimmer. This changes the rate of decrease on the neck, which is shaped on every fourth round rather than every other round.

You may notice that the borders are worked on a needle one size smaller than the body, rather than the usual rule of two sizes smaller. This is because the body is worked on a size 4 (3.5 mm) needle, and with such a small needle, going down one needle size is as big a change proportionally as going down two needles from a larger needle. Besides — you don't really want to have to work the borders on a size 2 (2.75 mm), do you?

Getting Started

- Using Periwinkle and smaller 16" (40 cm) circular needle, cast on 108 stitches. Join beginning and end of round, being careful not to twist the knitting (see Off to a Good Start: Casting On and Joining, page 13). You may want to mark the beginning and end of round with a stitch marker to prevent confusion.
- Ribbing: Work in K2, P2 ribbing for ¾" (2 cm).
- Setup Round 1 (increase round): Using larger 16" (40 cm) circular needle, knit around, increasing 12 stitches evenly spaced. (*120 stitches*)
- Next 3 Rounds: Knit 3 more rounds with Periwinkle.
- Next 30 Rounds: Using all four colors and stranded knitting, work Rounds 1–29 of chart (opposite). Work Round 30, stopping 5 stitches before the end of the round.

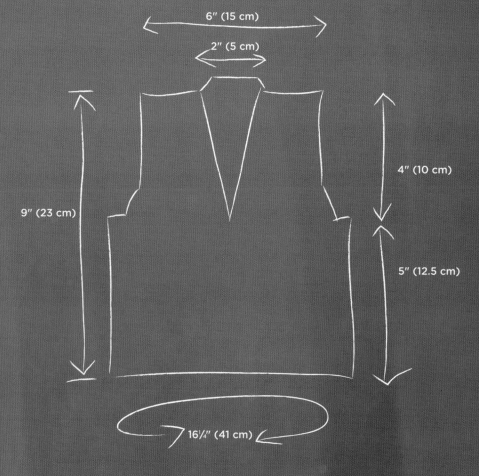

Schematic for Steeked V-neck Vest

6" (15 cm)

2" (5 cm)

4" (10 cm)

9" (23 cm)

5" (12.5 cm)

16¼" (41 cm)

Binding Off for the Armholes

You will bind off stitches at each underarm, leaving 49 stitches for the front and for the back. So you don't need to count stitches as you work around, you may want to place markers on each side of the 11 underarm stitches before working the next round, as described for the V-Neck Vest (pages 254–255). Because you are using both Periwinkle and China Blue, alternate the two colors as you bind off to carry them across the underarm, ready to be used on the other side of the underarm.

• Round 31: Bind off 11 stitches for the underarm. Work 48 more stitches, then bind off 11 stitches for the other underarm. (By knitting the 48 stitches, you bring the second underarm into alignment with the first.) Continue working in pattern as established until you get to the end of the round, where you bound off the first underarm stitches. Notice that you no longer start with stitch 1 of the chart on each round. Instead, as you begin each section of the front and the back, start with whatever stitch aligns the pattern properly with the fabric already knitted. For illustration of binding off the underarms, see the V-Neck Vest (page 255).

Before you work any farther, count the front and back stitches to be sure there are 49 of each. If not, unravel and correct the problem.

Casting On for the Steeks

In order to continue working circularly, you have to fill in the gaps above the bound-off underarms and also in the opening for the V-neck. Therefore, in Round 32 you will add *steeks* at the two armholes and the neck opening. These are just extra stitches that form seam allowances when you cut them later. Because you've just finished a round using Periwinkle and China Blue and the next round uses the same two colors, cast on stitches using these colors above the bound-off armholes and in the center front. When beginning steeks, you can use any cast on you like but must use both colors. If you use the Long-Tail Cast On, place one of the colors on your thumb and the other on your index finger (see Two-Color Long-Tail Cast On, page 303); if using Half-Hitch, Knitted, or Cable Cast On, alternate the colors as you cast on. Note that the beginning of round is at the center of the first armhole steek. This is where you change colors, if necessary, before beginning the following round. (See Working the Steeks, page 268.)

Stranded chart

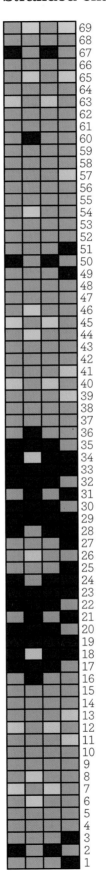

Periwinkle

China Blue

Firefly

Sunshine

- Round 32: Cast on 9 stitches, using both Periwinkle and China Blue 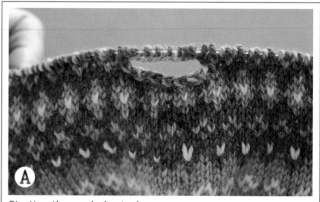. Continue around working in pattern for 24 stitches. The 25th stitch is the center front; take it off the needle and place it on a split marker. You'll use this stitch later when you pick up for the neck border. Cast on 9 stitches with both yarns for the neck steek . Continue in pattern until you reach the second armhole. Cast on 9 stitches with both yarns to bridge the gap, then continue in pattern across the back of the vest until you come to the steek at end of round.

Starting the armhole steek

Shaping the Armholes and Neck

To shape the armholes, decrease 1 stitch on both sides of each armhole every other round six times. To shape the neck, decrease 1 stitch on both sides of the neck opening every fourth round ten times. Round 33 is your first decrease round.

- Round 33 (decrease at both the armhole and the neck edges): For left front, *work steek stitches; K1, ssk, work in pattern as established for body until 3 stitches remain before the next steek, K2tog, K1; repeat from * once for right front, and once for back; then work to the center of the final steek.
- Round 34: Work in pattern as established (no decreases).

Starting the neck steek

WORKING THE STEEKS

Begin every round in the center of the first armhole steek, where you change colors if necessary, then continue around in pattern working the left front, the neck steek, the right front, the other armhole steek, and the back, ending at the center of the first armhole steek. If you're working just one color around, knit the steeks with that color. If you are working with two colors, alternate the two colors across the steeks to make vertical stripes while continuing to work the charted color pattern across the fronts and back. The noticeably different color patterns of the steeks function as visual markers between the different sections of the garment; the vertical stripes also serve as cutting lines when it's time to cut the garment open .

The beginning of round is now at the center of the armhole steek between the back and the left front. When you come to the center of that steek, stop and see what colors are required for the following round. Make the color change at the center of the steek. If there's a color you won't be using on the following round, check before you cut it to see how soon you'll need it again. If it's within a few rounds, just leave it attached and carry it straight up the center of the steek when you're ready to bring it back into use.

For example, Round 32 used China Blue and Periwinkle, but Round 33 requires only China Blue. Periwinkle comes in again just 2 rounds later, so there's no need to cut it. Continue across the second half of the steek using China Blue and complete Round 33. On Round 34, you need both China Blue and Sunshine. At the center of the steek, start alternating Sunshine with China Blue, leaving a short tail hanging. At the end of Round 34, you can either cut the Sunshine, or leave it attached to be used 4 rounds later. To prepare for Round 35, pick up Periwinkle again at the center of the steek and start alternating it with China Blue.

Working the steek

- Round 35: Repeat Round 33, but make decreases only at the armholes, not the neck.
- Round 36: Work in pattern as established (no decreases).
- Rounds 37–44: Repeat Rounds 33–36, continuing to work the charted stranded pattern while decreasing at both the armhole and neck edges. (*6 sets of armhole decreases and 3 sets of neck decreases completed, with 37 back stitches and 15 stitches each front remaining*)
- Rounds 45–69: Continue the steeks and complete the charted pattern, but decrease only at the neck edges every fourth round; on the last round, stop at the beginning of the armhole steek, just short of end of round **D**. (*8 stitches remain for each front shoulder*)

Binding Off the Steeks

- Round 70: Continuing to work with Periwinkle, bind off the 9 steek stitches at the first armhole, knit across the 8 front shoulder stitches, bind off 9 steek stitches at the neck, knit across 8 stitches for the second shoulder, bind off 9 steek stitches at the other armhole, and knit across the 37 remaining stitches of the back. Do not cut yarn **E**.

Ready to bind off steeks

Steeks bound off

Because this garment is so small, it can be difficult to prepare the steeks for cutting if you wait until after the shoulders have been joined. If you plan to use a sewing machine to secure the steek stitches, temporarily transfer the front and back stitches to pieces of waste yarn now and sew as described in Preparing and Cutting the Steeks below. When you make a full-sized garment, this is not a problem, so you can first join the shoulders to get the stitches off the needles and then worry about securing the steeks.

Joining the Shoulders

- Turn the vest inside out. Using another needle the same size, join the 8 stitches of the front shoulder to the first 8 stitches of the back using the Three-Needle Bind Off (page 69) **F**.
- Continue across the back, binding off until 8 stitches remain of the back.
- Use the Three-Needle Bind Off to join the second front shoulder to the back.
- Cut the yarn, leaving a tail about 4" (10 cm) long to weave in later, and turn the vest right side out again.

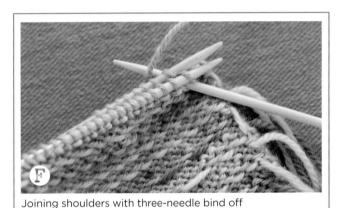

Joining shoulders with three-needle bind off

Preparing and Cutting the Steeks

The yarn I used for this vest is superwash wool, which means that it doesn't felt, even when machine washed. This presents a problem when working with steeks because they rely on the natural felting properties of animal fibers to secure them permanently so the cut areas don't unravel. To prevent this, prepare the steek by securing the stitches with machine or hand stitching on either side of the center stitch. Be careful not to sew across this center stitch, because the thread will be cut when you cut the steek.

My preference is to use a zigzag stitch when sewing by machine, and an overcast stitch when sewing by hand, because both of these stretch with the knitting. If you work a steeked garment in cotton, silk, a tightly spun tightly plied wool or any other fiber that doesn't felt, it's extremely important to secure the steek stitches this way

Steeks prepared for cutting

H
Cutting the steek

I
Picking up border stitches

before you cut **G**. On the other hand, if you're working with a natural wool that's loosely spun and plied, which you can rely on to felt, you can steam the steek, wash it and let it dry, or just let it sit for a few days before cutting. The wool will become crimped so it doesn't unravel immediately; felting will begin as soon as the sweater is worn, permanently securing the cut ends.

Cut straight up the center stitch of the steek. Use a pair of sharp sewing shears; dull ones will pull and distort the stitches and make the process even more nerve-wracking. Be very careful not to cut any of the strands on the inside of the opposite half of the garment. You can insert a folded newspaper, magazine, or piece of cardboard into the garment to protect the opposite side from your shears **H**.

Cut one steek at a time, work the border, and finish the cut edges before cutting the next steek. The steek at the beginning/end of round will almost certainly sport longer yarn tails from when you changed colors. Just trim these even with the edge so they don't get in your way while working the borders.

Working the Armhole Borders

See the V-Neck Vest for a detailed description of how to pick up stitches around an armhole (pages 256–257). This armhole is too small to fit around a 16" (40 cm) circular needle, so choose one of the alternative needles. It's easier to pick up the stitches with a circular needle than with double points. After you pick the stitches up, move them to double points or two circular needles, and rearrange them to work comfortably.

- Pickup Round: Use Periwinkle yarn and needles one size smaller than you used for the body. The steek naturally rolls to the inside after it's cut. Pinch the fabric to make a fold with the first stitch of the garment at the very edge and all the steek stitches to the inside. Pick up stitches for the border by inserting the needle under both strands of the edge stitch, wrapping the yarn, and knitting up a stitch. Starting at the center of the underarm bind off, pick up 1 stitch in each stitch of the bind off, then continue up the side of the armhole, picking up 3 stitches for every 4 rows **I**.

Because all the decreases are 1 stitch away from the edge, there is one neat, easy-to-follow column of stitches running all the way from the bottom of the armhole to the shoulder seam. The armhole border should have a total of about 72 stitches; make sure you have a multiple of 4 stitches. If you need to adjust, decrease a few stitches at the lower corners of the armhole when you work the first round.

- Rounds 1–3: Work in K2, P2 ribbing.
- Bind off in knitting. Cut the yarn, leaving a tail about 4" (10 cm) long to weave in later. Use it to make the beginning and end of the bind off continuous (see Making the Bind Off Look Continuous, pages 56–57), then weave it in.

Picking Up for the Neck Border

- Pickup Round: Use a circular needle one size smaller than the one you used for the body and Periwinkle yarn. Leaving a tail of about 6" (15 cm), begin by knitting the stitch you set aside at center front. Work your way up the right-hand side of the neck opening, folding the steek to the inside and picking up 3 stitches for every 4 rows exactly as you did for the armholes. (*about 28 stitches in addition to the center stitch*)
- Pick up 1 stitch in each stitch across the back neck. (*about 21 stitches*)
- Pick up along the second side of the neck as you did for the first side. (*about 28 stitches; a total of about 78 stitches*)

The ribbing is set up so that, on the right side, it begins and ends with two knit stitches. This will look nice and neat when you sew it down. You need a multiple of 4 stitches plus 2 to make the neckband begin and end with 2 knit stitches. If you don't end up with a multiple of 4 plus 2, adjust when you work the first row by decreasing a few stitches at the corners where the fronts meet the back and across the back neck, if necessary. The neck border is worked flat, not circularly, so turn and work the first row on the wrong side.

- Row 1 (wrong side): P2, *K2, P2; repeat from * to the end of the neck border.
- Row 2: K2, *P2, K2; repeat from * to the end of the neck border.
- Row 3: Repeat Row 1.
- Bind off in knitting on the right side.
- Cut the yarn, leaving a 6" (15 cm) tail. Overlap the two ends of the border and use the two tails (from the beginning and end of this border) to sew them down. On the outside of the garment you want your sewing to be as invisible as possible. Sew neatly up the center of the last stitch of the border, tacking it down or overcast directly over the slanted outer half of the knit stitches so that your sewing looks like it's part of the stitch.

Finishing the Steeks

After you finish each border, turn the vest inside out and finish the steek at that opening. The cut ends will have frayed; use your sharp sewing shears to trim the frayed yarn but avoid cutting the protective sewing thread. Tuck the cut edge of the steek to the inside to form a neat hem against the wrong side of the garment. Use a yarn needle and a strand of the background color (Periwinkle) to sew the hem to the strands on the back of the fabric. For less bulk, assuming you are using a plied yarn, you can pull the yarn apart and sew with just one or two plies. Take care not to sew all the way through so the stitches don't show on the outside of the garment.

As you can feel, the hemmed steek is fairly bulky even in sport-weight yarn. In worsted weight or thicker, it would be excessively thick and lumpy. If you wish to steek a sweater in a heavier yarn, don't tuck the edge under. Trim it as neatly as you can, flatten it against the inside of the garment, and work overcast stitches around, sewing the steek to the strands on the back of the fabric. If you have not secured the steek stitches by machine or hand sewing them, overcast a second time in the opposite direction, making crossed stitches that cover the edge and prevent it from fraying.

Finishing

- There will be lots of strands below the underarm at the beginning/end of round. Weave in these and all the other ends on the back of the fabric. Your knitting will look puckered and uneven until you've blocked it (see Stranded Knitting Basics: Blocking, page 209).

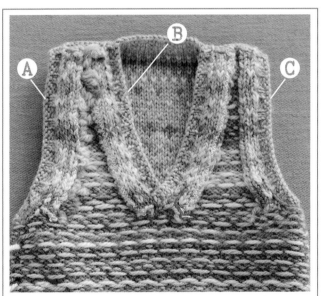

Ⓐ Left armhole border picked up; steek untrimmed, ready for finishing; Ⓑ neck border complete; raveled edges of steek trimmed; Ⓒ right armhole steek hemmed and complete

STEEKED V-NECK VEST

Any Size, Any Yarn

Because it's the same shape, follow the Any Size, Any Yarn guidelines for the V-Neck Vest (page 258) to calculate the number of stitches and shaping to design your own Steeked V-Neck Vest, with these exceptions:

- You'll need a multiple of four stitches for the ribbing and to start the body. Above the underarms, you must have an odd number of stitches for the front and back to center the pattern.

- Follow the general directions for the Steeked V-Neck Vest, using your own stitch counts and shaping.
- Repeat sections of the chart until the vest is as long as you want it. For example, repeat rounds 1–51 until you reach the narrow part of the shoulders, then finish it off with the simpler pattern in rounds 52–69.

For a Different Look, Try This

Round Neck

First chart the shape of the neck opening (see Designing the Neck Opening, pages 262–263). A round neck will start higher than the V-neck, so start the armhole steeks, but continue working the front without a steek until you reach the point where the bottom of the neck opening should be bound off. Handle this exactly as you did the armholes, by binding off the requisite stitches and then casting on 9 steek stitches on the next round. Shape the sides of the neck opening by working decreases at least 1 stitch away from the steek, working a K2tog decrease before the opening and an ssk decrease after it. Many neck shapings call for binding off a few stitches at each neck edge on several additional rows, but this can be problematic when working with steeks. Instead, if the neck shaping calls for binding off 2 stitches, simply decrease 1 stitch on each of the next 2 rounds. If the neck shaping entails binding off larger groups of stitches, bind off the first group at the center and start the steek. Figure out the total number of bound-off stitches plus decreases that remain to be worked on each side of the neck. Get rid of the first half of these by decreasing one stitch at each neck edge every round, and then decrease the rest by working the decreases every other round. This will give your neckline a perfect curve.

Cardigan

For an open cardigan front, you need a steek for the front opening. It can begin at the bottom edge when you cast on or, if the bottom border will be just one color, the steek can begin after the border is completed. To start the steek at the bottom edge, just cast on an additional 9 stitches and work the steek centered over the beginning of round and the bottom border on the remaining stitches. If you are working a single-color border, work the bottom border flat, with a knit rib at each end. When the border is complete, cast on 9 stitches for the front steek, join into a round and begin working circularly. Remember to alternate colors across the steek whenever two colors are in use and to change yarns at the center of the steek. Notice that the front steek rather than the underarm is the beginning of round. When you get to the neck shaping, you won't need to start a new steek for the neck: this steek just continues up to the shoulder line.

- **Back neck shaping** is worked exactly the same as round front neck shaping, but it's shallower and begins higher up. To design the back neck, see Designing the Neck Opening (pages 262–263). You'll need a fourth steek at the center back to accommodate it.

- **Sleeves** are most easily added if the garment is a simple drop-shouldered shape. When you get to the underarm, do not bind off any stitches, just cast on 9 steek stitches for each armhole and continue working the armholes straight up to the shoulder. After the shoulders have been joined, prepare and cut the steek, then pick up stitches around the armhole and work the sleeves, tapering down to the cuff. (See the Top-Down Raglan-Sleeve Sweater, page 284, for an example of this type of sleeve.)

- **Gussets.** If you are planning to add sleeves, then you can also add underarm gussets for additional shaping. These are made exactly like a thumb gusset (see Working the Hand, page 231), starting 2"–3" (5–7.5 cm) below the underarm on the body. When working stranded knitting, the gussets are usually worked in a simple checkerboard pattern, because they don't fit into the existing pattern repeat. When you reach the underarm, place the gusset stitches on a piece of waste yarn and then cast on the steek stitches above them on the following round. When you pick up the sleeve stitches around the armhole, knit the gusset stitches too. As you work the sleeve in its pattern stitch, continue to work the gusset stitches in their simpler pattern while decreasing the gusset stitches until they disappear. Work the gusset decreases just as for the thumb gusset (Working the Gusset, page 244), then taper the sleeve as usual down to the cuff.

Circular Yoked Sweater

Circular yoked sweaters are the simplest of seamless circular sweater constructions, popular particularly in Iceland where stranded patterns are worked just
above the bottom band and cuffs and throughout the yoke. This example is
worked with striped garter stitch borders and yoke instead.

For Project Shown You Need

YARN	Lorna's Laces Shepherd Worsted (100% superwash wool, 225 yards/4 oz)
YARN AMOUNT	225 yds/206 m Grapevine (3ns), 70 yds/64 m Periwinkle (49ns), and 40 yds/37 m China Blue (41ns)
GAUGE	20 stitches and 30 rounds = 4" (10 cm) in stockinette stitch
NEEDLE SIZE	US 7 (4.5 mm) and needles two sizes smaller for borders. Match the project's gauge if you want finished measurements to match pattern instructions. For specific information about the needles required for this project, see Needle Types for Circular Yoked Sweater, page 274.
OTHER SUPPLIES	Split markers, 18" (46 cm) of waste yarn or a spare circular needle or double points to use as a stitch holder, 1 yd (1 m) of waste yarn cut into four pieces to hold the underarm stitches, yarn needle
FINISHED SIZE	18.5" (47 cm) circumference and 10" (25.5 cm) length (shoulder to bottom)

New Techniques Used

- Tapering sleeves
- Garter stitch stripes
- Joining sleeves and body in a circular yoke
- Shaping a circular yoke
- Kitchener stitch to join underarms

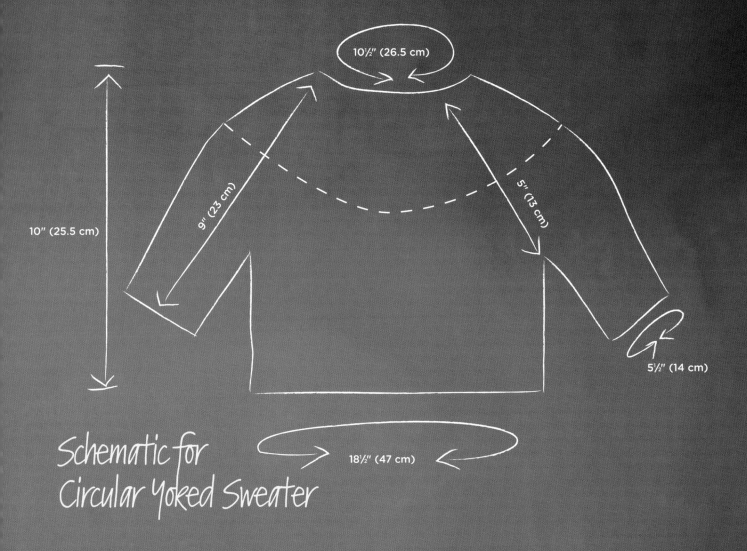

10½" (26.5 cm)

10" (25.5 cm)

9" (23 cm)

5" (13 cm)

5½" (14 cm)

Schematic for
Circular Yoked Sweater

18½" (47 cm)

NEEDLE TYPES FOR CIRCULAR YOKED SWEATER

You need quite an array of needles in order to complete this project. Notice that the bottom borders are worked on smaller needles. This is because garter stitch is wider than stockinette stitch — working it on smaller needles prevents the borders from flaring and flipping up.

For the bottom border, body, and beginning of yoke: The body and the beginning of the yoke are large enough that they can be worked on a single 16" (40 cm) circular needle. You'll need two sizes: one for the body and one 2 sizes smaller for the bottom border.

For the sleeves and neck: The sleeves and the area around the neck opening are narrow and must be worked using one of the methods for small tubes (see page 39-47): a set of four or five double-pointed needles, two circular needles at least 16" (40 cm), or a long (47"/120 cm) circular needle for Magic Loop. The instructions assume you are using double points. If you prefer to use two circular needles or Magic Loop, you may substitute these at any point.

Project Overview

- First, construct a large tube for the body, worked up to the underarms and then set aside.
- Work two smaller, tapered tubes for the sleeves up to the underarms. (The sleeves in this project are just three-quarter length, because you learn just as much by making a shorter sleeve as making a longer one.)
- Place the stitches for the underarms of the sleeves and the matching stitches for the underarms of the body on pieces of yarn; assemble the sleeves and body on one circular needle.
- Decrease the yoke up to the neck, ending with the neck border.
- To finish, Kitchener stitch (pages 70–74) the underarms together, and weave in the loose ends.
- The instructions call for you to cut the yarn each time you change colors. While it's not possible in garter stitch to make the color changes look absolutely perfect at the beginning/end of round jog, weaving in the ends behind the same color using duplicate stitch on the wrong side can still go a long way toward concealing it (see Stripes Without the Stair Step, pages 97–98). If you dislike weaving in ends and don't care about hiding the jog, then carry the Grapevine and Periwinkle yarns from round to round without cutting.

Border Pattern Stitch

The border pattern is worked in garter stitch. Every time you work one knit round followed by one purl round, it will make one garter stitch ridge. The first ridge, in Grapevine, is made by the cast-on round followed by Round 1. You'll change colors before starting the knit round that begins each ridge. When you cut each yarn, leave tails about 4" (10 cm) to weave in later.

- Round 1: Using Grapevine, purl 1 round, making one garter stitch ridge. Cut yarn.
- Rounds 2 and 3: Using Periwinkle, knit 1 round, then purl 1 round, making one garter stitch ridge. Cut yarn.
- Rounds 4 and 5: Using China blue, knit 1 round, then purl 1 round, making one garter stitch ridge. Cut yarn.
- Rounds 6 and 7: Using Periwinkle, knit 1 round, then purl 1 round, making one garter stitch ridge. Cut yarn.
- Rounds 8 and 9: Using Grapevine, knit 1 round, then purl 1 round, making one garter stitch ridge. Do not cut yarn.

You've completed five ridges of garter stitch.

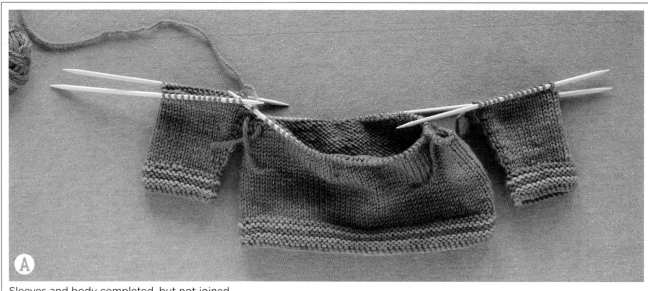

Sleeves and body completed, but not joined

Yoke Pattern Stitch

- Rounds 1 and 2: Using Grapevine, knit 1 round, then purl 1 round. Cut yarn.
- Rounds 3 and 4: Using Periwinkle, knit 1 round, then purl 1 round. Cut yarn.
- Rounds 5 and 6: Using China Blue, knit 1 round, then purl 1 round. Cut yarn.
- Rounds 7 and 8: Using Periwinkle, knit 1 round, then purl 1 round. Cut yarn.
- Rounds 9 and 10: Using Grapevine, knit 1 round, then purl 1 round. Do not cut yarn.
- Rounds 11 and 12: Using Grapevine, knit 1 round, then purl 1 round. Do not cut yarn.
- You've completed six ridges of garter stitch.

Working the Bottom Border

- Using smaller 16" (40 cm) circular needle and Grapevine, cast on 96 stitches. Join beginning and end of round, being careful not to twist the knitting (see Off to a Good Start: Casting On and Joining, page 13).
- Rounds 1–9: Work Border Pattern, page 275.

Working the Body

The body is just a straight tube worked in stockinette stitch.

- Continuing with Grapevine and larger 16" (40 cm) circular needle, knit all rounds until the sweater measures 4⅝" (12 cm) from the cast-on edge.
- Divide for underarms: K52, place the last 9 stitches you worked on a piece of waste yarn for the underarm; K48. You are now 4 stitches past the end of the round; place the last 9 stitches you worked on a piece of waste

yarn for the second underarm. Cut yarn, leaving a tail to weave in later. Leave stitches on a needle (preferably this needle) while you work the sleeves. (*39 stitches remain for the front; 39 stitches remain for the back*)

Working the Sleeves

The sleeves begin with a garter stitch border to match the body, then increases are worked along a "seam" stitch every fourth round to taper the sleeve. The increases should mirror each other on either side of the seam stitch. You can work your increases a number of different ways. Just a few examples are to work M1L before the seam stitch and M1R after it, or work M1R before and M1L after, or Kfb into the stitch before the seam stitch and into the seam stitch itself.

- Using Grapevine and double-pointed needles two sizes smaller than for body, cast on 28 stitches. Join beginning and end of round, being careful not to twist the cast on around the needle.
- Rounds 1–9: Work the Border Pattern, page 275. Place a marker in the last stitch of the round to identify it as the seam stitch.
- Next Rounds: Continuing with Grapevine and using double-pointed needles two sizes larger, work in stockinette to top of sleeve, increasing 1 stitch every fourth round before and after the marked stitch until there are 38 stitches and the sleeve measures about 4" (10 cm) from the cast on.
- Last Round: Knit 4 stitches past the marked stitch; place the last 9 stitches worked on a piece of waste yarn. The marked stitch should be at the center of these 9 stitches. Cut the yarn, leaving a tail about 4" (10 cm) long to weave in later and remove the marker. Leave the sleeve stitches on a circular needle, two

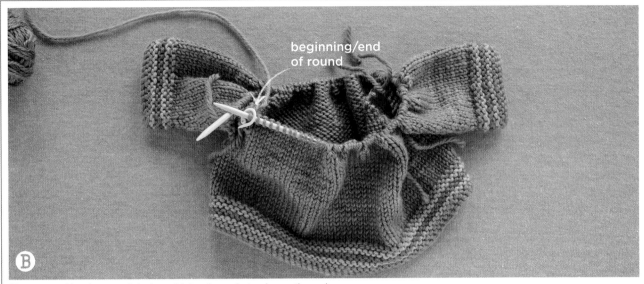

Sleeves and body completed, and joined, ready to shape the yoke.

extra double points, or a piece of waste yarn until the second sleeve is completed. (*29 stitches remain*)

- Make a second sleeve identical to the first one, but do not cut the yarn when it is completed. Leave it on the needles Ⓐ.

Joining Body and Sleeves

Before shaping the yoke, you'll assemble the body and the sleeves on one needle by knitting across each of them, then you'll work even for a while to ensure a comfortable fit. If you start decreasing a circular yoke immediately after the sleeves are joined to the body, the underarms will be tight and uncomfortable.

- Joining Round: Using the yarn still attached to the second sleeve, knit the stitches from this sleeve onto the same needle as the body. The 9 underarm stitches of the sleeve should face 9 matching underarm stitches of the body. Knit around the body to the second underarm. Knit the stitches from the other sleeve onto the same needle as the body. Again, the sleeve's underarm should face the body's underarm. Knit the remaining 39 stitches of the body. Place a marker at this point to indicate the beginning/end of round Ⓑ. (*136 stitches*)

A 16" (40 cm) circular needle may seem quite full with so many stitches on it. If it's more comfortable, you can work the yoke on a 24" (60 cm) needle until it becomes too narrow. As you approach the neckline, change to double points, two circular needles or Magic Loop.

- Work even in stockinette with Grapevine until the yoke measures 1½" (4 cm) from the underarm.

Shaping the Yoke

The Yoke Pattern on page 276 is a variation on the Border Pattern, with extra ridges of Grapevine added. In the upper section of the yoke, you'll decrease 8 stitches on each of the knit rounds. This is exactly the way that hats, bags, placemats, and coasters were shaped in chapters 6 and 7, with decreases and increases staggered so that they aren't noticeable (see Staggered vs. Swirled Increases, page 126). When you cut each yarn, leave tails about 4" (10 cm) long to weave in later.

- Rounds 1–12: Work Rounds 1–12 of the Yoke Pattern.
- Rounds 13–24: Work the garter-stripe Yoke Pattern Rounds 1–12, and decrease 8 stitches evenly spaced on all the knit rounds, being careful to stagger the decreases so they don't line up with decreases from preceding rounds. (*88 stitches remain*)
- Rounds 25–32: Work Rounds 1–8 of the Yoke Pattern, continuing to decrease on all the knit rounds. (*56 stitches remain*)

Working the Neck Band

- Work the entire band in Grapevine.
- Beginning with a knit round, work 5 rounds in garter stitch.
- Bind off loosely in purl (or turn to the wrong side and bind off in knitting).
- Cut the yarn, leaving a tail about 4" (10 cm) long to weave in later, and use it to make the beginning and end of the bind off look continuous (see pages 56–57).

Finishing the Underarms

- Place underarm stitches on two needles. Cut a piece of Grapevine about 21" (53 cm) long; this allows 1" (2.5 cm) for each stitch of the underarm, plus 6" (15 cm) on each end. Thread this piece of yarn into a yarn needle. Leaving a 6" (15 cm) tail hanging as you begin, use Kitchener stitch (pages 70–74) to join the underarm stitches . When all the stitches have been joined, use the tails to close up the holes that always remain at the ends of the seam. Weave in all other ends.

Underarm being joined with Kitchener stitch

Any Size, Any Yarn

Work a circular gauge swatch to determine your stitches per inch (or cm) in stockinette. Multiply this by the desired circumference for the body and round that to an even number. (See appendix for Craft Yarn Council website, which provides Garment Sizing Guidelines.) Cast on this number of stitches, make a bottom border any way you like (see Ribbed Borders on the facing page), then knit the desired length to the underarm. Transfer 9 percent of the body stitches to pieces of waste yarn for each of the underarms. To figure out how many stitches this is, multiply the number of body stitches by 0.09. (For example, in the Circular Yoked Sweater, 96 stitches × 0.09 = 8.64, which is rounded to 9 stitches.) Make sure that there are the same number of stitches for the front and the back, or your sleeves won't be opposite each other.

Begin the three-quarter-length sleeves with 30 percent of the body stitches. (For the Circular Yoked Sweater, 96 × 0.30 = 28.8, which I rounded down to 28 in order to have an even number.) If you prefer full-length sleeves, begin with 25 percent of the body stitches. Work the sleeve cuff, then increase 2 stitches at the beginning/end of round every fourth round until the sleeve is about 1½" (4 cm) below the underarm of the intended wearer. Set aside the same number of underarm stitches on waste yarn as for the body and make a second sleeve just like the first.

Join all three pieces just as described for the Circular Yoked Sweater; that is, work around, knitting across one sleeve, half of the body, the other sleeve, and the second half of the body, then place a marker for the beginning/end of round.

The length of the yoke from the underarm to the neck is about one-fourth the circumference of the body. In our little sweater, the body is 19" (48 cm), and the yoke is about 4¾" (12 cm). It is better to make the yoke a little longer rather than too short. Work the first half of it without any decreases. During the second half of the yoke, decrease 8 stitches every other round, staggering the decreases so they aren't noticeable (see Staggered vs. Swirled Increases, page 126). When you reach the number of stitches that will make your neck opening the correct size (if necessary, you can adjust by decreasing fewer stitches on the final decrease round), work the neck band without decreasing, then bind off. Join the underarm seams using Kitchener stitch.

I owe a great deal to Elizabeth Zimmermann's explanation of how to make a circular yoked sweater in *Knitting Without Tears,* but my proportions for sleeves and underarms differ slightly from hers because I prefer looser sleeves.

The Top-Down Approach

This sweater can very easily be made from the top down. Just cast on the 56 stitches for the neck, work the border, then increase 8 stitches on the knit rounds as you work the striped Yoke Pattern until you reach 136 stitches. Work even in established garter stitch pattern until you've worked the yoke pattern three times, ending with Round 10. Work even in stockinette for 1½" (4 cm). Separate the sleeves from the body, placing 29 stitches for each sleeve on waste yarn and cast on 9 stitches at the two underarms on the body. Work the body straight down, changing to smaller needles for the bottom border. Work one sleeve at a time. Pick up 9 stitches along the underarm of the body in addition to the stitches set aside for the sleeves when you divided the yoke. Taper the sleeves by decreasing 2 stitches, one on each side of the first stitch of the round, every fourth round until 28 stitches remain, then change to smaller needles and work the sleeve cuff. Repeat for the second sleeve.

For a Different Look, Try This

Ribbed Borders. If you prefer ribbed borders, substitute K1, P1 or K2, P2 ribbing, worked on needles two sizes smaller than for the body, but reduce the number of stitches by 10 percent. The body border would then be about 86 stitches; the sleeve borders about 25 stitches; and the neck border about 50 stitches. You'll need a stitch count that's a multiple of the ribbed pattern for each border, so adjust for that. Remember to increase to the correct number of stitches on the first round above the border when you change to the larger needles.

Stranded Knitting. Circular yoked sweaters are a traditional vehicle for stranded knitting (pages 206–209), placed just above the bottom and sleeve borders and throughout the yoke. This serves a functional purpose, making those sections thicker and warmer. Stranding also makes the knitting narrower, so if you want to work it instead of garter stitch, work a swatch in stranded knitting and use this to determine the correct number of stitches for the yoke area, estimate the number required by adding 10–15 percent, or work the yoke on larger needles. The proportion of the yoke will also change, because stockinette stitches are taller and narrower than garter stitches. To accommodate this, change the rate of decrease to prevent the yoke from being shaped like a long, tall funnel. It's easiest to work the decreases in plain areas between bands of stranded patterns. Remember to work the first half of the yoke without shaping. When you do begin shaping it, decrease severely by working (K1, K2tog) repeated all the way around (two-thirds of the stitches will remain). Work this again when you are about halfway through the shaped section. When you are ready to work the neck band, decrease to the correct number of stitches to make your neck the size you want. If you don't have the correct multiple of stitches at any point to work your stranded pattern, adjust the number of decrease stitches to accommodate your pattern.

Plain Stockinette. Like stranded knitting, stockinette has different proportions from those of garter stitch, so the yoke decreases must be worked at a different rate. If you are decreasing every other round, then decrease 9 stitches evenly spaced on each decrease round. If you line these up, you'll get a pleasing swirl of decreases up to the neck, but they will be asymmetrical because 9 is an odd number. You can achieve the same effect by working 18 decreases every fourth round, and the placement on the front and back will be symmetrical because 18 is an even number. Instead of decreasing gradually on alternate rounds, you may also work 3 rounds of many decreases as described for stranded knitting above.

Top-Down Raglan Sleeve Sweater

New Techniques Used

- Tubular cast on (pages 18–19)
- Increasing at four points to make raglan sleeves
- Separating sleeves and body at underarms
- Casting on and picking up stitches to join underarms
- Decreasing to taper sleeves
- Tubular Bind Off (pages 62–65)

This raglan-sleeved sweater is worked from the top down, the opposite direction from the Circular Yoked Sweater (pages 273–279). This means it is cast on at the neck, enlarged as it progresses down to the underarms, the sleeves are divorced from the body, and three separate tubes are worked down to the bottom. The circular yoke in the previous project was worked with eight decreases every other round, staggered so that there were no noticeable decrease lines. The rate of increase for this sweater (8 stitches every other round) is identical, but placing them in pairs at four points creates the distinctive diagonal "seams" that separate the raglan sleeves from the body. If you remember the lessons on increasing and decreasing to create circles versus squares (see Lacy Square Shawl, pages 158–161, Round Pot Holder, pages 167–168, and Mitered Rectangle Scarf, pages 162–166), this is exactly the same technique. In fact, as you begin the raglan-sleeved sweater, the shape you knit is a square with a hole in the center of it for the neck opening. You could also make a square collar for a sweater using this shaping, even if the sweater itself wasn't shaped this way. This project also introduces a few clever details: the neck border begins with a Tubular Cast On and the bottom borders end with Tubular Bind Off, so all the edges match perfectly.

For Project Shown You Need

YARN	Lorna's Laces Fisherman (100% wool, 500 yds/8 oz)
YARN AMOUNT	240 yds/220 m) Periwinkle (49ns)
GAUGE	20 stitches and 31 rounds = 4" (10 cm) in stockinette stitch
NEEDLE SIZE	US 8 (5 mm) and two sizes smaller for borders. Match the project's gauge if you want finished measurements to match pattern instructions.
NEEDLE TYPES	A wide variety of needles could be used at any point through the project. The Tubular cast on at the neck can be a little hard to control so is most easily worked on a single needle: a 12" (30 cm) needle works best. For the rest of the project, Magic Loop uses the smallest number of needles; for this you'll need: One circular needle 47" (120 cm) or longer, two sizes larger than the needles used for the borders. This will be used for the yoke, the body, and the sleeves, down to the borders. One circular needle 47" (120 cm) or longer, two sizes smaller than the needle used for the body. This will be used for the bottom border and the sleeve cuffs.
OTHER SUPPLIES	Four split markers; about 2 yds (2 m) waste yarn
FINISHED SIZE	19" (48 cm) circumference and 9½" (24 cm) length (shoulder to bottom)

A

Yoke completed to underarms

Working the Neck Band

- Following the directions for Tubular Cast On, pages 18–19, and using the 12" (30 cm) circular needle, cast on 64 stitches. You'll need about 1 yard (1 meter) of waste yarn. In step 1, be sure to cast on only 32 stitches, because you double the number of stitches in step 2. Complete the cast on through the tubular knitting in steps 3 and 4. Mark the beginning/end of round.
- Work K1, P1 ribbing for 4 rounds.

Raglan Shaping

Each of the four raglan seams in the yoke area is an increase point. Two stitches are increased at all four points every other round. Mark these points by retaining the marker at the beginning of the round and placing three more markers after every 16 stitches.

There will also be 16 stitches between the fourth marker and the first one.

- Knit around using the larger 47" (120 cm) circular needle and the Magic Loop method.
- Increase Round: Knit around, working Kfb into the stitches before and after each marker. (*8 stitches increased*)
- Continue in stockinette, working the increase round on alternate rounds until there are 160 stitches. (*12 increase rounds; 40 stitches between markers*)

Lay the knitting out flat, and notice that what you've made is a square with a hole in the middle. Fold this in half and you can see that two of the sides of the square make the top of the sleeves, while the other sides are the front and back of the body. At this point all four sections are identical Ⓐ.

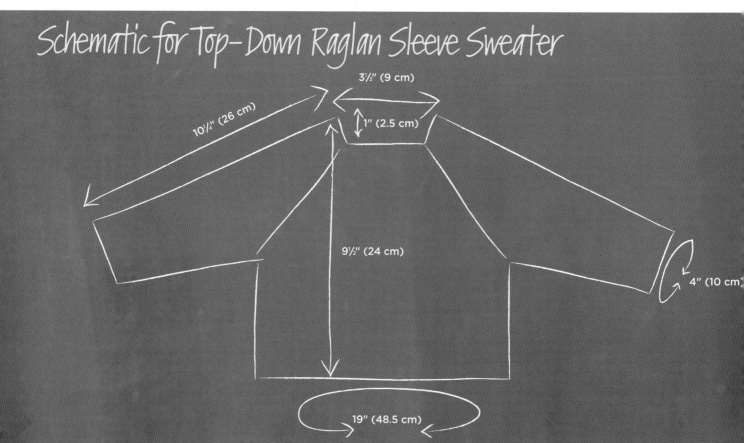

Schematic for Top-Down Raglan Sleeve Sweater

3½" (9 cm)

10¼" (26 cm)

1" (2.5 cm)

9½" (24 cm)

4" (10 cm)

19" (48.5 cm)

Sleeve stitches set aside on waste yarn (Magic Loop)

- Next Rounds: Knit around (no further increases) for 1" (2.5 cm). (Working even after the raglan increases are completed allows enough ease in the underarm area so that the sweater can be worn comfortably; if you omit this step, the underarms will be too tight.) Don't cut the yarn!

Separating the Body and Sleeves

You'll need two pieces of waste yarn, each about 18" (46 cm) long. You can re-use the piece from the Tubular cast on, if it's still intact.

- Place the first 40 stitches of the round on a piece of waste yarn.
- Slip the next 40 stitches to the other end of the needle.
- Place the third set of 40 stitches on another piece of waste yarn.

- Slip the last 40 stitches to the other end of the needle. You're now back at the beginning of the round, where the working yarn is still attached. The stitches on the waste yarn are reserved for the sleeves, which will be worked later **B**.

Working the Body

The 80 stitches still on the needle(s) are the front and back half of the body. You will work the body circularly, but first you need to cast on stitches for the underarms.

- Cast on 4 stitches, place a marker to indicate the beginning/end of round, cast on 4 more stitches, K40, cast on 8 stitches, knit to marker **C**. (*96 stitches, joined to work circularly*)
- Work in stockinette stitch until the body measures 8½" (21.5 cm) from the shoulder to the needle.

Underarm cast ons completed; body joined

Working the Bottom Border

- Setup: Using the smaller 47" (120 cm) needle, knit around, decreasing 10 stitches evenly spaced. (*86 stitches remain*)
- Work 3 rounds of K1, P1 ribbing.
- Work 4 rounds of tubular knitting to match the neck border (alternating rounds of Knit 1, Slip 1 and rounds of Slip 1, Purl 1).
- Bind off using the Tubular Bind Off (pages 62–65).

Working the Sleeves

- Slip 40 stitches from the waste yarn onto the 47" (120 cm) needle used for the body. Leaving a tail of about 12" (30.5 cm), pick up and knit 9 stitches across the underarm of the body, placing a marker after the fourth stitch ⓓ. The marker is at the beginning of round. The stitch following the marker will be your "seam" stitch: you will work decreases on both sides of this stitch every fourth round to taper the sleeve. (*49 stitches*)
- Knit 3 rounds.
- Decrease Round: K1, k2tog, knit until 2 stitches remain before the marker, ssk. (*2 stitches decreased*)
- Continuing in stockinette stitch, work the Decrease Round every fourth round until there are 29 stitches left and the sleeve measures about 9¾" (25 cm) from the neck edge.

Picking up sleeve stitches at underarm

Working the Sleeve Cuff

- Setup: Using smaller 47" (120 cm) needles, knit around, decreasing 5 stitches evenly spaced. (*24 stitches remain*)
- Work the ribbing and bind off as for the bottom of the body.

Finishing

There are holes at both sides of both of the underarms, but you will use the long tail that you left when you started each sleeve to eliminate the gaps. First use the tail to close up the hole closest to it, then weave the tail across the underarm to the other hole and close it up the same way. Weave in the tail for a few stitches, and trim. Weave in any other tails on the inside.

TOP-DOWN RAGLAN SLEEVE SWEATER

For a Different Look, Try This

Eyelet increases. Use yarn overs to increase on either side of a marked seam stitch instead of Kfb. Or use a double increase, such as K-yo-K (see the Mitered Rectangle Scarf, pages 162–166). These open increases look particularly nice if you add an eyelet border or a lace insert in the body or sleeves.

Pattern. Add a small pattern stitch to the body and sleeves. Begin immediately after the neck border and maintain the pattern as the yoke grows wider. You may limit the pattern to the yoke area, or continue it down into the sleeves and body. If your pattern has about the same proportion of stitches to rows as stockinette stitch (about 5 stitches = 7 rows/ rounds), then you can increase for the raglan shaping on every other round as in the original project. In garter stitch (where 1 stitch = 2 rows/rounds), you can increase at the same rate, but your yoke will be shorter in length when it reaches the desired width. To adjust for this, once the yoke is wide enough, work even until the yoke is the required length to the underarm. If your pattern is narrower in propor- tion, you'll need to increase more quickly, so work the increase rounds more frequently. If it's wider,

increase more slowly by working the increase rounds less frequently. To test your increase plan, make a cir- cular swatch, starting from the center and increasing 2 stitches at each of the 4 corners. You want the swatch to either lie flat or rise slightly in the middle.

Embellish the seams. For a more challenging project, separate the two increase stitches at each of the raglan "seams" by a few stitches and work a small pattern like a cable between the increases.

Bottom up. To make this sweater from the bottom up, cast on for the body and sleeves using the Tubular Cast On (pages 18–19) and follow the directions for the Circular Yoked Sweater, pages 273–279 until the sleeves and body have been joined and you've worked about 1" (2.5 cm) on all the stitches. Place markers at each of the four points where the body meets the sleeves. Decrease 2 stitches (one on either side of the center stitch) at each of the seams every other round. Stop when all of the sleeve stitches have been decreased, or when the neck opening is the desired size, whichever comes first. Add the neck border and finish with Tubular Bind Off (pages 62–65).

Any Size, Any Yarn

Work a gauge swatch to determine the number of stitches per inch (or centimeter), then calculate how many stitches you need for the circumference of the body. You can measure a sweater that fits to determine the body and neck measurements, or you can measure yourself (or the intended recipient). (See appendix for Craft Yarn Council website, which provides Garment Sizing Guidelines.) Be sure to add 4"–6" (10–15 cm) of ease to the body measurement so that the sweater will be comfortable to wear.

Also decide how big you want the neck opening and calculate how many stitches you need for it. The easiest way to measure for it is to use a piece of yarn. Put it around your neck, trim it to the length that lies where you'd like your neck opening to be, then measure the yarn to find the length. Round this to a multiple of 4 stitches.

Follow the directions for the sweater given above, but cast on the number of stitches you need for your neckline. Start the border, working K1, P1 ribbing until it's as wide as you like.

Mark the four increase points for the raglan shaping. This is where you control the fit of your sleeves. Dividing equally, with 25 percent of the stitches for each sleeve and for the front and back, results in a loose, comfortable sleeve and a generous armhole. For a more fitted sleeve, you can vary the proportions, down to as little as 15 percent of the stitches for each sleeve and 35 percent for the front and the back. In the Top-Down Raglan Sleeve Sweater, with 64 stitches cast on at the neck, this would result in 10 stitches for each sleeve and 22 stitches for the front and the back. The shoulder area of each sleeve will be much narrower, as will the rest of the sleeve. The neck will also be shaped differently: the back and front will be higher. Keep increasing until the sweater is long enough to reach the underarms and the sleeves are wide enough to reach around the arm. Depending on the desired measurements for the widest point of the sleeve and for the width of the body, you may need to continue increasing for the body sections after the sleeve increases are completed, or vice versa. To do this, simply work the increases on one side of the seam stitches while working even on the other side of the seam stitches. Because the sleeve sections and body sections will look identical at this point, be very careful to increase only in the two sections that need to be wider. Try the sweater on at this point to make sure it will fit. For an adult sweater, work about 2" (5 cm) more without increasing.

Place the sleeve stitches on waste yarn, and calculate the number of stitches to cast on at the underarms; this should be about 8 percent of the body stitches. In the Top-Down Raglan Sleeve Sweater, the body has 96 stitches, 8 percent of this is 7.68, which I rounded up to 8 stitches.

Cast on for the underarms on both sides of the body, work the body until it is the desired length to the bottom border. Change to smaller needles and decrease about 10 percent of the stitches (making sure you have an even number to accommodate your ribbing). Work K1, P1 ribbing for as long as you like, then finish off with 4 rounds of tubular knitting and the Tubular Bind Off (pages 62–65). Remember that, assuming your circular needles are long enough, you can try on the sweater as often as you like for fit.

When you work the sleeves, place the waiting stitches on needles and pick up 1 more stitch across body underarm than you cast on. In the Top-Down Raglan Sleeve Sweater, for example, you cast on 8 stitches at each underarm, and then picked up 9 when you started the sleeve. This provides a center stitch to serve as a seam line when you work the sleeve decreases. If you need to pick up an even number of stitches across the underarm, you can center the sleeve decreases by setting aside two stitches to serve as the "seam" rather than one. Work around, decreasing regularly on both sides of the "seam" to taper the sleeve down to the cuff. To calculate how often to decrease, see Sleeve and Armhole Options, pages 260–261. The Top-Down Raglan Sleeve Sweater instructions specify an ssk decrease before the seam stitch and a K2tog following it, because that makes the seam look only 1 stitch wide. On a larger sweater you could reverse the position of the two decreases, making the seam look 3 or 4 stitches wide. Try it on for fit as you work!

Continue until the sleeve reaches the desired length to the cuff, or until you have only 25 percent of the body stitches left (25 percent of 96 is 24), whichever comes first. If you aren't down to 25 percent, adjust for this when you change to smaller needles and prepare to work the cuff. You'd normally decrease the remaining stitches by 10 percent. If you have a few too many stitches remaining, decrease these away at the same time. Make sure you have an even number of stitches, then work the ribbing as for the body.

NECK VARIATIONS

You may have noticed that the only neck shaping so far in this chapter has been the front V-necks on the vests, although I did discuss how to change the V-neck to a round front neck. You can improve the fit of garments, especially V-necked garments, immensely by adding back neck shaping. If you're working a vest or sweater that's circular to the underarms and then flat to the shoulder, just follow normal flat pattern instructions to add back neck shaping or to work a different front neck shaping.

If you're making a sweater that's circular all the way to the neck, like the Circular Yoked and Top-Down Raglan Sleeve Sweaters, the front and back necks are usually identical. In actuality, this means that the front neck will be a little high and the back neck a little low when you put it on. It's easiest to adjust for this when working from the bottom up.

When you reach the point where you'd work the neck border, work around to the center back. Build the back of the neck up a bit by working short rows, going a few stitches past the center back, then turning and working an equal distance past the center in the opposite direction. Keep turning and working a few more stitches on each row until you've worked partway around the front, then begin working circularly again and finish it off with the border. See the appendix for details on working short rows (pages 308–309).

If you'd like a cardigan that opens down the front, prepare the center front as you would a steek, then cut it and add borders. Remember to finish the raw edges on the inside to prevent raveling.

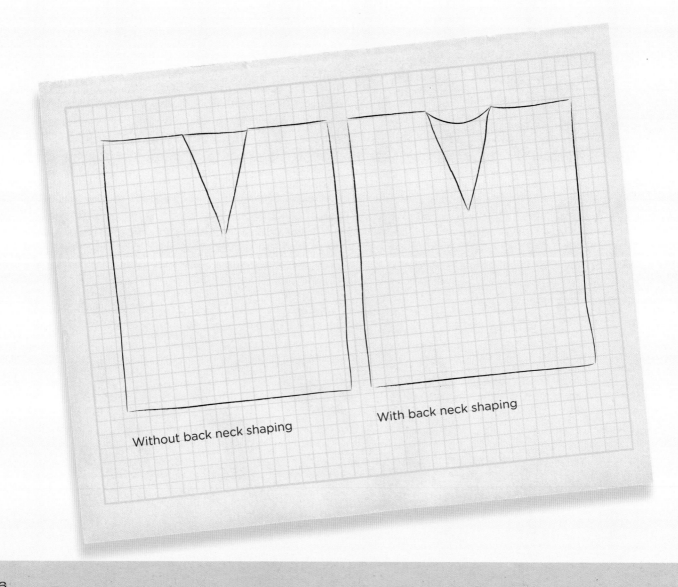

Without back neck shaping

With back neck shaping

Side-to-Side Sweater

By using steeks, it's possible to knit even cuff-to-cuff sweaters seamlessly. Sideways sweaters are, of course, a great choice when you want to make vertical stripes. Just change colors row by row, turn the fabric sideways, and there they are. To make single-row stripes in flat knitting, you'd need to knit across with one color, slide the knitting back to the beginning of the row and knit across with the second color, then turn to the wrong side and purl with the first color, slide back to the beginning and purl across with the second color. Working circularly, it's easy to make continuous single-round stripes using helix knitting. If you want to make stranded patterns where the colors change from side to side across the knitting, sideways sweaters allow you to do that as well. In either case, working the garment circularly means that you never need to work on the purl side while maintaining your color pattern, and you ensure that the patterning matches front to back and is continuous where the sleeves meet the body.

New Techniques Used

- Picot hem at cast on
- Helix pattern with changing colors
- Increasing at center of sleeve to taper sleeve and shape the sleeve cap at the same time
- Making a closed seam by casting on and picking up stitches along the bottom of the cast on
- Steek for bottom and neck openings
- Shaping a sideways neck

- Tapering the sleeve and shaping the sleeve cap at the same time by decreasing at center of sleeve
- Picot hem at bind off
- Cutting front for cardigan opening
- Finishing steeked neck edge with doubled picot band
- Finishing steeked bottom opening with binding
- Picot Bind Off (page 60) down front, around corner, and along bottom

For Project Shown You Need

YARN	Lorna's Laces Shepherd Sport (100% superwash wool, 200 yds/2.6 oz)
YARN AMOUNT	196 yds/179 m Bittersweet (630); 27 yds/25 m Grapevine (3ns); 32 yds/29 m China Blue (41ns); 53 yds/49 m Douglas Fir (6 ns); and 16 yds/15 m Turquoise (22ns)
GAUGE	26 stitches and 36 rounds = 4" (10 cm) in Helix Pattern
NEEDLE SIZE	US 4 (3.5 cm) for sleeves and body and one size smaller for inside of hems and borders. Match the project's gauge if you want finished measurements to match pattern instructions.
NEEDLE TYPE	Two circular needles 24" (60 cm) or longer
OTHER SUPPLIES	12" (30.5 cm) sport-weight waste yarn for Provisional Cast On, three stitch markers (two should be split markers), 1 yd (1 m) crochet cotton to hold front stitches (cut into two pieces), tapestry needle (smaller than a regular yarn needle, but is blunt and has a larger eye than a sewing needle), four 7/16" (11 mm) buttons
FINISHED SIZE	21" (53.5 cm) circumference, 10½" (26.5 cm) from center back to sleeve cuff, 10" (25.5 cm) long from shoulder to bottom edge

You'll notice that the gauge measurement is provided in rounds as well as stitches. In a conventional sweater, the stitch gauge is crucial to making the garment the proper circumference while you control the length as you knit. In a sideways sweater, this is true for the sleeves (which are actually knit the same way as in a conventional sweater), but the length of the body is controlled by the stitch gauge. You can adjust the width of the body as you knit by working more or fewer rounds. Both the stitch gauge and the row gauge are therefore required to ensure the fit of side-to-side sweaters.

You'll also notice that, unlike the other projects in the book, this one specifies the use of two circular needles throughout. Using the two needles makes it easy to keep track of the stitches for the front versus the stitches for the back and the placement of the steeks. It also means that you need to change needles only twice — once from the smaller needles to the larger needles after the first cuff and then back to the smaller needles before the second cuff.

This particular sweater uses a collection of related techniques to make all the edges match each other: picot hems at the sleeve cuffs, a picot border at the neck edge, and picot bind offs along the two fronts and the bottom edge. The cut edges at the two steeks are neatly enclosed — at the neck edge by a double-thickness border and at the bottom by a binding that is worked circularly. The end result is that the inside of the sweater looks almost as perfect as the outside.

This is a challenging project. If you'd like to try it, but want it to be a bit less challenging, check out the ideas for simplifying it in For a Different Look, Try This, page 300.

Helix Pattern

Before beginning, please review Helix Knitting (pages 128–129). The round-by-round instructions below make the color sequence seem more complex than it really is.

- The Bittersweet yarn is used throughout the sweater, alternating rounds with the solid colors, so you never need to cut it (except possibly to allow for the second side seam).
- The solid yarns are always used in the following order, always alternating with the Bittersweet. If you understand the logic of the pattern, it's easier to maintain. Notice that each yarn is always used for 3 rounds or 5 rounds, and that these numbers alternate. Notice also that the sequence goes from Grapevine through Turquoise, and then the colors reverse order.
- Grapevine (5 rounds)
- China Blue (3 rounds)
- Douglas Fir (5 rounds)
- Turquoise (3 rounds)

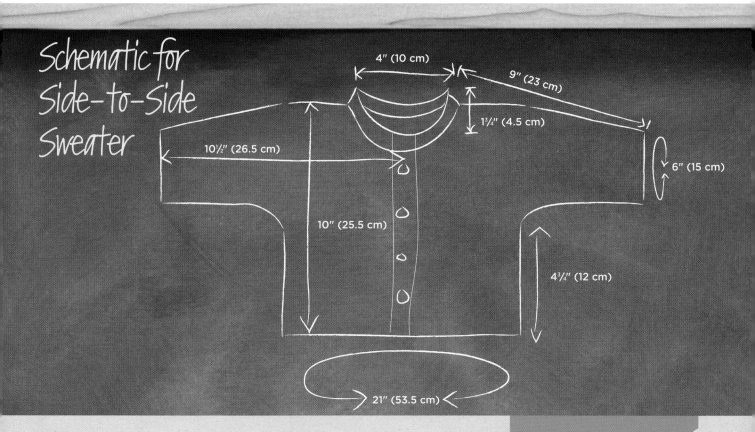

Schematic for Side-to-Side Sweater

4" (10 cm)
9" (23 cm)
1¾" (4.5 cm)
10½" (26.5 cm)
6" (15 cm)
10" (25.5 cm)
4¾" (12 cm)
21" (53.5 cm)

- Douglas Fir (5 rounds)
- China Blue (3 rounds)

When you finish a section of each solid color, cut the yarn, leaving a 4" (10 cm) tail.

- Round 1 and all odd-numbered rounds: Using Bittersweet, knit around.
- Rounds 2, 4, 6, 8, and 10: Using Grapevine, knit around.
- Rounds 12, 14, and 16: Using China Blue, knit around.
- Rounds 18, 20, 22, 24, and 26: Using Douglas Fir, knit around.
- Rounds 28, 30, and 32: Using Turquoise, knit around.
- Rounds 34, 36, 38, 40, and 42: Using Douglas Fir, knit around.
- Rounds 44, 46, and 48: Using China Blue, knit around.
- Repeat Rounds 1–48 for pattern.

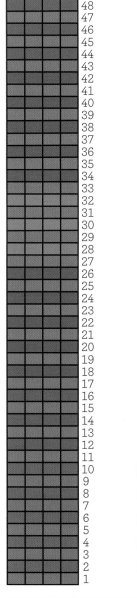

Bittersweet

Grapevine

China Blue

Douglas Fir

Turquoise

Working the First Sleeve

Throughout the sweater the first needle of the round is called Needle 1 and holds the back stitches. The second needle, Needle 2, holds the front stitches. The sleeve begins with a picot-edged hem, so please review this construction in Two Hems for a Finished Edge (page 21).

- Round 1: With smaller needles, waste yarn, and Bittersweet, cast on 39 stitches using a Provisional Cast On (pages 303–304). Place 20 of these stitches on the first needle for the sweater back and 19 on the second needle for the front. Join the beginning and end of round, being careful not to twist (see Off to a Good Start: Casting On and Joining, page 13).
- Rounds 2–6: Using Bittersweet knit around.
- Round 7: (Picot Round): Using Bittersweet, *K2tog, yo; repeat from *, ending K1. (*39 stitches*)
- Round 8: Using Bittersweet, knit around.
- Round 9: Change to larger needles. Using Grapevine, knit around.

Begin working the Helix Pattern on the following round. For the remainder of the sweater, work the Helix Pattern, even if not explicitly instructed to do so, until you reach the final sleeve hem, which is worked just in Bittersweet. The instructions tell you when to change.

- Rounds 1–3: Knit around in Helix Pattern, beginning with Round 1 of pattern.

There were six rounds up to the picot round. You have now completed 6 rounds above the picots, so it's time to join the two layers of the hem.

Joining the Hem Layers

- Turn the knitting inside out by pushing it up between the needles. Remove the waste yarn from the Provisional Cast On and transfer the live stitches at the bottom edge onto the smaller needles. Fold at the line of picots, with the bottom edge inside. Knit the two layers together using the larger needle and the yarn for Round 4 of Helix Pattern (Grapevine).
- Rounds 4–8: Knit Rounds 4–8 of the Helix Pattern.

After this, the instructions expect you to keep track of the Helix Pattern yourself. One way to do this is to stick a split marker in the knitting on Round 1 of the pattern and move it up to the next Round 1 when you start a new repeat of the pattern. It's easy to count the stripes from the marker to see what round you're on.

Tapering the Sleeve

- Setup: Place three markers on the sleeve to indicate increase points, as follows: a split marker in the first stitch of the round (seam stitch), one after the 14th stitch of the round, and one after the 26th stitch. The 12 stitches between the last two markers form the center panel of the sleeve. Increases are worked on either side of this center panel, making the sleeve wider and also shaping a sleeve cap, which improves the fit of the sweater Ⓐ. Move the split marker up closer to the needle as the sleeve grows to keep track of the first stitch of the round.

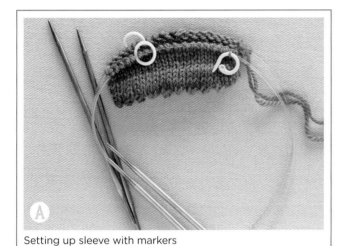

Setting up sleeve with markers

You can use whatever increase you prefer, but avoid the Kfb increase because it creates a bump at the base of the new stitch, making the left sleeve look noticeably different from the right sleeve. If you use M1 increases, you can make them symmetrical by twisting the two increases in opposite directions (see the appendix, page 306).

- Round 1 (increase round): Knit around in Helix Pattern, increasing 1 stitch before the second marker and 1 stitch after the third marker.
- Rounds 2–4: Knit around.
- Rounds 5–28: Repeat Rounds 1–4 six times. (*7 increase rounds; 53 stitches*)
- Round 29 (increase round): Continuing in Helix Pattern, knit the marked stitch at the beginning of round, increase 1, knit around increasing next to both of the other markers as in Round 1, knit to the end of round and increase once more. (*4 stitches increased*)
- Rounds 30–32: Knit around in Helix Pattern.
- Rounds 33–48: Repeat Rounds 29–32 four times. (*5 total increase rounds; 73 stitches*) The sleeve should measure about 6½" (16.5 cm) from the picot edge to the needle. Remove the two markers at the center of the sleeve.

Working the Left Shoulder and Body

You're now at the top of the sleeve, and the fabric needs to suddenly become wider to form the side seam for the body.

- Setup: At the end of the last sleeve round, cast on 25 stitches for the front of the sweater at the end of Needle 2. There are two strands of yarn attached. Use both of them and the Long-Tail Cast On (pages 302–303), with the color you just used over your index finger, and the color you need for the next round over your thumb Ⓑ.
- Slide the stitches you just cast on down the needle onto the cable.
- Next round: To begin the next round, pick up stitches along the bottom edge of the stitches you just cast on. To prepare for this, twist the cast on stitches so that the bottom of the cast on is above the cable of the needle, rather than below. (See Cast On and Pick Up, page 28.) Using the far end of Needle 1 and the yarn for the following round, pick up and knit 24 stitches for the back between each of the stitches you just cast on Ⓒ. The next stitch on the needle is the marked seam stitch. Remove the marker and knit across the rest of Needle 1, up to the top of the shoulder. Knit across Needle 2, down the front all the way to the bottom of the sweater. (*122 stitches, 61 on each needle*)

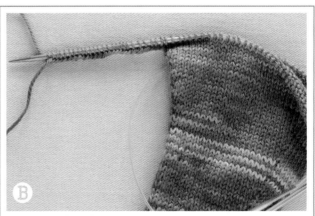

Casting on for side seam

Picking up side seam stitches along bottom of cast on

Creating the Bottom Steek

These instructions call for an 8-stitch steek. Look at the Steeked V-Neck Vest (pages 264–272) and note that its steeks are 9 stitches wide. There's no rule for the exact number of stitches in a steek: you just need enough fabric to work with after the steek is cut. For this project, it's simpler to keep the same number of stitches on both needles, which is only possible if the steek has an even number of stitches.

• Setup: Cast on 4 stitches for the bottom steek at the end of Needle 2, using both strands of yarn and the Long-Tail Cast On **D**. This carries both strands of yarn to the center of the steek, which is now the end of the round.

• Using the color for the following round and the Half-Hitch Cast On (page 302), cast on 4 more stitches for the second half of the steek at the beginning of Needle 1 **E**.

• Knit around, using the correct yarn to continue the Helix Pattern, until 4 stitches remain at the end of Needle 2. Because the steek consists of horizontal stripes with no vertical patterning, it can be difficult to tell where it begins and ends. To make this clear, purl the first and last stitch of the steek on every round, as follows: when 4 stitches remain on Needle 2, P1, K3; when you start Needle 1, K3, P1, then continue knit-

Casting on for first half of bottom steek

Casting on for second half of bottom steek

ting to the steek at the end of the round. (*122 stitches for body and shoulders, plus 8 stitches for steek; a total of 130 stitches, 65 on each needle*)

The beginning/end of round is at the center of the steek. Always purl the first and last stitch of the steek even if the instructions for the round just say "knit."

• Next 23 Rounds: Knit around in Helix Pattern, purling the first and last stitch of the steek and changing colors at the center of the steek, until you've worked 25 rounds beyond the side-seam cast on. The piece should measure a little less than 3" (7.5 cm) from the side seam to the needle and about 9½" (24 cm) from the bottom of the sleeve to the needle.

Shaping the Neck Opening

The neck shaping is charted on the facing page. Although it's not shown in the chart, after binding off the beginning of the opening, you'll cast on for a second steek on Round 2, exactly like the steek at the bottom of the sweater. Although these stitches are not shown on the Neck Opening Chart, the neck steek is worked across the opening from Rounds 3 to 45. On Round 45, you'll bind off the steek and on Round 46 you'll cast on to close the neck opening and begin the right shoulder.

The front neck is lower than the back, and the neck curve develops gradually. To achieve this, the shaping changes as the neck progresses, and it's different on the back than on the front. It begins on both sides with decreases every round, then every other round, and then less frequently. The decreases are worked on the first 2 and the last 2 stitches next to the steek stitches. This is intentional, so that they disappear behind the neck border when it is picked up. If they were worked a stitch away from the edge, they would show on the outside of the sweater, and because decreases look very different from increases, the right and left sides of the neck would appear unbalanced.

When you are halfway across the neck opening, you'll put stitches for both sides of the cardigan front opening on crochet cotton, so that cutting and picking up for the front borders is easier. When you reach the center front, you may either continue the Helix Pattern or reverse it so the stripes in the second half mirror those in the first half.

The second half of the neck reverses the process, increasing in a mirror image of the first half.

Remember to continue the Helix Pattern as you work the neck opening and to purl the first and last stitch of both steeks. To stay oriented in relation to the Neck Opening Chart, place a marker 10 stitches from the end of Needle 1 (the end opposite the bottom steek) and another marker 18 stitches from the beginning of Needle 2. These markers indicate the beginning and end of the stitches shown in the Neck Opening Chart.

- Round 1: On Needle 1, knit until 2 stitches remain, K2tog to begin the back neck opening. On Needle 2, bind off 5 stitches for the front neck, knit to end of round.
- Round 2: On Needle 1, knit to the last 2 stitches, K2tog, cast on 4 stitches at the end of the needle for the neck steek. On Needle 2, cast on 4 more stitches for the neck steek, ssk, knit to end of round.
- Rounds 3 and 4: On Needle 1, knit until 2 stitches remain before neck steek, K2tog; P1, K3 for neck steek. On Needle 2, K3, P1 for neck steek; ssk at front neck; knit to end of round.
- Round 5: On Needle 1, knit the back without decreasing. On Needle 2, work neck steek, ssk at front neck, knit to end of round.
- Round 6: Repeat Round 3 (decreases at both neck edges).
- Round 7: Knit around without decreasing, continuing to purl the first and last stitch of each steek.
- Rounds 8 and 9: Repeat Rounds 3 and 7.
- Round 10: Knit around, decreasing only at front neck on Needle 2.
- Round 11: Knit around without decreasing.

Neck Opening Chart

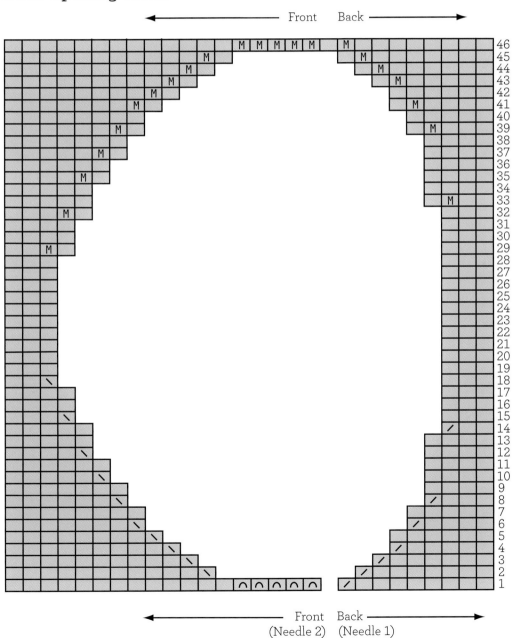

Front ← → Back

Front (Needle 2)   Back (Needle 1)

Front stitches set aside on white crochet cotton

- Round 12: Knit around, decreasing only at front neck on Needle 2.
- Round 13: Knit around without decreasing.
- Round 14: Knit around, decreasing only at back neck on Needle 1.
- Round 15: Knit around, decreasing only at front neck.
- Rounds 16 and 17: Knit around without decreasing.
- Round 18: Knit around, decreasing only at front neck.
- Rounds 19–22: Knit around without decreasing.
- Thread a piece of crochet cotton on a tapestry needle and run it through all the front stitches (not the steek stitches) on Needle 2 without removing the stitches from the needle. This piece of yarn will serve as a stitch holder when the front is cut open.
- Round 23: On Needle 1, knit without decreasing. On Needle 2, bind off the 4 neck steek stitches, then knit to the bottom steek and bind off the four bottom steek stitches. (Binding off the front half of the steek stitches prevents the steek from unraveling when you cut the front open.)
- Round 24: Knit around without decreasing, casting on 4 stitches at the beginning and end of Needle 2 to replace both sets of steek stitches that were bound off on the previous round.
- Round 25: Knit around without decreasing.
- Run another piece of crochet cotton through all the front stitches on Needle 2 (as you did at the completion of Round 22). This holds the stitches on the other side of the neck opening .
- Rounds 26–28: Knit around without decreasing.
- Round 29 (first increase round): On Needle 1, knit to end without increasing. On Needle 2, work across the steek; K1, M1 at front neck, work to end. (Place the increases 1 stitch away from the steek on both sides of the neck. This makes it easier to pick up stitches for the neck band later.)

- Rounds 30 and 31: Knit around without increasing.
- Round 32: Repeat Round 29.
- Round 33: On Needle 1, knit until 1 stitch remains before neck steek, M1 for back neck, K1; work neck steek. On Needle 2, knit without increasing.
- Round 34: Knit around without increasing.
- Round 35: Knit around, increasing only at front neck on Needle 2.
- Rounds 36 and 37: Repeat Rounds 34 and 35.
- Round 38: Knit around without increasing.
- Round 39: Knit around, increasing at both neck edges.
- Rounds 40 and 41: Repeat Rounds 38 and 39.
- Round 42: Knit around, increasing only at front neck on Needle 2.
- Rounds 43 and 44: Knit around, increasing at both neck edges.
- Round 45: Knit around, increasing at both neck edges and binding off the 8 neck steek stitches.
- Round 46: On Needle 1, knit until 1 stitch remains, M1, K1. On Needle 2, cast on 5 stitches using the Half-Hitch Cast On, knit to the end of the round. The cast-on stitches close the neck opening. (*130 stitches; 65 on each needle*)
- This completes the neck steek and neck opening.

Working the Right Shoulder and Body

- Rounds 1–23: Knit around in Helix Pattern. The right front should be one round shorter than the left front to the side seam. If you are one round off, don't worry about it.
- Round 24: Knit around to the steek at the bottom of the front, then bind off the 4 steek stitches. If this is a round where you would change solid colors, change now.
- Round 25: Bind off the 4 remaining steek stitches, alternating stitches with each color of yarn. Knit to the end of the round, and cut the yarn you just used, leaving a tail about 4" (10 cm) long to weave in later.

Side Seam

- Setup: Turn the knitting inside out by pushing it though the center of the needles. With right sides together, hold the front and back stitches together, and using the yarn color needed for the next round, work Three-Needle Bind Off (page 69) on the first 24 stitches from each needle.
- Slip the remaining stitch on the right needle point onto the back needle. (*37 stitches on Needle 1 for back of sleeve; 36 stitches on Needle 2 for front of sleeve; 73 stitches total*)
- Turn right side out by pushing the knitting through the open armhole. With the same color you used for

Body completed, ready to start second sleeve

Finishing hem at bind off

the bind off, slip the first stitch (you already worked it while binding off), then knit to end of round, which is now where the sleeve meets the side seam .

Right Sleeve

- Setup: As for the first sleeve, you need three markers to indicate your decrease points: Place a split marker in the first stitch of the round to indicate that it's the seam stitch; place the second marker after the 32nd stitch of the round (5 stitches from the shoulder at the end of Needle 1); place the third marker after the 42nd stitch (5 stitches from the shoulder at the beginning of Needle 2).

For the second sleeve, you will reverse the shaping from the first sleeve, decreasing rather than increasing. Begin with the correct color for this round in the Helix Pattern, and continue in Helix Pattern to Hem.

- Rounds 1–3: Knit around.
- Round 4 (decrease round): Knit marked stitch, K2tog, knit until 2 stitches remain before the second marker, K2tog, knit to third marker, ssk, knit until 2 stitches remain before end of round, ssk. (69 stitches remain)
- Rounds 5–7: Knit around without decreasing.
- Rounds 8–23: Repeat Rounds 4–7 four times. (5 total decrease rounds; 53 stitches remain)

Note: On the following rounds, you'll decrease only at the center of the sleeve, not at the beginning/end of round.

- Round 24 (decrease round): Knit until 2 stitches remain before the second marker, K2tog, knit to third marker, ssk, knit to end of round.
- Rounds 25–27: Knit around without decreasing.
- Rounds 28–51: Repeat Rounds 24–27 six times. Remove markers. (7 total decrease rounds; 39 stitches remain)
- Rounds 52–58: Knit around without decreasing, ending with a solid round.

Working the Picot Hem

The rest of the sleeve is worked only with Bittersweet.

- Round 1: Switch to smaller needles, and knit around with Bittersweet.
- Round 2 (Picot Round): *K2tog, yo; repeat from *, ending K1. (39 stitches)
- Rounds 3–7: Knit around.
- Weave in any ends that will be covered by the hem. Join the hem to the inside of the sleeve by sewing or weaving (see Hems, page 66–67). You won't be able to turn the sweater inside out until the steeks are cut open, so just tuck a section of the sleeve out through the needles to give access to the wrong side .

Cutting the Openings and Working their Borders

You will complete the finishing for the sweater in the following order. Complete instructions are provided below.

- *Cardigan front:* After cutting or unraveling the center two rows of the front, put the stitches on needles and work garter stitch button and buttonhole bands flat.
- *Neck border:* Prepare and cut the neck steek, then pick up stitches around the neck and work a bind-off hem with a picot fold to enclose all cut ends of the steek.
- *Bottom border:* Prepare and cut the bottom steek, then finish the raw edges by enclosing them in a circular binding. Pick up stitches on both the inside and the outside of the bottom, knit around on the inside and the outside of the binding, then knit the two layers together with all the cut ends hidden inside.
- *Picot trim:* Work a Picot Bind Off along the button band and bottom edge to match the picot hems on all the other edges.

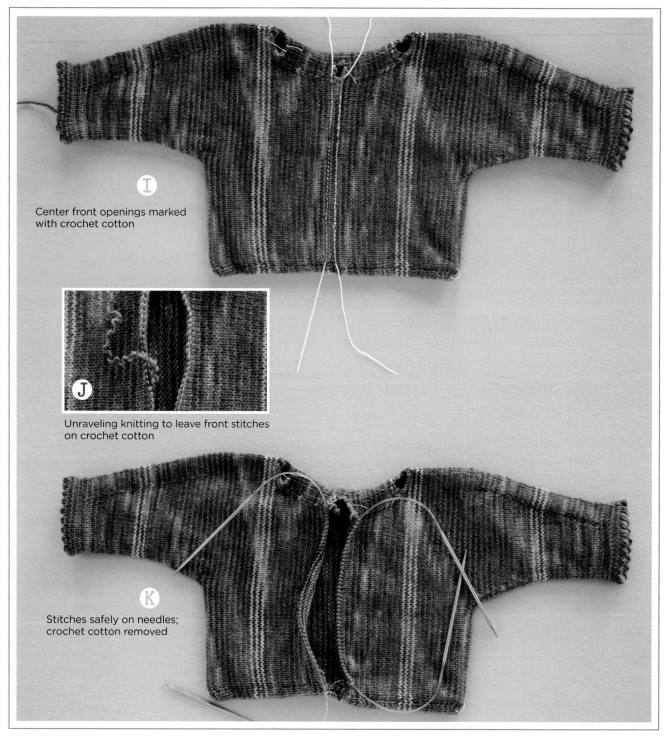

Center front openings marked with crochet cotton **I**

Unraveling knitting to leave front stitches on crochet cotton **J**

Stitches safely on needles; crochet cotton removed **K**

Opening the Front

The center front opening is clearly marked by the two strands of crochet cotton **I**. To open up the front, you have two choices: (1) Take a pair of sharp sewing shears and quickly cut straight up the center between the two strands of crochet cotton. Most of the tiny pieces of severed yarn will fall out as you work, so you can dispose of the remains later. If you are a cautious soul, however, this may be too traumatic, so instead, (2) snip one strand of yarn at the center of the row, halfway between

the two strands of crochet cotton. Pick out 1 row of knitting from this point, working up to the neck edge and down to the bottom edge. Unravel the intact row of knitting next to it to leave both the right and left front stitches on their respective pieces of crochet cotton **J**. Slide a smaller circular needle (the size for the borders, not the body) into the stitches for the left front. Once the stitches are safely on the needle, pull on the crochet cotton — it will slide right out. Place the right front stitches on a needle as you did for the left front **K**.

Save a piece of the cotton — you'll need it again soon. (*about 46 stitches for each front*)

Button Band, Left Front

- Row 1: Using Bittersweet and with the right side facing you, slip 1 knitwise wyib, knit to last stitch and at the same time decrease enough stitches evenly spaced so that band has 41 total stitches, P1.
- Rows 2–9: Slip 1, knit until 1 stitch remains, P1. (*4 garter stitch ridges on right side*)
- Bind off loosely in knitting on the wrong side. To avoid having the front edge pull in, be careful not to bind off too firmly.

Buttonhole Band, Right Front

- Rows 1–4: Work as for Button Band. There will be 2 garter ridges on the right side of the band. (*41 stitches*)
- Row 5 (start buttonhole, right side): Slip 1, K3, *K2tog, yo twice, ssk, K6; repeat from * twice more, K2tog, YO twice, ssk, K2, P1.
- Row 6 (finish buttonhole, wrong side): Slip 1, K2, *K1, (K1, P1 in double yo), K7; repeat from * twice more, K1, (K1, P1 in double yo), K4, P1.
- Cut the yarn, leaving a 4" (10 cm) tail to weave in later. Place the stitches on waste yarn or on a spare circular needle the same size or smaller than the one you used to make the border. You'll need both of the smaller circular needles for your borders when you work the bottom border.

Neck Opening and Border

See Preparing and Cutting the Steeks pages 269–270 for complete details on opening the neck. Stitch along both sides of the neck steek's center, sewing between the second and third stitches on each side. This is a little farther away from the center than normally recommended, because this steek will be trimmed to fit inside a narrow binding, rather than sewn down. Stitching far-

ther from the center means that you won't have to cut the sewing that secures the cut stitches, which in turn means that it's less likely those stitches will unravel after the garment is finished. Next, use sharp shears to cut straight up the center of the steek.

- Pickup Round: Using one of the smaller circular needles and Bittersweet yarn and starting at the right front corner of buttonhole band, pick up and knit about 87 stitches around neck edge. When picking up, work one stitch away from the steek. (This makes the edge stitch disappear behind the border.) Insert your needle straight through to the back of the fabric, wrap the yarn and knit up a stitch . Pick up 1 stitch for each ridge along the bands, 3 stitches for every 4 rows along the front and back, and 1 stitch for every stitch along the cast-on and bound-off shoulder edges.
- Row 1 (wrong side): Turn and purl across, decreasing (evenly spaced) to 78 stitches.
- Rows 2–6: Work flat in stockinette stitch.
- Row 7 (wrong side, Picot Row): *P2tog, yo; repeat from *, ending P2tog. (*77 stitches remain*) Ending up with 1 fewer stitch is useful here, allowing the inner layer of the border to fit better inside the outer layer.
- Rows 8–13: Work flat in stockinette stitch. Cut yarn, leaving a tail about 48" (120 cm) long.
- Sew down on inside (see Hems: Sewn Join, page 66).

Bottom Opening and Binding

Prepare and cut open the bottom steek exactly as you did the neck steek.

You will pick up stitches on both the front and the back of the fabric all the way across the bottom edge. First pick up and knit stitches along the bottom from the right side just as you did for the neck border . Between each stitch you picked up on the right side is a horizontal strand across the wrong side of the fabric. Turning to the wrong side and using a second circular needle, you'll knit up stitches in each of these horizontal strands. Be sure to keep the stitches very loose as you pick up on the right side, or the wrong-side pickup will be almost impossible. You may still find it difficult to get the right needle point under the strand on the back of the fabric; if so, hold the other end of the same needle in your left hand, pick up the strand on it, then knit it off onto the right point.

- Picking up on the right side: With the right side facing you, use one of the smaller circular needles to pick up *loosely*. Knit up 1 stitch for each slipped stitch across both front bands and 3 stitches for every 4 rows along the bottom of the body. (*About 155 stitches*) Cast on 1 stitch at the end of this needle (Half-Hitch Cast On is fine), then slide the stitches down onto the cable of the needle.

Picking up stitches along steek

- Picking up on the wrong side: Turn to the wrong side. Using a second circular needle the same size and continuing with the same strand of working yarn, knit up 1 stitch in the strand between each stitch you picked up on the right side. Cast on 1 stitch at the end of this needle **M**. (*about 311 stitches, divided between two needles*)

- Count the stitches on both needles. They should be the same, or there should be 1 fewer stitch on the wrong-side needle. If there are more stitches on the wrong-side needle, decrease just enough on that needle to make the numbers equal when you work the first round.

- Rounds 1–5: Knit across Needle 1 (right side), then Needle 2 (wrong side).

- Trim the steek so that it is just a bit narrower than the border you've made. Be careful not to cut the sewing or your steek may unravel.

- With the right side of the sweater facing you, hold the two layers of the bottom binding together. Using the end of one of the needles, knit across, working the front stitches together with the back stitches to close the binding around the steek **N**. This is exactly like working Three-Needle Bind Off, but you join the two layers without binding off the stitches. When you get to the end of round, there may be 1 extra stitch: just knit it. Do not cut the yarn. Leave the bottom stitches on the needle.

Picking up inner layer of bottom binding

Joining the two layers of the binding

Front and bottom stitches on needles, ready to work picot bind off

Binding Off the Buttonhole Band and Bottom

- Setup: Place the buttonhole band stitches on the smaller circular needle that was just freed from the bottom binding. Using the working yarn still attached at the bottom corner and the far end of this circular needle, pick up and knit 3 stitches along the end of the bottom binding, knit across the 41 front stitches already on the needle, then pick up and knit 3 stitches along the end of the neck border, working through both layers to join them **❶**. Turn to wrong side. (*47 front stitches on one needle; about 156 bottom stitches on a second needle*)
- Picot Bind Off: * Using the Knitted Cast On (page 302), cast on 1, bind off 3, slip the stitch on the right needle point back to the left needle point; repeat from * across. When you reach the end of the front stitches, abandon their needle and continue around the corner across the bottom until all stitches have been bound off.
- Cut the yarn and pull it through the last stitch.

Finishing

- Weave in all the remaining ends. Use the tail at the end of the bind off to make the bottom corner look neat before weaving it in. Use nearby tails to close the open end of the neck border and any looseness at the underarms before weaving them in.
- Sew on buttons, aligning them with the buttonholes. If the holes in the buttons are large enough, you may use yarn and a tapestry needle, otherwise use a sewing needle and thread.

For a Different Look, Try This

Note that many of these variations make the project less complicated.

- **Fewer balls of yarn.** Use just two yarns for the Helix Pattern, rather than changing solid colors throughout. You can use two different variegated yarns (one or both could be self-striping), a variegated and a solid, or two solids. You could also abandon helix knitting altogether and just use one yarn.

- **Single-layer cuffs.** Instead of starting with a hem, cast on and make a K1, P1 or garter-stitch cuff. Change to larger needles when the cuff is complete. Work a cuff to correspond at the other end of the sleeve. To make ribbed cuffs on the two sleeves identical, skip the cuff on the first sleeve. Instead, start with a Provisional Cast On (see pages 303–304) and begin the first sleeve on the first round above the cuff. When the sweater is complete, pick up these stitches and knit the cuff down.

- **Simpler sleeve shaping.** Avoid all sleeve shaping by increasing from 39 to 73 stitches immediately after the hem is completed. On the first round following the hem, K3, *M1, K1; repeat from * until 2 stitches remain, K2. Work the sleeve even on 73 stitches until it's time to cast on for the side seam. On the other side of the body, after joining the side seam, work even on 73 stitches until one round remains before the cuff. Decrease back to 39 stitches: K3, repeat (k2tog) until 2 stitches remain, K2. Note that this option will require additional yarn.

- **Buttons on the other side.** To make the button band on the right front rather than the left front, start by working the button band on that front, exactly as directed above. Then make the buttonhole band exactly as directed, but on the left front. Before you begin working on the bottom binding, cut and set aside a piece of Bittersweet about 1 yard (1 m) long. Work the bottom binding and do not cut the yarn. Place all the buttonhole band stitches on a second circular needle. With the right side facing you and using the cut piece of yarn, pick up and knit 3 stitches along the end of the neck border, joining the two layers; knit across the 41 band stitches already on the needle; then pick up and knit 3 stitches along the end of the bottom binding. (*47 stitches*)

Using the ball of yarn attached at the bottom, turn to the wrong side and work the Picot Bind Off as directed (page 60) across the bottom and up the front.

- **Make a pullover.** Don't bother with the crochet cotton at the center front, and don't bind off and cast on steek stitches at the center of the neck or the bottom edge. You'll have to prepare the steeks for cutting using hand sewing, because, with no opening at the front, you won't be able to use a sewing machine. For the neck border, pick up about 89 stitches all the way around, decrease about 10 percent of these on the first round, and then work the neck border as directed, except that you'll work circularly instead of flat, so there are no wrong-side rows. Because the picot round is worked on the right side of the fabric, work it exactly as you did for the two sleeve cuffs. Work the inner layer of the border and fasten down on the inside. Prepare and cut the bottom steek, then pick up stitches around the outside on one needle. Work the bottom border exactly like the neck border.

- **Standard borders.** Replace the double-thickness neck border and the bottom binding with a normal single-thickness ribbed or garter stitch border. Pick up stitches as described for the steeked vest (see page 270). If you like, work the Picot Bind Off on each of these so they match the cuffs. Turn the steeks under and sew them down on the inside.

- **Separate halves.** To avoid having to increase on one side of the sweater and decrease on the other side, make it in two pieces, increasing from cuff to center, but reversing the neck shaping on the second half. When you've completed Round 23 of the neck, bind off both the steeks. Put the back stitches on a piece of waste yarn. If you're making a cardigan, work the border on the front stitches now and bind it off, otherwise put these stitches on a second piece of waste yarn. When both halves have been completed, join them at the center using Kitchener stitch (pages 70–74). If you hate Kitchener, you can substitute Three-Needle Bind Off (page 69), but there will be a noticeable seam. Note that, although joining at the center means extra work, working the two halves separately makes it very easy to machine stitch the neck and bottom steeks before joining.

Any Size, Any Yarn

Make a gauge swatch and determine the number of stitches and rounds per inch (or centimeter). Decide how big the cuffs need to be, and multiply this by the stitches per inch to determine how many to cast on. (See appendix for Craft Yarn Council website, which provides garment sizing guidelines.)

- Work whatever border you like (ribbing, garter stitch, or a hem), then begin increasing to taper the sleeves. Plan your sleeve increases as described in Sleeve and Armhole Options (pages 260–261). Increase two stitches on each shaping round. You can do this at the center of the sleeve, or you can shift all the increases to the "seam," as in the Circular Yoked Sweater (pages 273–279). You may also want to add a gusset (just like a thumb gusset) by placing additional increases on either side of the seam stitch as you approach the underarm. This smooths the transition from the sleeve to the side seam of the sweater at the underarm. When the sleeve is the desired circumference at the underarm, check to see if it's also the correct length to the underarm. If not, work a few more rounds until it's long enough.

- Check your stitch gauge and decide how long the sweater should be from the underarm to the bottom (allowing for a bottom border to be added later). Multiply gauge by length to find the number of stitches for the side seam. Cast on this number of stitches at end of round. Pick up the same number of stitches, or perhaps 1 less, along the bottom of the stitches you just cast on. Work to the end of the round and cast on 8 stitches for the bottom steek. Work circularly on all these stitches until the shoulder is wide enough to reach the neck opening.

- At this point (or earlier, if you like to plan ahead), measure and chart the neck opening out on graph paper. See Designing the Neck Opening (pages 262–263). Once you've charted the shape, work to the neck edge and bind off the stitches at the shoulder to begin the neck opening. On the next round, work up the body to the neck opening, begin your shaping, and cast on for the neck steek. Continue working around, shaping the neck on both sides of the steek. If you plan a cardigan, stop and run crochet cotton through the 2 rows of stitches on either side of the center front. (If you are a brave soul, you can skip this step and just pick up the stitches without a "lifeline" after you cut.) When you are 1 round short of completing the neck opening, bind off the neck steek. On the following round, cast on stitches for the shoulder.

- The number of stitches you now have should match the first shoulder. When this half of the front is the same measurement to the side seam as the first half, bind off the bottom steek. At the end of the following round, turn inside out and use the Three-Needle Bind Off (page 69) to join the side seam.

- Turn right-side out and work around on the sleeve stitches, using decreases to shape this second sleeve identically to the first one and finish the sleeve off with a cuff or hem to match the first sleeve.

- For a cardigan, open up the front and add the front borders. Prepare the neck and bottom steeks, cut them, pick up stitches and work the borders.

Appendix

Glossary of Techniques and Terms

Bind Offs

Basic Bind Off. K1, *K1, insert the left needle into the stitch on the right, pass it over the other stitch and off the needle; repeat from *. When one stitch remains, cut the yarn and pull through the last stitch to prevent it from unraveling.

In pattern. Continue to work the pattern already in progress while binding off. For example, if working K1, P1 ribbing, knit the knit stitches and purl the purl stitches while binding off.

In purl. Instead of knitting while binding off, purl all of the stitches.

Blocking

Some projects benefit from blocking, either to straighten and flatten the fabric to make finishing easier, or to make pattern stitches or stranded knitting look better. You may block individual pieces of knitting before they are joined together, but the projects in this book are seamless, so you are more likely to block them either just before completing the finishing or after they are completed. There are two ways to block your knitting:

- Soak or wash the project gently by hand, roll in a towel to remove excess moisture, and lay out flat and neat to dry. You may want to stretch it by pinning out sections.

- Lay the project out flat, pinning or using blocking wires if desired. Mist it with cool water and leave it to dry or steam it gently using a clothing steamer or hovering a steam iron over it.

Blocking wires or woolly boards can make this process easier (see page 209).

Cast Ons

Cable Cast On. Cast on 2 stitches using the Knitted Cast On, below, right. *Insert the right needle between the 2 stitches **A**; knit up a stitch, leaving the 2 original stitches on the left needle **B**; insert the left needle up into the new stitch from the front and slip it off the right needle; repeat from *, knitting each new stitch between the last two stitches cast on.

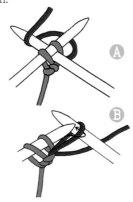

Alternating-Color Cable Cast On. This is a variation on the Cable Cast On. Using two colors of yarn held together, make a slipknot and put it on the needle. These are your first 2 stitches. *Using the yarn that matches the second stitch from the end of the needle **A**, knit up a stitch in this color between the last 2 stitches **B** and slip it onto the left needle. Twist the two yarns to change colors. Repeat from * until there are enough stitches. Be careful to always twist in the same direction when changing colors.

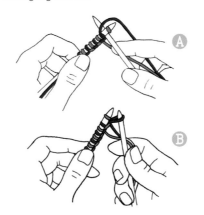

Half-Hitch Cast On. This is only one of many ways to work this cast on, which is just a series of half hitches placed on the needle: Hold a needle and the cut end of the yarn against your left palm. *Bring your thumb to the front under the yarn **A**; slip the needle up into the loop on your thumb **B**; slip your thumb out; repeat from * **C**.

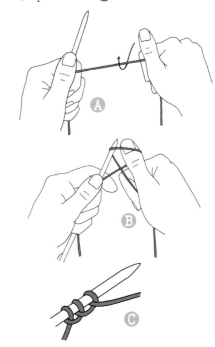

Knitted Cast On. Make a slipknot, leaving a short tail, and place it on your left needle. *Knit a stitch, leaving the original stitch on the needle **A**; insert the left needle into the new stitch from the front **B**; tighten up the stitch; repeat from * until you have enough stitches **C**.

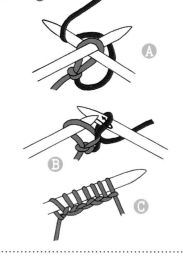

Long-Tail Cast On. Pull out a length of yarn for the long tail, about three times as long as the circumference of your knitting, plus a few inches. Make a slipknot at this point and place it on the needle. Hold the needle in your right hand with the index finger on the slipknot to prevent it from sliding off. Arrange the yarn in your left hand, with the tail over your thumb and the working yarn over your index finger 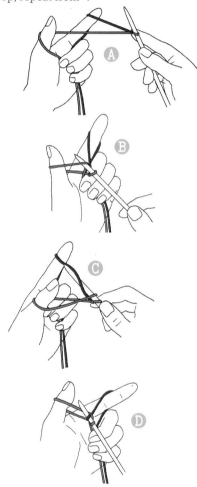. *Insert the needle up through the loop around your thumb, bring it over and behind the front strand on your index finger, then back out through the thumb loop to form a stitch; drop the thumb loop, place your thumb behind the long tail, and use it to tighten the loop; repeat from *.

Alternating-Color Long-Tail Cast On. Using two colors of yarn held together, make a slipknot and put it on the needle. Work as for the Long-Tail Cast On above, with one color on the thumb and the other on the index finger. Between each cast-on stitch, twist the two yarns and swap their positions on your finger and thumb. Be careful to always twist in the same direction. Do not include the slipknot in your stitch count. When the cast on is complete, remove the slipknot from the needle and unravel it.

Two-Color Long-Tail Cast On. Hold the ends of both colors together and make a slipknot. Place the slipknot on your needle, put one color on your thumb and the other on your index finger, and work the usual Long-Tail Cast On. Unlike the Alternating-Color Long-Tail Cast On at left, you do not swap the yarns between each stitch. The color on your thumb will appear at the bottom edge of the knitting. The color on your index finger will be the first row of the knitting. Do not include the slipknot in your stitch count. When the cast on is complete, remove the slipknot from the needle and unravel it.

Ribbed Cable Cast On. This is a variation on the Cable Cast On (page 302), alternating knits and purls. Cast on 2 stitches using the Knitted Cast On. *Purl up a stitch between the last 2 stitches on the left needle and slip the new stitch knitwise onto the left needle. Knit up a stitch between the last 2 stitches on the left needle (exactly like the Cable Cast On) and slip the new stitch knitwise onto the left needle. Repeat from * until desired number of stitches has been cast on. To work K1, P1 ribbing above this, knit the knit stitches and purl the purl stitches.

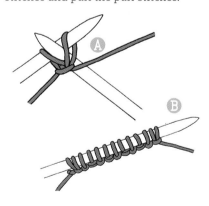

Cast Ons, Provisional

Provisional Cast Ons are worked using waste yarn so that you can easily remove the cast on and have live stitches at the beginning of your knitting. These are very useful for creating hems and seamless tubes.

Crocheted Cast On. You need waste yarn and a crochet hook the same size as your knitting needle. Using waste yarn, make a slipknot and place it on the crochet hook. The yarn, needle, and crochet hook may be held in either hand. Cross the crochet hook in front of the knitting needle. *Bring the yarn behind the knitting needle, chain a stitch with the crochet hook. Repeat from * until you have enough stitches on the needle. Cut the waste yarn and pull it through the loop on the crochet hook so it won't unravel. Change to the working yarn and knit one row, being careful to work into the stitches so that you do not twist them. To remove the waste yarn later, pick the ending tail back out and unravel the chain.

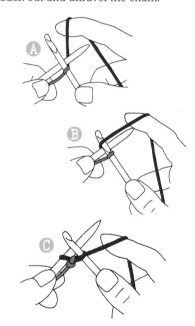

Invisible Cast On. Use waste yarn and your working yarn to begin this cast on. Tie the waste yarn around the end of the working yarn. Arrange the yarn with the waste yarn around your thumb and the working yarn over your index finger. Hold both strands taut against your palm and the point of the knitting needle under the knot; keep the knot from sliding off the needle with your index finger .

*Point your thumb up and insert the needle under the waste yarn from front to back and scoop up a strand of the working yarn; one stitch is now on the needle **B**; point your thumb down and take the needle behind the working yarn to scoop up a second stitch **C**; repeat from * until there are enough stitches. Cut the waste yarn and tie it to the working yarn to keep it from coming undone. To remove the waste yarn later, untie both ends and pull it horizontally out of the fabric.

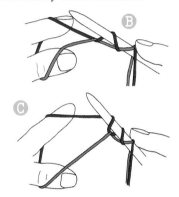

Center-Pull Ball

A ball of yarn where both ends are accessible: one can be unwound from the outside and the other can be pulled from the center. Center-pull balls can be wound using a hand-cranked ball winder, around a stick or nostepinne, or around your fingers.

Nostepinne or stick. The nostepinne or stick serves as the base for your ball. Make a slipknot to attach the end of the yarn to the top. Wrap diagonally around the shaft, turning it a tiny bit each time you wrap. Slip the ball off over the end, then disconnect the yarn from the tip of the tool. This makes a neat center pull ball. Nostepinnes are tapered to make it easy to remove the ball, but you can use any smooth round object in its place, such as a piece of dowel, a child's block, or a wooden spoon handle.

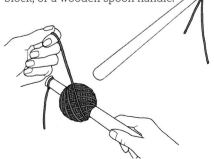

Fingers. Hold the end of the yarn against your palm and let it dangle down past your wrist. Bring the tips of two fingers together with your thumb and use them as a core for the ball you're winding. Wrap diagonally around your fingers, shifting the position of the wrap slightly each time so that the ball is evenly wound. As it grows larger, you can remove your thumb. Be careful to wrap fairly loosely or your fingers will feel the squeeze! When done, slip the ball off your fingers.

Decreases

Knit 2 together (K2tog). Insert the right needle into the first two stitches knitwise and knit them together. This decrease leans to the right on both the knit and the purl side of the fabric.

Purl 2 together (P2tog). Insert the right needle into the first two stitches and purl them together. This decrease leans to the right on both the knit and the purl side of the fabric.

Slip, slip, knit (ssk). Slip 1 stitch knitwise, slip another stitch knitwise, insert the left needle into these two stitches and knit them together. This decrease leans to the left on both the knit and the purl side of the fabric.

Slip, slip, purl (ssp). Slip 1 stitch knitwise, slip another stitch knitwise **A**. Pass both of the slipped stitches back to the left needle, being careful to maintain their current orientation **B**. Purl the two stitches together through the back loops **C**. This decrease leans to the left on both the knit and the purl side of the fabric **D**.

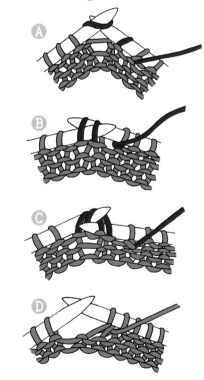

Double Decreases

Knit 3 together (K3tog). Insert the right needle into the first 3 stitches knitwise, and knit them together. This decreases 2 stitches and leans to the right.

Purl 3 together (P3tog). Insert the right needle into the first 3 stitches purlwise, and purl them together. This decreases 2 stitches and leans to the right.

Slip 1, knit 2 together, pass slipped stitch over (sk2p). Slip 1 knitwise; knit 2 together 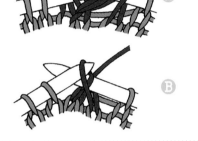; pass slipped stitch over **B**. This decreases 2 stitches and leans to the left.

Slip 2 together, knit 1, pass 2 slipped stitches over (s2kp2). Insert the right needle knitwise into the first two stitches, as if to knit them together, and slip them to the right needle; knit 1 **A**; pass the two slipped stitches over the knit stitch and off the needle **B**. This decreases 2 stitches and is centered.

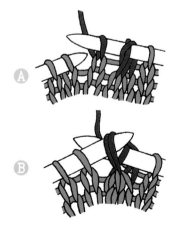

Duplicate Stitch

A method of embroidering with yarn on the surface of the knitting that follows the structure of the knitted stitch.

Knit side. Bring the point of the yarn needle up through the bottom of the stitch. *Sew behind two strands along the top of the stitch **A**; sew back through the bottom of the stitch and under two strands to the bottom of the next stitch **B**; repeat from *. You may work from either right to left or left to right.

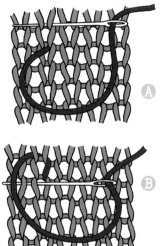

Purl side. The yarn should not show on the knit side of the fabric. This technique is used on the wrong side of the fabric for working in ends invisibly or to adjust the tension and alignment of stitches to improve the appearance on the right side.
* Sew under two purl bumps from bottom to top **A**; sew under the next two purl bumps from top to bottom **B**; repeat from *. Work right to left or left to right.

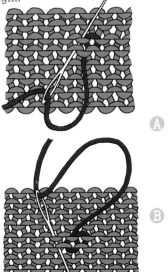

Evenly Spaced

When a series of increases or decreases are worked spaced across one row, you are instructed to increase (or decrease) a number of stitches "evenly spaced across." When working in circular knitting, the instructions will say "evenly spaced around." If you are mathematically inclined, you can calculate the positions of the increases/decreases by dividing the total number of stitches by the number of stitches to be increased/decreased. For flat knitting, you then adjust the position of the decreases to leave a few stitches at each edge.

For example, if there are 80 stitches and you need to decrease 9 stitches evenly spaced, 80 stitches divided by 9 decreases = 8.888 . . . Which means it's almost 9 stitches, so you'd knit around decreasing every 9 stitches (except that there will be one fewer stitch between the last decrease and the end of the round). But you must remember that each decrease uses 2 stitches out of the 9, so you'll need to work (K2tog, K7) around in order to decrease every ninth stitch.

But what if the answer is somewhere in the middle? For example, if you needed to decrease 7 stitches, 80 divided by 7 = 11.43. You need to decrease about every 11½ stitches, and 2 of these will be used by the decrease, so there will be 9½ stitches between each decrease. To accomplish this you'll alternate between 9 stitches and 10 stitches, repeating (K2tog, K9, K2tog, K10) until you get to the end of the round. You won't be able to complete the last repeat at the end of the round, but you should end up with 7 stitches decreased.

For increases, the calculation is worked the same way, but the adjustment for the number of stitches between increases differs depending on the increase you use. Some increases (the M1 or the lifted increase) fall between stitches, so you don't make any adjustment. Others (kfb, pfb, and "knit-and-purl into the stitch") use one stitch, so you adjust by one stitch. For example, if you have 70 stitches and need to increase 10, 70 stitches divided by 10 increases = 7; you need to increase every 7 stitches. To do this using M1 increases, repeat (K7, M1) around. To do it with Kfb increases, repeat (K6, Kfb) around.

If you dislike even the idea of calculating the stitches between increases or decreases, then it's just as effective to estimate the spacing. Divide the knitting into halves or quarters and divide the total number of decreases by the same. Place the correct number of split markers or safety pins in each section, so that they appear to be evenly spaced. To go back to our first example, if you have 80 stitches and want to increase or decrease 9, lay your knitting out flat, so that half is facing you and half is hidden underneath. Half of 9 is 4.5, so one half will need to have 4 increases and the other 5 increases. Place a marker at each side of the knitting, and three more markers spaced more or less evenly between them. You don't need to count stitches, just eyeball it. Turn the knitting over and place the remaining four markers spaced more or less evenly on this side. Adjust the positions of any markers that look noticeably closer together or farther apart. On the next round, work a decrease (or an increase) at each of the marked points. So long as they're spaced reasonably, it will look just fine.

Half Hitch

A simple knot formed from a twisted loop. The half hitch is used in the Half-Hitch Cast On and the Make 1 increase. The working yarn can also be tied in a half hitch around a ball of yarn to allow it to be dangled in the air and untwisted. To make a half hitch, see M1 (at right) with working yarn.

Increases

Knit into the front and back (Kfb). Knit into the stitch leaving it on the left needle. Bring the right needle to the back of the work, knit into the back loop of the stitch and slip it off the needle. Pfb is the purled equivalent of Kfb (see Purl into the Front and Back, below).

Knit-purl-knit into a stitch (K-P-K). This is a double increase. Knit into the stitch as usual, but leave it on the left needle. Bring the yarn to the front, purl into the stitch, yarn back, knit into the stitch, and slip it off the needle.

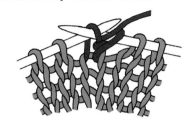

Knit-yarn over-knit into a stitch (K-yo-K). This is a double increase. Knit into the stitch as usual, but leave it on the left needle, yarn over 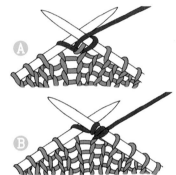, knit into the stitch again **B**, and slip it off the needle.

Make 1 (M1, M1L, M1R). There are many ways to work the M1 increase. Lifted M1s steal yarn from the stitches on either side, so are tighter than M1s made using the working yarn or with a yarn over.

Left slant: lifted (M1L). Insert the left needle from front under the top strand between the two needles **A**, then knit into the back of the stitch to twist it **B**.

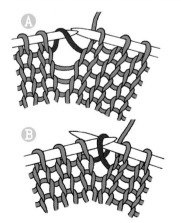

Left slant: working yarn (M1L). Make a small loop of the working yarn close to the needle, twist it clockwise and place it on the needle.

Right slant: lifted (M1R). Insert the left needle from back under the top strand between the two needles **A**, then knit into the front of the stitch to twist it **B**.

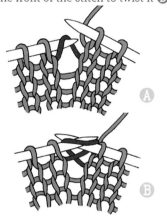

Right slant: working yarn (M1R). Make a small loop of the working yarn close to the needle, twist it counterclockwise and place it on the needle.

Yarn over. Work a yarn over on the increase row, then knit into the back of this stitch on the following row to twist it. This makes a left-slanting M1 and is useful when the other methods are too tight to work easily. To make a right-slanting version of the M1 using a yo, wrap the yo the opposite of the normal way (from back to front over the right needle), then work into the front of it on the following round.

Purl into the front and back (Pfb). Purl into the stitch, leaving it on the left needle. Bring the right needle to the back of the work, purl into the back loop of the stitch and slip it off the needle.

Row below. Knit the stitch normally. Then, from the back, insert the left needle into the left half of the stitch on the row below. Knit into this stitch **A**. To reverse the slant of this increase, reverse the order: lift up the stitch from the row below and knit it, then knit the stitch normally 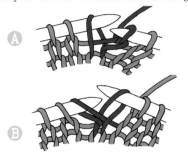. You may find it easiest to lift with the right needle and slip to the left needle before knitting.

Yarn over (yo). A stitch worked between two existing stitches that produces an eyelet. Note that the yarn always travels over the top of the right needle. If the next stitch will be a knit, the yarn over must end with the yarn in back. If the following stitch will be a purl, the yarn must continue under the needle from back to front in preparation for purling. *With yarn in left hand,* either wrap counterclockwise around the needle with your index finger, or take the right needle around the back and under the yarn 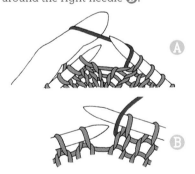. *With yarn in right hand,* wrap counterclockwise once around the right needle .

Knit Below

Insert the right needle into the stitch directly below the first stitch on the left needle, all the way through to the back of the fabric. Wrap or pick the yarn as usual and pull the new stitch out to the front, knitting the lower stitch together with the one on the needle. Slide the stitch off the left needle.

Knit Stitch

Yarn in left hand. Insert right-hand needle into the stitch 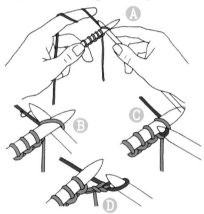; bring the tip of the needle over and behind the working yarn or use the left hand to wrap the yarn around the needle ; hook the yarn back through the stitch with a twist of the right-hand needle ; slip the old stitch off the left needle . Keep the yarn near the first joint of your index finger while you work. If it slides up and down, wrap it around the finger once to keep it in place. If the tension on the working yarn is too loose, wrap it once round your index or any other finger to control it. Once you get used to it, this becomes a smooth in-and-out movement, rather than separate steps.

Yarn in right hand. Insert right-hand needle into the front of the stitch; wrap the yarn around the needle counter-clockwise 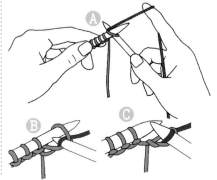; pull it through the stitch with tip of needle ; slip the old stitch off the left needle . With practice, you will work more quickly and this will become a smooth in-and-out-and-off motion, rather than separate steps. If you find it difficult to hold the yarn, try wrapping it once around one of your fingers or holding it against your palm with the little and ring fingers.

Knitwise

Designates the way the right needle is inserted into the stitch on the left needle. Knitwise is from the front of the fabric to the back under the needle, the same way you insert the needle when you knit a stitch.

Pick Up

Throughout this book, the terms *pick up* and *pick up and knit* are used inter-changeably.

Along the sides of garter stitch. There are two ways to pick up stitches in the edge of garter stitch. You can "pick up and knit" as for stockinette stitch (below), inserting the needle either a whole stitch or a half stitch in from the edge and knitting out a stitch with the working yarn. You can also "pick up" the stitches on one needle and then "knit" in a separate step. Working from left to right, insert a needle through the stitch closest to the edge of the fabric at each ridge of garter stitch 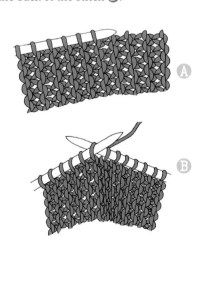. Using another needle, knit across these from right to left. These stitches will be on the needle the non-standard way. To avoid twisting them, be sure to knit into the back of the stitch .

Along the sides of stockinette stitch.
Insert the tip of your needle through the fabric and use the needle to knit up a stitch of the working yarn. Do this a whole stitch in from the edge.

Along the top or bottom edge. Insert the needle directly into a stitch, wrap the yarn, and knit up a stitch; if your knitting is upside down, this is actually the space between two stitches, but it looks just like a stitch. Do not attempt to pick up in the cast-on or bound-off stitch at the very edge; instead work into the stitches one row (or round) away from the edge. This will be easier to do, because the bind off and cast on are frequently tighter and it will also look much neater because the knitted fabric will look continuous.

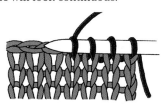

On sock heels with a slipped-stitch edge. Insert the needle into each slipped stitch (see page 200). Wrap the yarn around it and knit the stitch out to the front. You can also use the separate pick up and knit technique described for garter stitch edges. If the slipped stitches are loose, twist them to tighten them up by knitting into the front of each stitch.

Purl Below

Insert the right needle into the stitch directly below the first stitch on the left needle, from the back of the fabric all the way through to the front; wrap or pick the yarn as usual and pull the new stitch out to the back, purling the lower stitch together with the one on the needle.

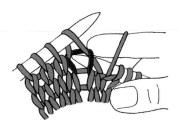

Purl Stitch

Yarn in left hand. Hold the yarn pulled taut (but not too tight!) in front of the left needle. Insert right-hand needle into the stitch from right to left. Make sure the tip of it is behind the yarn stretching up to your index finger **A**. Move your left index finger down and to the front so the yarn is taut over the tip of the right needle **B**. Hook the yarn back through the stitch with the right needle **C**. Slip the original stitch off the left needle **D**. (See also Knit Stitch, page 307.)

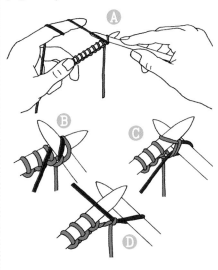

Yarn in right hand. Hold the yarn in front of the needles. Insert the right-hand needle into the stitch from right to left **A**. Wrap the yarn around the needle counterclockwise **B**. Pull it through the stitch with the right needle tip **C**. Slip the original stitch off the left needle **D**. (See also Knit Stitch, page 307.)

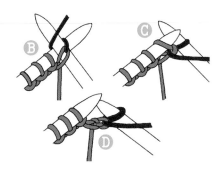

Purlwise

Designates the way the right needle is inserted into the stitch on the left needle. Purlwise is from the back of the fabric to the front under the needle, the same way you insert the needle when you purl a stitch.

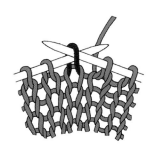

Salt and Pepper

A two-color stranded pattern where single stitches are alternated on every row or round to make a checkerboard.

Seed Stitch

A knit-purl pattern where single knits and purls are alternated on every row or round to make a checkerboard.

Short Rows

Short rows are a way of shaping knitting that involves working partway across a row and then turning back before finishing the row. Working a series of short rows makes it possible to shape sloped shoulders or neck edges without binding off. Each time you turn in the middle of a row, you leave a hole. To close the holes at each turning point, work a wrap-and-turn. To hide the wrap, when you come to a wrapped stitch from the row below, pick up the wrap and knit (or purl) it together with the stitch it's wrapped around. Short rows are also used to shape the turning of a sock heel, but wrapping is not required because the holes are closed using decreases.

Wrap-and-turn. Work across until you are ready to turn, slip the next stitch, change the position of the yarn (from front to back or from back to front), slip the stitch back to the left needle, then turn. Position the yarn wherever you need it to work the next stitch and continue back across the row.

Pick up the wrap. In garter stitch and some other pattern stitches, the wrap will be unnoticeable; if so, just ignore it. If it shows, hide it by knitting or purling it together with its stitch. When knitting: insert the right needle tip up into the wrap, then through the stitch on the needle and knit the two together. When purling: lift the back of the wrap (the side away from you, on the far side of the fabric) up onto the left needle, and then purl it together with the stitch. Whether knitting or purling, the wrap should fall to the purl side of the fabric so it will be hidden when viewed from the knit side. If you are working a pattern stitch, you may need to adjust how you handle the wrap so that it falls to the correct side.

Slip Stitch

A slipped stitch is one that is simply moved from the left needle to the right needle without working a knit or a purl. Stitches can be slipped knitwise (as if you were knitting a stitch) or purlwise (as if you were purling a stitch). They can also be slipped with the yarn in front of the needle (wyif) or in back of

the needle (wyib). If you need to change the position of the yarn to the location specified, do this before you slip the stitch. See also Knitwise (page 307) and Purlwise (facing page).

Slipknot

Holding the end of the yarn in your hand, wrap it around two fingers, and then a little farther to end in back **Ⓐ**; pull a loop of the working yarn through the wrap around your fingers **Ⓑ**; slip your fingers out and tighten by pulling the cut end and the loop **Ⓒ**.

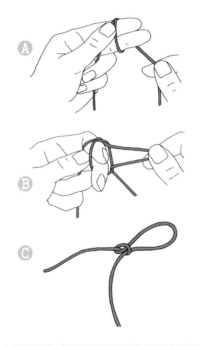

Tail

The cut end of a piece of yarn attached to the knitted fabric. Tails are created when you cast on, change colors, start a new ball of yarn, bind off, or cut the yarn for any reason.

Through the Back Loop

An alternative method of inserting the needle when working a stitch, causing it to twist. To knit through the back loop, insert the right needle from right to left into the back of the stitch on the left needle, then knit as usual.

Waste Yarn

Yarn used temporarily to hold stitches or when casting on. Waste yarn should be the same weight as the working yarn, smooth, nonfuzzy, and a different color from the working yarn, so that it knits up at the same gauge as the working yarn and can easily be removed later without leaving any residue.

Wind Yarn

To take yarn from a hanging skein, pull skein, or other "put up" and wind it into ball. See also Center-Pull Ball, page 304.

Woolly Nylon

A nylon thread that can be carried along with the main yarn to provide reinforcement, especially for socks. It is thin enough so it has little impact on the gauge of the knitting. It is used as thread for serger sewing machines so can be purchased on small spools or cones at sewing stores.

Work Even

Continue working without increasing or decreasing. If the instructions say to "work even in pattern," then continue with the pattern stitch that has already been established, without doing any shaping.

Working Yarn

The yarn that is attached both to the most recently worked stitch and to the ball of yarn currently in use. This term may be used to distinguish between the yarn in use and another not currently in use, between the yarn attached to the ball and the cut tail of yarn at the cast on, or between the project yarn and waste yarn.

Yarn Over

See Increases, page 307.

Knitting Symbols

☐	Knit on right side; purl on wrong side
−	Purl on right side; knit on wrong side
⋎	Slip with yarn on right side of fabric
∨	Slip with yarn on wrong side of fabric
⋒	Knit below on right side; purl below on wrong side
⋀	Purl below on right side; knit below on wrong side
▱	Cable 4: Slip 2 to cable needle and hold in back, K2, K2 from cable needle
○	Yarn over
M	Make 1 (increase)
╱	Knit 2 together on right side; Purl 2 together on wrong side
⊬	Purl 2 together on right side; Knit 2 together on wrong side
╲	Slip, slip, knit 2 together on right side; Slip, slip, purl 2 together on wrong side
⊢	Slip, slip, purl 2 together on right side; Slip, slip, knit 2 together on wrong side
⅄	Double Decrease: Slip 1, knit 2 together, pass slipped stitch over, or slip 2 together, knit 1, pass 2 slipped stitches over
∩	Bind off
∗	Indicates marked stitch
■	Not a stitch (a placeholder in chart for additional stitches on other rows/rounds)
V	Double increase; for example, K-yo-K in a single stitch

Knitting Abbreviations

For complete instruction on how to work the techniques below, see the Glossary of Techniques and Terms starting on page 302.

CC	Contrast color
K	Knit
Kfb	Knit into front and back (see Increases)
K-P-K	Knit-purl-knit into a single stitch (see Increases)
K-yo-K	Knit 1-yarn over-knit 1 all in one stitch (see Increases)
K2tog	Knit 2 together (see Decreases)
K3tog	Knit 3 together (see Double Decreases)
MC	Main color
M1	Make 1 (see Increases)
M1L	Make 1 left slant (see Increases)
M1R	Make 1 right slant (see Increases)
P	Purl
P-yo-P	Purl 1-yarn over-purl 1 all in one stitch (see Increases)
P2tog	Purl 2 together (see Decreases)
P3tog	Purl 3 together (see Double Decreases)
sk2p	Slip 1, knit 2 together, pass slipped stitch over (see Double Decreases)
ssk	Slip, slip, knit 2 together (see Decreases)
ssp	Slip, slip, purl 2 together (see Decreases)
s2kp2	Slip 2, knit 1, pass 2 slipped stitches over (see Double Decreases)
wyib	With yarn in back
wyif	With yarn in front
yo	Yarn over (see Increases)
-	Indicates a series of actions to be worked in one stitch. For example, "K-yo-K into the next stitch."
∗	Indicates the beginning of a section of instructions to be repeated
()	Indicates the beginning and end of a section of instructions to be repeated, usually used inside another repeat indicated by ∗
[]	Indicates the beginning and end of a section of instructions to be repeated, usually used within another repeat indicated by ()

Further Reading

Becker, Judy. *Beyond Toes: Knitting Adventures with Judy's Magic Cast On* (Indigo Frog Press, 2011)

Bernard, Wendy. *Custom Knits: Unleash Your Inner Designer with Top-Down and Improvisational Techniques* (Stewart, Tabori & Chang/STC Craft, 2008)

Bordhi, Cat. *Socks Soar on Two Circular Needles: A Manual of Elegant Knitting Techniques and Patterns* (Passing Paws Press, 2001)

Bush, Nancy. *Folk Socks: The History and Techniques of Hand-knitted Footwear* (Interweave, 2012)

Cookie A. *Sock Innovation: Knitting Techniques & Patterns for One-of-a-Kind Socks* (Interweave, 2009)

Craft Yarn Council, *Standards and Guidelines for Crochet and Knitting (2003)*. www.yarnstandards.com

Dandanell, Birgitta, and Ulla Danielsson. *Twined Knitting: A Swedish Folkcraft Technique*; translated by Robin Orm Hansen (Interweave, 1989)

Farson, Laura. *New Twists on Twined Knitting: A Fresh Look at a Traditional Technique* (Martingale, 2009)

Gibson-Roberts, Priscilla, and Deborah Robson. *Knitting in the Old Way: Designs and Techniques from Ethnic Sweaters* (Nomad, 2004)

Hansen, Robin. *Ultimate Mittens! 28 Classic Patterns to Keep You Warm* (Down East, 2011)

Kinzel, Marianne. *First Book of Modern Lace Knitting* (Dover, 1972)

Ling, Anne-Maj. *Two-End Knitting*; translated by Carol Huebscher Rhoades and Anne-Maj Ling (Schoolhouse, 2004)

Macdonald, Cecily Glowik, and Melissa Labarre. *Weekend Hats: 25 Knitted Caps, Berets, Cloches, and More* (Interweave, 2011)

McCarthy, Betsy Lee. *Knit Socks!: 17 Classic Patterns for Cozy Feet* (Storey, 2010)

Morgan-Oakes, Melissa. *2-at-a-time Socks: The Secret of Knitting Two at Once on One Circular Needle* (Storey, 2007)

New, Debbie. *Unexpected Knitting* (Schoolhouse, 2003)

Newton, Deborah. *Designing Knitwear* (Taunton, 1998)

Radcliffe, Margaret. *The Essential Guide to Color Knitting Techniques* (Storey, 2008)

Radcliffe, Margaret. *The Knitting Answer Book* (Storey, 2005)

Starmore, Alice. *Alice Starmore's Book of Fair Isle Knitting* (Dover, 2009)

Walker, Barbara G. *Knitting from the Top* (Schoolhouse, 1996)

Zilboorg, Anna. *Magnificent Mittens & Socks* (XRX Books, 2010)

Zimmermann, Elizabeth. *Knitting Without Tears: Basic Techniques and Easy-to-Follow Directions for Garments to Fit All Sizes* (Scribners, 1973)

Acknowledgments

As always, there are so many people and organizations that I need to thank for their help. Without them, this book might have been started, but it certainly would never have been completed.

My editor, Gwen Steege, and my agent, Linda Roghaar, who supported me throughout the lengthy process.

Charlotte Quiggle, who in addition to performing the painstaking technical editing made numerous suggestions for improvements and additions.

Mary Velgos for coming up with a beautiful and coherent design for yet another complicated book.

John Polak for his beautiful photography and Alison Kolesar for her clear and detailed drawings.

The businesses that generously provided crucial supplies and equipment:

Lorna's Laces, for providing the vast majority of the yarn for the book (www.lornaslaces.net)

Black Water Abbey, for Z-twist yarn for the Twined-Cuff Glove (www.abbeyyarns.com)

Skacel, for all the many sizes, types, and lengths of needles (www.skacelknitting.com)

Strauch Fiber Equipment, for the world's most reliable ball winder (www.strauchfiber.com)

The knitters who produced samples, tested instructions and made suggestions for improvement: Meredith Baber, Lyn Day, Caitlin Fass, Karen Greider, Cat Leonard, Lawre O'Leary, Allegra Radcliffe, Jeanne Rippere, Phil Sponenberg, Darcy Whitlock, and Cathy Williams.

The innovative knitters who have shared their techniques with me in person and through their writing. I can't thank everyone who has increased my knitting knowledge over a lifetime, but particular contributions that informed this book came from Lucy Neatby (Sock Toe Chimney, www.lucyneatby.com), Debbie New (working Kitchener stitch on the purl side), Elizabeth Zimmermann (my favorite heel flap and circular sweater construction), and Sarah Hauschka and Bev Galeskas (Magic Loop, www.fibertrends.com).

I also must thank the John C. Campbell Folk School, Brasstown, North Carolina, for providing an environment where, over the last fifteen years, I have found the space, time, and inspiration to work on my knitting and writing projects (www.folkschool.org).

Finally, a heartfelt thank you to the businesses that provided knitting space, endless cups of coffee, and gluten-free sustenance: Posana Café, Asheville, North Carolina; Blackfriars Theatre, American Shakespeare Center, Staunton, Virginia; and the Windjammer *J.&E. Riggin*, out of Rockland, Maine.

Index

Page numbers in *italics* indicate photographs; **bold** indicates pattern instructions and charts.

Other Storey Titles You Will Enjoy

By the same author

The Knitting Answer Book, by Margaret Radcliffe.
Answers for every knitting quandry — an indispensable addition
to every knitter's project bag.
400 pages. Flexibind. ISBN 978-1-58017-599-9.

The Essential Guide to Color Knitting Techniques,
by Margaret Radcliffe.
Stripes, stranded knitting, intarsia and more multicolor knitting
methods, clearly explained with step-by-step photographs.
320 pages. Hardcover with jacket. ISBN 978-1-60342-0402.

2-at-a-Time Socks, by Melissa Morgan-Oakes.
An easy-to-learn new technique to banish Second Sock Syndrome forever!
144 pages. Hardcover with concealed wire-o. ISBN 978-1-58017-691-0.

Toe-Up 2-at-a-Time Socks, by Melissa Morgan-Oakes.
The practicality of toe-up knitting combined with the convenience
of the 2-at-a-time technique!
176 pages. Hardcover with concealed wire-o. ISBN 978-1-60342-533-9.

Knit Socks!, by Betsy Lee McCarthy.
Classic patterns for cozy feet — 17 patterns, plus valuable advice on
using alternative yarns and adapting patterns to any type of needle.
176 pages. Paper. ISBN 978-1-60342-549-0.

The Knitter's Life List, by Gwen W. Steege.
A road map to a lifetime of knitting challenges and adventures.
320 pages. Paper with flaps. ISBN 978-1-60342-996-2.